SO-BAQ-800

3 5674 02085764 6

CH-R

UNTOLD TALES,
UNSUNG HEROES

African American Life Series

A complete listing of the books in this series can be found at the back of this volume.

General Editors

Toni Cade Bambara
Author and Filmmaker

Geneva Smitherman
Michigan State University

Wilbur C. Rich
Wellesley College

Ronald W. Walters
Howard University

UNTOLD TALES, UNSUNG HEROES

An Oral History

of Detroit's

African American

Community,

1918–1967

Elaine Latzman Moon
DETROIT URBAN LEAGUE, INC.

WAYNE STATE UNIVERSITY PRESS   DETROIT

Library of Congress Cataloging-in-Publication Data

Moon, Elaine Latzman.
Untold tales, unsung heroes : an oral history of Detroit's African
American community, 1918–1967 / Elaine Latzman Moon.
    p.   cm. — (African American life series)
Includes index.
ISBN 0-8143-2464-9 (hard : alk. paper). — ISBN 0-8143-2465-7
(pbk. : alk. paper)
    1. Afro-Americans—Michigan—Detroit—History—20th century.
2. Civil rights movements—Michigan—Detroit—History—20th century.
3. Afro-Americans—Michigan—Detroit—Biography.   4. Detroit
(Mich.)—Race relations.   5. Oral history.   I. Title.   II. Series.
F574.D49N476   1994
977.4'3400496073—dc20   93-26073

Designer: Joanne Elkin Kinney
Jacket photo: Paul B. Shirley

TO THE
CHILDREN
OF
DETROIT

For, while the tale of how we suffer,
and how we are delighted,
and how we may triumph is never new,
it always must be heard.
There isn't any other tale to tell,
it's the only light we've got
in all this darkness.

James Baldwin

CONTENTS

9

FOREWORD

In 1916 the Detroit Urban League was founded to address the needs of the large number of blacks who were migrating to Detroit in hopes of finding a better life. The major needs of this large influx of blacks were in the areas of housing, employment, social services, and recreation.

Blacks had heard that Detroit had many opportunities from which they could benefit. They heard that they would get much better treatment in Detroit and would not have to deal with many of the racial problems they were experiencing in the southern communities from which they were moving. Of course, this was not really the case, and so the Urban League was formed to provide the much needed employment training programs and services for Detroit's rapidly growing minority population.

Over the course of the next seventy-five years, much of the work and efforts of blacks seemingly went unreported and undocumented. There have been some reports written about Detroit's black population, but many of these histories have had a limited and often negative focus. So when the Detroit Urban League had the opportunity to do an oral history project that would recapture some of the lost history of black Detroiters, we felt this enterprise was something in which we absolutely had to participate.

This oral history project represents a labor of love and commitment on the part of the Detroit Urban League, led by the hard work and dedication of Elaine Latzman Moon. Extraordinary efforts were devoted to writing proposals for financial support of the project and conducting hundreds of face-to-face interviews, telephone calls, and communications with the people whose oral histories have made this book possible.

13

For their financial support the Detroit Urban League wishes to thank the Henry Ford II Fund, the Gannett Foundation and Community Freedom Fund, Hudson's Corporation, the Black United Fund, and the Community Foundation for Southeastern Michigan. We also want to thank the individuals and groups that gave of their time and wisdom either by interviewing or consulting on this oral history project. For their graphic and photographic support in kind, we thank the Detroit Edison Company. *Royalties earned from the sale of this book will benefit the Detroit Urban League.*

Detroit has a great heritage, and it must not be allowed to vanish or become clouded because we failed to capture it in its true form. The Urban League has a mission and duty to do its part in presenting the history of black Detroit. We are a part of this history and have played a critical part in helping many people to achieve their goals in this community.

We remember those who have traveled this way before us; and we leave this legacy, *Untold Tales, Unsung Heroes: An Oral History of Detroit's African American Community, 1918–1967*, for later generations to read about and, hopefully, not forget those who came before them.

N. Charles Anderson, President
Detroit Urban League

This is a history of Detroit's African American community over fifty years—from the period of great migration in the early 1900s to the turbulence of the 1960s. It is told by the men and women who lived it.

These stories are moving, sometimes contradictory views of life. They tell of the migration of African Americans to Detroit early in this century; of their search for equality in education, housing, and employment; of their struggles against racism and their experiences of goodness; of their activities in the union movement and the civil rights movement; and the pain and losses that flowed from the years of discrimination against their race.

This book strives to present a panorama which relates the experiences of housekeepers, business owners, factory workers, union organizers, executives, children raised on welfare, and those members of the elite. It brings to light the contributions of many true heroes who will never be the namesakes for buildings, streets, or holidays.

This project evolved because I am a native Detroiter who has written extensively about Detroit history; because I have noted that the African American community is not represented in the city's written history; because I have worked with many people in the black community and heard their stories; because many have said to me, "People tell me I should write a book," and because they may not do it but still need to have their story told.

While Detroit's past has been depicted in many books, typically the history of the black community is allocated to a single chapter; even then it is usually no more than a recitation of events considered noteworthy—slavery and the underground railroad, the riot of 1943, the civil disturbance of 1967—and such phenomena as Joe Louis's prizefighting career and the Motown sound.

15

With the belief that the reminiscence of African Americans has more validity than a history based on secondary research, we have compiled a document based on the experiences of men and women who lived in this city during the fifty-year period from 1918 to 1967.

This compilation of personal experiences does not make up for all the histories of Detroit that have excluded African Americans or have relegated "coloreds," "Negroes," "blacks," "Afro-Americans," or "African Americans" to segregated chapters in books on the city's history. It does provide a balanced perspective by chronicling the African American experience and providing a complement to existing histories.

The effort began in 1989, when I approached N. Charles Anderson, president of the Detroit Urban League, with the idea and made the commitment to find funding to support the project. I credit him with having the vision to hire me and trust that I could do it.

The first step was a series of conversations with thirty-five individuals who were well respected in Detroit's African American community. They were asked to recommend topics to be included and individuals to be interviewed.

Michele Tunstall assisted me in researching seventy potential topics. She was very helpful and thorough in compiling background material in preparation for interviews. Our primary resources were the Bentley Historical Library of the University of Michigan, the Burton Historical Collection of the Detroit Public Library, and the Archives of Labor and Urban Affairs, Walter P. Reuther Library at Wayne State University.

Through various recommendations we developed a mailing list of two hundred potential interviewees. A media release inviting the general public to discussion groups at the Detroit Urban League on February 3 and 6, 1990, generated additional participants. From a total of three hundred prospects, I interviewed more than two hundred persons in either an individual or group session. Of these, one hundred and ten were selected for inclusion in the final manuscript.

A small number of white people were interviewed, and some are included in the history. These are all individuals who have been recognized by the African American community as heroes in civil rights and human rights efforts (Frank Angelo, Ernest Goodman, Richard V. Marks, Harold Norris, Stanley Nowak, Mel Ravitz, George Romney, John F. "Jack" White, and Carl Winter). Most of these have been honored as Distinguished Warriors by the Detroit Urban League.

Extensive interviews with participants were conducted individually, in groups, and sometimes both. Group interviews focused on selected topics recommended by participants. The goal was to allow the participants to create the history—from structure to content. Those who had expressed an interest in a specific topic were invited to meet in small group sessions held to discuss such subjects as crime, the labor movement, civil rights, neighborhoods, and churches. Often the participants knew each other. Sometimes they did not. These sessions were generally held in the evening, lasted about two hours, and were supplemented by light refreshments.

Individual sessions were frequently held in the home of the interviewee and usually lasted about one hour. A serendipitous approach allowed the interviewee to share his or her most profound memories— either good or bad. Typically the first question was, "What are your earliest memories of living in Detroit?" Rather than lead, I tried to follow as the interview progressed. Often the subject I had expected a person to discuss was not the one they focused on. Individuals usually favored a certain period of their lives and skipped over other times.

The manuscripts which were most representative of the African American experience were selected for inclusion in the history. Each manuscript was edited and given to the interviewee to review and correct. A great deal of time and care was devoted to this process. Every attempt was made to retain the conversational quality of the material while at the same time respecting the wishes of the interviewee.

The oral history was divided into decades representative of certain periods of history. The years from 1918 to 1927 represented a period of migration to Detroit. From 1928 to 1937 the country was in the throes of the depression. From 1938 to 1947 World War II and the 1943 race riot profoundly affected the lives of Detroiters. In the decade from 1948 to 1957 the beginnings of civil unrest became apparent. From 1958 to 1967 America was shaken by the upheaval of war and assassination, and Detroit marked by the violence of a civil disturbance.

The interviews are ordered according to the time of the interviewees' experiences. For example, Oscar Lee begins our history with his journey to Detroit in 1919. Some interviews cover a short period of time; others cover several decades. Rather than dividing parts of the interviews among separate sections of the book in order to achieve a strictly chronological account, they were left intact. It is hoped that the reader will find it a journey worthy of its meanderings.

The experience of compiling this book was a wonderful one. In my own past I did not have an extended family to tell me stories; my mother often had to repeat her experiences of picking blueberries on a hill in Pennsylvania, or crocheting with a bent pin, or working in the factory as a child. I have never tired of listening to stories, and so listening to more than two hundred of them was a pleasure.

We hope that this book will be enjoyed by all who read it and that it will prove beneficial to the entire community. Older people will have been a part of it. Young people will have a better understanding of their past. Blacks and whites will gain an understanding of the historical issues of racism in this city and in the United States. This document is significant to both Detroiters and to the nation, as this city is in so many ways a microcosm of our country.

It is our hope that this oral history will provide an understanding of the past and present and an insight for those who can affect the future. Perhaps it can serve as a bridge between black and white. Hopefully it will provide for those who are not aware of their history a sense of community and family.

Finally, we hope it will be an inspiration to others to complete the story—to tell the tales we have not yet told.

ACKNOWLEDGMENTS

We are profoundly grateful to the more than two hundred men and women from the ages of forty to ninety who participated in an interview, and particularly those who worked with us to edit their manuscript for use in this book. Thanks also to the participants for sharing the photographs used in this publication.

We are also grateful to those who were interviewed but whose contributions were not published. They, too, provided valuable insight and inspiration to this history.

The following is a list of persons who have contributed to the project in some way—participating in an interview, providing valuable resources, or being a friend.

Clara Adams
Dorothy Aldridge
Ronald Alpern
Christopher Alston
Dr. Carleton Ardrey
Fentriss Armmer
Kiersten Armstrong
Muriel Berry
Charles Blakely
Barbara Bommarito
Thelma Booker
Dr. James Boyce
Dr. Horace Bradfield
Edgar Brazelton
Johnetta Brazzell
Thomas Briscoe

William Broyles, Jr.
David Campbell
Nathaniel Carr
Dr. Leon Chestang
William Colburn
Alfred Cole
Douglas Crawford
Rev. William H. Crews
Malcolm Dade
Carolyn Davis
Bernadine Denning
Thomas Dietz
Samuel Dixon
Walter Downs
Herbert Dudley
Todd Duncan

Joe Dunmore
Jack Dwyer
Lucille Dwyer
Marty Eddy
Lillian Edwards
Arthur Evans
Deborah Evans
Thomas Fentin
Dorothy Ford
Edsel Ford II
Joyce Garrett
Norma Gatliff
Robert Giles
Adelaide Graham
Irene Graves
Dr. Karl Gregory
Felix Guitterez
Mary Wright Hastings
Raymond Hatcher
Kaiser Hayes
Carrie Hayes-Gaskins
Treamon Hicks
Lorenzo Holloway
Rhemelda Houston
Gloria Hudson
Mildred Jeffrey
Richard Jennings
Arthur Johnson
Felix Jones
Patricia Jones
Thomas Jones
Susan Kelly
Earl Kennedy
Robert Lawrence
Dr. William Lawson
Walton Lewis
Ernest Lofton
Sam Logan
Gil Maddox
Benson Manlove
Scott Martelle
Fred Martin
Philip Mason
Eva Matthews

William McClinic
Floretta McCreary-Harvey
George McFall
Ollie McFarland
Reginald McGhee
Harold McKinney
Helen Moderville
Dave Moore
Dr. Charles Morton
Theresa Moss
Alberta Motley
Richard Mulvey
Lorraine Needham
Mariam Noland
Elma W. Peddy
Wentz Perkins
Hilanius Phillips
Margaret Piper
Dianna Pleasant
Wardell Polk
William Ransom
Brenda Rayford
Louise Reid Ritchey
Walter Robinson
Verbel Ross
John Roundtree
Hazel Roxborough
Rosetta Sadler
Kenneth Scheffel
Horace Sheffield
Mary Barnes Simmons
Susan Simpson
Fred Smith
Patricia Whitby Steinberg
Phy Stevens
Alma Swain
Helen Thomas
Julia Thomas
Fr. Norman Thomas
Tyrone Tillery
Homer Townsend
Lynn Trease
Neely Tucker
Michele Tunstall

Rev. Kevin Turman
Taft Upshaw
Elizabeth Walker
Lucius Watkins
Susan Watson
Joseph Walker Williams
Lawton Williams
Maxine Broyles Williams
Hayward Wilson
Reginald Witherspoon
Dr. William Womack
Joe Zainea

CHRONOLOGY:
AFRICAN AMERICANS IN DETROIT TO 1917

The presence of the Negro in Detroit dates to the beginnings of the city's history. Many arrived in Detroit by way of the underground railroad.

1773   There were 93 slaves in the settlement along the Detroit River.

1782   There were 179 Negro slaves in Detroit, of whom 78 were males and 100 were females.

1805   There were six free Negro men and seven free Negro women in the community.

1807   Governor Hall organized a company of Negro militia in Detroit.
       Judge Woodward handed down the decision that no new slaves could be brought into the settlement and that slavery was not permissible except in the case of persons already in the possession of British subjects on July 11, 1798.

1830   There were only 32 slaves in the state of Michigan.

1836   All former slaves in the state were either dead or manumitted. Second Baptist Church was established.

1837   The Detroit Anti-Slavery Society was organized for the purpose of opposing slavery.

1839   Bethel A.M.E. Church formed.
       The Detroit Board of Education organized a separate school for colored children.

1840   The American Presbyterian Church ordered all Presbyterians in the country to give up their slaves. The Gradual Emancipation laws of New York, Pennsylvania, New Jersey, and Delaware began to take effect.

1850   On September 18 Congress passed the Fugitive Slave Act, providing that slaves might be arrested in any state. During the period from 1850–51 many slaves emigrated to Canada from Detroit.

1856   Anti-intermarriage law passed.

1859   On March 12 John Brown arrived in Detroit, met with Frederick Douglas, and planned the raid at Harpers Ferry.

1863   The Negroes of Detroit organized the First Michigan Colored Regiment, the 102nd Infantry, comprising 895 men.
The first celebration of the Emancipation Proclamation held anywhere in the United States took place on January 6 in the Colored (Second) Baptist Church.

1865   The Fourteenth Amendment was passed, abolishing slavery.

1866   American born Negroes were made citizens.

1870   The Fifteenth Amendment gave Negroes the right to vote.

1889   Anti-intermarriage law abolished.

1890   A rift developed in the cordial relations which had existed between the white and colored races in Detroit. Among the reasons for this racial antipathy was the increasing number of Negroes in Michigan.

1895   Negroes gradually lost their hold on the financially rewarding positions they had held. The large number of people immigrating from Europe enabled employers to obtain highly trained servants at a lower wage than they had been paying Negroes.

1913   A new anti-marriage bill was introduced.

1914   Beginning of African American migration north.
Henry Ford offers wages of $5.00 a day (January 12).

1917   United States enters World War I (April 8). African Americans were not allowed in the Marines, Coast Guard, or Air Force. During May, June and July, 1,000 Negroes a month arrived in Detroit.

African Americans
in Detroit and the United States,
1918–1927

1918	World War I ended (November 11).
	Prohibition went into effect (May 1).
1910–20	Detroit's total population grew from 465,776 to 993,678.
	Detroit's African American population grew from less than 6,000 to 41,000. By the spring of 1920 more than 1,000 black migrants were arriving in Detroit by train every week from the South.
1923	1,000 admitted to membership in Ku Klux Klan; crosses were burned in front of City Hall and the Wayne County Building.
1925	Dr. Ossian Sweet purchased a home at Garland and Charlevoix. Whites harassed the family and a man living nearby was killed. Sweet and his brother were tried for murder and successfully defended by Clarence Darrow.

OSCAR LEE

When I hit this town, I was seventeen years old. 1919. I'll never forget that as long as I live. I didn't pay my way here. I hoboed here.

I have never wanted to be a boy in my life. I wanted to be a man. I left home kind of early, but I wouldn't tell nobody where I was going. I'd just walk off. I stayed right here. My momma didn't know I was coming here. I didn't tell nobody I was coming here. I didn't tell my momma nothing.

I got married on my seventeenth birthday. Never should have done it. I wasn't making enough money. I told my wife, "I'm going to Pittsburgh. I'm going to Detroit." So I have twelve dollars. I give it to her. I kept one dollar and fifty cents and I left. I was in Alabama then. I was leaving.

"Gots your clothes, boy?"

"Yes sir!"

"Got everything you need?"

I said, "Yes sir!"

I put an overcoat and two big old bricks in a red paper suitcase. The suitcase didn't cost me but two dollars and fifty cents. I locked it. If I'm going to the steel mill in Ohio, I've got to go. I ain't got time to fool with no suitcase. I'm not going to tell you what I said. I cussed, something I don't do now. There was a sign there, and that sign's right there today. I threwed the key over the sign with a, "Go you son-of-a-bitch, cause I don't need you no more." I had a brand new suit of clothes on me. I paid fifty dollars for that suit. I don't buy no cheap clothes.

We left that evening at six o'clock, and we didn't get to Steubenville, Ohio till four o'clock in the morning, which ain't too far, about three hundred and seven miles. I had 60 miles to go.

I walked back down like four miles to the next local passenger station where they stop cars. I walked down them four miles, and that was lucky. I never wore nothing but a cap, and I looked on the ground and I see a hat check. I picked it up. Ain't I lucky? The train had stopped and I got this hat check.

Then I got on the train. What was I going to do? I was going in the bathroom and shut the door. What they do to keep somebody from getting on the train is lock the bathroom door. So I sat down, and a guy came by and said, "Hey, where's your hat check?"

I said, "Here it is."

He said, "I ain't seen you on this train before."

I said, "I was here all the time."

He said, "Let me see your hat check."

In Pennsylvania the only thing you could do was get a job in a steel mill, so I decided I'd come here. Now I'm coming to Detroit.

This detective pulled us off the train three times. And he said: "Listen, I'm going to tell you, if I pull you off this train again, I'm going to take you downtown and you'll get thirty days. I'm going to give you a break." He said: "You see this road here? This is Telegraph. There's fifty-nine miles to that damn Indian at Cadillac Square at Michigan Avenue, and you're going to walk it."

He pulled me off the train, so now I've got a quarter, and I got a little hungry. A hot dog was a dime, a great big hot dog. A coke was a nickel. So I went in there and got me a hot dog and a bottle of coca cola. He gave me two buffalo nickels. I got 'em today.

I listened to these two fellows talking on this truck. They had a load of trucks come out of Cincinnati, the Hudson Motor Car Company; and I listened to them. Well, I'm going to Detroit too. So what I did I listened to 'em good, and he told this driver: "We're going down Telegraph Road; and when I get to Michigan Avenue, I make a right turn. I go to East Jefferson and make a left turn." I'm sitting there listening. So I crawled under the back truck, not the front truck where they had the axles.

When they said, "This is Michigan Avenue and Woodward," that's when I jumped off. I jumped off right at that Indian. I wasn't but a block from Gratiot Avenue. I went to the McGregor Hotel, half a block off of Gratiot Avenue.

I stayed there three days, in the same suit of clothes. I almost cried. They're scared you're going to have lice on you. I went in there, and they washed my brand new suit of clothes. They thought I had lice. And they washed my suit of clothes. I hated it. I paid fifty dollars for that suit of clothes. It wasn't that good a wash, but it was all right when he gave it back to me.

I was seventeen years old. Now I'm eighty-eight. That was the fifteenth of May.

BIOGRAPHY

Oscar Lee was born on May 15, 1902, and came to Detroit in 1919. He has been employed as a factory worker at American Curler Company, Cadillac Motors, City Metal Refining, Ford Motor Company, and Excello. He was married to the late Helen Johnson for sixty years and helped raise her two children as his own.

Rosa Lee Kirkman Wheeler enjoyed her childhood and adolescence in her east side neighborhood; her home was on Joseph Campau near Lafayette. This picture was taken in the late 1920s.

ROSA LEE
KIRKMAN WHEELER

I was born in Detroit on October 17, 1916. I was born on the east side. I went to kindergarten and first grade at Lincoln Elementary. Then I went to second grade in a school called Fort Street School on Fort Street which was, as I understood it, the last one-room schoolhouse in Detroit. It was a one-story frame building or one-room schoolhouse, just like you see on picture postcards.

I forget what street, but it was right around the corner, because I lived on Joseph Campau near Lafayette. The next block up is Fort, and I went down Fort Street about two blocks. It was within walking distance. And that was the most wonderful experience I remember.

We had two or three grades in the one room. I can remember the teacher, she had a little harmonica about two inches long. We had all the subjects, but they were in this one room; and at certain times she'd change from one subject to another. And when you had music, this little harmonica would give us a pitch.

We had a coal- and wood-burning stove, and the wood and the coal was in the schoolyard next to the door. The boys in the class would go out in the morning and bring in the wood. They had a coal scuttle, and they would bring in a scuttle of coal for the stove.

We had books, and there was a blackboard in front of us behind the teacher's desk. We had reading and writing and arithmetic and geography and music; we had different subjects on different days. She would teach one grade and then give them desk work, then go to the next grade, instruct them, and then give them desk work and go to the next. I think there were three grades.

Well, if you got your desk work done you could listen to what the next grade was learning. So when you got to the next grade, it wasn't completely foreign to you; you were sort of prepared for it.

My best girlfriend's grandmother was Joe Louis's aunt. Her name was Louise, and Joe was Louise's cousin. I also knew his sister, Vuniece. We used to go to the show together on Saturdays—Vuniece, Louise and I—the girls. So we would get together. I'd go to Louise's house. From her house we'd walk to Joe's house, then pick up Vuniece and go around the corner to the show. I think they changed the name of the street to Madison, but years back it was known as Catherine Street, and the name of the show was the Catherine Show.

When we were in middle school, another one of my girlfriends had a crush on Joe. He used to work on a wagon. He sold coal in the wintertime and ice in the summertime. So we used to tease her because she liked this boy that rode on the coal wagon.

We all knew him. We went to school with him. He went from Duffield School to Miller School. We all lived in the area. He lived about six or eight blocks, within walking distance. At that time he lived on Catherine, right around the corner from the show. We all went through school together.

Our mothers used to give us fifteen cents to go to the show, ten cents to get in the show and a nickel to spend. So if you got penny candy, a nickel for the candy was a lot of candy. "Mary Janes," you got four for a penny. A scoop of red hearts, they used to sell 'em in bulk. I guess you got about two spoonfuls. And they had these aluminum or tin cars that had licorice in them. One of my favorites, and I think all it was, was just maple sugar, in this little tin dish. Some of the girls used to collect the tins and use them for doll dishes.

The Monroe streetcar, we called it "the Dinky" because it was a small streetcar, just ran on Monroe from Elmwood Cemetery to downtown, which is now Greektown. And the old Ferry Seed Company building was at the end of the line. So we would skate down the street and jump the car tracks. It was an obstacle to us, just one set of tracks, it was daring. Our parents didn't want us to do it.

In the summertime, when it was real hot, we'd get together and get our skates and skate to Belle Isle and cool off. There was a grocery store on the corner, and we could get a pound of bologna for a nickel. And a small-size loaf of bread, I think, was six cents. We would go in my mama's kitchen, get mustard and stuff, and make sandwiches, and take them and skate to Belle Isle.

When we got to Belle Isle, if we had money we'd buy a soft drink and eat our sandwich and rest. And then we got all rested and played around and around. Depending what our mood was, we'd go to the diamonds and see a baseball game or go to the tennis courts and watch them play tennis, or go to the aquariums. There are a number of things on Belle Isle to do, so we could find something different to do every time.

When I was growing up, little girls didn't ride bicycles, and I always wanted a bicycle. The little boy next door to me had one, and he let me ride his bicycle. I had a two-wheel scooter. I had another girlfriend that had a scooter, and we would take our scooters and ride down Monroe right to the gate of Elmwood Cemetery. The gatekeeper knew us, so he would let us come in. It was cool over there. There was a house outside the cemetery, a yellow frame house, and the upstairs had a turret type arrangement of windows; and we were told that that was the lookout during the Battle of Bloody Run.

They said if you dig deep enough in certain parts of Elmwood Cemetery, the earth is red from the blood that was shed. That's why it was a cemetery. They just made a cemetery out of that area because so many soldiers died there. Once we dug right around a tree. We dug down, and we did get red clay. I don't know if it was the blood or not, but when we were going to school taking history, the teacher brought that up. And Duffield is right up the street from it. So that weekend we went over to the cemetery and we dug just a little patch and put the grass back. We were careful not to disturb anything. At that time there were areas where there were no graves. It was just big trees, and it was cool and peaceful.

BIOGRAPHY

Rosa Lee Kirkman Wheeler was born on October 17, 1916, in Detroit. Ms. Wheeler has been active in the community since she was a teenager. She has worked as a laboratory technician, seamstress, school librarian, and clerk at Catholic Social Services. Organizations in which she has participated as a volunteer include the Detroit Urban League, NAACP, Lucy Thurman YWCA, Brewster Center, Midwest Aquatic Club, Draft Board and Ration Board during World War II, Focus Hope, 25th Street Block Club, Core City Neighborhood, and Girl Scouts. In 1991 she was recipient of the Core City Neighborhood—Prayer, Hope, and Determination (CCN-PHD) Award.

James E. Cummings was known throughout the community for his philanthropic efforts. He made significant contributions to the Detroit Urban League and the NAACP.

JAMES E. CUMMINGS

I moved to Detroit in the latter part of 1918. I came with my family. My father was already here with two of the children. There were nine of us, seven children and mother and father. He couldn't find employment in the South. He came first and then sent for my older brother and my sister who was older than me. He found living accommodations for the three of them. After about six months, he sent for the balance of us, and that's the way we got to Detroit in 1918. I think he first started at one of the paint factories, Berry Brothers. Detroit at that time was noted for automobiles, paints and stoves. We had a lot of stove works here out on East Jefferson.

The Urban League helped find a home for us on East Congress Street after the whole family was together. Later it became known as Black Bottom. Blacks were only up to, beyond Riopelle. There were no blacks except the ones who had lived here way back during the Civil War times. A few were sprinkled here and there all over the city. There was no such thing as resistance to blacks until that surge of blacks coming up during World War I. That's when attitudes began to change and resistance set in.

I had a brother younger than me. As youngsters we sold newspapers. Our routes were from downtown, from the old City Hall right out Congress Street, Jefferson Avenue and Larned Street, all the way out to where we lived.

I was ten when we moved here. We started delivering papers right off because as now, with the auto industry, they had their ups and downs. Immediately after World War I there was a big demand for cars. In 1922 I remember my folks saying, "It looks like a panic is coming on. The factories are all laying off." That lasted about two or three years. The family relied on the income from our paper routes, and we were able to make as much as fifty dollars a week. At that time there were three of us. We all had good-sized routes, and we made a cent a piece off of every paper. We had the *Detroit News* and the *Detroit Free Press.*

Later on, I was getting to be about thirteen, the Hearsts came in and set the *Detroit Times* up and gave out prizes to all newsboys as an incentive to get the paper started. For twenty-five subscriptions you'd get a brand new, Rollfast Bicycle. That was a popular make at that time. I was one of the first to get one. They gave the newsboys wagons to haul the papers in and gave them other little things like baseball gloves and footballs.

I remember when we had to depend entirely on the newspapers. That's when we made a lot of money selling the papers. Radio began, as far as I can remember, about 1921–22. I didn't know of any radios before World War I. It was right after that. Everybody's ears were at the radio during World War II. They had no television, although television had been developed in New York but not put on for sale. It didn't get out here until after World War II. People read more, too. It was a nice time despite what we were up against. We didn't know any better, at least we youngsters didn't. We accepted what it was because it was the way it was and had been. We thought that was the way it was supposed to be, and we didn't know any kind of way to change it.

There were others among us who were educated and who had a vision. Booker T. was one, but he came later. He had a vision, and he had the right vision too. He wanted black teachers and the black public to be taught the trades, and he was right. He was definitely right. From the trades we would get the professionals. The money even today is made with the tradesmen.

DuBois wanted to train the professionals . . . doctors and lawyers. They would be up against the system. That's the way I saw it. If the system didn't want them to move, they wouldn't.

When I graduated from high school I started to work in a hotel as a bellhop. Things were still kind of bad. We were hitting kind of close to the '30s then. They built the LaSalle Hotel in 1927 or '28 over there on Woodward Avenue, a big eight hundred room hotel. I tried to get a job in there. I was going to leave the job I had and go over there, but the reputation of it was destroyed.

Did you ever hear about the Buckley case? He was a radio announcer; the radio station was headquartered in the penthouse of the hotel. The gangsters had infiltrated and were living in there as soon as the hotel opened up. Jerry Buckley was his name, and it was in the late 1920s. They had two or three widely publicized killings. They killed him, Jerry Buckley. He would get on the air and expose the gangsters. He would say, "We're going to drive them out of Detroit," and all like that. People who they called the mob now, the first name they gave them was the Black Hand Gang. They were mostly Sicilians. Detroit had a few of them, and they finally killed Jerry Buckley for trying to expose them; and that kind of gave it a bad name. He was a newsman, giving out the nightly news. He thought they wouldn't dare. They caught him coming out the door after the eleven o'clock news.

I worked in the Hotel Fort Wayne and another one. I was never abused, as some say they were, because you were acting in a servant capacity. I did very well at that. I saved my money.

After that I began to buy up some property. That was right after World War II. The buildings that I have now are the last thing I bought. I had a Standard Oil gasoline station that furnished me some income. I was in the service for about two years, and I took that insurance policy and converted it into enough money to make a down payment on a station and in turn from a station to the building.

The way the buildings were bought was because we had a riot in 1943. It was a real riot. It was not like this in 1967 where it was mostly looting. That was a real race riot. They had boundaries set up which, if you would pass, you would certainly get killed or hurt. The owners of the property became afraid, and they began to sell all of this property right from Harper Hospital north and sold it almost on your terms. They thought it would break out again.

BIOGRAPHY

James E. Cummings was a successful Detroit businessman who gave generously to many human rights efforts. He was a major financial backer of the Detroit chapter of the National Association for the Advancement of Colored People and the Detroit Urban League. He also raised money for Green Pastures Camp. He was born on January 18, 1908, in Greenville, Alabama—the son of African Methodist Episcopal Zion minister, Rev. Felix X. Cummings. He attended Wayne State

University. Mr. Cummings served in the U. S. Army in World War II. He was married to the late Dorothy L. Daniel. His children are James E. Cummings, Jr., and Judith Cummings. Mr. Cummings died on March 11, 1991.

HELEN NUTTALL BROWN

Black Bottom was an area very near to the downtown section but very far removed in terms of being isolated economically and geographically. It was home to me; it was a safe place. It was a neighborhood mainly of single homes with a number of businesses on corners, but they were family businesses. The people who had the businesses were ethnics, like Italians or Germans.

I was on the corner of St. Aubin and Chestnut. It was a magnificent home, and had a slate roof and double-brick construction. It had a cork floor in the kitchen and bathroom which was very easy on the feet. It had central vacuuming. You just plug into the wall, and you vacuumed. It had hot water heat, which was very expensive. It had stained glass windows. The neighborhood was not consistent. Most of the homes were frame; many of them were two-family; a few four-family, very few. People trusted each other; people knew each other. It was safe.

We went to neighborhood schools. When the students finished Miller, which was called a junior high school at that time, it was converted all the way through the twelfth grade so that blacks wouldn't transfer to Eastern. We knew the pattern. We didn't have the facilities that a high school had; we didn't have a swimming pool.

My father owned a drugstore and the funeral home on the corner next to ours at St. Aubin and Maple. My father was Dr. Harry M. Nuttall. He didn't operate the funeral home, but he rented it out to people. He rented it out to Charles Diggs. He didn't really rent it to him; he just let him be the undertaker. Charlie was a little boy at that time. He would hire pharmacists at the drugstore. My father never allowed us to work.

The drugstore was very well stocked, and it was just two aisles. The drugstore was on the corner. The funeral home was next to it. There was a flat upstairs, and there was an up-and-down flat behind it. It was a very beautiful building. It was just across the street from Coleman Young's family. They had the cleaners and lived behind it. On the corner was a grocery story, Mike's grocery store. The grocery store on the other corner was Louie's. We could walk and get almost anything we wanted—bakeries, hardware, cleaners, grocery stores.

It was Coleman's uncle who owned the barbecue at that time, and he wouldn't give away one rib. I went around there many a time with Coleman's sisters, and we would just stand there; and he would not give them a rib.

BIOGRAPHY

Helen Nuttall Brown was born in Detroit in the 1920s. She is daughter of Harry M. Nuttall, M.D., and Mrs. Susie Neola Nuttall, and wife of Russell S. Brown, Jr. She is mother of Judge Helen E. Brown and Russell S. Brown III, and grandmother to three—two girls and one boy. She earned a master's degree in elementary education and is a retired teacher from Detroit Public Schools. She also worked for the Children's Aid Society. Ms. Brown has served as a member of the Historic Designation Advisory Committee and on the board of the Boston Edison Historic District. She is a member of Delta Sigma Theta Sorority.

Through his writing and civic activities, Frank Angelo has achieved recognition as a champion of human rights for all people. Mr. Angelo rose to managing editor during his forty year tenure, from 1941 to 1981, at the Detroit Free Press.

FRANK ANGELO

I was born on Hunt Street, about three blocks east of the famous Hunt Street Police Station. My first recollection is going to Pingree School which was on McClellan. That's where I started kindergarten in Detroit.

One of the things I remember, and I guess it's true today, every school always had a confectionery store across the street from it. I remember one incident. My grandmother came over from Italy for a short time. She was a fairly large, stocky woman and wore a dress that had great big pockets. She had, literally, almost a pocket full of Italian coins. They were parts of a lire; but they looked like dimes, nickels, and quarters. Grandma gave my oldest sister Frances and me a handful of these coins. We were about five or six years old. We went to the confectionery store, and we thought we were in heaven. We had all this money, and we could spend it. There were other kids milling around and, my God, we got candy. At that moment the storekeeper didn't realize he was getting Italian money, but he obviously spotted it that night; and, oh, did he chew us out the next day, I'm telling you.

I was probably about seven or eight years old, which would make it about 1922, when Detroit was just beginning to explode. In terms of population, it was a million then. One of the major explosions in growth was on the east side, particularly the area around Joseph Campau and Davison. Those were the two important cross streets; and the Baker Streetcar Line, which was a major lifeline of Detroit, began at Davison and Joseph Campau. Then it ran down Joseph Campau through Hamtramck, picked up at Chene, and came down to Gratiot. Then from Gratiot it crossed onto Michigan and wound up at the Ford Rouge plant.

We moved to Shields, between Davison and Six Mile Road. I went to Northeastern High School. We took what amounted to a "Toonerville trolley" type of car from where I lived to Davison and Joseph Campau. We changed there and picked up the Baker streetcar. I'd have to leave quite early in the morning. You'd get on that Baker streetcar, and the odors of the Ford Motor Company workingman were all over the place. I was a bright young kid and dressed in my school clothes, and everybody else was in denim, dark clothes, and headed for work at Ford. Everybody just sat silently.

There were some black children at Northeastern. I didn't realize it until I was looking at the graduation picture a couple years ago, but all the black children were clustered in one corner.

I was graduated in June 1930, which was sort of the official start of the depression. But what people don't understand is that the so-called big depression had started in Detroit about two years before when the Ford Motor Company shut down all its plants to end the production of the Model T.

Generally speaking, I'm not hard-nosed about the good old days. When I look back, they weren't all that good. I used to come home from college, and if there was a bowl of pea soup on the table, it was pretty damn good. In terms of family, in terms of interpersonal relationships and so on, the times were good, because if I was only eating a bowl of soup, that's what everybody in the family did. And if there was only one bowl of soup, and there were five of us, then we got five spoons.

World War II shattered the social structure of the city. That, plus the fact that in the '30s you had come through the tremendous depression, and you had seen a tremendous battle going on for unionism. People overlook that fact. We look now and say, "Gee, unions were great." But the fact of the matter was that the '30s were a tremendously traumatic thing because of the union movement. Unions were not universally embraced.

Detroit at the time also had a black community that had deep roots in the city. They had been here for a long time. There was sort of a black establishment, the Pecks and the Pelhams, for example. The ministers also were part of this hierarchy. Basically, the community was separate; it was within itself, with a lot of good people. Then the War came along and shattered many relationships.

40

Take my own family. I had four sisters and myself. Until 1939–41, we were very close, very intimate. We lived together, and we worried about having to go to war. All of a sudden, I was in the Navy. My sister married a soldier, and she took off for Carolina. Another sister married somebody and wound up in California. The other sister wound up in Boulder, Colorado. You know, boom, there goes the family. And now you say, "My God, what's happened?" But those are the things the war impacted. In addition, you had a massive migration from the South.

The neighborhoods on the east side, until the late '30s and '40s, were very distinct. You had your Polish area. Out where we lived on Shields was a mixture of Italian, a lot of Polish. They had spread out from Hamtramck. The north Detroit area boasted a lot of Italians, and if you went out Gratiot, around Harper, there were a lot of Italians. Below Gratiot and McDougall you were all Italian. Beyond that it was mostly German. As you went further east, you began to run into the Belgians.

At that time there was a black community. It was downtown on the east side and was very distinct. It was locked in there, and gradually began to move north on Brush Street, then St. Antoine and Hastings. As the Jewish community moved north, the black community expanded behind it. When the Jewish community hit the Boulevard, that was it. They didn't cross the Boulevard directly, and so they leapfrogged and went from the east side at the [Grand] Boulevard to Dexter, 12th, and 14th. It was just understood that if you were Jewish, you didn't move into a WASP area, which it was at that time. The historical path is clear, and the blacks followed the Jewish people up the St. Antoine route to the Boulevard; and they, too, leapfrogged and took over the 12th, 14th, and Dexter-Boulevard area.

One of the absolutely great untold stories in this country is the greatest migration of people that's ever happened anywhere. It gained momentum in the '50s, particularly right after the war. And it brought millions of blacks from the South. They were fleeing since the intensity of attacks in the South was increasing. Take a city like Detroit where the population ratio was maybe fifteen to twenty percent black, but a black community that had roots. In the next two decades large numbers of blacks came into a community which was not prepared to absorb this huge inflow. Many of the people who came were poor, with little education. The massive numbers really shook the city up, and at that point whites began to say, "My God, we're being engulfed; I'm going to get out of here." At the same time expressways opened up, making it very easy for people to get out. And with FHA the government was making it easy to build new housing wherever you wanted it. The white population was the only part of the population that was able to take advantage of that, because blacks in most cases didn't have the money or were blocked by racial attitudes.

BIOGRAPHY

Frank Angelo was born on September 6, 1914, in Detroit. He attended Detroit Public Schools and earned a B.A. degree from Wayne State University in 1934. He wrote for the *Detroit News* from 1934–41 and the *Detroit Free Press* from 1941–81, where he rose to managing editor. He has served on the boards of several social service agencies, including the Detroit Urban League. Mr. Angelo was awarded an honorary doctorate by Wayne State University and was elected to the Michigan Journalism Hall of Fame. He was honored as a Distinguished Warrior by the Detroit Urban League in 1985.

*Reginald R. Larrie is a historian. He grew up on
Scoville Place near Scotten. He is pictured in front of the
family car, at the far left.*

DISCUSSION ON EMPLOYMENT OPPORTUNITIES
HENRY BIGGS AND REGINALD R. LARRIE

REGINALD R. LARRIE: The phenomenon in terms of blacks coming to Detroit was like a domino effect. If someone came from the South and got a job, as soon as they heard about another job, they would write for another family member to come here. That's how my father, Robert Larrie, came to Detroit. He came from Indiana. The whole family came from Indiana. He came to Detroit in the 1920s.

Some of the best paying jobs at that time were porters. According to my father, most porter jobs in Detroit were at Michigan Central and Pennsylvania train stations. There was also the Interurban Railroad Station, which was down on Jefferson near Randolph Street. The system used electric rail cars. It was transportation from Detroit to outlying areas, such as Pontiac, Toledo, and Grosse Pointe. We're talking about four or five cars of people. It ran down to Toledo in about fifty minutes.

Ben Turpin, who was hired as a policeman in the 1920s, got his job because a white man recommended him. Ben only had an eighth-grade education. He had been a porter in Cincinnati. He wanted to come to Detroit, and this white fellow who was politically powerful, he made a recommendation; and they hired Ben because the city was searching for a certain kind of black male to bring on to the police department, and Ben fit that mold.

HENRY BIGGS: I know Detroit quite well. Me being a native born of Detroit in 1911 and my father preached here in 1900. My father was Reverend Robert L. Biggs.

As a fair boy, I knew from Beaubien Street to Woodward. Unless you were working as a maid or houseman or chauffeur, there were no blacks over there. When you come to Grand Boulevard, there was no police protection north of the Boulevard except mounted police. Of course the city wasn't extended as far then as it is now. They had to send a mounted police out to investigate, because they didn't have the transportation then. This is going back to the 1920s.

After World War I is the time they began to come from the South when Ford announced the five-dollars-a-day pay. From Europe, they were coming by the shiploads. The foreigners would come in from all parts of Europe, and they would come to Ellis Island and stay thirty days, because they didn't have planes flying. There was no rapid transportation like they have now. You come into Ellis Island and stayed for thirty days, and then if you didn't have a disease or you weren't wanted for murder or something, why they would pass you on into the United States. If they wanted apple pie or something, they would point. They couldn't speak English.

They mostly came here because Detroit was the "Motor City" of the world at that time. Everybody wanted to get to Detroit where the big money was. People were renting out their basements, their attics. They were putting in partitions and sleeping two people in the same room. If you worked days and I worked afternoons, you would sleep there in the night, and I would sleep in the same bed during the day.

When the depression came in the early '30s, for three years as a young man I walked the streets of Detroit and couldn't find a job, couldn't buy a job. It just wasn't there. White and blacks were looking for work, and you could not find it. It just wasn't there.

Well, I shined shoes. I cleaned and blocked hats. At that time, people were burning a lot of coal. If I seen five tons of coal, I would ring their bell and ask them if they wanted it put in their basement. I didn't ask how much you'd pay. I'd just go ahead and put it in there with their approval, and whatever they'd pay me was acceptable.

I remember one time, it was near Christmas. I shoveled three tons of coal and the people gave me some food and three dollars; and I was all day doing that and part of the night. It was night when I went home. I was happy to have that money because I could take it to my sisters and they could buy food for the table. My mother and father were deceased.

I was just in my teens at that time. I'd travel from here to Chicago. I went to Chicago on my own and paid my own fare which at that time was two dollars on the bus. From there I went into Brooklyn, New

York, and then into Harlem. I turned nineteen in Harlem, New York. I did this all on my own. I wasn't going to uncle's house or auntie's house like they do now. I was a perfect stranger everywhere I went, but I made it on my own. I had to be a man of my own, and today that's the only way I believe in doing it. Earn what you get.

I worked on the WPA for approximately a year and a half, during the depression, and I tried to get to be foreman on the job. That was when they made me a supervisor over the repair work—shovels, and picks, and so on. That was as high as I could go. I went to the GAR Building to try and get a promotion. I protested, and I still couldn't get past that barrier that was there due to the color of my skin, not because of knowledge or what I could do.

REGINALD R. LARRIE: I'm an African American history teacher now, and an author of two books. I've done some traveling. In Detroit, I used to get up on Saturday morning and go over on the Boulevard—at the time wealthy people lived on the street—and I would go from door to door asking if they needed any work done. Usually someone would say, "Yes, come on in, I have a bathroom that needs cleaning." And I'd go in and mop the bathroom or do whatever work they had. I was only nine then. . . . I had a little job for two hours a day and I made fifteen cents for two hours work. I would get ten cents from the store owner and a nickel tip for delivering this lady's items. I started paying rent at home when I was twelve. I worked at Wise's Drugstore at the time as a soda fountain clerk. Mr. Wise, the store owner, taught me how to handle and count money.

After the army I worked for the DSR operating streetcars on Woodward Avenue. It was the last cars the city had. If there was a commotion, I could stop the streetcar and say, "Okay, stop it," and people would stop whatever they were doing because they respected your position. Now, they would throw the operator off the car and tear it up.

My father worked for the DPW in the Sanitation Department. Lots of times we fed five or six families in the block, because he would pick up the garbage at fish markets and chicken places. They would intentionally throw out a couple cases of fresh chicken, and so he would come home in the evening and go up and down the block and give them away. At Christmastime he would come home with three or four hams.

We used to go out to Belle Isle all the time. My father worked for the city, and they used to have city picnics every year. The city would provide food for the city employees. You could invite your neighbors. My father had an eight-passenger limousine, Buick. We would go by and pick up the Gibson family. There were five in their family, and sometimes we would pick up the Strong family. There were three in their family and four of us.

45

HENRY BIGGS: I was working at the LaSalle Hotel. I was there when Jerry Buckley was killed. It was July 23, 1930. I was bellhopping. Jerry Buckley was a radio announcer. He was exposing the Purple Gang. The Purple Gang was here when Prohibition was in; and he was exposing the bigwigs, the main men in the Purple Gang. He was naming them. I got there right after that happened. Oh my, I couldn't even get in the place, and I worked there. That was the broadcasting station.

REGINALD R. LARRIE: During Prohibition the bootleggers put a tunnel under the Detroit River, and it was wide enough to pull a cart through. It was like a dumbwaiter, and they ran whiskey from Canada under the river. They had speed boats on top of the water as decoys. The police thought they were chasing the bootleggers, and the bootleggers were bringing the liquor under the water.

HENRY BIGGS: How many nights I would dance all night at the Graystone and have to go to work the next morning, after taking my lady friend home. The old Roxy Theater was on Woodward, near Adelaide, on the west side of the street. It's torn down now. Next door was Levinson's Restaurant which, was the headquarters for the mob. I have seen police with motorcycles escort the bootleggers up Woodward Avenue from the dock that he's speaking of. There was a speakeasy on the corner, a cigar store it was supposed to be, but you could go in there if you were known . . . because there was always a guard there. When they let you in, they just pushed a little button underneath the counter, and this wall would go back, and you could go in the closed back apartment. They had gambling, roulette tables in there, and everything.

REGINALD R. LARRIE: Mr. Black was the first Detroiter to drive an electric streetcar up Woodward Avenue when they first brought the streetcars in. He said nobody would get on the streetcar. There was two things. First, because he was black, and secondly, they didn't know how the electricity worked. He said the first day they got very few riders. The only way he got the job was that no one understood when they set the system up that they needed somebody skilled to operate this thing. They bought it, and they could never find anybody. He was trained as a crane operator and used the same skills.

HENRY BIGGS: On the streetcars, do you know what they use to brake, when they want to stop? It was sand. It was sand that helped stop the momentum, the speed. Overhead cranes use this, and that's how he knew this.

It was driven by a lever, instead of a wheel. You had a certain lever according to your speed, just like you use your foot for your brake. You know how far to start braking before you have to stop. The same way with the streetcar. When driving a streetcar, you begin to brake a little at a time and slow it so you won't have what we call a brick-wall stop, a real hard stop. This way you would make a smooth stop. The sand was on the track. It was steel against steel. The sand would fall down on the track. The track was steel and the sand would break your speed.

The streetcars had a conductor, and he kept the fires going. Then when the war started you had the motorettes. That's when they hired the women.

REGINALD R. LARRIE: There was a man shortage, and they had to have somebody to take people to the defense plants. In World War II, if you were working on the job, say at Ford's, and you wanted to quit that job and, say, go to General Motors, well you couldn't quit that job. You were frozen on that job from the time war was declared until the end of it. The only way you could transfer jobs was to get a release from this employer, Ford Motor Company, and go to the unemployment office, and then they would send you on the other job. That was the only way you could transfer from one job to another. You either do that or you go in the service.

There were very few blacks on the transportation system except for Mr. Black and a few other people, and when he would go to church and put on his bus driver's uniform, and he'd walk in, they'd stop the service. "We have with us this morning, folks, Motorman Black is here." Everybody would stand up and acknowledge him.

BIOGRAPHIES

Henry Biggs was born on July 23, 1911 in Detroit. His mother was born in Chatham, Ontario, and his father was a native of Haiti. He is one of twelve children. A retiree from General Motors, Mr. Biggs is owner of Henry's Janitorial Service in Detroit.

Reginald R. Larrie was born on September 5, 1928 in Detroit. He earned a B.A. from Upper Iowa University, an M.A. from Marygrove College, and a Ph.D. from Western Michigan University. His written work has appeared in many publications; he is the author of *Corners of Black History*. Dr. Larrie is also an instructor of African American History at Wayne County Community College. He has produced a radio series and appeared on television and radio programs. Dr. Larrie has received the City of Detroit Distinguished Service Award and the Montgomery Ward Bicentennial Award.

Paul B. Shirley lived at 512 Watson as a boy and has vivid memories of the face of the city early in this century.

PAUL B. SHIRLEY

Around 1918 I came from Bedford, Kentucky. When I came here, they were getting these factories together. I knew a man named Mr. Cassius Cain had a Model T, and the wheels looked like bicycle wheels today; and this little Ford was just as shiny and pretty as it could be. He had to wind it up to get it started. They had traffic jams. I don't think they went over thirty miles an hour if they went that fast. The "Tin Lizzie" was a skinny car. Ford was the one that had a lot to do with cars on the road, although there were other cars. There was the Pierce Arrow and Stanley Steamer. They had a song about the Stanley Steamer: "Take me for a ride in your Stanley Steamer, Stanley Steamer Automobile." They sang that in vaudeville.

You didn't see very many women driving. Women just stayed in their place then. A woman might also have trouble cranking it up, but I noticed that men don't think much of women being in power, do they? "She should be over there somewhere, watching me do it." All my life I was wondering, don't the fools realize who got them here in the first place?

Detroit was dotted with beautiful little theaters. The black people had a theater called the Koppin. They had revues like Lou Leslie's

Blackbirds and the Brown Skinned Models, and they had Drake and Walker. A company would have thirty-five to forty people in it. They were specialty dancers—tap dancing, comedy, and the girls. The more girls you had, the bigger the production. The Brown Skinned Models was a favorite. Every one of those girls ranged from tea-color brown until a high brown. They didn't have what they called the "high yellows," but they'd have these pretty brown-skinned girls. They were gorgeous. Some of them could sing and dance, but they didn't do no more than walk across the stage.

In the '20s was the blues. The blues and jazz was controversial then. A lot of people didn't want jazz in their house because jazz came from whorehouses. "I don't want that devil music in here." My grandmother wouldn't allow you to play it in her parlor. You could play it in the kitchen, or you could play it on the back porch, but you couldn't bring jazz into her parlor.

I've been on earth since 1912, and I was raised in a place here called Black Bottom. I always lived with a mixture of people from various countries and places and times. The Italians that I knew, they'd have Wednesday for spaghetti day; and they will argue and fight, but they fought largely among themselves. Blacks will argue and fight, but they did it among themselves. When you go over to Miss Bagliotti's place, you either go over there to get some spaghetti or come in and have some vino. I don't know, we just blended. When I was a kid, we'd take our laundry to the Chinese laundry, and they could iron and wash your clothes. I don't know anybody who beats the Chinese when it comes to laundry. They had it together.

The blacks didn't have much business here. I think their biggest business, around 1922–23, was chili parlors. They had nice little places. They had chairs like ice cream chairs with wire backs and tables. You either had the chili there or you'd have it to go. To go, they'd put it in ice cream containers with crackers on the side. That was the best chili you ever wanted to taste. The restaurants didn't start coming in until the '30s, I think.

It was on a Sunday in 1943 that the riot was supposed to have started. At that time I was working out on Seven Mile Road and Woodward at a place that was run by a princess and her husband. They had this beautiful, beautiful dinner on Sunday, only one day a week; and they had beautifully flaky biscuits, fried chicken, mashed potatoes with gravy, and salads. It was just so gorgeous.

This particular Sunday, as I was coming down Woodward Avenue, the conductor asked us was anybody going across town, because a race riot had erupted. Instead of going straight home I stopped at Sunnie Wilson's bar. At that time it was very popular, on Forest and Hastings. Finally about dusk I left. I hadn't thought about the riot because we were laughing and talking. I then remembered I should go home. I was just casually walking along, and I was at Sherman and Gratiot.

A young policeman seemed to come out of nowhere and wanted to know what I was doing walking out there by myself, and he said, "Don't you know there's a riot going on?" It didn't bother, me because I told him I had heard about it, but I still don't understand all of it. So he said, "I'll walk you home," and he walked me from Sherman on Gratiot to Clinton and Russell where I lived. I thought it was so nice of him. He was a lone policeman. I don't know what he was doing out there by himself. I knew he wanted to protect me or else he would have let me go home by myself.

Hastings Street—there will never be another street like it, and it is known all over the world. Hastings Street in Detroit. I've felt pretty bad about it, because I've played up and down Hastings Street as a child, and it wasn't anything that could be done about it 'cause they were putting the freeway in anyway.

I remember heroin. The first time I heard about it, it was brought here by three dancers. They were a dancing team, and they would come here from Spanish Harlem. At that time they were dressed in the latest jitterbug, you know, the "Big Apple," gangster-type hats and the pocket chains hanging down to their knees; and they had brought this substance into Paradise Valley. Well, the kids in Paradise Valley always drank whiskey, beer, wine, and smoked reefer; but they didn't know anything about heroin. And this was in the 1940s. But when I came back to Detroit from Chicago, it was 1961, and it had taken its toll. There's a strange thing about people. They didn't know about this heroin, but they're willing to try it because it came from New York. Detroit wanted to be like New York—Hip!

BIOGRAPHY

Paul B. Shirley was born on July 30, 1912, in Dayton, Ohio. He moved to Detroit in November, 1919. He worked as a waiter at the Barlum Hotel from 1928–33, and he has also worked at the Downtown Club and Penobscot Club. During the Roosevelt administration, under the National Recovery Program, he dug ditches, cleaned alleys, set out trees, and blacktopped roads. He has entertained as a singer, dancer, and stand-up comedian in clubs such as Lark's Grill, Turf Bar, and Flame Show Bar. Mr. Shirley is currently a participant in the Detroit Urban League's Seniors in Community Service Program.

Charles C. Diggs, Jr., was Michigan's first black congressman; he was elected in 1955. Diggs previously served as the youngest member of the Michigan Senate.

CHARLES C. DIGGS, JR.

I was born December 2, 1922. My mother was Mayme Diggs. My father was Charles C. Diggs, Sr. I was their first child, and at that time our residence was 1391 Mullett, at the northwest corner of Russell.

Our property was my earliest recollection. There was a picket fence around it, and besides our residence on the second floor, the first floor was a funeral parlor, as my father was an undertaker. I remember looking through the fence on the Russell Street side, where the local headquarters of the United Negro Improvement Association (UNIA), founded by Marcus Garvey, was located. I frequently saw people in uniforms, parades, and other activity around that building, as the movement was quite popular.

When I was four years old, we moved to 580 and 584 Frederick. Those buildings were previously the famed Dunbar Hospital. We lived in 584, but crossed through the overpass to 580, where the mortuary was housed. Across the street was Bethel A.M.E. Church, pastored by Reverend William Peck, one of the community's most prominent black ministers, and his wife, who founded the highly respected Detroit Housewives League.

In 1933 Michigan elected its first Democratic party governor, and he appointed my activist father as the state's first black parole commis-

51

sioner. However, the devastatingly negative impact of the Great Depression at that time prompted my mother and I to move to Chicago, Illinois, where we had relatives on both sides of our families.

After my father settled into his new job with the state in early 1933, he sent for my mother and me to return to Detroit. For a short while we lived in an apartment at Montcalm and Brush, but then he obtained rental property at 301 East Warren between Brush and John R, to which we moved and reopened the funeral parlor.

In 1934 we moved to 1939 St. Aubin, corner of Maple, back to Black Bottom, as the lower east side was then known. The property had been a funeral home. The building was owned by a black physician, Dr. Nuttall. The funeral home was just part of its southwest side, for the rest of the segmented building contained a pharmacy and several apartments. Dr. Nuttall had three daughters and one son. One of his daughters is Helen Nuttall Brown, whose attorney daughter won a judgeship in Detroit's last election for the Recorder's Court.

From 1934 to 1936 I was enrolled in Duffield Elementary School, across the street from Calvary Baptist Church at 1330 Joseph Campau. I graduated from Duffield in 1936 and transferred to Miller Junior/Senior High School, which still stands on DuBois.

I only remember getting into two mischiefs. The first was "hitching," which was quite popular in those days, I guess because fewer people had cars, at least in most black neighborhoods. "Hitching" was jumping, unnoticed by the driver, on the back of a truck and just riding a few blocks through the streets. One day, however, a policeman in a car saw me "hitch" a truck, which he stopped, took me off, and carried me home. After the policeman left and I started upstairs to my bedroom at 1939 St. Aubin, my father, who was only about 5'6" and weighed about 135–140 pounds, took off his belt and whipped me up the steps to the second floor. I never "hitched" again.

Another time, when we were living on Rowena and Mack, my mother gave me a dollar to buy some fish on Hastings Street, a half-block away. At the mouth of the alley, a group of men were engaged in "Three Card Monte," a game in which three playing cards are displayed face down on a table. You pick one of the cards, not showing the dealer which one. He then shuffles the cards and turns one face up. If it's your card, you win; but if not, you lose. I had never seen such a game before, and it seemed so easy to win; but, of course, I lost my dollar and therefore couldn't buy the fish. When I returned home and my mother asked me for the fish, I told her what happened. She told my father, who led me back over to the game. He demanded return of the dollar; but when the dealer refused, he began to take his coat off to fight for it. However, one of the dealer's allies quickly intervened, saying, "Hey, man, this guy is Senator Diggs. Give him his dollar back." My father took the dollar with his left hand, but with his right hit me in the face, breaking my glasses, and then ushered me back home. I never played "Three Card Monte" again.

1936 was the year my father was elected to the Michigan State Senate; he was the only black senator in the country.

1937 was my father's first legislative session in Lansing, which in those days only met every two years, and the compensation was just three dollars per day. Having been refused rental of a room at the Olds Hotel across the street from the Michigan State Capitol because of his race, it further motivated him to introduce legislation banning discrimination in public accommodations based on race, creed, or color—the first such proposal in the country. The Diggs civil rights bill was passed and signed into law by the governor. It was the cornerstone not only of his active political career, but the foundation of additional civil rights legislation in other states, including the outlawing of discrimination in employment and other areas, plus policy changes within the structure and organization of the Democratic party.

On an official inspection visit that same year to Eloise (Wayne County General Hospital) in Wayne, Michigan, my father discovered that burial of decedent former patients in the cemetery on the premises and their transportation to the Wayne Medical School in Detroit was handled by hospital inmates and employees. This was contrary to state law, which requires such functions to be conducted and/or supervised by licensed morticians. After confirming the legal details, the hospital authorities gave my father the contract to take care of said decedents. Because he was dark-brown-skinned, however, and especially since that was the 1937–38 period, and almost all deceased patients and families were white, my father delegated his "high-yellow" wife and light-skinned son to carry out the contract.

Although I was only fourteen years old, I was 5'10" and weighed 150 pounds. I already had a driver's license, which I was permitted to use until I was sixteen if accompanied by an adult. Therefore, when the hospital called for our services, I would drive my mother the some twenty miles from Detroit to their morgue, a red brick building on their premises called the Round House because of its shape. Most of the time there were no friends or relatives for the interment. However, when their presence was anticipated, we were notified in advance. On those occasions we would come early, close the decedent's mouth, shave them, comb their hair, etc. We rarely had a female body, because with very few exceptions, females had primary family members who buried them privately elsewhere. Using plain white sheets from the hospital inventory, we would line their plain, wooden-box caskets. If they had clothes, we would dress them. If not, the bodies would be covered with a sheet up to their neck. The cemetery was just a short distance away; but for those in attendance who had their own transportation, we would form a cortege, have them follow our hearse in formation to the graveside, and conduct a regular interment ceremony. In the absence of such attendees, we would merely take the boxed decedents to the graveside, and the inmates would just bury them.

Despite our modest compensation for these services, the accumulation of those funds helped my parents purchase two houses at 689–693 Rowena—later named Mack Avenue—directly across the street from the North End of the commodious Brewster Public Housing Project. A brick front was erected across the entire face of the two houses, together with a cement and brick front porch of proportionate size, making it seem like one building.

Ordinarily, the completion of my high school requirements for graduation would not have permitted me to enter college until January 1941. However, I wanted to enter in September of 1940. After consultation with the Miller High principal, because of my scholarship and extracurricular activities, I was authorized to double up in the January–June 1940 semester and finish my last twelve hours in summer school, readying me for the entrance to the University of Michigan in Ann Arbor in September 1940, where I was enrolled until June 1942.

Out of the 25,000 students on the campus in those days, only fifty were black. So when the university monkeyed around about admitting me to the dormitory, my father confronted the president of the University of Michigan, who then had me assigned to the George Palmer Williams House, the men's dormitory right behind the Michigan Union, making me the first black to break the barrier.

Herman Hudson was a graduate of Detroit's Northwestern High who was legally blind and admitted to the University of Michigan in the same class as mine. He and I both entered a university public speaking class. There were thirty such classes, each containing between thirty to thirty-five students, but with only us two blacks in that number. Each class had an annual contest within their group, and the winners of those classes met in a semifinal, then a final to determine the universitywide champions. The contests had two divisions—oratorical, where a contestant spoke for ten minutes from a prepared, memorized text; and extemporaneous, wherein subjects for a ten-minute speech were passed out about ten minutes before delivery. I entered on the oratorical side and Herman on the extemporaneous. I won first place universitywide in my division and later attended the finals for the extemporaneous contest, where Herman was a contestant, and he won! Leaving the auditorium after the contest, I heard a group of mad students exclaiming, "Damn niggers are winning everything around here!"

In early 1942, I tried to join the Navy, but they rejected my application, saying I couldn't see well enough. Of course, that was just an excuse, because they knew my father was a state senator at that time, who was very well known; and they were afraid to recruit me, as conventional procedure at that time was to assign all black recruits to Great Lakes Naval Training Station in Illinois. But their jobs were confined to cooks or laborers swabbing ships' decks or doing other menial tasks. They figured dad would raise hell against such discrimination, and he would have. So I entered Fisk University in September 1942, but just completed one semester before, at age nineteen, being drafted into the U.S. Army.

After basic training I was sent to the Army Administrative School at Atlanta University in Georgia. I was the only black on that shipment. I traveled by train, and once I crossed the geographic line into the South, I was transferred to the coach next to the locomotive. When I was seated to eat in the dining car, a green curtain was pulled around me, technically separating me, southern-segregation style, until my arrival in Atlanta.

I was assigned on special duty to another army administrative school, this time at South Dakota State College, in Brookings, South Dakota, where I was promoted to corporal. Out of a population of five thousand people in Brookings, only two were black besides me—my roommate and a cook at the local hotel. Whenever we went into town, people would stare and point at us. I remember a little kid at one point tugging his mother's arm exclaiming, "Look, ma, there are some niggers!"

After graduation in September 1943, my orders returned me to the 3rd EAUTC Headquarters in Tampa; and shortly thereafter I was promoted to buck sergeant, my third stripe. In October I applied for entrance into the Army Air Force Officer Candidate School, at that time located in Miami Beach, Florida. In December I was authorized to come home to Detroit for the Christmas holidays. Upon my return to the installation and arrival at the gate, guys started congratulating me, and innocently I inquired, "What's going on?"

On the first day after my actual arrival at the Officers Candidate School, all black officer candidates were gathered together and officially told that although they could be "hazed" by upperclassmen, they could not "haze" lowerclassmen as they were elevated in the four-month program prior to graduation. Further, when in formation, marching or otherwise, we were instructed to place ourselves on the inside and to the rear, so we would not be so easily seen.

I returned home and entered Detroit's Wayne University College of Mortuary Science in September 1945. I was an only child, and I wanted to complete that course and join my parents in their mortuary business. Actually, my father had obtained a charter in 1942 to open the Metropolitan Funeral System, a burial insurance company, the only one in the state. The sale of those policies went like wildfire, as so many black people there at that time came from the South, where there was burial insurance in each state in that region. Obviously this boosted our funeral business dramatically, and I was very much needed.

In September 1950 I entered the night curriculum of the Detroit College of Law. After only one semester, however, I succeeded my father in the Michigan State Senate, which terminated me in law school, as Lansing is eighty-five miles from Detroit, and the round-trip was too physically exacting to continue. After two terms in the state senate, I ran for Congress in 1954 and was elected for thirteen straight terms before my retirement in 1980.

In June 1957 I was appointed by President Eisenhower to the U.S. Delegation for the Independence of Ghana. The delegation was chaired by Vice President Richard Nixon. Moreover, my paternal grandfather, who died before I was born, had been a Baptist missionary to Liberia in West Africa. Both these matters laid the foundation for my keen interest in Africa. So when I returned to the states after that ceremony, I applied in Congress for a change in my committee assignments. I had to wait until after the 1958 elections, following which the House Foreign Relations Committee had nine vacancies and eighteen replacement applications, including mine, which reflected the popularity of such an assignment. Nevertheless, I was unanimously elected to one of the vacancies, becoming the first black in history on that committee. I asked for and was also granted assignment to the Subcommittee on Africa, of which I became chairman in 1969.

I had made several applications to visit South Africa before, but they had always turned me down. After I became chairman of the Africa subcommittee, I was finally permitted to visit. Upon arrival at one of their airports, our U.S. Ambassador to South Africa met the plane but told me the authorities would not meet with me. I then decided to leave immediately, but there were no more flights that day. I had to at least stay overnight. My staff director, Attorney Goler Butcher, and I then visited Soweto, the huge, black, South African ghetto several miles from Johannesburg, where I met the Soweto City Counsel, other activists, and spoke to a large, open-air crowd.

On another subsequent visit, I was invited to a luncheon at the home of one of the members of the South African Sugar Growers Association, then a very prominent organization. After that affair, upon leaving, I noticed there was a segregated area where that plantation's laborers were housed. Unbeknownst to the owner at that time, I visited the laborers' camp, where the men were paid twelve dollars per month, slept in little, concrete cell-like rooms; and their waste was disposed of through a hole in the floor. Upon returning to the city, I held a press conference about the luncheon, but I also described the aforementioned conditions, which were well publicized. The Sugar Growers Association was very upset at such references and held their own conference to blast my criticisms.

Another highlight of my career was my first trip to Mississippi in 1955. The black movement down there at the time, headed by a physician in Mound Bayou, where he practiced medicine, invited me to make the main speech at their annual convention in Issequena County, where my father had been born and where the Baptist church founded and pastored by his father, who died before I was born, was located.

In 1956, I had a twice-a-week radio program in Detroit that was very, very popular. The Montgomery, Alabama, bus boycott had been started, and through a fund raiser sponsored by solicitations on the radio program, I collected ten thousand dollars which I took down there to give to the young preacher, who was heading the movement, at a rally at his church. His name—Reverend Martin Luther King, Jr. He never forgot that presentation, which was the seminal motivation of his distinguished career. In 1962, he came to Detroit and was the principal at a testimonial for me.

BIOGRAPHY

Charles C. Diggs, Jr., was born in Detroit to Charles C. Diggs, Sr., and Mayme E. Diggs on December 2, 1922. He is a graduate of Wayne State University and an alumnus of Howard University. He has been awarded honorary doctorate from several universities. While a student at Detroit College of Law, he was elected the youngest member of the Michigan State Senate in 1951. He became Michigan's first black congressman in 1955. Two years later Congressman Diggs was selected by President Eisenhower to be part of the U.S. Delegation to the Independence of Ghana. He was appointed to the U. S. House Subcommittee on Africa, and became its chairman. In 1971 he founded the Congressional Black Caucus. Retired Congressman Diggs is the recipient of more than one hundred awards and citations for community service. He is a licensed mortician in several states. He belongs to Ebenezer A.M.E. Church in Fort Washington, Maryland.

FREDERICK N. CURETON

I lived on the east side before I went to school. A lot of the families moved to the east side because that was the only available housing for blacks. See, ninety-eight percent of the houses in Detroit, white people once lived in them. So, when the people made a transition from the east side to the west side to the north end, they were able to live there awhile, and put a nest egg away, and were able to put a down payment on a house. That's how they escaped. But everybody over here was not able to put a down payment on a house, so they were not able to escape. They had mishaps, and families, and they just stayed there. And living in that type of environment, you just couldn't get your way out of there. And when the blacks come from the South, the area became crowded, because there were far more people living in this area than once white people lived.

In 1925 I lived on the east side when we went to grade school. They built that school in 1911, and I started going in 1925. That's about fourteen years after the school was built. It was all white, and there were very few Jews, relatively few. They had a small synagogue, a wooden building that was about half the size of this [building] on the corner of Begole and Milford that was used for a tabernacle. On the Sabbath I used to blow the candles out and take the ashes out, and I was a young-ster.

They had two or three families, or more, living in that house. I had an aunt downstairs. I had an uncle; I had cousins started coming in from the South. The first thing I know we ain't got a house without twelve people in the house. And then when they got money enough to get them a house, they broke away.

BIOGRAPHY

Frederick N. Cureton was born on October 20, 1918, in Green-ville, South Carolina. He moved to Detroit in 1921 and was raised on the west side. He remembers the crowded conditions of the time and re-calls that his family often shared their home with many aunts, uncles, and cousins.

ERNEST GOODMAN

I was born in Hemlock, Michigan, on August 21, 1906, moved to nearby Kawkawlin until the age of five, then lived in Detroit to the present. I lived the life of a young Jewish kid growing up in Detroit's ghetto. I went to Hebrew school and to synagogue services regularly. My family kept a kosher house. I had that sort of upbringing. We lived first on Adelaide Street, which is part of downtown now. Over the years we moved north to Brady Street, to Garfield, to Palmer, to Euclid, then across Woodward Avenue to the west side—Clairmount, then Burlingame.

The Jewish ghetto, before it moved to the west side of Woodward Avenue, consisted of housing which was always infested by cockroaches and bedbugs. Rats were another enemy which you had to be constantly chasing, avoiding, and destroying. These ghetto scenes have always been a sharp part of the recollection of my childhood.

To the south of the Jewish ghetto lived the black community in its own ghetto. As we moved north, the black people would take over the ghetto housing of the Jewish people.

I lived in this way, within a completely Jewish environment. I hardly knew any gentiles. We, like most families, didn't own a car. We traveled primarily by streetcar and lived, when we could, near where we worked and where our synagogue was located. Ours was an insular life for most of my childhood years.

I went through Central High School, and the experiences there were tied into the Jewishness of my life, especially in being singled out as Jewish and not being able to participate in the life of the non-Jewish WASP students who politically ran the school. It resulted, during the last part of my high school life, in a bloody battle that occurred at the school between the WASPS and the roughhouse Jewish guys, out of whom arose the notorious Purple Gang in the late 1920s. We considered them our friends because they protected us. This battle between the WASPS and the Jews helped open my eyes to the racial, religious, and ethnic divisions within our society. Where we lived too, in the process of moving from place to place, there were battles going on, in our neighborhoods, between the Poles and the Jews. If you walked past the border line, you were likely to get beaten up. If they came over, some of the guys on our side would reciprocate.

When the depression came and I was faced with it, I began to find out that the work that I was doing as a lawyer, all of it, was on behalf of small retail stores that sold furniture and jewelry on credit to working people. Our job was to try to collect these accounts or repossess if they couldn't pay, especially when they were laid off. The black community was particularly victimized by this practice. The more I did that kind of work, the more I felt that it was something I didn't want to spend my life on. I read and studied. I became aware that the Thirteenth, Fourteenth, and Fifteenth Amendments had utterly failed to provide any protection to black people.

Over the next five or six years, from 1929–1935, I made the decision to leave the practice of law or at least my kind of practice. Fortunately, as it turned out, all the different enterprises my partners and I entered into in terms of making money didn't go very well, and we went broke. I heaved a sigh of relief. I had escaped this rat trap, this cage in which I had found myself enclosed.

Then I began to find something else to do on behalf of people individually—human beings, not companies. I joined a number of organizations—the American Civil Liberties Union, very early, probably in 1935; then the Professional League for Civil Rights; and the Civil Rights Federation.

I saw people, unemployed, walking aimlessly, doing nothing, selling apples on the corner. These were people who looked able and intelligent; they just didn't have any money. I saw my father losing his source of work, his little business. Then I began to read the sources and causes of the depression, and began to understand what was happening, not only in Detroit but over the entire country.

I began to understand that people were being destroyed for no reason I could see that was logical or necessary. I then began to understand what I had been doing as an individual, as a lawyer. I had been working on behalf of a system that was destroying the people around me. I began to realize that I was becoming a part of this system. I made a decision I didn't want that. I wanted to fight on behalf of the people who were being oppressed and do something to help them. The only thing I began to feel sorry about was that I had wasted all these years when I could have been doing something that was useful and constructive.

For the first time, I met black people. I had never before met black people on a social level. In the organizations I had joined were black people as well as white people. Also, non-citizens who were living here, from different countries, different cultures, with different personalities. I began to find out all the wonderful things I could learn from them. Their ideas were so different, and they helped me to expand my view of life and of the world at the same time.

As I began to engage in political work, I was asked to speak from time to time at meetings. I was invited to speak at a black church on a Sunday morning. It was a church service. I forget what the subject was. What I do remember is that I put on my Sunday clothes, which means my older, comfortable clothes. I thought, "Well, it's Sunday; I'll just go over there." It was a store-front church on Hastings Street. I had never been in a store-front church. I walked in, in a shirt and trousers, without a jacket and without a tie. As I walked in, I saw all these people dressed up in their Sunday best. I hesitated but realized I couldn't walk out. I sheepishly sat down. Everybody was looking at me. I felt like shrinking up into myself. Finally, the pastor saw me and called on me to speak. He introduced me by saying that Mr. Goodman doesn't understand the custom about Sunday church and has just come from home. I felt so embarrassed. I began to realize that I just didn't understand the culture of the black community. I wouldn't have gone to a white church the way I was dressed, but I did to a black church because I didn't understand. It was lessons of this kind, over a period of years, that helped me to feel comfortable with black people.

I'm getting into about 1935, 1936, and 1937. These were great years in the sense that there were tremendous organizing movements all over the city—organizing labor unions, organizing tenants, trying to get food for people in some fashion. All these were political struggles. Of course, most important was the labor union struggle. Detroit was nationally known as an open shop-town with no unions of any consequence. They had been kept out for years.

The state laws made it very, very difficult for a union to organize. Peaceful picketing was not permitted. Injunctions would be issued, people put in jail for peaceful picketing. There was no way in which working people could peacefully organize a labor union except in the small, side businesses. What we now consider a right under the Constitution, necessary to a democratic society, was not then possible in cities like Detroit. Other means had to be used. Usually it was by violating the law—going on a picket line, trying to close the plant in order to force the employer to bargain for a contract so they'd be arrested, put in jail as law breakers.

A few of us at that time, who were concerned with organizing labor unions, were doing much of the legal work. Labor unions were considered, and usually treated as, communist organizers at that time. The press and the radio were all under the influence of the employers. Only a few minor alternative newspapers were open to take the side of working people or people who were being evicted from their houses.

There was no way in which a lawyer could make a living doing that kind of work because none of these people had any money to pay a lawyer. In addition, a lawyer became a social and professional pariah. There was no such thing as a labor lawyer. Labor law was then examined under the heading of "master and servant" in the law books.

It was this kind of atmosphere that presented just the kind of opportunity I was looking for. As a lawyer, I could fight effectively within a larger struggle with which I identified myself, on behalf of the oppressed and virtually defenseless, against the clearly etched wealthy and powerful. It was a wonderful opportunity to be of help, instead of using the instrumentalities of law to evict people from houses and to take away their furniture when they failed to make the payments.

To my parents, anything I did must be right or else I wouldn't be doing it. Their view of their only son was somewhat naive, but sometimes it was helpful. The CIO was organized in 1936. It was attacked throughout the country as a communist organization. I remember billboards in 1936, during the Roosevelt reelection campaign, reading, "Join the CIO and build a Soviet America." This red-scare attack never stopped. I was continuously involved in handling labor cases. My name got into the paper quite often, sometime front page: strike, picket line confrontation, injunction, arrests, trials. I was always representing the CIO unions.

My mother and her friends read or heard about it. I'll never forget, one day she came to me and said, very cautiously and quietly: "Ernie, friends say you're active in the CIO, that you represent the CIO. They tell me that the CIO is bad. Maybe you should think about it." She was hesitant to criticize me, so she had put it that way. I realized that I couldn't give a dissertation on the nature of society, and that there are two sides to much of it—the workers and the boss—and that we were in a struggle for something that the workers believed in.

So I said, "Look, mama, do you think I would do anything wrong?"

She said, "Oh no, Ernie."

So I said, "Then don't worry about it." That satisfied her.

When the National Lawyers Guild was formed in 1937, I finally had an opportunity of belonging to a law society which embodied the concepts I held. The American Bar Association primarily represented big business and finance. It opposed everything Roosevelt and his New Deal represented, and excluded black lawyers. Through the Guild I became acquainted with lawyers across the country who held social and political views similar to my own. They formed a network of lawyers who were involved in the development of labor law, civil rights and liberties, and other areas of people's struggles. During the so-called McCarthy period of repression, our ability to exchange experiences and develop legal theories kept us from despair.

One important event occurred to me in 1935. I was campaigning for my then-partner for Circuit Judge, just before we dissolved. I said I would speak for him. At a meeting in the home of a black man on the near west side, I was one of five speakers. We were sitting at a dining room table facing the small living room. Only two or three black people were present. The host was understandably embarrassed. He excused himself, hustled up seven or eight neighbors and finally got the meeting started.

One of the speakers was a man named Maurice Sugar, whom I had heard of but never met. What he said, I never forgot. This was the first time I heard somebody speak intelligently about the nature of society, analyzing it clearly and simply so that I could understand what had been so confusing to me. Suddenly it hit me that the only political candidates I'd ever heard talk to a black audience spoke only in terms of, "Look, I help black people, I have a black chauffeur," or, "My wife hires a black housekeeper, who our children love." That was the level of political speaking. This man Sugar spoke about the domination of the few of great wealth over the many who do the work or are unemployed—of the racial prejudice which is used to keep the working people divided and prevent the formation of unions. He told them his election as judge would enable him to bring into the system the concept of equality which the Constitution guaranteed to everyone.

I soon found out more about Sugar. He was one of the organizers of the National Lawyers Guild. I went to visit him. He was one of the two or three lawyers in the United States who were known as labor lawyers. He had spent his life developing, fighting for, and working on behalf of labor unions. He had specific ideas about the nature of society. He had known all the great radicals of his time.

When he saw my interest in the union movement he began to call on me to handle some union work, which I knew absolutely nothing about. I began to handle labor related cases for him in 1936 and 1937.

In those days the police were solely under the control of the employers of this state. They dominated them top to bottom, in addition to which the employers had private detectives and agencies working full-time for them. We called them goons or company goons. As the number of strikes increased, violence increased. The employers used every means at their disposal to preserve Detroit as an open-shop town.

Most of the violence came from the police, and much of it was directed toward black people. They were treated differently than whites in all encounters with the judicial system. In the first place, black lawyers could not rent offices in downtown office buildings. Many had their offices on Broadway just off Gratiot. They were treated differently in court. They were usually called by their first name. When blacks, in the criminal courts especially, were witnesses or defendants, they were always called by their first name. Nobody ever called them "Mr. so-and-so." At a point later on, when I was handling criminal cases, I began to call a black witness or defendant, "Mr. so-and-so," and the judge would look up. He didn't stop me, but he did wonder what was going on.

Black lawyers had very few opportunities to practice law other than criminal cases, divorces, small business transactions, or real estate transactions. There were some very good lawyers who managed to survive at a somewhat higher economic level, but it was very difficult.

I soon observed the treatment by the police of the black community was in complete disregard of their rights. They would arrest a black person, hold him for about as long as they wanted—a week, two weeks, sometimes even longer. If a lawyer attempted to get him out because no charges had been brought against him, the police could transfer him from one precinct to another, and the judges would not acknowledge this common practice. Unless you served the subpoena at the precinct where the prisoner actually was at the time, the police would win this merry-go-round game.

White policemen—there were only a few that were black—didn't want to go into the black community to try to solve a crime. They had little communication within the black community. But they wanted to solve some crimes in the black community so as it wouldn't look as though they were overlooking criminal conduct. So they used the easy method—beat out a confession. The crime was solved. That was typical. I don't know how many hundreds or thousands of people were sent to prison for crimes to which they confessed but didn't commit.

In these cases the prosecutor's case rested primarily on the confession. Without the confession they had no case. The defendant takes the stand and testifies he didn't voluntarily give the confession; that he had been held in jail for several days, questioned constantly, threatened or beaten. Most of the time the all-white jury would believe the all-white police force before the white judge and all-white clerks. I'd look through this confession and try to find something that I could prove was not factually true. Now and then my own investigation would disclose solid evidence that was inconsistent with a specific statement in the "confession." In the face of such disclosure it was shown that the defendant could not have created the statement which was proved false by the evidence, and that the confession was coerced by the police. One got some satisfaction in showing that these cops can and do lie. In those cases the jury would frequently acquit.

We have to eradicate these four hundred years of slavery which makes a distinction between the white and black color, which emphasizes all the other attitudes and makes it something different from and greater than the kind of difficulty that people generally have in relating.

BIOGRAPHY

Ernest Goodman was born on August 21, 1906, in Hemlock, Michigan. He attended school in Detroit and graduated from the Detroit College of Law. He has been fighting the legal battles of the poor and oppressed since 1928. From 1939–47 he served as general counsel for the UAW-CIO and was responsible for the original Ford, Chrysler, and General Motors labor board cases. In 1950 he and George Crockett formed the first interracial law firm in the country. He is a practicing attorney with the firm Goodman, Eden, Millender & Bedrosian.

Carl Winter led many battles to preserve the rights of African Americans and was jailed for his leadership in the Communist party.

CARL WINTER

In my early childhood I had an occasion to experience many labor struggles, many labor strikes. My family was very conscious of labor development and supported those labor struggles. I can remember a bakers' strike when I was about eleven years old. I remember my father saying: "Don't buy that bread. There is blood on that bread." What he referred to was that the striking pickets had been brutally assaulted. That was an example of my early upbringing.

May Day, 1919, I was thirteen years old. My parents marched in that demonstration. It was a demonstration soon after the end of World War I, and it was primarily motivated by anti-war sentiment. The head of the parade consisted of returned army men in uniform who carried the flag and called for no more war. Participants were brutally assaulted by the police in an organized attack. It wasn't just a matter of the police barring a procession. I saw young men in Boy Scout uniforms and others in Western Union uniforms equipped with baseball bats and billiard cues with spikes driven through them which they swung against the marchers from flatbed trucks which were provided for them. In other words, this was an organized, planned assault. It wasn't just the usual police confrontation with a procession that they were trying to stop. In fact, the first thing I recall being struck by, before the parade started, was that there were no police in sight. I thought that was strange, because ordinarily you expected the police to lead a parade and be there in an organized way; but there were no police whatsoever.

Certainly a very important thing is the organization of the UAW at the Ford Rouge plant, because Reverend Hill played an important and a very likely decisive role in bringing the workers in the Ford Rouge plant to support the union. That was no mean achievement, because to talk in favor of the union usually resulted in immediate dismissal. Black workers had been coming up north at the time and getting jobs in the Ford plant, but they were discriminated against. They were permitted to work only in the foundry or in the coke oven, the dirtiest and the hardest and the most dangerous jobs. They were not permitted in any of the skilled trades, no matter what their qualifications might be. Many of the white workers were themselves practicing prevailing discrimination against black people.

When the union organizers called for a strike in support of the demand for recognition of the union, black workers at first felt that they had no stake in it. Reverend Hill played a very active part in appearing in the picket lines and talking to black workers and inviting them to come out and join the strike. In fact, it was a turning point in the strike when the black workers came out and joined the strike, because the company had figured that it could play the black workers against the others and get more black workers to come to Detroit and take the strikers' jobs. That didn't succeed, and the union succeeded in gaining recognition.

I was here at the time that Paul Robeson was barred from public appearance in most places. I participated in efforts to secure meeting places for concerts with Paul Robeson. I got to know Reverend Charles Hill and was part of the group that asked him if he would receive Paul Robeson at his home, which he did, and made his church available for Robeson's concert. I also participated in the Civil Rights Congress which organized for the security of Paul Robeson when he was in Detroit. I chaired some public meetings for Paul Robeson.

As a member of the Civil Rights Congress, I had to make arrangements for refuge for one of the Scottsboro Nine who escaped from a prison farm. There were nine young black men, teenagers, who were apprehended by the railroad police for riding the freight train, which was very commonly used in those days for traveling across the country. They'd hitch onto them and travel, looking for work. When the police took them off the train in Mississippi, there were two young white women in the freight train, and the police immediately charged all nine of them with rape. In 1931 they were all convicted. The women were used as government witnesses against them, though one of them later repudiated her testimony and said it was under coercion by the police and the prosecuting attorney. That didn't affect the jury. That was standard practice in the South. A black man could be charged with rape if he simply was accused by a white woman of having looked at her.

I participated actively in the campaign for the freedom of the nine Scottsboro youths. Later one of them was on a prison farm; that was where he was doing his time and doing work as a prisoner under guard. He escaped, and I got together with the Civil Rights Congress and arranged for his refuge on a farm here in Michigan. Later, of course, all of the prisoners were released; but that was after they had served many years in prison in the South.

The women had nothing to do with them. They weren't any part of any other group, nor were the nine an organized group of any sort. It was characteristic of the times. Unemployment was such that young people would hop on a freight train in hopes that it might be better someplace else. These happened to be on the same train. I'm not even sure that they were in the same boxcar. When the railroad police cleared freights, as they frequently did of hoboes, they found these nine youths and the two women. Ruby Bates, as I recall, was the name of the one who repudiated her testimony and said that while she testified that she had been raped, it was not true.

In 1946 the police shot and killed a thirteen-year-old black lad for no reason, no provocation whatsoever. He happened to be running through the alley in the neighborhood where he lived, and he was shot down. His name was Leon Mosely. I mention that because I participated in an effort to arouse the city's attention to the prevailing police brutality in the black community. The family was devastated by the murder, but it didn't know where to turn and was even reluctant to make any public outcry for fear of reprisals, which others had experienced in such situations.

I became involved after reading about Mosely's murder in the papers. The press made nothing of the action of the police and simply reported that this boy had been killed. I suspected that what was involved there was the usual. Police shoot first and ask questions afterwards. They often didn't ask any questions in the case of black youth in particular. At that time it was notorious that police were stopping and searching black people on no excuse whatsoever. Stopping people on the street, demanding to know what they were doing in the neighborhood, searching them without warrant, searching people's cars without warrant, if the driver was black. This was well known in the mid-'40s.

When I learned about the funeral arrangements that the family had made at a church on the east side, I contacted the Civil Rights Congress. It was an organization that had come to the defense of victims of police brutality. It had helped arrange legal assistance where people were unjustly arrested and charged. Wherever there was a case of racial discrimination, the Civil Rights Congress took an active part in mobilizing public sentiment against the perpetrators. We talked the situation over, and we decided to get as many white people as possible to attend the funeral services in sympathy and solidarity. However, we had other plans as well as to how to bring this to public attention. We prepared placards which each of the people that we got to attend the service put under their coats to be used later. When the services ended and the funeral cortege formed out in the street, we joined in the procession. As it proceeded down the street, we whipped out these placards denouncing police brutality, particularly focusing on Police Commissioner Toy, whom we charged with responsibility for the brutal behavior of the police, calling for Toy's removal. Then when the cortege reached downtown, we urged onlookers to join us as we formed a procession headed towards City Hall.

The old City Hall was in the area that is now Kennedy Square. I led the march to the steps of City Hall and mounted them. The police were very much alarmed. They thought we were going to invade City Hall. They locked the doors; they barred them and set up a cordon of police on the landing. By that time we had close to one hundred people with us. I addressed the crowd from the City Hall steps, pointing out that this murder of the young lad was typical of the brutality that the city police engaged in against black people in general. It was part of an effort to terrorize the community and to prevent it from joining in any demand for equal treatment, whether in employment or in housing opportunities or in welfare and so on. I raised the call for the removal of Police Commissioner Toy. There was no interference with the gathering. The police were extremely alarmed. They thought that this was going to be a raid and they acted that way, but took no action against the gathering.

I was one of those who was arrested with the national board of the Communist Party under the Smith Act and served a five-year sentence. That was from 1951–1955. It was a jury trial. It later went to the Supreme Court, which in about 1958 found the Smith Act could not be applied to an organization like the Communist party exercising freedom of speech.

When I was on trial under the Smith Act, I asked for Mr. George Crockett to be my attorney and he accepted. For his pains he served four months in prison on the contempt charge which the judge put in effect. There were eight attorneys and eleven defendants. Judge Medina cited all the attorneys in that case for contempt. They had repeatedly called attention to his illegal rulings, any number of them, all through the trial. He was outraged that anybody would dare to challenge him, but they called him on legal points. They raised objections, and he'd say, "Sit down!"

"But I have a right to make an objection."

And he'd say, "If you don't sit down, I'll cite you for contempt." He did this all through the trial, but didn't cite anyone until the trial was ended. Then he summoned all the lawyers to the bench; and he cited every one of them; and he gave them six months, four months, and so on—distributing sentences which they all then served. In fact, some of them were disbarred, lost their legal rights as attorneys. It was some years later that they regained the right to practice law. Crockett was not disbarred; he served that four-month term and returned to legal practice.

BIOGRAPHY

Carl Winter's life was dedicated to the struggle for equal rights, social and economic justice for the working class and all oppressed people. As a civil engineer for the New York City Subway System; he became a member of the Union of Technical Men and active in the struggles of the unemployed. He held leading positions in the Communist party in several states. In 1948 Winter was found guilty of conspiring to advocate and teach the overthrow of the government. Carl and Helen Winter moved to New York in 1965, where they held many leading positions in the Communist party. In 1982 they moved back to Michigan, where he established the Midwest Labor Institute. In 1985 he was honored as a Distinguished Warrior. Mr. Winter died on November 16, 1991.

*Alice E. M. Cain Newman's father, Jimmy Cain, was
the owner of several businesses, and was a musician and
producer of stage shows. His daughter, Alice, earned a
quarter a week for performing in his shows when she was
nine years old. As a young woman she worked as a
model.*

ALICE E. M. CAIN NEWMAN

I lived downtown. I remember we went to church which was on Rowena Street, which is now Mack Avenue. We went to Mt. Olive Baptist Church. The pastor was Reverend Glover. I remember the house was a little frame house.

The races weren't as separated then, I don't believe, because I'm remembering some of the people. I don't know if they were Hungarian or Jewish or what. I'm remembering when they had a wedding that there was a lot of dancing and going on. I remember a little girl I used to go to school with. We used to trade sandwiches in school. She would bring bean sandwiches, and I loved beans, and I don't know what kind of sandwiches I must have had. She and I would trade sandwiches. That's about all I can remember about downtown Detroit.

We moved out of that area when I was very young. My grandmother and father bought property out on Eight Mile Road when it was first developed, and that's where my memories really begin. We were right on Eight Mile Road, because my dad had a business. On both sides of Eight Mile was a black-owned commercial strip. One side of Eight Mile was Ferndale; that's the side we lived on. The other side was Detroit. So we were in Ferndale, but it was right on Eight Mile. 164 Parkside.

The community, as far as I can remember, was all black, and all had built their own homes. They were frame houses. It was very nice. It was safe, it was clean, and the businesses were black-owned. Down farther, I remember there was a Kroger on the Detroit side, further down toward Woodward.

This is the part that I think you might find interesting. We black kids had to go to school over in Ferndale. I went to Jefferson School first. They really didn't want us. They treated us horribly. They treated us very, very bad. I can't remember how many black kids were there. They just didn't want us there. They let the children abuse us. They would call us nigger. They'd call us black, and teachers wouldn't do anything about it, not a thing. If they were reprimanding the children, they didn't let us blacks know anything about it, which made us hostile too.

My grades were terrible. At home and in the community I was so well-loved and respected; and at school, where I was spending so many hours a day, I was treated like dirt. At that time they marked with one, two, three, four, and five. I got nothing but red fives. I would just be devastated.

The whites decided that they were going to put a school in the black community, and that was the Grant School. My grandmother was Mrs. Robinson. She and another woman and I don't know how many others really fought the school because they knew it was just for segregation reasons. However, the more I think about it, the happier I am that it happened, because I was doing so poorly before then.

When that black school finally got up there, they brought in young black teachers who were college graduates. There was a lady out there named Mrs. Pearl Wright who was the assistant principal. They put in a white principal, Mr. Kern; but all of the teachers were young, black women. I'm going to tell you the difference in my grades was remarkable. I remember they had some kind of a citywide intelligence test, and my intelligence score was one of the highest in the city.

There was one white family who lived in the area, had a little boy. She was a widow or not married; there was no husband. The people got together and moved her out of that community so that her little boy wouldn't have to go to school with all the blacks. The people in the white area moved her out. They got together, with her permission, and found her a house near to where her child would go to Jefferson School.

We had a nice house. It was newly built, and it was big. Everybody in the community who got married didn't get married at church, they got married at our house. It was a nice settlement. If you go out there now, most of those homes are very, very old.

My father had his business, a restaurant on the front part of Eight Mile, and then our house was behind that facing Parkside. The restaurant was facing Eight Mile. My dad made a lot of money, he made a very lot of money. It was called "Jimmy's"—Jimmy Cain's hot dog stand. I think hot dogs were a nickel. I think pop was a nickel. Chili was probably a quarter. My grandmother made sweet potato pies. I don't know what they sold for. There was a slot machine that you pulled down, and the lemons and the other fruits all came up. It cost a nickel to play. There was gum and candy, just little small things like that. I worked there.

Just the young people came. They came, and they hung out, and they would play the machine. They'd sit and talk and kid each other, buy hot dogs and whatever. My dad also had an orchestra that played for the city recreation department. He had a semiprofessional baseball team out there. He and another man had a partnership in a recreation room. I found out later that may have been a pool hall.

There was a man out there who was a candy manufacturer. There was another restaurant owned by a lady. She was the first person I knew to have barbecue in a store. There was a grocery store. Just all up and down. My aunt died and was buried at Oak Grove Methodist Church which is still here. I don't know if the theater was owned by blacks, but I know it was operated by blacks because my father used to put on a stage show there every week. I'd earn a quarter a week; I'd dance in it. A quarter a week was a lot of money for me then.

We moved from there, forcibly, because of urban renewal. I think it was about 1930. The city wanted to widen Eight Mile Road. When the city came through to buy the property, the owners fought it for a long time. They had to hire an attorney. Eventually they had to sell. I'm using the word urban renewal; and, of course, that wasn't a word I knew at that time; but I know what they would call it now. They broke up the community. They broke up the business.

I've noticed a pattern. The city did the same thing in the '40s down at Paradise Valley. That was a thriving black business community, probably one of the most thriving in the United States that was owned by blacks, not just fronted by blacks but it was owned. They came through and did the same darn thing and let that land stay vacant ten solid years before they put up housing down there.

I was resentful because, when I had to leave, it broke up my life, my whole life pattern—the friends I had made, the teachers that I loved. We moved up north, up into the Idlewild area. My grandmother had fine china, fine silver, linens and really the best of everything. My dad had a Graham Page car. Have you ever heard of that? It was a big car. He bought it used as well as a Model T Ford. I guess it was made by Graham Page Company. It was a big car, real big car. I remember my dad never drove. My uncle drove. We were on Woodward Avenue, in Highland Park, and the police officer stopped my uncle because he had that big car. Of course, he could show that the ownership was legal. He stopped him just because he was black with a big car.

We left the cars right on up there in Idlewild and Big Rapids, and my grandmother put the furniture in storage that she was never able to get out. I used to see her just sit and cry. I said nothing would ever mean that much to me. I determined that, when I was a kid. Nothing would mean that much to me that I'd cry about it.

BIOGRAPHY

Alice E. M. Cain Newman was born in Pittsburgh, Pennsylvania. She attended Lewis Business College, Wayne State University, and Ruby Trimble's School of Cosmetology. She worked for Allen's Millinery and for the U. S. government for thirty years as a tax technician, exempt organizations specialist. She is now a licensed realtor. She is married to Leroy C. Newman and is mother to Aldine R. Dickens, Connie L. Scott, and Erva Jones. She is grandmother to seven children and great-grandmother to seven. Ms. Newman is a member of Eta Phi Beta Sorority, National Council of Negro Women and is a life member of the NAACP. She attends the Church in the Light.

WILLIAM HINES

We came here from the South in 1919 from Albany, Georgia. You started to Bible School at fifteen cents a week when you were three years old where you were already exposed to some things at that early age. I'll never forget the first address. It was 998 High Street. I was born in 1915.

In reference to the era that I was here in the Hastings area, the Detroit Paper Station was across the street. That station carried the *News*, the *Times*, the *Free Press* and the *Daily Mirror*. This was the extent of our little world.

Every house along here was a one- or two-story flat. In the middle of the block that's where the Buckner boys were raised. One played the piano with Lionel Hampton. Over them, upstairs, was the singing cowboy family. We were all kids together in those days.

The only two-family house was where the music store was and where the Buckner boys all lived. The music shop was in the front, and their residence was in back. On the corner was a barber shop. In the next block was Cole's Funeral Home, off the corner of St. Antoine and High Street.

In 1919, Shiloh Baptist Church was in the basement at this corner;

and it was covered over by one of those tents; and then they built and moved into what is still Shiloh Baptist Church. The unique thing about it, our minister at that time was Reverend Ross. Reverend Ross and Turkey Stern married two sisters. Turkey Stern was one of the greatest baseball players in black history.

On this corner was a baker's shop. At the end of evenings, if there were any bagels left over, we got them.

Walking from here to Belle Isle was nothing. If you had six cents, you didn't ride the streetcar with it, you saved it for a hot dog.

I remember the Swift Packing Company trucks coming down Hastings, and we'd see the boys jump on the back of that truck and throw hams, sides of beef off it. You cooked hot dogs in the alley there called "Apes Alley." That was where the tough guys hung around. They were tough, but they never came on the playground, only watched us. We're seen some famous fights in that area, but never on Brewster Playground.

Brewster Center here motivated a lot of young men who were headed to stay in the street. I remember when Dave Clark, the famous fighter and stable mate of Joe Louis, had a gang called Blackstone. They were kind of rough fellows in the neighborhood. They then decided to come into the center. We can say that this particular building helped a lot of boys turn around. We challenged a fighting team to come up and play basketball. You know how it was trying to play basketball with boxing shoes. They were sliding all over the floor, and we were really making clowns out of them. After the game was over, it was time for us to go down to their gym and put the gloves on. We all got very sick, and we had to go home.

When Will Robinson came into the city of Detroit, his team was waiting for him. They were already playing. All he had to do was discipline, he and Mr. Leroy Dues down at Miller School.

For our championship games, Mr. John White kept our team up at the Gotham Hotel. We stayed in the penthouse. Mr. White would come down and sit on the gym floor and watch the games.

The first facilities we had for recreation was when we took over the old Jewish Center. Robinson Furniture Store was there, and the first black hospital was to the right side of the Jewish Center.

The Brewster Center's original name was Central Community Center. The building was originally the Ginsberg Library. For the first two years we slid up and down that floor. This is a unique neighborhood, and it was occupied by Jewish people at that time.

Then the Urban League was over by Eastern Market. That used to be a cemetery. Then it was the House of Corrections. We used to go over there and watch the guards patrolling the high wall. That was after they took up the graveyard. There's a restaurant that's always been there at Erskine and Riopelle—Roma Café.

77

John Dancy was a great athlete. He was good at everything. He was one of those people who could call Henry Ford on the phone and say, "I need to see you," and not have to wait a long time for him or anybody else like you. He would say, "I need, not a party for these kids, but some shoes to put on their feet." He had the personality. He could talk to anybody. Never any pretense. We would all get into the back of Mr. Jones's car. Did you ever see nine kids in the back of a rumble seat? We would all get in on a Saturday to play ball in the Urban League. There would be nine of us hanging all over that convertible Dodge.

The black businesses—the largest laundry service was Allen Supreme Laundry. He at the time supplied all black businesses with their coats and their pants. Mr. Porter had the largest black-owned cleaners. Mr. Howell had the first beauty supply business.

I can remember Mr. Barthwell was very close to us. I went to his store and bought ice cream from him as a young boy. Then I went back to him as one of the first black liquor salesmen in the state of Michigan. Mr. Barthwell had five liquor licenses, so they hired me to crash the market. Mr. Barthwell did accept me, but he let me know that I had to make my own way. It wasn't easy, because my competition was Jewish, and that was heavy in the wine business. I'm very grateful for the fact that I can remember all of the good things.

One of the areas that is not talked about, and why our dollars turned over in the community, was the black numbers business. Our local people here developed it, and we controlled it. Of course, it was considered illegal, but that money was put to good use in the black community, with the dollar turning over in the community five or six times. The pickup man, the lady that wrote the number, pickup man, the other pickup man, to the owner. The owner had all blacks working for his area.

I remember the destroying of the Gotham Hotel, which surpassed all black-owned businesses at the time as the number one hotel in America, even superseding New York's. This was entirely Class A. Harper Hospital fought us over getting a liquor license so we could have a beautiful lounge. They did everything to stop us. Sure, every black was aware that that was the resting place for the numbers. That's when the officials discovered how much money was in the black community, and they proceeded to destroy it when they discovered it.

I recall the signs that store owners put up during the riot. A Chinese laundry put on his door, "Me colored too."

At a cleaning place up there one guy said, "Oh my God, all my clothes was in there. I forgot them."

My experience here was very, very good in terms of my young life, because I knew my limitations. There was no bell to ring or no mother to holler, but when the sun went down, you knew where you were supposed to be.

BIOGRAPHY

William Hines was born on September 20, 1915 in Albany, Georgia. He came to Detroit four years later. He graduated from Northern High School and attended Wayne State University. Mr. Hines was a paper boy, one of the first Negro clerks for C. F. Smith, and worked on Joe Louis's farm as a promoter. He was also a sales representative for the St. Julian Wine Company. A founder of the Brewster Old Timers in 1958, Mr Hines participated in the organization of the Detroit Athletic Association of Businessmen for Youth. He is an active member of New Bethel Baptist Church.

M. Kelly Fritz was married during the 1943 riots to Johnnie Mae McConico. The National Guard provided a protective escort.

M. KELLY FRITZ

I came as a youngster, fourteen years old. I came alone. My parents were still in Alabama. They didn't have a damn thing to do with it. By the time I was eleven years old I was on my own. I left my little hometown at eleven and went to Birmingham, which is one hundred and fifty miles away. I worked and did what else. I was a good boy. Then I ended up in Sharon, Pennsylvania then Washington, Pennsylvania, and finally to Detroit.

In the South they had labor trains bringing people north. They'd come into your town and they would conscript you, follow you around and pick you up: "Where you wanna go?" Labor agents would go around town and recruit you, and you got a free ride to this part of the country.

What happened is they would get on those cars; and they were supposed to come to Detroit. And then they'd go on to Flint, because they were building a new General Motors plant then. And some of them would get off other places. So sometimes when they got where they're going, they didn't deliver many people. So they got smart and locked the cars, and you couldn't get out until you got where you're going.

Companies were bringing people to supply their labor needs. Sounds gruesome doesn't it? So, myself and two other fellows, older men, came up. But we paid our own way. When we were in Cincinnati a fellow said, "So where'd you come from?" We told him. He said, "Why didn't you come on the labor train?" We didn't want any part of it. I told him we wanted to go when we wanted to go. Police did everything they could to keep you from going, because companies in the South were losing their employees.

There were three of us leaving, but the three of us wouldn't go to the window at once because, if three of you went up to buy a ticket they would charge one as being a labor agent, and you'd end up in jail. So you'd go individually and buy your tickets. When we got on the train, it sat quite awhile before it left and finally the whistle blew and at the same time we said, "Wheeee . . . free at last!" And we worked that day up until five o'clock. The train left about seven. We rushed home and changed clothes. We had our bags packed; and we took a circuitous route. The streetcar went way around the back to go to the depot because we were trying to avoid anyone observing us, because it's a possibility we might have been stopped or arrested.

I was here from 1919 to 1924 the first time. I was almost twenty. When I walked through the dining room at the Detroit Athletic Club, there must have been three hundred people sitting in there. I thought everybody in the world was looking at me. There wasn't a soul seeing me. Who in the hell is going to see a busboy? I was so self-conscious about it.

I had never heard of a cabaret, didn't know what it was. All this singing and dancing, I loved it. I wasn't old enough at that time to be in there, but I was a big boy, so nobody questioned me. I was in there the minute I got off of work at night until they closed. Went home and got a little sleep and back to work the next morning.

There was a place called the Royal Garden which was the most outstanding at that time. The Graystone was just built. It was brand new. It was on Canfield and Woodward. Blacks were only allowed to dance starting at midnight when the whites left. We would crowd in there starting at midnight and dance till morning. St. Antoine was quite a mecca. We'd all proceed down St. Antoine to the restaurants. There were all sorts of cafés and what-not there. If it were a weekend, we'd go on to a morning dance. The Graystone started at about 9:00 A.M. and stayed until 1:00 P.M. It was called a breakfast dance. After having danced the night before you'd think we would have had enough, but it was quite the contrary. I guess you'd consider me a good dancer. I still dance, shake a mean foot, I guess.

Picnics were quite the quite then. Second Baptist at Monroe and Beaubien is one of the oldest churches in town, established in 1836 by ex-slaves. It was the most prominent church in town. They used to have these picnics and boat rides. They had a lot of boats here then. We'd take the boat down to Sugar Island and another place. They'd run one boat down at about 9:00 A.M. People would line up until about 11:30 or 12:00. Then that boat would come back and take another load down. That was quite the thing. I got on the boat and didn't pay any attention. It was like most islands. It had camping, amusements, etc. It was mostly blacks. We haven't used Sugar Island in years. It's probably weeds now. There was another place called Put-in-Bay, I can't tell you the area. We'd get on the boat, and it was a couple hours ride. We'd be so busy on the boat enjoying it we didn't pay any attention to where it was. We just went there. We would swim, picnic, and play ball.

When I came to town, the people I lived with went to Bethel A.M.E. Church, which was located on Hastings and Napoleon. It's all torn away now, just expressway. I went there temporarily. I was looking for pretty girls and what we called the "high-yellow" gals. Almost white. Mostly went to St. Matthew's, where the pretty girls were. We had some friends at Second Baptist, so I'd go there occasionally, but I didn't belong. Everybody was looking for pretty girls. They were half-white or mixed and had pretty hair and all that stuff. That was quite the quite.

I came to Detroit because I had a friend here that I knew. He said come on over, and I'll get you a job. That was it. It was a busboy job at the Detroit Athletic Club. Then I stayed here a few years and went back to Pennsylvania.

I finished Eckles College of Mortuary Science in 1925 in Philadelphia, then came back to Detroit. A chap by the name of Samuel W. Franklin, who was one of the outstanding funeral directors in town, gave me an apprenticeship in 1929. In 1931 he made me a partner. I laugh about the partnership now because it didn't mean a darn thing. I was working the hotels and taking the money I made there to pay the rent on the funeral home. In 1937 he died. By that time we had moved up on Garfield and Brush Street. We lived upstairs and had the funeral home downstairs. I carried on there from 1937 to 1947. Then I bought this place and have been here since 1947.

Up until the late 1930s we were laying people out at home. We'd hold funerals in the homes. We'd haul chairs to the house and set them up in the house. Then we would have a green carpet running from the door clear out to the walk. They used to call us and say, "My mother's dead," and they'd want you to embalm her in the home. Didn't want you to take her out. Finally the Health Department ended all that. We'd haul them into the home and lay them out. We had to stand the casket on end and work it up the stairway until we got it into the house. When you look back on it today, it looks very foolish, but we did it because that was what folks wanted.

I took a funeral from Flint to Roseland Park one day. I got to the front gate with a great huge group of cars behind me. The attendant wouldn't open the gate. He said to go around to the side. I asked why. He said, "That's where we bury. . . ." In other words, go around to the back gate because you're burying a Negro.

We had a very prominent man in this town. He was a doctor. His child died. We took him out to the cemetery, and they said, "Go around to the back gate." He pulled his pistol out and made them open the door. A few years later his wife died, and the same thing happened. They still wouldn't let him in. He pulled his pistol out. His name was Dr. Ossian Sweet.

He went along for years and married again. He bought a home on Garland. Soon as he moved in a race riot started. People gathered in great numbers around the house, threatening him and all. Those in the house wanted to protect themselves. One of his brothers shot out into the crowd, and I think he killed a man. They had the biggest trial ever, the Sweet trial it was called. There was a prominent lawyer from Chicago, Clarence Darrow. He conducted the trial. We had another prominent Negro lawyer name Mahoney, and they conducted it together. I was head waiter at the Wolverine Hotel. Mr. Darrow brought Mr. Sweet and Mrs. Sweet and Mr. Mahoney down, and they sat down to have lunch. It was the first time I had ever seen a black sit down in a dining room in Detroit.

There were two race riots—1943 and 1967. Our first one in 1943 was the worst thing that I've ever seen. People killed like flies. It was all over the city. I remember one particular thing. I went down on Alfred and Hastings Street, picked up a man down there that the police just took an automatic gun and, he was lying on the ground, cut him in two. You had to pick up one part of him and then pick up the other part. I shipped him back to his home in Mississippi. It was a race riot, and anything could happen. He had an altercation with the police, I guess. That stands out as the most gruesome thing I'd ever seen.

I remember there was a chap that worked over at the Famous Cleaners, which is at the corner of Beaubien and Garfield, and he used to pass our house every day going and coming to work. As he got along by our house, five or six of those youngsters grabbed him and proceeded to beat him terrifically. My mother had just come here. She raced out and put her arms around him and held onto him. They knew her and respected her, so they didn't hurt her, and she saved the man from being beat up terribly.

In 1943 I got married to my second wife, Johnnie Mae. We're still together. We were married over here at Bethel A.M.E. Church. We had to have the National Guard patrolling around the whole time so that we could have a marriage without being interrupted. We had hired one of the outstanding florists to decorate the church. The wedding was at 6:00. At 6:30 he came rushing in, with shirt sleeves, full of sweat, said the police had stopped him. Never got up some of the flowers. I thought since he didn't get them up I shouldn't have to pay for them. I paid just the same. I was fuming because the wedding was late and the flowers hadn't come. The pastor, Reverend William H. Peck, one of the most revered men in town, said: "Now, brother Fritz, don't worry about it. Sister Peck and I didn't have any flowers when we got married." They were still together after some sixty years. In other words, he was indicating the flowers didn't matter.

I don't know what happened that all these Negroes went out of business. We had a hotel—Gotham Hotel. It was one of the finest hotels run by Negroes anywhere in the country. People came from everywhere. All the major black acts that came to town used to stay there. Soon as the white places opened, they all stayed downtown.

There's an old saying among us that we laugh about. Two men are selling ice across the street. One is black, and one is white. "I need some ice," said one.

"Are you going to the black fellow?"

"No, I'm going to the white fellow, because his ice is colder."

We make a joke of it, but apparently it prevails. Negro businesses are just gone in this time. It's a shame. The thing that we have now are funeral homes and cemeteries.

One day, I think it was in Mayor James Couzens' time, we business people held our businessmen's luncheon every Wednesday at noon at the Lucy Thurman YWCA at Elizabeth and St. Antoine. Mayor Couzens came down and said: "As of tomorrow, segregation ends in Detroit. Every place will be open to you."

There was one Negro sitting there named Sidney Barthwell. Sid had nine drugstores at that time. He got up and said: "As far as I'm concerned, I don't want any integration because it's only a one-way street. All the Negroes are going to go over to the white places, but none of the white folks are going to come over to us." He was a prophet.

BIOGRAPHY

M. Kelly Fritz was born on July 6, 1904, in Uniontown, Alabama. He completed Eckles College of Mortuary Science in Philadelphia. He came to Detroit in 1919 and worked as a waiter. Six years later he moved here permanently with his wife and son. Mr. Fritz passed the Mortuary Science Board in 1929. He received an apprenticeship with Samuel W. Franklin, was made a partner in 1931, and became sole owner of the business in 1937. Mr. Fritz has been active in many civic organizations including the Kiwanis. He, and his son, James B. Fritz, operate the Fritz Funeral Home on Ferry Street in Detroit.

Sidney Barthwell was a successful businessman and proprietor of nine drugstores in Detroit. He was featured in Ambitions That Would Not Be Fenced In, *in 1945, a book by Snow Grigsby.*

SIDNEY BARTHWELL

I graduated from Cass Tech in 1925. I went to Wayne University Pharmacy School. When I graduated, I didn't have the twenty-five dollars to pay to get my degree, and the dean loaned me the twenty-five dollars. His name was Roland P. Lakey. I got a lot of help along the way from different people.

I spent quite a bit of time job hunting and finally found a job with a small black drugstore. At that time there were a lot of drugstores on Hastings, but all except one were operated by people of the Jewish faith. They didn't seem interested in hiring a black pharmacist at that time.

I went to work for a fellow named Fred Green. He had a store on Russell and Alger, so it was my first job as a pharmacist.

I opened my store in 1933. The store I was working at failed, so I went into a partnership with another pharmacist, and we changed their store into our store.

Back in those days, all the small drugstores had a fountain in them. The store that we leased had a fountain. A couple had opened up in the black neighborhoods that were double-dip specialists. They were selling huge ice cream cones for a nickel. So they took all the fountain business. Just as I was doing fairly good, this company came down the block from me and opened up the place. I never knew you could sell that much ice cream at one place till they opened. They had throngs of people every night, and my little fountain business just went down to nothing.

One morning a circular came in the mail about a kind of freezer for soft-serve ice cream, so I got the guy up here. He finally came, and I told him I was interested in getting a freezer. This is when I made the rude discovery that I didn't have any credit. I gave the man what he said was a down payment. I kept looking for them to deliver the freezer. I didn't know what happened. I guess this man was working behind the scenes frantically trying to get me approved so he could make his delivery. What happened was he finally came back and told me that my problem was that I didn't have any credit established, and he had finally gotten me straightened out. He told them that he had so much faith in me, if they would ship it to me, he would let them hold his commission until I paid for the freezer. This is how I got in the soft ice cream business.

I put a sign in my window. Those guys were selling a double-dip for a nickel so I started selling a triple-dip for a nickel. So then I certainly got going in the ice cream business. The crowd was at my store at nights.

I went ahead. About every two years I'd open a store. I finally opened two stores where we were selling just ice cream. One on Hastings was the first. It had a low counter with stools. We were operating that store from twelve noon until 2:00 A.M. I forgot how many seats we had, maybe twenty or something like that. My father had been laid off from Ford's, so he was helping me all he could. One night I was working a shift at the store on Oakland. He called up and said, "Son, close up and come down here. They're lined up on every seat and standing against the wall waiting for a guy to finish so they can get in." We did a tremendous business. I just went from one thing to another until I had nine stores.

I purchased a parcel of land on the corner of Hague and Oakland avenues. I had decided to build a building. But once again I ran into a problem of getting the credit that I needed to be successful. The contractor had given me an estimate of twenty thousand dollars. However, when I went to the bank, it refused to give me a loan unless the creamery which I dealt with would give me a loan subordinate to the bank's. The creamery agreed to do this. But the bank still wasn't satisfied. Now they were requiring that I get a term life insurance policy. Incredible although it might seem, I couldn't find a company to write the policy. Finally Occidental agreed to write the policy. But the catch was that I had to pass an extremely rigorous physical exam to qualify. I had to run up and down five flights of stairs three times and then have my pulse rate checked.

We had meetings every two weeks with my employees. I had maybe 140 employees, so every two weeks we had a meeting after we closed. We would talk to the people about things that were very essential to you being a good clerk in the store. One, we told them, don't be chewing gum in the store. Don't be cross-talking. We told them that taking a bath was not enough, that you had to use deodorants and take a bath daily. It helped a lot. We just told the people that they had to conduct themselves in an acceptable manner. I think we were doing a lot of things almost like a family that helped us along.

I was the first black member of the Detroit Retail Druggist Association. I had a very good rapport with everybody. When the race riot came, various store owners that I knew would call up and ask me whether it was safe or not to come back. I told them all to come back. There wasn't nothing pointed directly at them.

During the riots they called me up about 3:30 A.M. and told me, don't go to work because hell had broke loose. Naturally I got up and drove over to Hastings Street, and it made my flesh crawl. Where you'd see all those steel bars, the guys had just put a tow chain on the back of the truck and drove off and just pulled them off. All of Hastings Street was wide open, full of people just looting all the stores. Some of the stores that had whiskey, they had gone as far as getting trucks, backing them up and loading them up.

I saw children pull children over the broken glass to throw merchandise out of the store. Guys would go back to their homes with half a shoulder of meat on their shoulder. I remember one funny thing. Up on Oakland there was a shoe store. They had broken in, and there were street guys in there. They were calling the ladies in: "Baby, don't you need some shoes? Come on in here." So they were grabbing everything.

A guy said to them: "Ain't no use getting something that hurts your feet. Sit up here and let me try them on."

The funny thing about it, I think there was some racism, because the police department had a large percentage of southerners. I think they were almost as much against the Jewish people as they were against blacks. Two and three police were on each side of the street, and they did absolutely nothing to try to stop these things.

I had a friend who told me that when they were tearing out the Jewish stores across the street from him he stood and laughed, because he thought, "It's good they're gone, then my business will be better." But he told me that a couple of months later, he was locking up one night, and a guy put a gun in his side and made him go home and give him money. It just came to him then that crime was a way of life for some people. When they had the choice, they didn't bother you. When the choice was gone, they had to still live, so you became the target.

The Booker T. Washington Business Association was a great inspiration to black business people. It concentrated on black ownership. They used to have a noontime luncheon in a small hotel up on Adams with a basement lunchroom. We would have 250 in attendance. It started in 1930. At that time, Mr. Carlton Gaines was the chairman and used to always refer to me as Mr. Cunningham. The organization had many things that would contribute to a small business being successful. There were several different ministers in it—Reverend Bradby and Reverend Peck. They formed a branch called the Housewives League. I believe Mrs. Peck founded it. They had the housewives boosting black business. They would shop, canvas the neighborhood, have meetings, and support them.

I think World War II was the greatest setback to Negro relations in general. I think that one of the mistakes that black people made was when they thought they had integration, they gave up their own institutions. I think every ethnic group needs a place where they can get together to discuss things that are peculiar to their problems.

BIOGRAPHY

Sidney Barthwell was born in Cordele, Georgia, in 1906. He attended the Holsey Academy, a C.M.E. school. He came to Detroit when he was fourteen to join his father, and found work in a meat packing plant. He attended Cass Technical High School and then Wayne State University. He graduated with a degree in pharmacy. Mr. Barthwell served as president of the Booker T. Washington Business Association in 1953–54.

LILLIAN DUPLESSIS

My mother first came to Detroit to live, she and her family, from Lansing. She started school at the Trowbridge School up on Forest and Hastings. Then they left the city of Detroit and moved to Howell, and that's where she grew up. And they stayed there until she was in the tenth grade. She was the only colored girl in the whole town, and it was lonesome for her.

So my mother prevailed upon her family to move back to Detroit; and I think she was in about the tenth grade, and so she graduated from high school, the old Central High School which is now Wayne State University. Then eventually she married my father and I was born. And then she and my father separated and eventually divorced.

But I always tell people I grew up in the house with a liberated woman, my grandmother. So my grandmother said to my mother, "You don't have a husband to take care of you, so what do you intend to do with your life?"

Well, she had had piano and voice lessons. So she said, "Well, I think I would like to be a public school music teacher."

My grandfather had a beauty shop, and they had a mail order business. He made a hair pomade, and they used to sell hairpieces. So when he died, my grandmother took over. She had never worked outside the home, but she took over his business. And then, she eventually got into real estate; and that's what she was buying and selling, real estate, and renting property.

So, my grandmother had this building down on St. Antoine Street; and where they had had the beauty shop, there were some rooms they rented out. But, anyhow, she put a five-room flat on top of the main building, and that's where we moved to when I was three years old. And she took care of me while my mother went to the Detroit Teachers' College. She graduated in 1925 and became a public school music teacher. I went to St. Matthew's Episcopal Church, which was on the corner of St. Antoine and Elizabeth.

I lived at home with my mother and grandmother; and all of our entertainment, more or less, centered around our church, St. Matthew's Episcopal Church.

Father Daniel, I heard them say, he was lonesome. He came to Detroit from New York, and the community went to the church where he was assistant rector. But at the time he came to Detroit, the community around St. Matthew's was not involved with the church. People came from all over the city to St. Matthew's. He missed the children, and I was the only child that went to the church, that lived nearby. So when his son Langton would come home from school, he would send Langton across the street to get me. He and his wife taught me how to answer the telephone, and Mrs. Daniel said that he used to write sermons with me sitting on his desk; and I would fall asleep over there almost every night, and then he'd have to carry me home.

Father Daniel appeared to be a very gruff person but he had a heart of gold. He believed that every man should have a job so that he could support his family. Father Daniel was responsible for a lot of men getting to work at the Ford Motor Company. There was also another man in the church. He was superintendent of the Sunday School—Donald Marshall. He worked at Ford's.

When I was about ten, I remember when I would go to St. Matthew's to take my dancing and music lessons on Saturday. We would stay down there till about 5:00 or 5:30; and then we would start home. We now lived on Rohn near Mack. The sidewalks between St. Matthew's and Gratiot Avenue were just packed with men waiting to see what the policy number was gonna be, and they would write it on a little blackboard and put it up in the window. Well, my mother told me: "Those men aren't gonna bother you. You just walk straight through and act like you know where you're going, and don't look around like you're looking for anything, and they won't bother you."

And sure enough, they didn't. They would just make a path; and if someone didn't see us coming, someone would say, "Hey man, get out of the way. Don't you see that little girl coming down the street?"

We were living on St. Antoine Street when I started kindergarten. So they wanted to move to a better neighborhood because my grandmother used to pay some boy to walk me to school, to keep me from gettin' beaten up by the kids that lived around here. We didn't really associate with them, and so they just didn't like, not that we'd ever done anything to 'em but, you know how mean people are? They just decide to pick on you, and a little girl would be easy prey.

BIOGRAPHY

Lillian Duplessis was born on March 1, 1919, in Detroit. She was married on April 19, 1947, in the parlor of the Detroit Urban League. She is a retired clerk of the 36th District Court. Mrs. Duplessis has been a volunteer for a number of community organizations, including the Salvation Army. She is a longtime member of St. Matthew's-St. Joseph's Episcopal Church.

Left: *In 1947 Arthur Michael Carter III joined his parents and younger brother, Raymond, in attending service at Second Baptist Church.* Right: *Nathaniel Leach is a long-time member of Second Baptist Church; he serves as the church's historian.*

DISCUSSION WITH SECOND BAPTIST CHURCH MEMBERS

ARTHUR MICHAEL CARTER III, NATHANIEL LEACH, WILHELMINA LEWIS MEANS, KATHERINE E. REID, AND ERNESTINE E. WRIGHT

KATHERINE E. REID: I arrived in Detroit on the third of July, 1923, as a youngster, with my mother and dad and my brother. During that time, it was difficult to find a place to stay, so we ended up on the east side where my dad had rented a room for us. That was 4529 Hastings Street; it was near Forest, I believe. It was new to me, because I lived in a small town in the South. And hearing voices talking loud all during the night and early mornings, it frightened me.

My dad wasn't satisfied, so we moved over near Eastern Market. We lived on Russell Street. That was almost as bad. So finally my dad found a house on Binder. They were building new houses out there. And we lived near Nevada on Binder. Anytime my mother forgot some groceries, I had to walk from there to Davison to the market to get them. So I wanted to always remember everything so I wouldn't have to walk. About that time, my Dad was working at Ford's, out at Ford Rouge plant. And that meant he had to get up around two o'clock in the morning in order to get to Ford, because he had to walk to Davison to get the Baker streetcar. So finally we moved to the west side, and I was a little bit happier over there.

At that time I had visited all kinds of churches, and I wasn't satisfied. So the people where we lived at that time, it was at 1344 Wabash, some of them belonged to Second Baptist, and I visited with them. I liked Second Baptist. I liked Reverend Bradby. He seemed to be warm, not like some of the ministers. And I finally asked my mother and dad if I could join. And they said yes, so I joined in March of 1924. And I've been a member ever since then.

Reverend Bradby was warm, and he'd always come down and talk to the young people and start an argument among us and sit back and laugh. Not to provoke, but start us discussing something, something that was new, that was in the city, something that young people would know about. And then I had the opportunity to work in the church office for about a year. And he was very, very strict. At nine o'clock in the morning, he wanted to get a telephone call, no matter who was there. And with me being a teenager I was shy, and I wanted to wait until the secretary got there to call for fear I'd get something mixed up. But one minute after nine, or two minutes after nine, he was on the phone. I had to answer the phone sometimes 'cause the secretary wasn't there. He said, "Well, Catherine, I thought I told you to call me at nine o'clock."

I said, "I was waiting for you."

"Wait a minute. I didn't say you wasn't. I told you to call me at any cost." He would scold me for waiting to call.

WILHELMINA LEWIS MEANS: I was practically born here. Reverend Bradby blessed me as a baby. My father was a member here, but my mother was a member of Bethel A.M.E. And I had a little brother who was ill, so my mother could not take me to Bethel. So I started attending Second Baptist. I lived at 1464 Macomb, which is now Nicolet Street. And the kids that lived in the neighborhood would walk to Second from there, and I'd started walking after my mother couldn't take me to Bethel. So I finally joined here. And after my brother passed, my mother said, "We'll keep the family together." She joined.

When I got a little older I joined the Sunshine Band in here. That was a little missionary group of small children. When I was eight years old, I was secretary of the Sunshine Band, and Mrs. Jenkins was the advisor or group leader of that group. And then, as Katherine said, later on the youth missionary group, Second Baptist Red Circle, was one of the largest in the state, because we at one time had three hundred members. Ernestine was also in the Red Circle. And we had a very active group. We would go to nursing homes and give programs, and we did a lot of things.

During the First World War Reverend Bradby would have members of the community to meet the people coming from the South, at train stations, to bring them in, to see that they had housing and food, and got them jobs. Even though our membership has diminished over the years, it's because the city has expanded and there are many churches that have grown up.

ERNESTINE E. WRIGHT: I arrived in Detroit, Michigan, the 29th of January, 1929, from Parma, Louisiana, where I had lived all my life. My grandmother heard it was very cold up north in the wintertime. She gave me a union suit. I was well organized from neck to ankle. So you can see I knew all about unions before industry did. It was like Noah's Ark—one door you got in from the front, and they had a sliding back window in the back. And when I arrived, sure enough, it was one of the coldest winters since I've been here. I had eight dollars over and above my fare. My sister Sally believed in saving, so I put that in her savings account.

In the early '30s, the rich were jumping off the Belle Isle Bridge. Blacks didn't have any decent jobs anyway and lost what they did have, which was domestic work. Many Negro men left their families, came north to work at the Ford factory for five dollars a day. They paid them off in cash that same day so we could buy food and pay room rent. Reverend Bradby would meet the trains, give them a place to stay overnight. As soon as they were able to, they sent and got their families here. Second Baptist membership grew to four thousand soon.

Reverend Bradby was pastor from 1910 to 1946. He was a strong leader, with lots of dignity. No one rattled in and out of their coat before the benediction was given. Nor did they walk out of the service, chewing gum, nor pass any notes unless it was an emergency. If anyone became ill, he would ask if there was a doctor in the house.

Reverend Bradby preached his last sermon—let's see if I got this right, "The Old Ship of Zion"—and died in his office that Monday morning. He stepped on board and went to heaven.

I love Second Baptist Church because their vespers meant so much to me through the years when my husband was sick. I have known times when I didn't have my meal for the next day, but I didn't cry. I did come to the church, and I told them I wanted to borrow some money. They gave me eighty dollars that I wanted to borrow. When I got able to pay them back, I said I would pay them back on installment plan. They said: "No, you don't pay nothing back. This is for you. You don't pay it back." So that made me more and more dear to Second Baptist Church.

NATHANIEL LEACH: I came to Detroit in 1922, a young lad from Tuscaloosa, Alabama. My mother lived there on Sherman near Riopelle. Sherman Street was south of Gratiot. Gratiot represented a dividing line

94

for blacks to live. My first job was as porter in a barber shop right next door. Actually a porter has all kinds of cleaning jobs. My job was to clean the spittoons. I'd pick up about a dollar, a dollar and a half on Sunday, so that I'd go to church. Sunday School then was after church. It was a rule that you couldn't go to the show with the kids unless you went to Sunday School.

So, we'd make sure we could go to the show, so we came to Sunday School. Only the old-timers would remember Monroe, Gratiot, Hastings. You'd have the Jewel, the Rosebud, Castle, Bijou. Those are the theaters that would show you a movie and a comedy, and you could make about three shows a Sunday. They didn't last that long. A regular feature plus a comedy. You'd be in the show about an hour and a half.

You'd go down Gratiot and up Hastings and finally end up on Gratiot and Orleans, and I'd be close to home.

Well, we saw cowboy movies . . . always a cowboy . . . continued next week. Or some thriller that would keep you in suspense till next week, so you'd have to come back and see what happened. It was some type of a serial movie and a comedy. And you'd go to another show and you would see the same thing. So that was a regular Sunday routine, after Sunday School.

As I said, I was a Sunday School student, joined in 1922. So in April of 1924, two years later, I joined the church and was baptized. And to tell you a story about the pool, and baptism, I often relate that Ralph Bunche was baptized September 4th in 1927. But I point out that I was baptized in the same pool before Ralph Bunche.

Bradby was very influential by being hired by Ford to represent Ford Motor Car Company and okay the blacks getting jobs and then to act as a troubleshooter. They had a factory in Highland Park and River Rouge. Bradby would go back and forth. When the whites did not want to work with blacks or didn't get along with blacks or vice versa, Bradby was the trouble shooter. So those were some of the things that come to mind.

ARTHUR MICHAEL CARTER III: My family joined Second Baptist back before 1920. My great-grandparents, Gussie and Appleton Lawrence, joined Second Baptist in about 1918, when they first came to Detroit. My great-great-grandparents, Luke and Anna Lawrence, also joined the church. As more family members came, everyone in our family was more or less required to join Second Baptist Church. My great grandmother brought her granddaughter, my mother, to Detroit in 1925 when she was a child of nine, from Memphis, Tennessee. My father, a native of Millidgeville, Georgia, became a member upon his marriage to mother in 1939.

In 1948, I was eight and my brother four. In those days it was acceptable for an eight-year-old to take a four-year-old and walk up Gratiot Avenue and feel perfectly safe. I would sometimes walk my brother Raymond to our church at 441 Monroe from our house at 1938 Waterloo.

So I guess my earliest memories of Second Baptist Church were as a kid. I sat there with my great-grandmother, and I remember Reverend Bradby vaguely. But I do remember the day he died, because our house was very, very sad. My great grandmother announced that Reverend Bradby had died. It was a tremendous shock to our family, as it was to many other families in Detroit. Reverend Bradby had been the minister of the church since 1911 and was a patriarch of the African American community in Detroit. He was one of the most important church leaders since the founding of the church by thirteen former slaves in 1836.

Mrs. Louise Reid, the junior church director at Second Baptist, had a profound influence on me, along with many other people in those days. I attended the junior church from about 1947 until 1958. It was from that time that I began learning a great deal about Africa. Most people in the 1940s and '50s did not know a great deal about Africa. Conversation about Africa within the African American community was not very popular until the revolutionary activities in the '60s. We were taught about Africa very early before that time. Mrs. Reid had been there and had spent a great deal of time over there as a missionary. I believe she was a missionary in Liberia. She'd give vivid descriptions of the churches, of the people, and she would tell us great stories about the simple choices between good and evil faced by the children in the villages there.

In 1963 I learned that the vice president of the United States was going to be at Second Baptist. I went to the 3:00 P.M. service that Sunday with my great-grandmother. I was a young man by this time, twenty-three years of age. After we waited for a long time, this very large, red-faced man came down the aisle with his entourage, including Secret Service men. It was Lyndon Johnson. John Fitzgerald Kennedy was president at the time. Vice President Johnson delivered a plaque to the church commemorating the reading of the Emancipation Proclamation at Second Baptist Church back in 1863.

I remember getting off the bus as a child, walking with my great grandparents, Appleton and Gussie Lawrence, and passing the spot where the Fellowship Hall now stands. There was a store that sold pots and pans. I remember an old parrot who used to sit there on the corner. He sometimes would talk, and that was the highlight of my day. I would say, "Hi, Polly, Polly Parrot." He would sometimes respond, if he felt like it. I have a vivid memory of that old parrot.

The story goes that Reverend Bradby could pick up the phone and call Henry Ford and was able to secure jobs for his members. That word, of course, got into the community and certainly beyond the boundaries of the city of Detroit.

I can remember my great-grandfather coming to church along with the men of that era in the late '40s. They would wear their badges to church, which was an interesting phenomenon, because they were proud of the fact that they were working. During that period, there was also a new hope for economic security and freedom with the establishment of the United Auto Workers (UAW).

NATHANIEL LEACH: A word or two about the badges and working at Ford's. Bradby had the inside track to Ford Motor Company that hired blacks. Reverend Charles Hill, our associate pastor, was active in organizing, and Ford Motor Company didn't want no organization. They didn't want the union. There was a split there. Reverend Bradby, hired by Ford, could not afford to displease Henry Ford. So he tried to be neutral. But Hill courted the organization. So there was a sort of a split there. And Bradby had to remain, in a way, neutral. He couldn't say yes or no. But that became sort of a split because people sprang up all over the city, the so-called leaders—the YMCA, YWCA, and so forth, other churches. So each one was in a contest to have an "in" in hiring blacks. And this sort of left Bradby to slip down and down and caused him to lose power. And he could no longer send blacks to get jobs, because if he said he would support unionizing, he would be on the outs with Ford's. So that's the one thing that happened about wearing the badges to church.

In those days, we only had one place we could eat downtown; that was the Broadway Market. They would serve us, us blacks, at the market. At first it was all right; then the whites complained that more blacks were occupying the seats than the whites, so eventually they took out all the chairs and had everyone standing up. Broadway Market then was across on Broadway from the Board of Education. So, gradually, Crowley's would let blacks eat there. Hudson's had blacks eat in the cafeteria on the balcony. But in the main dining room, which I think was on the fourth floor, we weren't allowed to eat up there.

Someone mentioned about streetcars. Well, on the streetcars . . . a motorman could be black, but the conductor had to be white. That was a standard rule; you just couldn't get that job if you were black. So blacks could not handle the money or deal with the public as such because the conductor would have the right to put someone off the bus that didn't pay his fare. So black people couldn't do this, so we'd be the motorman. The motorman often would stop his streetcar right in front of his house, if he lived there, and go in and take five or ten minutes and get a bite to eat; so you'd go on waiting till he was done. Then they had the type of streetcar one time where it was open in the back, and the conductor operated it from the back more than up front. And the conductor in the back let people on, and sometimes you'd get on and hold on from the outside; and by the time he would ask the person for money, he'd get off.

Another thing, I don't want to let us forget that coming downtown to the theater, there was only one, where we'd go to see plays or stage shows—the Koppin Theater, which was on Gratiot between Beaubien and Brush. And that's where we saw all of these stars making records— Mavis Smith, Becky Smith, and Butter Beans and Suzie. See, the old-timers remember those, 'cause that's where you really saw vaudeville at its best.

BIOGRAPHIES

Arthur Michael Carter III was born April 27, 1940 in Detroit to Arthur and Alberta Carter. He attended Detroit Public Schools and was baptized at the Second Baptist Church in Detroit. He graduated from Wayne State University with a B.A., M.Ed., and Ed.D. He taught in the Detroit Public Schools and served as dean at Wayne County Community College. He was elected Wayne County commissioner in 1974 and served as chairman. In 1989 Dr. Carter became deputy superintendent of Detroit Public Schools.

Nathaniel Leach was born on January 19, 1911 in Tuscaloosa, Alabama, and moved to Detroit in 1922. In 1938 he received an M.A. in French, with a minor in Italian. He has a Ph.D. in religious education from Kensington University in California. He worked as a teacher, counselor, assistant principal, and evening school principal in the Detroit Public Schools for thirty-nine years. He has been a member of Second Baptist Church, where he is church historian, since 1924. Married to Justina Leach since 1940, he has four sons and six grandchildren.

Wilhelmina Lewis Means was born in Detroit. She attended Detroit Public Schools, graduated from Northwestern High School, and attended City College (now Wayne State University). She is retired from a lifelong career with the Visiting Nurses Association, where she was an E.E.N.T. specialist. She has been at Second Baptist Church since she was a baby. She has taught Sunday School, been assistant church clerk for more than sixty years, and volunteers with the Friday Fellowship Luncheon Committee. She is a member of the female order of the Masons (Prince Hall Affiliation), where she has attained the highest office.

Katherine E. Reid was born on July 29, 1911, in Okolona, Arkansas. She came to Detroit on July 3, 1923, with her mother, the late Lula Jones Anderson, her brother William, and her sister Kathleen to join their father. Soon after, the family become members of the Second Baptist Church. Ms. Reid was a charter member of Detroit's first black

Girl Scout troop. She and her husband Mr. Thomas Reid are the parents of a daughter, Mary.

Ms. Reid worked in a clerical position at the Veterans Administration until her retirement in 1976. She entered Madonna College and earned a bachelor's degree in 1984. She is an active member of Second Baptist Church, participating in Group 2500 and the Altar Circle.

Ernestine E. Wright was born on March 4, 1908, in Eudora, Kansas, and moved to Detroit in 1929. As a child she worked on her grandmother's farm. She married Herbert Hendrix in 1939 and adopted a son, Carver Hendrix. Ms. Wright worked at Lakeside and Herman Keifer hospitals. She was a member of Second Baptist Church for sixty three years and was active in Sunday School, Baptist Young People's Union, Women's Council, Group 500, Historical Committee, and Choir Number Two. After the passing of her first husband, she married William Wright. Mrs. Wright died on March 30, 1993.

William St. Clair Billups worked for the Detroit Board of Education for forty-eight years as a teacher, principal, and regional superintendent.

DISCUSSION ON EDUCATION
WILLIAM ST. CLAIR BILLUPS
AND EARLIE M. POOLE

WILLIAM ST. CLAIR BILLUPS: On Canfield, one block over, was St. Antoine. There was a butcher shop. And the butcher shop was typical, complete with the butcher with the sleeves on his white coat. I think his name was Schwartz, but don't quote me on that.

I was five years old, and I was standing on the corner experimenting with four-letter words I had heard, and I didn't know what they meant. I just heard them and thought it was the thing to do. I was standing right in front of the open shop door. And suddenly, I was up off of the sidewalk. Something hit me across my backside, and it was Mr. Schwartz. He had me by the scruff of my neck, and he walloped me twice. Wow, my teeth were shaking. My middle name is St. Clair. He said, "St. Clair, if I hear you talking like that again, I will tell your mother." Well, now that's invoking the ultimate in punishment. Tell my mother? He could have beat on me all day, and I will never, never say a word when I went home. First of all, my mother would know if Mr. Schwartz hit me, he would have a good reason for it. He hit me twice, and I will always remember that. I think that's the reason I avoid four-letter words, unless I'm looking around to see if Mr. Schwartz is still around.

But if I had gone home and said to my mother that Mr. Schwartz hit me, the very first thing she would have said was, "He had a reason; you must have been doing something." And if he had told her, I might not be here today.

EARLIE M. POOLE: I think sometimes we have given children too much, or we feel that we don't want them to live like we did. We fail to realize that they need to earn some of it.

I went to Northwestern as a student. We had more whites there than we did have blacks. As time went on, the area built up with more blacks. Then more blacks got into schools, and they began to offer different curriculums. Instead of wanting us to take a college preparatory course, which they called it, they wanted us to take sewing and cooking, which was valuable; but it wasn't that which would allow us to go to college. They didn't give us the background to go to college, so very few of the people were really prepared to go.

They did say—where would we get a job? Who would hire us as typists? I remember that very well.

WILLIAM ST. CLAIR BILLUPS: I started school at four years old at the Trowbridge. It was an integrated neighborhood—Jewish and black. The boundary lines were pretty clear. If you got to the east, on the other side of Hastings, you found the Polish Catholics attending those large churches around there.

I then went to Northwestern High School in 1927. I finished, and because money was in short supply, I didn't go to college. I was fifteen when I finished, and I didn't get into college till I was twenty years old. There was a five-year interval, during which I took post-graduate courses. When it came time to register, the principal, Mr. Frost, looked at my application; and he said: "St. Clair, would you sit down and wait until I talk to you?" He said, "Now, you're a boy. Boys don't get jobs in business too often, and you're colored. Where do you think you're gonna get a job?" There was nothing mean. It was just a question. He wanted to know whether I was going to waste my time.

EARLIE M. POOLE: I don't think they did it to be unkind. I think it was just a sign of the times. If you want a job, where you gonna get a job? And they weren't really hiring too many blacks in the schools, as a matter a fact, because we didn't have but maybe two black teachers at that time anyway. There was a Miss Denmark who was a teacher over on the west side where I was. If you didn't get A's and B's, then there was nothing for you. So that was part of it, I suppose. I don't think it was malicious; I think it was just a sign of the times.

As I went through high school at Northwestern, we were beginning to integrate the area, and that was causing a lot of problems. And even in picking people to go to concerts, they were very choosy about who they picked. We had a principal who was very anti-black. He was determined that we weren't going to go. They would even have operas, and we couldn't sing in it, and we had good voices and would have been very qualified. He canceled the picnic one year because we had wanted to go.

St. Clair, don't you think that the neighborhoods in our day were more stable than they are today? On your way to school you met everybody and you knew everybody. If you had PTA, the parents were there, and you baked cookies or whatever. You were more involved.

When you got home, you changed your clothes and you did your homework, and then you did your chores. And you didn't stay up. We had a radio; but you didn't have too much of it at that time because by the time your mother and dad listened to it, you didn't have time to listen to it anyway.

WILLIAM ST. CLAIR BILLUPS: Television has had its impact on education like I don't think many people realize. We didn't have a television. You came home and did your homework, and I did my chores. We had two stoves, what we called a base burner, where you had to put coal in the top, and the ashes had to be taken out. I had to cut wood and bring in the soft coal for the kitchen stove which we cooked in.

It was not uncommon for all of us to sit around the dining-room table. It was a sense of unity. My three sisters and my brother, we were all working on our lessons.

EARLIE M. POOLE: When we grew up, there was a father in the home. He went out to work. He came back from work. You sat down and had your dinner, and you took your bath, or you did what you had to do because there was a head of the house. And in the morning you got up, and you had breakfast, and you combed your hair, and got ready for school.

I blame it on social service. I guess I shouldn't do that, because I have a daughter who works in social services. But I think we have given them too much and not demanding something in return for it. Now, I didn't go for this idea that they would help mothers and then the people would come out and go in your house at night to see if there was a man hanging around or some of that type of stuff. But I think they gave 'em too much. It's not enough to take care, mind you, but they don't use it wisely, and I think that today they are able to be idle. We looked for a job; we had to work. But these mothers don't work now.

WILLIAM ST. CLAIR BILLUPS: It was usually a two-person family. The mothers, in those days, were not career women, going out the door even before the kids went off to school. They were there. They were a stabilizing force.

But then you had, also, the revolution of the '60s, the social revolution. This has changed. There's an attitude on the part of many people that, "I'm entitled. . . . Give me. . . . and I don't have to measure up."

You even hear people saying, "Because I am a minority group member, I don't have to meet these requirements because I have been deprived in my background." And you find an attitude where people are not willing to spend the effort and the time in applying themselves to getting ahead. We have a built-in source of paranoia that says, "They're against us."

EARLIE M. POOLE: We didn't know to be angry. We had been given nothing, and so we didn't know that we could be angry at that time. When they were telling us just to take sewing, this was just what was expected. There were a few who would challenge. But those of us who just went to school, and parents were just ordinary people, we didn't know to fight back. And what could you fight? You couldn't fight the system.

BIOGRAPHIES

William St. Clair Billups was born on May 14, 1915, in Detroit. He attended Detroit Public Schools. He received both A.B. and M.A. degrees from Wayne State University and did graduate work at the University of Michigan. For forty-eight years he worked for the Detroit Board of Education as teacher, elementary and secondary school principal, and regional superintendent. Mr. Billups has been active in community and professional organizations and was president of the Detroit Institute of Commerce from 1978–79. He is retired.

Earlie M. Poole was born on August 2, 1914, in Tuscaloosa, Alabama. She moved to Detroit in 1917. She is married to Franklin E. Poole. She is mother of one son, Franklin, Jr., and three daughters, Nancy Bass, Christine Simmons, and Denise Taylor. She is grandmother of Rickardo Johns, Joddest Taylor, Dah'nia Taylor, Ericka Simmons, and Elisha Simmons. She is a member of St. Matthew's A.M.E. Church.

SHELTON TAPPES

I came to Michigan in 1926. At the time I was sixteen years old. When I came to Michigan, I came to Saginaw. That's where my Dad lived. My mother and father were divorced when I was ten, going on eleven. I stayed with my mother until she remarried, and there was that kind of friction that does occur on occasions. I went to school for a short while but I was over-anxious to meet my brother and sister and mother and stepfather, who had also migrated to Michigan by then. I left Saginaw and came to Detroit.

This neighborhood [LaSalle and Longfellow] at one time was fairly exclusive, just a little above the norm. My mother worked in this neighborhood as a day worker, as a cook, and in various other positions. When I was in school, I used to come in this neighborhood; and while she worked, I would get a job washing windows or cutting the grass. That was my money that I used to go to the Graystone, to the dances.

As I got acquainted with the neighborhood, I would work for other people. Wash the windows for the ladies and things like that. I would bring my pail, and a chamois, and squeegee when I went to visit my mother; and I would find other work. I was walking through the neighborhood one day; I was on Calvert. I had the pail in my hand, and the squeegee, and the chamois. The police stopped me and asked what I was doing in that neighborhood. I said: "You can see what I'm doing. I'm washing windows." They asked who sent for me. I said my mother works in this neighborhood. They put me in the police car and drove me all the way to Grand Boulevard and Woodward and let me out. They said they didn't want to catch me in this neighborhood anymore. These are the kind of experiences that can create a bitterness that will stay with you all your life.

Detroit in those days was quite different from what it is now, I can assure you of that. The black community was not organized. Those who were, were organized as Republicans, because they felt a responsibility to support the party that had produced Abraham Lincoln. Those who didn't agree with them didn't vote at all, because they didn't feel welcomed to the Democratic party, which was primarily based in the South at the time. Almost every southern state in those days was Democratic.

After I graduated from high school, I had a scholarship. Being a young black, there were not too many inducements to encourage you to do too much, but I did have the scholarship—four hundred dollars—and I could choose the school that I wanted to utilize this scholarship at. It was enough money for a half-term, so I decided I wanted to go to the University of Nebraska. Most discouraging six months I ever spent in my life. I couldn't stay on campus or any of the student establishments. I had to find a black family to stay with. The teachers were very cold and indifferent, not all of them, but too many of them. Even before the term expired, I left and came home. Discouragement put a very sour note in my mental makeup, to the point where I decided I would just go get a job somewhere and forget it.

Well, this is depression days. So jobs, especially for a young black in Detroit, Michigan, meant find a job washing dishes in a restaurant or similar work of that type. Any other type of job, such as porter in a store, went to men who had families. Street cleaning was the property of the immigrants—Russians and Italians and Poles. So you couldn't get a job sweeping streets. Most of the more menial jobs were manned by Polish Americans, German Americans, Swedish Americans, Italian Americans. So there was this poor element of the city vying against each other for position. Welfare was not an organized thing then. If a family was fortunate enough to get some welfare help, that was for a month or two or three. It was not a permanent thing. There was quite a scratching among the people to live, to exist.

The black people were forced to live in the downtown area below Jefferson, below Vernor, down toward the river and east of Russell, east of Riopelle. That was called Black Bottom. Before I came here, my family lived in that area too. But as the neighborhood spread as a consequence of the migration of blacks from the South, they advanced east of Beaubien, and as far north as Canfield, Garfield, and Willis.

Some time in the '30s, maybe in the latter part of the '20s, President Roosevelt, who was at that time governor of New York, indicated that he would be a candidate for the Democratic party. There was some activity in the black neighborhood. A fellow by the name of Bledsoe, an attorney, was very outspoken in favor of blacks being involved with the democratic party, especially on behalf of Roosevelt. He, in my opinion, was the vanguard leader of the transition of blacks into the Democratic party and losing their loyalty to the Republicans because they "freed the slaves." Because of him there were quite a few others who gradually swelled the ranks of black Democrats. This was particularly interesting to me, because at the time I was not old enough to vote.

I have always boasted that when I became eligible to vote that Roosevelt was the Messiah that we had been hoping would come along, so I voted for Roosevelt. The young blacks who were able to vote and who had been activated were very strongly Democratic. In many cases they had problems with family because of the Republican loyalty. Most of their families in those days were the sons and daughters of ex-slaves who had been freed by Abraham Lincoln. There was a considerable amount of confusion in the black neighborhoods. I say the black neighborhoods because they were herded in those days, herded into neighborhoods. These are the late '20s and early '30s.

With the success of President Roosevelt, so-called alphabet programs were enacted—WPA, PWA, CWA. These were works programs. Then the CCC camps, Civilian Conservation Corps. It was semi-military, because they had the camps and uniforms and things like that. They supplied the youngsters with a certain stipend that was sent to the family. Many of the forests in Colorado, Minnesota, Michigan, Ohio, Illinois, and New York were replanted by these youngsters. My brother was in the CCC camp.

The support wasn't so much for Roosevelt as it was against Hoover. President Hoover had been seemingly indifferent to the plight of the unemployed. There were thousands and thousands of people out of work, and there was no organized assistance to any extent. Here in Michigan, the Ford Motor Company, which was the largest employer at that time, had closed down because the Model T had become so passe that they weren't selling. The General Motors Corporation had begun to concentrate on the Chevrolet. It had outsold Fords for two consecutive years. Ford closed the plant down for a transition into an eight-cylinder automobile. This was for months and months that the plant was closed, and it just seemed like the whole city became stagnant. The pressure intensified.

One of the events that brought it into focus was the so-called Ford Hunger March, in 1932. This is where a number of Ford workers and allies, under the leadership of an organization that was called the Unemployed Council, imposed this march on the Ford Motor Company. They made this trek out there, and the organization called for them to march back and forth down Miller Road in front of the plant. This was in April 1932. The plant had closed a year or so before that. There were still people working in there, but for all intents and purposes massive production was over.

Their purpose was to bring attention to the plight of Ford workers who were out of work, but they were greeted with water hoses and shots. Harry Bennett was in charge. Five men were killed—four whites and one black. We were able to discover the graves of the four whites in later years. I was a catalyst behind that in that I got the union to mark the graves. The black fellow had been refused permission to be buried in the cemetery with his brothers, so his body lay in the undertaker's for several weeks, until finally a group got together and had it cremated. They flew the ashes over the Rouge plant and scattered them over the plant. That's one of those untold stories.

When the shots were fired, people scattered. A number of people were injured with shots in their arm, leg, or whatever. They were dragged and hidden away, because, as Ford workers, that meant that they never would work at Ford's anymore. They never went to hospitals or anything like that. There were so many organizations that joined in this hunger march, some by invitation, others just because they had heard of it. Some church groups, some revolutionary party groups, the Communist party, the Socialist party, the Proletariat party. Then there was a group of Baptists. It was a white Sunday School. Then there were several black groups.

Stanley Nowak was very much involved in organizing Ford. He was part of a weekly radio program sponsored by one of the Polish newspapers. When we were organizing Ford Motor Company, he helped us to get some time on the program. I spoke on that program three times during the Ford organizing days.

Shortly after this hunger march took place, an effort was made to organize the Ford workers into what was known as the Auto Workers Union. The way I got into this was, being young and attending all of these rallies and meetings, I found that you didn't have to be a Ford worker to join the Auto Workers Union. You didn't have to be an auto worker. If you were the wife or daughter or son of an auto worker, you were still eligible, so I joined the Auto Workers Union. It cost me a quarter a month.

BIOGRAPHY

Shelton Tappes was born on March 27, 1911, in Omaha, Nebraska. He moved to Detroit in 1927. He was hired to work at the Ford Rouge plant in 1936. He was fired in 1939 for his participation in a

Labor Day parade. The Union Organizing Committee hired Tappes to assist in their efforts. He was elected chairman of Local 600 Foundry Unit and served as a member of the committee that negotiated the first contract with Ford Motor Company. Until his retirement in 1976 he held various positions within the union. Before his death on April 19, 1991, Mr. Tappes committed his energy to advocacy for the aging.

African Americans
in Detroit and the United States,
1928–1937

1929	Stock market crashes (October 29).
1930	Total population of Detroit 993,578; Negro population 120,000.
1931	Scottsboro Trial. Nine Negro men were maliciously accused, tried, and convicted in Alabama for allegedly raping two white girls.
1932	Ford Hunger March—3,000 people marched in Dearborn demanding help and were dispersed by gunfire (March 7).
1933	Repeal of Prohibition.
1935	United Auto Workers organized (August 26).
1937	Battle of the Rouge Overpass—confrontation between Ford Motor Company guards and UAW leaders (May 26).
	Joe Louis won the heavyweight boxing championship.
1930s	During the depression years Negro unemployment reached seventy-five percent.
	By the late 1930s Negro employment in the auto industry had dropped from 30,000 to 20,000. Of these, 10,000 were at Ford Motor Company; they represented less than four per cent of the total work force in Detroit.

FRED W. GUINYARD

I met Joe Louis in Sunday School—Calvary Baptist Church. We were both young fellows, thirteen years old.

We used to go to Eastern Market to work before we went to school during the week. They had tissue paper on the apples and oranges. You take the tissue paper off and set 'em up so you could see the quality of the oranges.

When we were in intermediate school, we worked on an ice wagon together—a horse and wagon. At first we used to go and get a job with somebody else. A man would give us a dollar a day to work for him. Then we said, we'll go get us an ice wagon ourselves and try it. We bought our ice at Stroh's. Our mothers would give us enough money to buy a three-hundred-pound block of ice. They'd slide the ice onto the wagon right out of the chute. You'd take an ice pick and pick it down to the size you wanted—twenty-five to one hundred pounds. The ice was marked when it came out of the chute. There was a line on it, like a scratch. You could break it with a plain ice pick. The lines went a quarter-inch deep.

Joe was much larger than myself, and every time somebody would say, oh, twenty-five pounds, I says, "Your turn, buddy." We would buy

111

four three-hundred-pound pieces of ice; then on Saturdays you'd get more, because people would buy more ice on Saturdays because they churned ice cream on Sunday.

We rented the horse and wagon for three dollars a day. We went to St. Aubin and Antietam. We would drag the horse and wagon from the barn to the ice house, load your ice, and then pick your route that you think that you could sell more ice on.

You couldn't go on Jefferson Avenue. You couldn't go on the Boulevard. You couldn't go on Gratiot Avenue. But all the side streets you could go on.

Other people who were selling ice tried to get territories, but you would say a few things that would make him know you were gonna be there, that I wouldn't say in front of you. But you had a license on your wagon that said you could go anywhere.

This was '29, '30, and '31.

I was secretary to the trainer of Joe Louis in training camp with Joe. I worked with him for fifteen years when he was fighting. He and I were friends. We went all over everywhere together, all over the world, even when he was going on fighting for the Army Relief Fund and Navy Relief Fund, we were together then.

One time they asked Joe Louis what did he think of managers, and Joe said, "Well, I think of managers the same as I think of my buddy, Freddie Guinyard." He said, "He hauled ice, and I carried it."

Joe Louis was much smarter than people gave him credit to be. During the army, when we were traveling to different army camps, he would never say what he would do for somebody. Somebody would ask him, "Joe, can you give me this or loan me this?"

He'd say, "I'll see what my buddy can do for you."

I had the hardest time explaining to people that this is Joe Louis doing this, not me. He just didn't want to take any bows for a lot of things.

BIOGRAPHY

Fred W. Guinyard was born on August 16, 1914 in St. Matthew's, South Carolina, and moved to Detroit in 1923. He worked for Joe Louis for fifteen years. During World War II, from 1942–45, he traveled with the boxer, who performed twenty-one exhibitions all over the world for the benefit of army navy relief. Along with his wife Margaret ("Mike") he worked at Joe Louis's Brown Bomber Chicken Shack. Currently Fred and "Mike" Guinyard are agents with Book Couzens Travel.

〰

Ernestine E. Wright came to Detroit as a young woman. The only work she could find was as day worker or housekeeper in the homes of wealthy and often ungenerous white people.

ERNESTINE E. WRIGHT

I came to Detroit in 1929, and shortly after I was here, the depression came. In the early '30s there was no jobs for anyone, especially black people. Anyplace you saw a home, you would see rooms for rent.

Most of the time it was day work. For me it was living in, staying nights. They would have children, and I would take care of the children at times when they had to go shopping. And sometimes they would leave me sleeping in the same room with the baby's crib, so if the baby needed a changing during the night, well, that was for me to get up and take care of the infant.

We had half-a-day off on Wednesday and a half-a-day on Sundays, some Sundays. If they were going out of town or someplace, and you had to stay there and take care of children while they were away, you probably had to work all day Sunday.

I never had a chance to go to my church on Sunday morning because of staying on the premises. Even if I got off, that half-a-day, they would sleep late because they'd been out carousing and partying all night. So I'd have to wait until they got up and had their breakfast, and wash up the dishes and make the beds, and tidy up the bathroom, and then I would get off.

It rolled on and on till I got tired of staying on the place, and some of them paid $2.50, a week, and sometimes you wouldn't even get the $2.50 because they'd kinda fall out with something because they didn't need you. They would let you go and call the employment office after another month or so, and then they'd get someone else to come in for that $2.50 a week.

Then finally I got to where I wanted to do day work, and I was so light behind, I had nothing going for me like those large women. They would go out, and they would have an enormous shopping bag, and I just wondered about that. I said, "I want day work, and I'll get me a shopping bag." I didn't know why they were carrying the shopping bag. I learned later that they would bring stuff home in them shopping bags.

Sometimes they would say, "I'll give you a dollar a day and tote, or seventy-five cents and tote, and a dollar and no tote." That was for the day's work. The lady has several children, and she would say, "Well, I'll take seventy-five cents and tote." Tote meant she would let us have food to take home to the children. Most times they would have children that they had to feed.

I would get a dollar a day, and you couldn't always get a day. You'd go to the employment office and sit there for hours all day, and sometimes you wouldn't get a call to come in and do a day's work.

I went to work for a day, and when I got there they would have the clothes all sorted out, and I'd go downstairs and wash. At that time they had washing machines with the little gas burner to heat the water in the tub to wash. I have washed on washboards in the home. After you got through doing the laundry, you put it in a big old dryer.

When I'd go upstairs for lunch, you know what I got for lunch? A little bit of tuna fish or salmon poured right out of the can, and two or three crackers, and a bowl of Jello, and two or three cookies and a cup of tea. That was my lunch. When I was at lunch, I would have to go and tidy up the bathroom. You know what tidy up a bathroom means? That means you clean that bathroom, and then you scrub the kitchen floor. You didn't know what color the linoleum was on the floor until you washed it. That was a day of doing laundry.

Then when you went to houseclean, you would have all the rooms to clean, and white people would have that long hair; and by the time you get through with that floor, you'd have a bunch of hair all on the rag. You didn't use a mop, because they had white woodwork. They didn't want it slopped up with the mop. I had to get on my knees and clean the baseboards and mop the kitchen floors. Under the bed there would be rolls of dust big as your thumb.

They would go downtown every day to Hudson's and Crowley's. They were the main stores. They'd go down there every day and go shopping and leave me to do my work. When they came home, they'd say, "Did you do this?" on the window sill, "Did you do that?" They knew very well that it wasn't the color that it was when they left there.

One day a lady set the clock back. I didn't have no watch or nothing except for an old alarm clock that would dance off the whole table if you let it go long enough. So when I got home I found out that she come in, I was down in the basement working, and set the clock back so that made me work one hour longer than I was supposed to for that dollar. For one dollar a day. One dollar. This was in 1929 and 1930.

They didn't want you but once a month. That's why the dust was so heavy under the beds, and that's why the floors were so dirty you didn't know the color of them. They would call when they got ready for another person for once a month; they would call the employment office, "That girl you sent me, she stole such and such a thing."

Mr. Phillips, he was one of the heads of the employment office, would say: "Well, I'm going to send you another one. This is a good girl."

They was afraid if you sent a young person that their husband would flirt with them, which they did. They said, "Send me an Aunt Jemima type," because they didn't want their husbands to be flirting with me.

I remember one lady I worked for would have me once a week to come in and clean for her, and she told her neighbor what a nice person I was. I did like to keep things clean. I wasn't jealous of them having pretty things, but I lived in a dull, drab neighborhood, and I wanted pretty things too.

This one lady asked me, she said, "My friend wants you to come and give her a day."

I said, "All right."

She had asked the lady I was working for how much she paid. She told her one dollar, I'm sure she did. But when I went to work for her, I didn't say, "Well now, you pay a dollar too," because I know'd it was understood that she had recommended me to her. So when I got through working that day, boy did I have a day's work, and she came out with a pair of old muddy shoes, with mud dried on them, cracking and peeling on the living-room floor, right where I had cleaned it, and the mud fell all over it, and fifty cents. She meant to pay me with those shoes. So I said: "You get me some more money. You know what I mean." She went back and got another quarter, which made seventy-five cents.

I told my sister, "I took that and come on out because the lady was pregnant, and I didn't want to get into it with her because she'd have that baby." I was just so disgusted with that woman to come into the room with those muddy shoes.

BIOGRAPHY

Ernestine E. Wright: See p. 99.

As the eldest girl, Dorothy Elizabeth Lawson cared for her brothers and sisters. She and her brothers, Kenneth (center) and Earl (left) are pictured in the back yard of their home on the east side of Detroit.

DOROTHY ELIZABETH LAWSON

I was born in Charleston, West Virginia, July 15, 1926. I was three weeks old when my parents brought me here to Detroit. I've been here ever since then.

I lived at 1990 Jay and St. Aubin. My grandparents lived on Maple and St. Aubin. I went to Duffield School. I remember some of the streets over there—Sherman, Joseph Campau, Orleans. We had fun. We were a close family. The whole family sometimes would get together and we'd go out to Belle Isle and spend the weekend on Belle Isle. We didn't even come back home. We didn't have to worry about locking our doors or windows. Nobody bothered back then. In fact, that was the only air conditioning we had in the summer time, with the windows open, the front and back door open.

My father worked at the packing house. He was a beef-boner, and he was rated with the ten best in the city. He was fast. We used to go down there and watch him. We would freeze because it was so cold in there where he worked. He would reach up and get that cow off the hook; and zip, zip, zip, and he'd have steaks over here and roasts over there. I don't know how he did it so fast. He was also a minister. I was born and raised in the Church of God till I got older and went out on my own.

I lived on Vernor Highway. It was near the old Silvercup Bakery. That bread smelled so good in the morning. We would be going to school, and the bakers would give us a small loaf of bread. Near the Elmwood Cemetery we used to tell each other spooky stories about the cemetery. Me, I was always the instigator, because I'm the second oldest of eight children; so I more or less had to take care of the younger kids. I knew how to make them behave, because I'd tell them somebody's going to come out of the cemetery and get 'em.

We used to make a lot of the things we played with; like we would take an old crate, tear up a pair of roller skates, put wheels on it, and have a scooter. We would take tin cans and bend them in the middle and put them on our shoes and zip up and down the street.

I was a tomboy. I had one brother older than I. I had some uncles that were close in age. I've been around men all my life, so I picked up their language. If they had a fight, I had a fight. I fought all of my brothers' battles, and nobody bothered them because they didn't want to bother me.

I used to drink dago wine with some Italians that lived on the block and my uncles. I wouldn't get drunk, but I was drinking it. My grandfather used to give me whiskey. He'd say whiskey was good for the heart. I guess I was his favorite, because he used to tell me some tales. He used to be a grave digger. He's also from West Virginia. And he used to tell me some of the things he used to dig up. He brought a skull home one day, and my mother put it on the end of the broom. When Grandma and Papa came home everyone was sitting on the porch. I guess I got some of that from my mom, too, because I used to do devilish things.

At one neighborhood we lived in there were mixed families. There were Italians, Polish, Negroes. It was just like one big happy family, because my girlfriend was a Polish girl. One day she would come to my house for lunch, and the next day I would go to her house for lunch. We would be eating the same thing, because it was during the depression. No one was working and there was little money.

When everybody had the same thing on their table, you couldn't think you were better than I was when you didn't have any more on your table then I did. You had the same size hole in your shoe that I did. You used the piece of cardboard from the same box to cover that hole so you wouldn't be walking on the sidewalk. So you couldn't say you were better than I was because we both had the same thing basically.

I used to take care of my brothers and sister just like I was the mother of the house. My mom and dad would get up on Saturday morning and go to the market to shop, and we didn't have a refrigerator that we could freeze and store. We had an icebox. Cab Calloway used to live in Black Bottom. He used to ride on the back of an ice cart hollering, "Hi-de, hi-de-ho," and we used to buy blocks of ice and put it in the ice-box.

While they were gone, she didn't have to tell me to watch the children, or give them their breakfast, and wash them up, and put their clothes on. My oldest brother and I had everybody in the house cleaned up, the house cleaned; and all she had to do was come home and put the groceries away.

If someone took sick, a mother or father, in that block, almost everybody on that block would come over and help clean up the house and cook. Color didn't make any difference; nobody ever thought about color. In fact, we have more prejudice now than I can ever remember in our childhood. And my father didn't allow us to use the word black. Even if we wanted to say "black," forget it. We couldn't do that, or he would really tan our hides.

I got older and loved to dance. I went to every dance that I could at the Graystone Ballroom.

I met my first husband in school. It was just before the war. When I first met him, my father said I was too young. He didn't want me courting. So it was one of these things, "I'll see you in school." The only time I could go out to a party was if my older brother went. Then I would have to bribe him to get him to take me there so I could see him.

One day I was talking to my dad about marriage. It took him about three hours to tell me all the pros and cons of getting married. He never did tell me. He said, "Ask your mother." That was his favorite thing, "Ask your mother." So they decided they were going to let me get married, and I had one child.

Shortly after we got married he went into the service for two and one-half years. He came home and was home seven months and got killed. For awhile marriage or anything else wasn't on my mind. I was young. I should have been taking myself to Paris instead of getting married. What has brought me through a lot of my experiences was the way my parents raised me. My mother and I were very close. I would tell her everything. If I did something bad, I told her.

During the war my husband and brother were both stationed in Illinois. My husband was at Fort Sheridan, and my brother was at Great Lakes Naval Station; and every time I would go there, we would go out or meet somebody and they would say, "Where are you from?"

I would say, "Detroit."

And they would say, "Where, on Hastings Street?"

Everybody thought everybody from Detroit was from Hastings Street or Black Bottom; and then it was changed to Paradise Valley. We used to go to the bars down there in Black Bottom and have sing-alongs. Everybody would come. Before you knew it, the whole bar was singing. They were friendly times. And people fought, but they fought with their fists. They would have a knockdown, drag-out fight, and in ten minutes they'd be drinking out of the same bottle. People never carried grudges or chips on their shoulders. I don't know what's wrong with this world today.

I met my second husband in 1948, shortly after my first husband died. He said he had been seeing me all the time and he loved me. I said, "You're crazy." He would tell everybody from the first time he saw me, he fell in love with me. I used to wear my hair long. He just watched me from a distance because my husband was still living when he first saw me. But we used to go out a lot up to a bar on Warren. So he would just watch. And then after my husband got killed, shortly after that, he started talking to me.

He died last year. I told him I wasn't in love with him. I told him as long as he treated me nice, and he acted like a gentleman, and he was willing to settle for that. . . . I told him I liked him or, "I wouldn't be bothered with you, but I'm not going to say I love you." I never told him I loved him, because I didn't.

I decided to marry him because he was nice, and he was a good person. To me, he was beautiful. We were together twenty-seven years. He used to like to dance. We would go dancing every weekend. I love to dance, and he did, too. He treated me nice and was a fun person to be with. He treated my oldest son nice, and that's what mattered to me. He was a nice person and had a lot of friends. Everybody liked him.

BIOGRAPHY

Dorothy Elizabeth Lawson was born on July 15, 1926, in Charleston, West Virginia, and came to Detroit three weeks later. She has worked for Children's Hospital of Michigan, Veterans Administration Medical Facility, and the U.S. Postal Service. She was an employee of the Detroit Urban League and participated in the Seniors in Community Service Program. She also is a Boy Scout leader.

Mrs. Lawson is the mother of four children—Robert, Sandra Gayle, Karen Lynne, and the late Steven. She has six grandchildren—Dwayne, RaShawn, Monique, Matthew, Antoine, and Andre and two great-grandchildren. She enjoys making and selling her crafts.

Shiloh Baptist Church choir in the early 1900s.

DISCUSSION WITH SHILOH BAPTIST CHURCH MEMBERS

MARY RUTH CHAPMAN HARRIS, MARGUERITE RHODES McINTOSH, O. DAVENE ROSS McKINNEY, AND MARY O. BROOKINS ROSS, D.D.

MARY O. BROOKINS ROSS, D.D.: I came to Shiloh in June 1930 as a bride of Pastor Solomon D. Ross. My husband lost his first wife by death. Four children were left. From our marriage, Davene Ross was added, giving us five children to rear.

Having been my senior by some years, my husband was at one time my high school teacher. After high school, I went to college, and we lost track of each other. Having graduated from Spelman College, I began teaching in Augusta, Georgia. It was in Augusta where the Reverend S. D. Ross came to conduct a revival meeting for a minister friend. His business there was to help to gain souls. And, yes, he gained one soul, who became his wife for thirty-eight years. It was during his Augusta trip that he proposed to me, and I soon found myself the wife of the minister of Shiloh Baptist Church.

Our first home was 950 Medbury Street, which later became Edsel Ford Freeway. Davene was born at this address, for I was afraid to go to the hospital. My doctor, J. J. Rucker, a member of Shiloh, delivered the baby.

Of course there were many widows in Detroit, and in our church, who wondered why the minister had to go all the way back to Georgia to get a wife. But that is where he went, and I am happy to say I have served happily and, I hope, helpfully in Shiloh Baptist Church, the second-oldest black Baptist church in Detroit.

When I came to Detroit, the city and many parts of our country were hard hit by a depression. We had to work much to survive, and keep our self-esteem. Our church, however, kept the faith and served many people in need of food and jobs.

Many men in Shiloh were told if they brought a letter from the pastor to Ford Motor Company, they might be hired. Our pastor was in a position to get jobs for some men, which was a help to the church.

Interestingly enough, from the steps of Shiloh, Governor Romney made one of his campaign speeches.

Shiloh was left here for a reason. During the preparation for the building of the Brewster Housing Project many buildings, including a number of churches, had to be demolished.

Shiloh always enjoyed presenting distinguished artists. When some other churches were afraid to present Paul Robeson because he was accused of being a communist, Shiloh was one of two churches which presented Paul Robeson in concert. Hartford Avenue was the other church. Robeson blessed Detroit with his songs and his speeches, which emphasized desire for real freedom of voice. He was saying to us that he just wants to be free, and that was the main thing that he was talking about, about being free. He was not a communist, but he wanted freedom, and he found some of it, in some countries other than in the United States. He sang a lot of spirituals and, of course, we know that he had a great voice.

In our church the pastor emphasized a lot of things. Two things I particularly recall. He always put emphasis on education. He wanted that the people of this church and community would see to it that their children went to school and got an education. And then he emphasized buying homes, buy a place for yourselves to live.

MARGUERITE RHODES McINTOSH: I came to Shiloh in 1937. My mother was the organist at the time. We were youngsters; five sisters followed her on the streetcar; we lived on the west side.

My fondest memory, I must say, was when I was singing with the a cappella choir. My mother asked me to help the tenor section, because they were on the weak side. I met a young man whose name was Willie B. McIntosh who was in the a cappella choir. He was the lone tenor at that time. He asked me to go to the show and I went; he came on the streetcar to see me. He was the secretary of the trustee board. From the time I met him, until about three years before he passed, he was the secretary of the board. When the pastor would call for a meeting, no matter what time, night or day, he would respond; and there were many times Pastor Ross would call my house at two o'clock in the morning and say, "'Sweet Thing,' let me speak to your beloved." I would put him on the phone, and he would say, "Brother McIntosh, how are you? I was just sitting here thinking that I need some money before ten o'-clock. There's something that's urgent at the church, and it must be taken care of before ten o'clock."

And no matter what, my husband would say, "Reverend, it's kind of early in the morning. I have to be to work at five o'clock."

Reverend Ross said, "That's all right. You write out the check, and I'll have my daughter, Angeline, pick it up before she goes to school."

And often at 6:30 in the morning Angie would come by the house, and she'd say, "I told Father not to bother Willie."

Her father would say, "But Willie's my son."

When we were younger, many of us went on hayrides, and we went to Belle Isle together, the younger set. Of course the younger set is now the mature set.

Lula Divens was one of the persons who stood on the corner with a bank, asking people to put a dime in the bank for a brick to build Shiloh. She did this until they started the building, which was in 1922.

O. DAVENE ROSS McKINNEY: I came in that half-generation after Marguerite, the generation that we couldn't run with. They were too big for us. They shooed us away, so we had to make our own little fun the best way we could. And along with me were Mary, Minnie, Pauline, Gloria, and Marguerite's sisters, Agnes and Daisy, Geraldine, Nellie, and two Josephines. Dorothy was sort of between. She was accepted by that group for awhile, but sometime along the way she ended up with us. We visited each other's homes, sometimes spending the night.

Being the preacher's daughter, I spent the night or day at various houses. You can't imagine how they treated me. I used to go over to Mary's house, and we'd run up and down 17th and 18th together. And I would go over to the Rhodes's house, and they knew I was afraid of the dark. On Sunday they would turn out all the lights in the house, and I'm laying there shaking, and put on the "Hermit's Cave." That wasn't the worst of it. They would say, "We're going to the show."

I would think, "Oh, goodie goodie, I'm so glad." And you know what we would see? "I Walk with a Zombie." That was at the Granada.

I went to a hairdresser named "Sweetie Arthur." My mother used to tell him, "Get it as straight as a stick, 'Sweetie,' as straight as a stick." And I mean, "Sweetie" would have it as straight as a stick. In those days this is what we thought was the best thing to do.

MARY O. BROOKINS ROSS, D.D.: And your head would be burning.

O. DAVENE ROSS McKINNEY: Burning and greasy, just as greasy as it could be.

As I understand it, mother came to church almost until the time for me to be born. And this particular Wednesday she went on home from Missionary Society, and I got here at 2:20 that Thursday morning.

MARY O. BROOKINS ROSS, D.D.: Women in those days went in after a certain time, after so many months. They stayed home. They didn't want anybody to see them. But I didn't stop, I came right on. A woman in our church, by the name of Sue Johnson, said, "My God, if you're going to have that child down here at the church, just be at the Missionary Society on time."

O. DAVENE ROSS McKINNEY: Shiloh had some pretty lean years, and it seems to me God has a way of letting me know that there is such a thing as miracles still existing. This church was filthy, and we didn't have the money as a congregation to get it painted. It's one of the highest domes that you have in the city, making it have very good acoustics, but it's expensive to get scaffolds to paint it.

And I wanted to get married. Most of my friends were married. My mother told me, "If you just get out of school, then fine. You do what you want to do."

So in 1953, I graduated from college. I am inclined to believe that the Lord started a little fire right up here in this vestibule as you're going through that door coming up on the east of the northeast side. A little column of smoke got into the main sanctuary. Because of that small damage, Shiloh Baptist Church was completely painted by the time of my wedding. So I was able to get married at Shiloh in a clean sanctuary.

After church we all loved to go to Barthwell's. We would get ice cream, and we would run up and down Hastings, because we had friends that lived on Hastings.

A girlfriend of mine would take me down into the basement of her unit on Erskine, and we'd come all the way through the basement to the unit right outside the church. It was just that safe in those days.

We have experienced bitter-and-thin times at Shiloh. Mother touched upon some phase of racism that we have had here at Shiloh, such as the Baptist Ministers' Union trying to jack up mortgage rates for black churches. We have had some other experiences here. Shiloh, of course, was here during the only race rioting we've really had in my lifetime, and that was in 1943.

MARY RUTH CHAPMAN HARRIS: I came to Shiloh as a babe in arms. My grandmother was a member of this church and also my grandfather. We got baptized in 1938 by Reverend Ross. There were a lot of people instrumental in getting us to church. Brother King, Brother Galloway, Mrs. Thomas, and the streetcar. As we got older, we went to the corner and got on the Buchanan streetcar, and we came to this church. We came every Sunday and stayed all day. We were in church from the very beginning until church let out.

There was a lady friend of my grandmother's who we called Aunt Bethel that lived over on Rowena and St. Antoine, and my grandmother would come later on; and they had shoe boxes, which your shoes come in, and that's what they brought our food in. Then we would go over to Aunt Bethel's and eat our food, and then we would come back to church.

Mother Hudson, and Mother Wheeler, and all those ladies used to take us around to different churches, and they would somehow know that they couldn't find a ride. They would get enough money to put us all in a cab, and we went from church to church to Third Sunday Meetings.

BIOGRAPHIES

Mary Ruth Chapman Harris was born on January 27, 1930 in Detroit. The third child of seven, she was born in her grandmother's house on 18th Street. She attended Detroit Public Schools. She was employed at Henry Ford Hospital for thirty-eight years and retired in January, 1992. Mrs. Chapman Harris is the mother of two, grandmother of two, and a great-grandmother.

When Marguerite Rhodes McIntosh traveled south for Sunday school meetings in the 1940s, she stayed in private homes which was common practice at that time.

Marguerite Rhodes McIntosh was born on November 17, 1922, in Pulaski, Tennessee, and moved to Detroit in 1929. She was a music instructor with the Detroit Board of Education. Her family has been members of Shiloh for five generations. She is a choir member, a deaconess, and a Sunday School teacher. She is the mother of five children.

O. Davene Ross McKinney grew up at Shiloh Baptist Church as the child of S. D. Ross and Mary O. Brookins Ross, D. D.

O. Davene Ross McKinney was born on May 14, 1931 at home, on Medbury between Hastings and Rivard. She graduated from Cass Technical High School. She earned a B.S. in elementary education and an M.S. in special education from Eastern Michigan University. She taught for sixteen years in the Inkster School System. In 1953 she married Robert V. McKinney, Jr. She has two sons and two grandsons.

Reverend S. D. Ross and his wife, Dr. Mary O. Brookins Ross, served the congregation of Greater Shiloh Missionary Baptist Church for several decades. Reverend Ross was pastor for nearly fifty years.

Dr. Mary O. Brookins Ross was born in Dawson, Georgia in Terrill County and moved to Detroit in June, 1930. Her father was her teacher through the first eight grades. After high school she entered Spelman College. She married Reverend Solomon David Ross who brought her to Detroit where she became active at Shiloh Baptist Church. She received an honorary doctorate of divinity from Morehouse

School of Religion. She recently served seven years as a member of the Governing Board of the World Council of Churches and is currently the president of the Women's Auxiliary of the National Baptist Convention.

Left: *Gwendolyn Ruth Edwards made a significant contribution to the formation of the UAW. She was the first woman to serve as sergeant at arms at a national labor convention.* **Right:** *In 1944 Hodges E. Mason became president of UAW Local 208. He was the first African American in the Detroit area to hold the presidency of a UAW local. Mason was also a champion of equal opportunity for women. He is pictured third from the left.*

DISCUSSION ON THE LABOR MOVEMENT
HILDRED J. DREW DALE, GWENDOLYN RUTH EDWARDS, HODGES E. MASON, STANLEY NOWAK, AND JOHN J. "JACK" WHITE

STANLEY NOWAK: During the war there was a shortage of labor, and many came from the South, and the black population increased.

When the war was over, at first the wages were the same as before the war started, so wages were frozen; but prices during that same period went sky high, so there was sort of a strike not only there but the whole country, from Boston to Seattle. During that strike there were carloads of trains obviously hired by the packing house companies that brought black people from the South to Chicago to the packing houses. They were not told there was a strike there. They were placed in some private hotels, then driven by elevator trains into the packing house yards where the people were on strike. That strike they didn't know anything about. They were looking for jobs. That's all. Then quite a fight developed, and the union movement in the whole country was crushed.

There was very close cooperation between the blacks who came there during the war and understood. The new ones who were brought

127

in were just completely ignorant and were brought in as strikebreakers. The pickets would detest them, and there was a bloody fight.

That would be 1918, 1919, right up to the war. Actually that was the encounter of these ethnic groups from Eastern Europe. Of course, Irish were involved and the Germans. But the bulk of them were Polish, Ukrainian, Russian. That's the first time they were in contact with black people. When they brought these black people in as scabs, they didn't know they were scabs. The shoemaker who was reading the paper and the news for me, he explained that to me.

It was not until I came to Detroit many years later, when I started to work for the UAW in 1936, that I was introduced to black people.

At Cadillac the man in charge was Dave Miller, who came to me and said, "We have organized the white workers very well. But we have problems with black people." And he said, "The one way we can get to them is because they all are working in the foundry, and the other white people in the foundry are Poles and they all joined."

I went and talked to these Poles, as I speak their language, and they gave me the name of an individual who was a leading black person. One of them said, "They have a sports organization. There's one individual who is sort of a leader of it. If you can talk to him and win him over, you'll have the whole black community."

I went to see Mr. Keyes. He received me very friendly and told me that some of my Polish friends spoke to him. He told me that the company gave them uniforms to play ball. I visited him once. I visited him twice, but he admitted when I asked, "Did you ever take up the question of wages with them?"

"No, those things are out of the question. They give us uniforms to play ball, but wages are out of the question."

So I convinced him that something should be done to change that.

They had in Dearborn and other places, either small bars and restaurants, people who were selling jobs for the Ford Motor Company. The only thing you had to do was go there, leave your name, address and phone number; and in a few days you were called to work. You worked there for about three months, and then you were fired. How I discovered this, when I came there for the summer, I ran into a very elderly lady who had a restaurant at that time that closed, and she told me that she had sold probably five hundred jobs.

We worked on a proposal that the matter should be investigated. A law would forbid anyone selling jobs who had no permission, who was not a regular agency selling jobs. What happened in the meantime was that a strike took place at the Ford Motor Company and resulted in an agreement. Once the union signed an agreement, job sales would be out of the question.

During the strike a group of black people at Ford remained inside when others walked out. Paul Robeson came here and sang for them and talked to them with a loud speaker and they walked out.

One reason why I became a candidate for the senate was because when we organized meetings with the union, nobody would come. The workers were afraid. They would be spotted and fired. So the idea came that if one of us would run for public office, we would speak at public meetings. They said I would probably have the best chance as there are twenty thousand Poles working at Ford. So I became a candidate. Otherwise it was a surprise that I got the nomination. The Democratic nomination was practically election.

GWENDOLYN RUTH EDWARDS: I was a maid at Hudson's for many years, and I used to be in the millinery department. The people who owned Hudson's used to come in, and I was real friendly with them, and they'd say, "How do I look, Gwendolyn?" I'd say, you look fine, or you don't look fine. I was a maid. Normally the J. L. Hudson Company put very fair girls on the elevator, so when I went down there I got a maid job. I didn't particularly care what job I got, so they gave me a maid job. Finally they gave all the dark black people maid jobs. All the pretty ones went on the elevator.

Hudson's was a nice place to work. It didn't pay nothing. We may have got paid less than the elevator operators, but we had better times. I did at least. Mrs. Webber, the people that owned Hudson's, would come in. I'd lean on my broom and advise her not to buy that hat or whatever. We got to know them all really well. It was fun. The millinery department needed a full-time maid to keep things tidy. I kept the floor swept up and dusted off. The millinery department was the whole floor. That was my job. I'd go in and clean the offices in the morning and straighten up. Then all during the day I'd mop and pick things up. We had about sixty to seventy maids on the staff.

When I went to work for Ford's, I had worked at J. L. Hudson for many years as a maid. I decided that I wanted to make some more money. Well, I got very active in the union, and we started a women's committee out there because we felt the women were being discriminated against for the good jobs. I worked in the glass plant for ten years. I made windshields. I was one of the first black women they hired.

I got involved in the labor movement because I was getting the runaround from a lot of people. And I went to the union and said, "They're not treating me fairly," and they started working on my case. If I wanted to apply for a different job, they would have some excuse to keep me from doing it if it was more money. So I got tired of it, so I got real active in the union. As a matter of fact, I was an international rep for the union for several years because they discriminated against me.

We'd have conferences where we would teach the women what to do and what not to do in the plant. Then we would go all over, to every Ford plant, and have a conference once a year. We'd take maybe fifty or sixty women out of the plant and pay them the wages they would be losing and teach them how to be good union members.

JOHN J. "JACK" WHITE: At the plant where I worked there was a twenty-cent differential in wages between men and women. Before the union we worked thirteen hours a night. The women could only work ten hours a day and fifty-four hours a week. They could work four hours on Saturday and five ten-hour days. That necessitated the men working thirteen hours a night, because the women worked from seven until five, and then we would come in and stay until seven in the morning.

In 1932 the wage was eighteen to twenty-four cents an hour for women. For a man the maximum production wage was thirty-two cents per hour. It would have been quite a bit different if you could have collected the thirty-two cents for the thirteen hours you spent there. That was not the way it operated. You only got paid for the hours you were on that machine or line. If the line had to stop or broke down, you checked out and went to sit in the locker room on your own time until they found a job for you. You could be there five or six hours without any compensation. You worked about three months out of the year. That was the length of the production. They would dump it all out, then shut down or reduce the employment.

Once I got fired because I asked for the weekend off to get married. They told me, if I wasn't there Saturday and Sunday, don't bother coming back. I went back Monday; and, of course, they had pulled my card and told me they had no job for me.

HODGES E. MASON: I worked for a roofing company. I was anti-union. I was sent to Ford's as one of the roofers. They moved us around the pig-iron foundry. They roped off sections, and people going through would walk around. They were pouring pig-iron ingots. Those guys were working right under us. That's what burned me up. The tile that we were laying weighed 160 pounds. They were made out of cement. If they fell that 210 feet to the ground, it would kill a person instantly.

Outside was twelve degrees below zero. The guys would fall out from the excessive heat inside. One man would get under his arms and the other would get his feet and try to get him outside in that weather until he would come to. He was supposed to come back in and resume his work. He was so weak he could hardly stand up. I said to the guy, "Don't you have a union in here?"

In 1928 I went to Packard Motor Car Company. They had a guy they called "Skinny." He was the foreman. He walked up to me and said, "I want to tell you something, something that will do you good for years to come." He said: "Do you know how to pull enamel? Go over

130

there, and let that guy teach you." They had an assembly line along the wall. Each guy was taking a certain part of the crank case. They were chipping crank cases. I was considered darn good. I was fast.

A guy they called "Buddy" came to me and said, "Hey, Sonny, you think you're pretty damn good, don't you?"

I said, "Well I know I'm good."

He asked, "Do you think you could beat me?"

I said, "Sure." He asked how much, and I said ten dollars. I beat him out. Then we went for double or nothing, and I beat him again. But he was a stooge. They were working piecework. They were running bonuses, and they wanted to run the bonus up to two hundred percent. They didn't have enough sense to know that they were giving the company production.

In 1930, that was the heart of the depression, I got a job shoveling sand at Bohn Aluminum and Brass Corporation. It was piecework. They paid by the ton. You took the foreman's word about how much sand was in there. The old-timers knew just about, but they were afraid to do any talking. They had forty-ton, sixty-ton, ninety-ton, one hundred ton cars that come in there. They'd pay you fifty cents a ton. They'd get a car that weighed seventy ton, eighty ton, and tell you you had forty.

It was in 1936, I had established myself quite well in the plant. I was back at Bohn Aluminum as a chipper. You got so much for each casting. On the roof there was a time-study man, and the guys didn't know it. They would cut the prices on the job. You could make as much as five dollars and two cents working piecework, but you could only make forty-five cents an hour on an hourly rate. The blacks made forty-five cents and the whites made fifty-five, sixty-five, and seventy-five cents for the same job. All the Negroes were in the knockout department, the band saws and stationary grinding and chipping. That's where you knock out the cores of the castings that have been poured.

They would have the castings stacked up on a platform. The foreman would go to the extreme end of the plant; then he'd take the metal guys; then all the various departments. He would call them castings scrap. They weren't scrap. Then he would dock everyone of them, which meant that somebody had goofed on them, maybe. So after he docked all them, he would go and get a truck driver and have him pick the castings up. There may have been a few bad ones, but eighty-five percent of those castings were good, but almost four departments had been docked.

That went on for some time. One day a big guy that was pouring metal said: "We want to shut this so-and-so down. Can you shut down your department?"

I said: "I haven't been here very long. I haven't got as much seniority."

"But you should be able to do it."

I said, "Yes, I'll shut it down. When do you want to do it?" It was about 7:45 A.M.

He said, "Nine o'clock."

In December 1936, I remember very well. I went through the department talking to the guys, told them what we planned, and they said they would go for it. At nine o'clock he spread his hands, calling the strike.

I said, "Hit the button. Everybody in this plant, not just this department, is on strike." They sent me upstairs representing my department. We didn't have any union. We just went up ourselves. At 2:45 P.M. we came back. We had gained a ten-percent increase in pay. They liked my way of negotiating, not raising the devil, just telling them what the score really was.

We worked from December until March. Then the company's seven other plants went on strike. They closed down the plants. They were on strike on Wednesday, Thursday, and Friday. Friday morning the foreman said to us, "Everyone goes home at noon."

I didn't realize what the score was, but when I got home there was a telegram saying, "Do not report for work until further notice." They had locked us out. I was mad.

On Monday I went out to a meeting at the Local 306 hall. I said, "I'm going down there to turn it down."

They started talking about what their strategy was going to be. They said, "We need a steward."

I said, "Don't make me a steward, because I don't belong to your union and I don't intend to.

"You will be; that's all right."

We went on, and they discovered they had to have somebody on the negotiating committee. They recommended I be put on the negotiating committee. "I told you damn guys that I'm not in your union, and I'm not interested in being in it. I don't need you fellows to tell me what to do, and I'm not going to pay you a dollar a month."

They elected me anyway. They said, "You'll be a member."

I went down to the Book Cadillac Hotel. Went home, changed clothes and went down there and asked for the Bohn suite. They told me it was 2224. "Thank you very much."

He said, "Wait just a minute," and I stopped. The bellhop came. "Show this man up the service elevator."

"I didn't come down here to do any damn service. I'm on the negotiating committee."

My overcoat cost seventy-five dollars, and my suit cost sixty-nine dollars. I was well-dressed, there was no question about that. That was money then.

He said, "This way please." He walked past the passenger elevator as he was taking me to the service elevator. I stepped on the passenger elevator and said, "Twenty-two." At that time I weighed 236 pounds.

He said, "But. . . ."

"But, hell," I said, "twenty-two." He took me up then.

The life in the union was entirely different then. When we went to the picket line in 1937, '38, '39 we didn't know whether we were coming back alive or not. April 26, 1938, 125 police jumped thirty-two of us on the picket line. They were using the police to bring in scabs. I wasn't doing anything but walking the picket line, and they brought the scabs in; and this guy said to them, "You see that big nigger over there? He's dangerous. When trouble breaks out, get him."

They started hitting, and I put my hands up to let the clubs slide off. I thought I had to get out of there somehow. I was up against the wall in a suit costing sixty-nine dollars and wearing eyeglasses. Those guys came in, and the first thing they did was pound on my arms and hands. I picked up a little guy and put him over my head. That was a mistake. They were able to hit us on the head. I turned around to run. Whenever you went to the picket line, you knew about going around the place and finding how to get out of there.

Our local union had to go along with the union that agreed to accept the Chrysler contract and use it as a pattern. We lost a lot. I went into the plant after I joined the union and went all-out. Some of the Negroes told me that if you vote a union in there, they're gonna kick all the Negroes out. Management, they brainwashed them to a great extent.

I said: "Look, I'm gonna tell you fellas something. I'm Negro, and I don't take any foolishness. I just want to tell you one thing. When you build a building, you have to put down a foundation. In that foundation you put lime, cement, stone, and sand. Is that right?"

"Yep, that's right."

I said: "When you pour it and let it set, it hardens. And if you take one of them ingredients out, you'll wreck the foundation. I'm saying that you should be in the foundation."

There was a Frenchman that was an inspector before we had the lockout. He was making seventy-five cents an hour. The Negroes were getting forty-five cents an hour. The whites were making fifty-five, sixty-five, and seventy-five cents an hour. He came out after we had been on strike for two weeks, and he came in like a slimy turtle, quiet as he could be after the strike was over. When we decided we were going to officially organize the plant, get chief stewards, assistant stewards, committeemen, there was a guy by the name of Bill Cross. He was married to the Frenchman's sister. He said: "Boy, this union is sure going along fine. You know who we should get for chief steward in this department?" That department was seventy-five percent white.

"Nope, who?"

"That so and so Frenchman. Boy, he'll fight like hell."

I said: "What's wrong with me? I've been carrying the ball."

"You've done a good job, but that so and so Frenchman is the guy."

When we had an organization meeting that night, they jumped up and nominated me, and they nominated the Frenchman. He beat me by a landslide. I said to a guy, "Johnson, loan me your hat." He handed it to me. "Mr. Chairman, I told these guys if I should find one semblance of discrimination in this union that I'd be the first to talk about it. I've built the union in this so-and-so plant, and I'm asking everyone of you guys that believe I'm right to pull off your buttons and bring them and put them in this hat." I pulled mine off and put it in the hat.

The business agent said: "Brother Chairman, I'd like to make a motion. I move that we split the department in half. Have the inspection department in one jurisdiction and the bandsaw men, the chippers, the grinders, the knockout saw men in another." They passed it. That endeared me to the blacks and whites alike, because they saw that I wasn't going to take any foolishness.

There was a guy named James Walters. They ran him for president when I had been vice president for three years. Then they wanted to run more guys. I said: "What the hell is this? That guy can't put a motion on his wall much less put it before a house."

"Yeah, but we want him for president. After all, he has you."

I said: "Have me, hell! He doesn't have me. I'm not going to run. I'm the best chief steward in this local and one of the best in the country, and here's a guy that doesn't know anything at all, and you're going to reach down and bring him up and make him president. You can go to hell." I didn't run. They lost.

I had the distinction of being the president of the local for five years and simultaneously vice president of Wayne County CIO Council. I was dedicated to the union movement. I jumped into it with both feet because I felt I had disappointed my mother by not having become a doctor.

The next year they nominated me. I ran. My opponent said his slogan was, "No Negro president!" I won by a landslide.

HILDRED J. DREW DALE: My name is Hildred Drew, and I'm a retired international representative for the UAW. I became involved with the labor movement because I was hired in with Chrysler during the War. That, of course, was the time of "Rosie the Riveter," and the time for people who were patriotic to come forward. At the time I was hired it was so different from what it is now. They needed workers. The people needed jobs.

The labor movement is so much a part of me because I began working years and years ago, and what it provided was a decent income. The concern is that every worker is a person, and that worker has rights. One of the rights in particular is the right to be an individual, a right to get a decent wage for a fair day's work, and not only that but the involvement of the labor movement not only where you work but where you live—their commitment and concern with what is happening out in the community.

One of the things our late President Reuther said that stays with us and will always be with us is that you cannot separate the bread box from the ballot box.

Many of the things that we have accomplished at the negotiating table were accomplished at that time because of sitting down and talking. If you don't really protect yourself when it comes time for elections, and in community and political activity, much of that can be taken away with just the stroke of a pen.

I got involved in the labor movement because I saw the needs of the workers. And I saw many times the lack of dignity that was shown them by management, and taking advantage of them, because many who were not educated did not understand the contract. I got involved because I want to help people.

When I was coming along, my dad worked at Ford's, and there were family discussions. There was a time when families sat around a table together, and ate together and talked. We were a union family. My father worked at Ford Motor Car Company; and in so doing my brother became a medical doctor. My mother never worked. That income was sufficient.

The structure of the labor movement and the union is that there are elected officers. People who run for office get elected, and they represent people within the city area. So I ran for chief steward, and I ran for committeewoman. I ran for recording secretary. I was always running and/ or supporting others that I felt were the most qualified or I felt were sincerely concerned about helping other people, not just themselves.

There was a time when you couldn't find a seat at union meetings. It didn't have to be about something that just applied to Hildred Drew or to Gwendolyn Edwards. It was all of us working together, pulling the same way.

I didn't have any slogans, but I had secret strategies. I learned after a defeat or two that you can't take anyone for granted. Even those who work around you. You would assume that the people wearing your cap that says, "Vote for Hildred Dangerfield" would vote for Hildred Dangerfield. But a number of people who had the caps on didn't, because I took them for granted. You learn a lesson, because when you've lost, you've lost. So I learned some strategies—to talk to everybody and don't wait till it's time for you to run. Be involved in people's activities. Be involved with their families. Be involved with their feelings. Be involved with their government. Just be interested in people.

BIOGRAPHIES

Hildred J. Drew Dale was born on August 11, 1924, in Opelika, Alabama, and came to Detroit when she was six months old. A graduate of Miller High School, she attended Wayne State University. She first worked as a cosmetologist. During World War II she was hired to work at the Chrysler Corporation, and she remained there until her retirement in 1989. Ms. Dale was active in Local 372 at the Chrysler Trenton Engine plant and held the offices of chief steward and recording secretary—the first black woman to hold this position. She served as commissioner on the Detroit Board of Zoning Appeals. Presently she serves as a representative for UAW President Owen Bieber on the Retired Workers Advisory Council.

Gwendolyn Ruth Edwards was born on September 29, 1905, in Kansas City, Missouri. She was employed by the J. L. Hudson Company, and she also worked in the glass plant at Ford Motor Company. She was one of the first black women selected to participate in the Women in Industry Summer School at Brynmawr College. She was active in the YWCA and in the UAW. In recent years she was a member of the State of Michigan Commission on Services to the Aging.

Hodges E. Mason was born at Talbotton, Georgia on August 1, 1907 and moved to Detroit on June 13, 1936. Mr. Mason has been active in the unions and in activities to promote equal treatment for all persons. He fought to gain employment for black women in the automobile industry. He worked to assure that the union carried out the contract provision for seniority. He was largely responsible for the formation of Local 208 at Bohn Aluminum and Brass Company, and he was the first black president of that UAW local.

Stanley Nowak was born on March 14, 1903 in Poland; he came to Detroit in 1932. An early UAW organizer, he helped organize major automobile shops on Detroit's west side. He served in the Michigan State Senate for ten years, from 1939 to 1949. He was editor of the Polish weekly, *Glos Ludowy* (Voice of the Workers), for over twenty years. His wife, Margaret, has worked closely with him. They are parents of Lisa Nowak and have two grandchildren.

John J. "Jack" White was born on February 19, 1912, in Ottawa, Ontario of Irish-Canadian parents. He is a veteran of the U.S. Navy and served in World War II. He has been employed as an auto worker,

136

chemical worker, truck driver, and as a union member, officer, and staff member. He retired from the Teamster's Union in 1974. He has become a senior citizens' advocate, currently holding leadership roles in several organizations.

WALTER ROSSER

At about age twelve I developed a trace of tuberculosis, and then I had
to attend an open-air school. The open-air school was located over in the
Clifford and Michigan area, which was deep in the heart of the Polish
neighborhood in Detroit at that time. I went to school at Clifford open-
air for about two years, and I was deemed as being healthy enough to go
back to public school.

The feeling was that the more good, wholesome food a person got
and the more rest, the more apt he was to recover. So when they would
find a child with tuberculosis or the trace of tuberculosis, they would
segregate him into the open-air school. The main difference was, the
curriculum was the same, except there was no gym. The authorities saw
to it that you got a very wholesome breakfast and a very wholesome
midday meal and that you got at least an hour rest. Now it was called
an open-air school because the top had a big cage-like, heavy wire top
that opened. When the weather was permissible, they would open up
the roof and you'd get the open air, so that's where the name "open-air"
came from.

Prior to World War II the ill child and the needy child was taken
care of through the school system. I suppose that's one reason why I always go for a millage regardless of the merits.

It wasn't the question of the black children being segregated in the class or, when you go to the dentist, "black children only"; that was not the case.

I vividly remember the gray depression years in Detroit. I have seen people foraging in garbage cans. I have almost been trampled to death; as a little fellow I didn't know what I was doing. I'd go up to the packing house; and in those days certain parts of the animal—such as a heart, kidneys, lungs, or chitterlings or the intestines, that are sold now and converted into sausage—they dumped these parts in a tub and then threw them out to hungry people. I almost got trampled one day.

Well, we'd go to the packing house, and they'd bring out two or three tubs of kidneys, hearts, and all the intestines and just put them in some type of a bag, and just throw them out into a crowd of people and the people would be scrambling.

We did have a welfare system, and it was organized but there was no ongoing permanent thing like Aid To Dependent Children. The first welfare system, I'm just going from my personal memory as a youngster, if it did not originate during the depression here in Detroit, it's the first time that it ever operated on a large scale. People were given scrip. Detroit printed its own money for awhile. Paid it's own employees in scrip —schoolteachers, policemen, firemen. I would dare to say that a good seventy-five percent of the black community was receiving welfare. Because when the automobile plants went down, except for the few who had jobs in the service sector, that was it.

Well, I attended the Condon Middle School, then I attended Northwestern High School. I graduated from Northwestern High in June of 1939, and a few months later I got a job at the Ford Motor Company. My dad was able to go in and talk to Don Marshall.

Don Marshall was a black man, a former policeman, who Henry Ford met. I believe he met him through some of the Episcopalian church officials. At any rate, Mr. Marshall was given what is known as a star rank, which made him, more or less, on the general staff of the Ford Motor Company. Mr. Marshall had the power to hire and to fire. He hired all blacks at the company. Mr. Marshall also had the authority to, when there was a problem, if a black person could convince him that he had been discriminated against or mistreated, rectify the situation.

Well, I've known of people who got laid off or they'd get fired, and Marshall would investigate and determine that they were maltreated, and the people were put back to work. That's the good side of the coin. The other side of the coin was Mr. Marshall was anti-union, and he'd use his influence to do his very best to keep the UAW from becoming organized. Marshall had tremendous influence with the black ministers and black leadership in Detroit, because he's the guy who held the key to "who gets the job." And he who worked for Ford in those days, even though they were almost slave-like conditions, economically, was looked up to.

The American industry was not organized in the mass production industries. The employers got as much work out of a man as they possibly could, and you had to almost run to keep up with an assembly line job. And I was so shocked. I was hired at the age of eighteen and about five months. After I was hired, there was a layoff; and I assumed that being one of the latest hired, I would be the first to go, and I didn't understand it. Being only eighteen years of age and, at that time, in wonderful health, I didn't realize that I was probably performing the work of two or three men and doing it satisfactorily. Well, I never got laid off, and it amazed me. The boss seldom got on my back. I didn't understand that that alone was proof that my work was very satisfactory, but I was young and I was strong.

I wanted to keep the boss off my back, and I had the strength and I had the health, and I did nothing but eat well, come in from work and then go home and sleep. I didn't drink or smoke. I can realize now that in those days the average man, forty or forty-five years of age, actually, was almost at the end of his rope.

The advances in health care hadn't been made, then, that are made now, and medicine hadn't been developed to prolong life. Again, those who had to work in industry had to work in desperate conditions, because employers at that time didn't particularly provide proper ventilation. They didn't provide proper, safe working conditions, healthy working conditions.

Ironically, the Ford Motor Company was a place where you could almost eat off the floor. At the Rouge Plant they employed possibly ninety thousand people, and old Henry Ford wanted his plants clean, and so they were kept clean. There were about five thousand people in the janitorial division, which is a huge number of people. And almost every time that there would be a breakdown, maybe for half a day or half an hour, instead of being sent home we would assist in cleaning up or paint over and paint over again. The place was much cleaner then than it is now. That's a fact.

BIOGRAPHY

Walter Rosser was born on March 16, 1921 in Detroit. He was a UAW activist while employed at Ford Motor Company. He has served on the board of directors of the Virginia Park Community Investment Associates. He currently devotes time to four community service organizations striving for better housing, community support for schools, assistance for seniors, and support of libraries.

❦

RUTH WILLS-CLEMONS

When we first moved to Detroit in 1924 we lived on the west side for one year, and I went to Sampson Elementary School. Then we moved to the east side, and I went to Miller Intermediate School.

Our neighbors were concerned about us, and we would mind them the same as we did our parents. I was always fascinated with rain, and I remember once it was storming, and I put on my raincoat and cap and was going out for a walk. At that time, in the 1930s, we lived in a four-family flat, and there was a two-family flat next door to us, across the courtyard. The lady upstairs heard the door slam. I guess she was wondering what was going on. She raised the window and called me. "Ruth, where are you going?"

I said, "To take a walk."

She said, "If you don't go in that house and take your things off and wait 'til your mother comes home. . . ." Mother was at choir rehearsal.

I answered, "Well, I'm just going to be away for a short time."

She said, "You go back in the house and stay until your mother comes home!" I turned around, went back into the house, took my wraps off, and waited until mother came. So that was it! Yes, we obeyed our neighbors.

For fun we played all types of table games such as "Monopoly" and "Old Maid" or whatever types of games the entire family could play around the dining-room table. We could never play for pennies. There never was any gambling in the house. We played for buttons, and I still have that big can of buttons. Maybe each one of us started out with fifty buttons, and at the end of the evening we would see how many buttons had been won or lost. Then the buttons were put back into the can for next time.

My sister, Lilliane Wills, graduated from Cass Technical High School; I graduated from Northeastern High. After graduation I tried to apply for City College; my sister and I both did. We were turned down because they told us that we had to pay all of our tuition at one time. It was during the depression, and we were barely eating, so it was impossible to pay the tuition at one time. Later we found out that this was not a requirement.

Well, that kept me from going to college for about two or three years, but my sister went to St. Louis City Hospital No. 2 School of Nursing. Since I knew I had to work, I started into clerical work. And the reason I knew so much about the WPA [Works Progress Administration] is because that's the way I got my first job. In the daily newspaper they advertised for fifteen hundred clerical workers. I had taken college prep because I knew I was going to college, and my counselor was foresighted enough to give me typing. She said I would be able to type my own papers in college because I was college material, and she was trying to get me ready to enter. After seeing the newspaper article, I said, "Well, mother, do you think they will hire me?"

And my mother was always this way, she said, "Whatever you want, you try to get it." So she dressed me like I was supposed to go to an office, in my neat suit and white blouse, and I went down and applied for the job. There were so many applying that I started to return home, but I remembered what my mother said, "If you want something, you go for it."

When I saw so many girls and women there, I felt they were not going to hire me. I was down there six, seven, eight hours before I even reached the door and got in. And I'll always remember the interviewer asked me, "Why do you want a job?"

I said, "Because I can't go to college, and I must work and save enough money until I can enter some college.

He looked at me and said, "Well, you go to such and such a room." To my great surprise they hired me.

BIOGRAPHY

Ruth Wills-Clemons was born on May 29, 1912, in Middletown, Ohio, and moved to Detroit in 1923. She is a religious and community leader, official historian of Metropolitan Baptist Church, member and past president of Elliottorian Business and Professional Women's Club, and member Eta Phi Beta Sorority. She served as administrative assistant to the president, Progressive National Baptist Convention and was chair and editor of the 25th Anniversary Book. She is listed in *Black Women in Michigan: 1785–1985.*

Left: *Ernest Timothy Marshall (left) was the well-liked director of Green Pastures Camp in 1936 and 1937.* **Right:** *Eleanor Boykin Jones (first woman on left) was a counselor for several years at the Detroit Urban League's Green Pastures Camp.*

DISCUSSION ON GREEN PASTURES CAMP

ELEANOR BOYKIN JONES, ERNEST TIMOTHY MARSHALL, AND CECIL WHITTAKER McFADDEN

ERNEST TIMOTHY MARSHALL: Green Pastures Camp was John Dancy's idea. He patterned it after the play *Green Pastures.* He got the Children's Fund of Michigan, which was established by the late Senator James Couzens, to fund the camp. At that period, black children were not accepted at any of the other camps. It started around 1931.

It was on lovely Little Pleasant Lake out near Chelsea, closer to Jackson. It was also near Grass Lake. There were lovely beech trees out there.
ELEANOR BOYKIN JONES: The girls' cottages were at the entrance of the camp, and the boys' were way over on the other side. In the center we had a big dining hall, and there were quarters for some of the folks that worked there. You had to go all the way over the hill, and down there were the five boys' cottages.
ERNEST TIMOTHY MARSHALL: I was chosen because Mr. Dancy thought I would make a good director with my background. I was a social worker, a recreation worker with the City of Detroit and health education teacher with the Detroit Public Schools. Mr. Dancy was very selective in choosing his counseling staff. They represented a cross-section of people from all economic levels. He always saw to it that some of the counselors were real black with a lot of talent. So many of our young

people would be from middle-class black families, and he wanted to make sure that this would be an inspiration to young people.

ELEANOR BOYKIN JONES: All the counselors had to have had at least a year of college. The first year I got sixty dollars for twelve weeks, but we ate well. When I came back home I had to wear my mother's clothes, I was so fat!

ERNEST TIMOTHY MARSHALL: We had excellent counselors. The only problem was that after five weeks and that moon came out big, they started romancing.

ELEANOR BOYKIN JONES: Sunday afternoons a whole lot of folk would come out from Detroit, all the socialites. That was the place to go on Sunday afternoon, to drive up to Green Pastures Camp.

ERNEST TIMOTHY MARSHALL: Every Sunday we had chicken, corn on the cob, string beans, hot rolls, cake, and homemade ice cream.

ELEANOR BOYKIN JONES: It really was a well-built establishment. It was on a par with any campsite you would see anywhere, with a health cottage and the five cottages nicely spaced.

The girls slept inside the cottages. The counselors slept on the screened in porches, the same width as the cottages. The counselors slept on one side of the porch, and there was another cot there. The counselor got to choose a camper that she felt was a strong person or leader, and that camper got to sleep on the other cot. The other ten girls and no boys were inside this one large room that had five beds on either side.

They had to learn how to make up their beds, the hospital way to do the sheets and all that. The counselors taught them how to make their own beds. We had inspection every morning to be sure their clothes and all were put away carefully under the bed. We had space, but it was close.

The lavatory for the girls was downhill, and that was difficult for some of the girls, who had problems because they were frightened at night, even though there was a light. The lavatory was down there, and it was similar in that they had the lavatory and the bowls for them to wash in. By the time you went swimming three times a day you weren't very dirty. It seems that there was some kind of shower so that you could wash the sand from your feet, but it was cold water.

The counselors' part was separated from the students, but it was all cold water. I never felt hot water. We swam in the morning, before lunch; and then we swam in the afternoon. Three times a day you got into the lake.

CECIL WHITTAKER McFADDEN: I know my father had taken me around town trying to get me into a camp because I was what was known as a sickly child. I spent four weeks at Herman Kiefer with scarlet fever, and I was very much underweight. As I remember, he tried to get me into the *Free Press* Fresh Air Camp, but they did not take any little colored children.

We came on the bus, and as we got off the bus, kids were lined up watching us get off. They were shouting things over to us. I can remember one especially yelling at me: "Oh, you got good hair now, but you'll be going swimming three times a day. Your hair is going to beat you back home!"

Before we went to sleep, they talked about different things. Some of the girls were much older and much more sophisticated. My vocabulary increased. I heard words I had never heard before, and I began to get an idea about some sexual things I had never heard before, because some of them were more sophisticated than others.

They named each cottage after some famous black person, and you had to find out something about their background and who they were.

ERNEST TIMOTHY MARSHALL: Dancy would stop a child and say, "Who was Colonel Young?"

And the kid would say, "He rode a horse all the way to Washington, D.C." He came out every weekend and sometimes during the week. He loved that place. He had a room in the director's cottage set aside for himself.

CECIL WHITTAKER McFADDEN: If you were a good camper you got to go over there and dust the director's cottage.

Another thing that impressed me as a camper, I loved that ceremony where you came out every morning and you raised the flag. It was very solemn. In the evening, after supper and before sundown, they'd lower it. I was very impressed. We sang "Taps."

I can remember the main thing that we missed and that we wrote home for and were very frantic to get was candy.

ERNEST TIMOTHY MARSHALL: Mr. Dancy said it was unheard of to have a runaway from Green Pastures. Kids would get lonely, but they wouldn't run away. Mr. Dancy met this one kid walking down the road. Mr. Dancy was a House of Corrections commissioner and had a badge. He asked the kid where he was going. He said he was going somewhere; he didn't know who Mr. Dancy was. Dancy told him: "Boy, I'm going to take you back. I'm a commissioner," and showed him his badge.

The boy said, "Oh, you can buy those at the pawn shop."

ELEANOR BOYKIN JONES: In the morning we took a dip first; then we washed up and got dressed. Then they had the flag raising, and we went to breakfast. After breakfast, that's when they had some kind of class like nature study or performing arts. Then you took another dip, and you had dinner. Right after that middle meal of dinner you had quiet hour. That was your big meal of the day. That's when you went back and you could lie down in your bunk, or you could write letters, or you were just quiet. After that there were other activities. We would maybe go for a hike or have a nature study lesson or something like that. Then you took another dip, and you had supper. After that, sometimes in the dining hall they would have singing. Always on Saturday nights you had a big program. You had a big show and a dance following that. You went to bed fairly early because you got up so early, and you were pretty tired.

CECIL WHITTAKER McFADDEN: The children seemed to get along very well. I just remember there was teasing. I can remember these two girls were friendly, and one of them had let the other girl borrow an outfit she had. It was kind of like a romper suit. This girl liked it so well she wore it two or three times; and then later on, when the girl who owned it put it on, everybody said, "You've got on so-and-so's suit."

ERNEST TIMOTHY MARSHALL: We used to take the boys out on a snipe hunt. You take the boys out in the woods, and we'd tell them about this snipe. It's a wild animal out there. You go out, and two boys have to hold the bag and a flashlight. The snipe would appear and go into the bag. What you would do is leave them out there. You'd take them way out in the woods, and you'd leave them. We always had a snipe hunt with every group. We'd make sure that nothing happened to them, but they would think they were lost.

BIOGRAPHIES

Eleanor Boykin Jones was born on January 7, 1917, in Knoxville, Tennessee, and came to Detroit in 1926. Her parents are Ulysses and Curtis Boykin. Two brothers are Ulysses and Wade. She attended Detroit Public Schools and Michigan State Normal College, where she earned an A.B. degree and teacher certification. She has a master's degree from Wayne State University in counseling and administration. Ms. Jones was director of the Detroit Public Schools' Guidance and Counseling Department and worked for the Detroit Board of Education for more than forty-seven years.

Ernest Timothy Marshall was born on July 1, 1908, in Delta City, Mississippi and moved to Detroit in 1919. He was the only child of Tim and Elizabeth Marshall. His father died in the flu epidemic of 1918. He was educated in Detroit Public Schools and graduated from Cass Technical High School. He was a teacher and counselor with the Detroit Public Schools for forty years. He was director of Green Pastures Camp in 1936 and 1937. He married Louise Conger on April 4, 1936. Their children are Ernest T. Marshall, Jr., and Michael Alva, both of whom are physicians. He is grandfather to eight children.

Cecil Whittaker McFadden was born January 2, 1918, in Kansas City, Missouri. She attended Detroit Public Schools, South Carolina

State A & M College, and Wayne State University. She was on the board of Delta Home for Girls. She was secretary, Publicity Department, Ford Local 600, UAW-CIO from 1941–45. She was assistant editor, *Detroit Tribune*, 1945–48. She was also on the Detroit City Planning Committee in 1948. Ms. McFadden taught at Roosevelt Elementary School for twenty years and was elected to the Detroit Board of Education for the 1981–84 term. She was on the board of directors of the International Institute from 1983–85. She is president of the Detroit Alumnae chapter, Delta Sigma Theta Sorority.

James Boggs was an activist for more than fifty years, both in union affairs and in the community.

JAMES BOGGS

I came here in 1937, and I came here on the freight train, as most people were doing during those days. I was eighteen going on nineteen. I graduated from high school in Bessemer, Alabama, in 1937. I had brothers and uncles in Detroit. This was in the period when it was the Great Depression.

The way people would travel mostly at that time, you were a hobo. Black and white and everything else. You had a very tough time being a hobo at that time; primarily because they had the Scottsboro case down South; and it was a question of, if they caught black and whites hoboing together, they was just going to beat the hell out of blacks. It was tough.

Nevertheless, myself and one of my friends from Alabama, he was from my hometown of Marion Junction, which is below Selma, him and I got on the freight train and hoboed up north. We had nothing but what we had on our backs, that's all. Didn't even have a change of clothes which we learned about later after we hoboed some more that you always take along several pair of clothes. I had about fifty cents; he had about fifty cents. We ran out of money the second day.

We bummed up to people and said, "Would you please give me something to eat?" and people would generally give you some bread and a little meat. You'd go up to the nearest house and knock on the back door. I went over to a farmer's house, and a lady gave us some cabbage and hamhocks. This is in the summer. In Cincinnati we went down to the bakery, and they gave us some cinnamon rolls and stuff. Cincinnati was a bum town at that time, bums just by the hundreds, lying around. People built a shantytown there on the river. Every day you'd go uptown to bum.

In St. Louis people took railroad cross ties and made houses all down the Mississippi River. Sometimes you'd get on the freight train. There'd be fifty people on the freight train scattered all over, some sitting on top, some inside, some in gondolas, just riding where you could ride. The big thing you had to worry about was, when you come into a town and the freight train slowed down, everybody jumped off and walked around the town to catch the train when it would leave out the other end of town. Down South in Tennessee, if they'd catch you, they'd put you on a peanut farm to pick peanuts.

I came in on a train from Toledo. Got off at the Ford River Rouge plant, and I walked down Michigan Avenue to downtown Detroit, asking the police in Dearborn and all down that route where was Theodore and Hastings. That's where my uncle was living. I come to 940 Theodore, early in the day in June 1937. This is the first time I had ever been to a big city. I had been to cities like in Alabama, but they wasn't nothing like Detroit. Detroit was the first big city I'd ever been to. My brothers were here. I had two brothers here, and my uncle lived here. My uncle was the first black person that worked at Budd Wheel over here on Charlevoix. So all of us thought we was going to get a job over there. I don't know why we thought we would. We didn't get none. That's the year I came to Detroit—1937.

There's depression all over. So what do you do? You get a job washing cars or like bums do now. Or somebody picks you up and you go out in the country somewhere and work in cabins, where people had their summer cabins. I had never heard about that before until I come here. Or you'd do a little painting with somebody. Get about three dollars for a room to paint in those days. But mainly I went to car washing places.

Weren't many blacks working in the auto industry at all. Ford was the one where blacks worked, and they worked in the foundry. I used to have a cousin working at Ford. Even at that time, they was big shots. Big shots because they was always the ones who had a paycheck, getting about twenty-five to twenty-six dollars a week. At that time it was lots of money. Most people had them ten-, eleven-, and twelve-dollar-a-week jobs.

I went and worked on the Works Progress Administration. I worked on Orangelawn, Greenlawn, Cherrylawn, Southfield, State

Street, and all those streets, digging the curbstones before they put in the curbs and put in cement streets, 'cause most all the streets was dirt roads in those days. I went back South in 1938 and got married. Come back and still was on the WPA, because there wasn't nothing here to do.

When my first kid was born, I was still rooming. I paid three dollars, and the lady made me pay an extra fifty cents a week for the lights. The lights didn't cost no more than two dollars for the whole month, so I paid the whole light bill. But that's what they would do. They say you burn more light when you have a baby. And the baby couldn't cry. I remember I had to have a little song, "Peter, Peter, go to sleep. . . .Peter, Peter. . . ." I'd sit up half the night, 'cause if the baby cried the landlord was going to tell you, "Move!"

So practically all folks was rooming and rent wasn't high—three dollars. You could get a fancy room for four dollars. And there were kitchen privileges, and there would be all kind of notes up on the wall over the sink: "Don't do this. . . . Wash the dishes when you get through. . . ." That lasted until after World War II.

I lived in one house where there was one man and his wife and daughter, then me and my wife and kid and the landlady. That's it. Anybody who had a six-room house could rent out two rooms or more to help pay the rent. Those days people were still having rent parties to help pay the rent. This was the depression. People would go down to Eastern Market on Saturday afternoon to pick up all that food there free.

They also had a lot of soup kitchens in Detroit in those days. That's the first time I ever saw white people who were hungry. Down South nobody was hungry, not even black folks. We always had chickens, hogs and cows down South. Down South people were ragged. We didn't have no shoes, no clothes much; but you had food. When I came to Detroit, people didn't have no food. They'd be in line at the soup kitchens and soup lines. They weren't segregated.

Did eighteen months in George Washington Trade School. Pattern makers and all that stuff. Well, it was about that time the war industry was starting, and I got called to Aeronautic Tool Company out on Ryan Road. But I wouldn't take it because I had got called to Chrysler, and I thought I'd make more money at Chrysler, because they were going to give me sixty cents an hour as a template maker, pattern maker at this here aircraft plant. That was an apprentice program, whereas at Chrysler's I got sixty-eight cents an hour as a factory worker.

Most factory workers in that day was getting about a dollar and two cents an hour tops for skilled trades. I eventually worked up to ninety-eight cents an hour to a dollar and two cents an hour. I worked for a dollar and two cents an hour from 1940 until the war was over in 1945. The highest wages in Chrysler at that time was running about a dollar and thirty-six cents an hour, and that was for a tool cutter or gear cutter in the machine shop, and the skilled trade workers were getting a dollar and forty-two cents. All of us got less than two dollars an hour throughout the war, with lots of overtime.

You could get a job anywhere you went. Everybody would hire you. They was getting cost plus. If Chrysler was paying you a dollar an hour, the government would add a dollar to it, so they made a dollar off of me every hour that I was getting paid. That's what the war was doing. Therefore, the companies wanted to hire lots of folks anyway. Even if they wasn't doing much work, you hired them. They was getting so much a head for every one they'd keep. In fact, it was hard to get fired in those days, because they all wanted to keep you.

Out around Chrysler at them old houses they used to rent out, they used to rent the houses by shift, rent the rooms by shift. You slept in the bed during the morning shift and somebody else slept in it that night while you was at work.

Cost of living was lots cheaper. We had lots of money, comparatively speaking. In fact, everybody saved some money during the War. That's how they bought all those houses when the War was over, because people had four years there when they just worked and there wasn't nothing to buy. Didn't make no cars, so didn't nobody buy them new cars. Nobody bought refrigerators and stuff like that or big heavy appliances. Nobody bought nothing but house furniture. When the war was over, and they had been working all them long hours, they'd all accumulated a little money. I accumulated some, and I didn't have all that fancy a job. During the war this town was booming, because everybody was working.

I was active in the unions. I belonged to the goon squads. Our job was, when there was a strike, we was trying to make people join the union. Our job was to force folks to join up to the union, threaten them and certain things. More people joined the union because we forced them in the union than joined automatic. Because they didn't want to pay no dues. We told them they had to pay.

Every once in awhile we'd have a dues push. We'd line up out at the gate and wouldn't let them in unless they belonged to the union. They'd go around the back and jump over the fence and go to work anyway. The next day or so, we'd go out to their house and throw bricks through there or beat the hell out of them and they'd join. That was a part of the organizing. Then we used to go out and help other locals organize.

Smaller guys than me was goons, and there was smaller women. One of the best fighters I knew was a little old woman. Fought like a tomcat out there on the line. We had all different sizes.

I was very active in the union in the period when they was organizing. I guess you would say I was in the old left-wing group. I was with

152

George Addes and R. J. Thomas. R. J. Thomas was nothing but a welder. They was all political activists because they belonged to lots of little organizations at that time. Gotta remember there was the Socialist Workers party, Communist party, the Labor Movement, Shackmanites, Olerites, the Wobblers, IWW. All these different groups were in the union. There was three or four different political machines inside the union struggling for power.

You had lots of factions all fighting over who was going to have leadership. They wasn't divided being or not being union. They was divided on which direction should the union go. Some was a little more militant than the others. Thomas-Addes was a very militant group. Before Reuther come in we used to strike all the time, but when Reuther come in he cut the strikes out, most of them. We used to have wildcats, they called them. We sometimes had maybe one hundred and fifty strikes in a year. Anytime we didn't like something, we'd walk out. That's the way we forced the issue.

Wildcats are unauthorized strikes when people just spontaneously walk out over issues. They wanted to kick so many people off the line, and you say: "Like hell, you ain't taking nobody off. We need some more."

They outlawed wildcats, made them illegal. For years we only had wildcats. That's when the union was at its best, because there was pressure all the time. Then once they got check-off, when you had to be in the union whether you wanted to join or not, it was kind of a bad thing, because as long as everybody had to pay their dues each month instead of out of their pocket, they was always complaining.

Once they had check-off the union didn't have to do nothing, and it's still going to get the dues. It changed the whole tempo of the thing. A department would say, "Look, we ain't paying no dues this month unless you all get something did." That kept the union jumping like hell. The idea of having check-off was to have everybody be in the union. You had to be in the union from the day you walked into the plant and got hired. The union would have not only a steady income, but we had everybody being a unionized worker whether they wanted to be or not. But it also had a bad side to it. The negative side was, once everybody was in the union, the union didn't have to be militant no more. Because they was going to get the dues whether they was doing anything or not. So it had its positive and negative effects.

Being in the union meant something in those days—I'm a union member. Guys stopped going to church and go to the union meetings. But then it wasn't long before people was back at the church and the union meetings was down. My early experience was in the union, and that's where I got my real organizing skills—in strikes, wildcats, picketing, goon squads, stuff like that.

In 1946 the UAW set up the Fair Employment Practices Committee. The purpose of that committee was to break up discrimination in and around the plant. Not so much the hiring, because at that time everybody could get hired, but putting all black people in one particular classification or in one particular section of the plant. We was also trying to upgrade people to different skills. It was always based on seniority then. We didn't have what they got in affirmative action. We just meant that if, say, I have been working at the plant for a year, I should be able to go into skilled trades before somebody got hired off the street could go into skilled trades.

Around '46, '47, '48, '50, the Fair Practice Committee was very active. We used to go out on a Friday night downtown and picket all the different restaurants that wouldn't serve black people. We had to go up and down Woodward Avenue. Ernest Dillard, me and him, we used to work together.

They would tell us, "We don't serve black folks in here." So we'd file a complaint under the Diggs Act. The Diggs Act was, there should be no discrimination in Michigan under land, sea or air and all that stuff. We would go in, and we would be refused service. So we'd call the police, and we'd tell them we'd want to file a complaint.

They would say: "What you complaining about? If they don't want you over here, why don't you go over on Hastings Street and get yourself something?"

We said, "We don't want to eat on Hastings. We want to eat at this place."

He said, "Well, the man said he don't want to serve you."

"Yes, but the law says he has to serve us."

So we'd have an argument with the police, but he eventually would write up the case. Then we'd go down to 1300 Beaubien that Monday and follow up the complaint and file the case on them. Then finally they would have to agree that they would serve us, and then we would have to send back a team to see that they did serve you. We would keep going back until we'd break it up. But at that time we'd have lots of people that didn't want us in there. Even the customers in there would say, "We're going home, get our guns, and run these niggers out of here," but still we stayed.

This was up and down Woodward Avenue. We broke up all the bars and eating places from downtown up to Grand Boulevard, and then we went on up as far as Clairmount, because there was lots of white restaurants up on Woodward in those days that wouldn't serve blacks.

We went to the Hotel Detroiter. They put salt in our food. We called the manager and said it was full of salt, and he'd say, "It don't taste like no salt to me." He knowed they put salt in it. Lots of times we'd go in and they'd deliberately break the glasses up in front of us to let us know they wasn't going to eat out of something some nigger ate out of. All of this took place under the Fair Employment Practices Committee working with the NAACP. This went on throughout the '50s. At the same time, we were still active in the union.

The movement didn't come until after four little girls was burned in Birmingham. That was 1963. That's when we had all the big marches all over the country. I was in all of them. I was in the march here with Martin Luther King.

That was the biggest march they ever had in the United States anywhere. Bigger than the one in Washington. They didn't say that, but we knew we had over three hundred thousand people. That day I was just with family. All of our friends were together. I think the union marched, too, with a different group. But a lot of people didn't go with the union. They went with their own families and their block clubs.

What had happened, the blacks had organized all over the city and the churches. Reverend Cleage did lots of organizing. All of the preachers agreed that they would have a rally, and every one of their churches had a pre-march rally. That's what got out so many people. The day that they had it, from Warren Avenue and Woodward to downtown, from Woodward over to Brush Street on one side and to Cass on the other side, it was a solid wave. Now all these people wasn't black. Lots of whites were there too. Then people came from the suburbs and joined in, so it was a tremendous march.

They marched down Woodward Avenue. It was like a Thanksgiving parade. They marched to Cobo Hall, where Reuther spoke and where King spoke, but none of us could get near there. It was just impossible. Only the people who marched up there with them actually got in at that time. I don't think that place held many people back in those days. So people stood out there on the street, on Jefferson and all the streets up there, and listened to it over the loud speaker.

The black movement starts in the labor movement. I think it was coming from out of the south with the belief that people ought to relate to each other better than what they were doing and a sense of believing in fair play. I was put on lots of times. When I didn't want to do something, I did it. The call got bigger than me, so I didn't get limited by, "Hell, all I have to do is take care of Jimmy." I always knew that the world could only be made better if a lot of other people was involved in it. That I was not going to change the world by myself and, therefore, it was my responsibility to work with others or try to give some leadership to others for both of us to participate.

I was well aware of how divisive things could be when one group is torn against each other. I think by being in the labor movement, around particularly the Wobblers, I learned a deep sense of what I would call at that time class struggle, which meant that I recognized that it wasn't just a black struggle. Blacks and whites were in the struggle. So I come out of that too. I knew that it was important that all the different ethnic groups should struggle together. It didn't always happen that way. Those were the things that I think motivated me to try to always broaden my horizons.

BIOGRAPHY

James Boggs was born on May 28, 1919, in Marion Junction, Alabama, which is just fourteen miles below Selma. He was active in labor, black power, youth, and environmental movements throughout his adult life. He authored *Racism and the Class Struggle; The American Revolution: Pages From A Negro Worker's Notebook*; and *Revolution and Evolution in the Twentieth Century*, co-authored by Grace Boggs. After coming to Detroit in 1938, Mr. Boggs became active in the union movement, the Marxist movement, and the black movement. He was married to Grace Boggs, with whom he worked continually on critical causes with organizations such as Save Our Sons and Daughters (SOSAD), We the People Reclaim Our Streets (WEPROS), and Detroiters Uniting. James Boggs died on July 22, 1993.

Ernest C. Dillard, Sr., began to break down barriers in Detroit restaurants before the officially recognized start of the civil rights movement.

ERNEST C. DILLARD, SR.

I've been in Detroit since June of 1937. It was the next day after Joe Louis won from Jim Braddock. I left the night of the fight. The reason I remember that so well was that I had to borrow a suitcase, and I walked across town to a friend's to get it. He and I didn't have radios but the few people who had them, it seemed that they had a public service in mind: they played them loud. I could follow the fight as I walked across town. Down there we couldn't talk about black folks knocking out white folks, not even in a mixed group.

The next morning I grabbed the bus and took off. I came from Montgomery, Alabama. Eleven months later I was able to send for my wife and our children, Marilyn and Ernest, Jr. Jessie Mae Dawson and I had married at the Hutchinson Street Baptist Church in Montgomery, Alabama, on December 25, 1934.

In 1942 I was hired at the General Motors Fisher Body Fleetwood Plant, and while I was working there I joined UAW Local 15 and became a dues-collecting steward. At that time General Motors recognized only committeemen and not the stewards. I was a steward that was not recognized by the company. The local union recognized the stewards for the purpose of collecting dues. There was a time when you didn't have a

157

check-off. Check-off is when the company takes your dues off. We used to have a hell of a time getting them to do that. When you join the union now, you sign something and your dues are taken out of your pay. A lot of people say the union would be better if they had that now. In those days people were more eager to give because they could see unions blossoming before their eyes.

I was the first black everything in Local 15: chairman of the Fair Employment Practice Committee, member of the Executive Board, committeeman of the Paint Shop, editor of the local union paper, *Fleetwood Organizer*, chairman of the Shop Committee, and recording secretary. That Fisher Body Fleetwood Plant was old; it was home of the Cadillac—high scale, high quality car. They called it "the old man's home." Craftsmen worked there. There weren't any blacks. Those guys would come out at lunchtime and sit on the curb, and you'd have to go into the street to get around them. You knew damn well they weren't going to let you work in there, but the War put us in there. Almost no women were there either, black or white.

In 1949 I became a member of the Board of Directors for the NAACP. I was on the board when Arthur Johnson came from the South and was hired as executive secretary. Arthur Johnson's first Detroit contact with the NAACP was through our group, the Discrimination Action Committee, which I organized and chaired. This committee came into existence because of the Michigan Equal Accommodations Act which prohibited discrimination in public places.

We had this little left-wing group. One day we were in the back yard at Brewster Housing Projects, and this white fellow said to me: "Ernie, they just passed this Diggs law about eating in these places. If the colored people don't start going into these places, that law is just going to rust on the books. It's going to get dust covered." I didn't know what he meant then. He was talking about the Michigan Equal Accommodations Act. He made me aware of that, so what I began to do was figure out how you got something done about it.

While I was on the NAACP board, I started this committee to break down restaurants. In the process of breaking down restaurants, you just couldn't make a legal case unless you had some white folks with you. That is why I've had some experiences that give me a leg up on people who cry "black."

That's why in the United States the last thing blacks need to do is to go on a corner and start hollering, "Black! Black! Black!" You cannot win. That's very unpopular these days. You can get elected and stay there for life, but you can't do nothing. I learned that in the process. First of all it was a white guy who told me about the law. No black guy told me nothing about it. When we got ready to make a case, when you wanted a legal tight case, you had to have somebody who they had served under the same circumstances. You couldn't get nobody black because they weren't serving blacks. So we had white people do it.

I come home one day, still in Brewster, and I had dinner, and I went out and caught the streetcar and rode all the way up to beyond the Boulevard. I got off and went into every place on the way back to downtown. Didn't a single one serve me. I was getting what you folks now call raw data. If I would ask for coffee, they would say, "We don't serve coffee." I'd put down the names. They would say, "I'll serve you in the back," or, "Do you want to take it out? We're closing." This was about in '49. If you remember the old days, they had all kind of nice little coffee shops. I went to every one of them. I did this during the week.

On Friday night I had called this meeting, and I told the guys in the plant. I'd be telling them about what I'd been doing. They all showed up at the Y. The Y was segregated too. It was a black men's Y on St. Antoine. We rented it for twenty-five cents a night. I had all these guys come in there, and a friend of ours, Jesse Williams, who's a lawyer, I had him come in and explain the law. I was the chairman, and my wife, Jessie, our two children, and other community people were there. He explained everything you should do. "You go in there; you comb your hair; you wear your tie, and I don't care what the hell they do to you, you don't respond." We were ahead of King because this was 1949. "Just go in there and ask for coffee, and I don't care what they do, don't respond. If they refuse you, you go call the police. When the police come, you tell them you think you should be served under the Michigan Equal Accommodations Act. You get the policeman's badge number, in a very demonstrable way. You get that in such a way that it's buried in his mind and you put it down."

The reason we needed a group is because, I noticed when I used to go in a place, the Professional Building, down at Peterboro; I went in there, and they had a counter, and they had tables. I went in there, and she came up and said, "Can I help you sir?"

I said, "I'll have coffee."

And she said, "Yes sir." After awhile, she said, "As soon as I get to you sir, but there's somebody ahead of you."

I sat there and sat there and they just never came. Then we found out what we had to do. If you went to a table, they'd do the same thing. They'd say they'd be right back and just never come back. So we put a black at every table. The white folks would come in and they'd go. Then what they started doing was closing up at 7:00 P.M. They'd say the place was closed. When we'd leave they'd reopen.

Do you remember the old Detroiter Hotel? When it was running full bloom, the Korean War was going on. We went into that place one time, we had about five or six of us. It had a cafeteria. When we went in there, everybody disappeared. We kept standing there, and finally a guy came out and said he was the manager. Jessie did her speech. He was saying, "We just serve guests."

Jessie said, "How do you know we're not guests?" She went into this speech. She said, "Our money's just like anybody else's, and our boys died in the war," and so on.

He said: "If you feel that way about it, I'll serve you myself. What do you want?" He was giving us too much potatoes, all kinds of gravy, no kidding. He served everybody.

She was dropping the patriotic thing on him. The Korean thing was just ending, and she said how would he feel if we had just come back from serving over there. "We're Americans; our money's just as good as anybody else's." For whatever reason, she really got to him. It was so funny. We sat right up in the front by the window facing Woodward Avenue for all to see.

BIOGRAPHY

Ernest C. Dillard, Sr., was born on January 24, 1915, in Montgomery, Alabama. He moved to Detroit on June 1937. He married the late Jessie Mae Dawson in December 25, 1934, at Hutchinson Street Baptist Church. Their two children are Marilyn Frances and Ernest C. Dillard, Jr. During World War II he was an arc welder of exhaust systems on B-29 bombers. From 1964–1980 he worked on the UAW professional staff, in political action and education. He was assistant director of National Community Action Programs. After retirement and until 1993 he taught leadership development classes sponsored by the UAW and Detroit Association of Black Organizations (DABO). He is now working with the UAW in Los Angeles where he currently resides.

Richard L. King was manager of the Club Three 666 during its most memorable years.

RICHARD L. KING

My dad, James Calvin King, came to Detroit in 1924 from a small city, Thomaston, Georgia. In 1925 he brought the family to Detroit. I was a little boy, and we first lived on Jay Street. As I listened to people talk, they referred to the area as Black Bottom, and its boundaries actually started south of Vernor Highway. Jay Street runs east and west, and we lived in a large flat between McDougall and Elmwood at the cemetery. I don't remember when we moved, but our next move was to Vernor Highway, and the last place was on Heidelberg Street.

My father worked in the Copper and Brass Rolling Mill, located in Wyandotte, Michigan. I attended Eastern High School and went to Detroit School of Technology until the depression when the bottom fell out and I had to quit school. I quit school because I was the only one in the family who had a chance to get a job after my father lost his job. I was only out of school for a couple of years when I was able to return and graduate from Eastern in 1932. I then was lucky to be able to attend night school at Detroit Tech where, I studied business administration.

Fortunately, at this time I was working at the downtown YMCA, and Detroit Tech was in the same building. The president was a gentleman whose name was Dr. Paul Hickey. One day I wandered into his office and told him I wanted to go to school, but I had no money. He said: "Dick, you go and talk to the person in charge of enrollment; he'll make out your program and then you bring it to me. I'll get it okayed and it won't cost you anything." He kept his word, and that's the way I was able to attend my classes. Mr. Hickey was my benefactor and one of the finest gentlemen I have ever met. I shall always be grateful to him for giving me that opportunity.

At the time I attended Detroit Tech, which was located on Adams at Grand Circus Park, they had a great athletic program, which included basketball and football teams. I worked at the YMCA until 1942.

When I left the YMCA, I started working for a gentleman by the name of "Jap" Sneed, who had opened a dance hall known as Dance Paradise. Since it was only open on weekends, we discovered that we were not making any money. Jap Sneed applied for a beer and wine license, which he was able to get; then we decided to change the name. Jap asked me, "What shall we name it?"

I said, "Let's name it the "Club Three 666," since our address was 666 East Adams Avenue, located between St. Antoine and Hastings Street. This area was called Paradise Valley.

The Norwood Hotel was also located in the same vicinity, between Beaubien and St. Antoine. It was owned by Walter Norwood, and the Club Plantation was in the basement of the hotel. In later years the name was changed to the Club Congo and operated by Slim Jones.

Even though we had opened the Club Three 666, we had a contract with the Wagners, who owned the Graystone Ballroom located at Woodward and Canfield, and we continued to promote dances there. The Wagners also owned the Eastwood Ballroom on Gratiot Avenue and Eight Mile Road.

Paradise Valley started on the north side of Vernor Highway, to the east side of Hastings, down to Gratiot Avenue, from Gratiot to Brush Street, up Brush to Columbia on the west side. There were two prominent bars at that location.

The Brown Bomber Chicken Shack was included in Paradise Valley. It was located on the south side of Vernor Highway. Ed Davis, who had the Studebaker sales, was on the north side of the street across from the Chicken Shack. Located on the north side of Adams at Brush was a bar called the Adams Palms. Most of their clientele were waiters who were working downtown. It wasn't too far from the Detroit Athletic Club. Then they were working split shifts. Across from the Adams Palms was the Pythian Hall, also on Adams. Now we travel up Brush, cross Elizabeth Street, and you're at Columbia. On the south side of Columbia was Roy Mapp's Bar; across the street on the north side was the Columbia Bar, on the west side of Brush Street. Columbia ran east and west. Brush ran north and south. McInerney's Poultry place was located on

Elizabeth Street, off Beaubien Street; Beaubien ran north and south like Brush Street. Located on Beaubien between Columbia and Vernor you had another bar, named the Heatwave. It was a small family bar, ran by a family.

Now we shall go over on Vernor Highway to Hastings Street. On Vernor, after you passed Ed Davis's Studebaker business, at Beaubien was the Cole Funeral Home. Traveling down Vernor Highway over to Hastings there was a black hospital. This was between Hastings and St. Antoine. On the corner of Hastings and St. Antoine there was a drugstore, and on the west side of Hastings there was a bar, but I can't recall the name. Further down on the east side of Hastings was another bar owned by Sportree Jackson, called Sportree's Bar. It was located at Hastings off of Adams. On the corner of Hastings and Adams there was a seafood place called The Fry. You could smell their food all over that area. The Club Three 666 was located on Adams between Hastings and St. Antoine Street.

On the north side of Gratiot there were pawn shops and two bars. One of them was owned by Lee Lucky and was called the Prosperity Bar; it was on Gratiot between Hastings and St. Antoine. I don't remember the name of the other bar. On the corner of Gratiot and St. Antoine was the Detroit Bank and Trust. In that area there must have been three pawn shops. After you crossed St. Antoine Street, there was the Diamond Drugstore. Past the drugstore there were two or three bars between there and Beaubien. On the south side of Gratiot, at one time, there was a theater by the name of Koppin.

Starting at Gratiot, let's travel up St. Antoine; and on the east side there was a barber shop, a bar, and up over the bank some lawyers had offices. In fact, that's where most of the black lawyers worked. Near the barber shop there was another bar named the B & C, and it was owned by Roy Lightfoot. When you left the B & C, Earl Walton had a place upstairs. It was an after-hours place where you had lockers and brought your own whiskey. It stayed open all night.

Earl Walton's place was upstairs, and beneath it on the first level was a flower shop owned by C. T. Collins, who is still living; and we belong to the same church. I see him often. C. T., as he was called, had a flower shop on Wyoming, the West Side, and later a shop on Mack Avenue and Woodward Avenue. Next to C. T's flower shop on St. Antoine was a barber shop, and then the Biltmore Hotel located on St. Antoine between Beacon and Adams. There was a restaurant in the basement of the hotel, and on the corner was the Metropolitan Cleaners.

On the other side of St. Antoine, coming up from Beacon, there was another drugstore. Further down, between Gratiot and Beacon, there was a laundry. Beacon ran parallel to Adams, and it was a short street that went from St. Antoine to Brush. On the west side of St. Antoine and Beacon was a laundry. Beacon was the shortest street and is still there, while Elizabeth was the longest street; it went from Hastings across the city to Grand River. Detroit Edison is still in that neighborhood. Between Beacon and Gratiot was Ferguson's Restaurant. Also, on Beacon and St. Antoine there was a drugstore, and across the street after you left Ferguson's Restaurant there was a bank building; and Mr. Everett Watson had a real estate office there. Upstairs, over the real estate office, John Roxborough had his office. Around the corner on Beacon was Ray's Music Company and another laundry. There was a lot of action in that vicinity over the weekend. Everybody came to Paradise Valley; that's why we did such a terrific business at the Club Three 666.

One time on Adams there was a cleaning business right on the corner and a club next door named the 606 Horseshoe Bar. Across the street from the 606 were three apartment buildings, and on the south side was a large parking lot we used for parking the cars of patrons coming to the club.

Next to the parking lot was a bowling alley, which was owned by John Roxborough, Everett Watson, Joe Louis, Grady, T. J. Jackson, and a man named Cain. All of them are dead, with the exception of T. J. Jackson who lives in California. That is the bulk of the operation that I can remember. After you crossed Adams, there was Gold's Drugstore.

Let me tell you how Paradise Valley got its name. There was a newspaper, but I don't know whether Rollo Vest was working for the *Michigan Chronicle* or the *Tribune*, but he called himself the "Bow Tie Kid." He wrote about everything connected with night life. He had a contest to name this area, and someone came up with Paradise Valley. Many people think he named it, since it was his idea. I'm positive that Rollo named that section himself.

When we lost the white business that we were getting, it was time to get out of the business. We sold the business in 1949 to a syndicate, and they couldn't make it because two of the partners stayed at the race track most of the time. I worked for them when they first opened, because they knew nothing about how to run or manage the business. I woke up one night and thought, I'm with the wrong outfit. I opened the safe one day and found there was no money in it; then I was convinced it was time to make a change.

When we opened the Club Three 666 as a night club, we presented Doc Wheeler and the Sunset Royals, with Ralph Cooper as the emcee. In the late years, we added a chorus line with a choreographer by the name of Betty Taylor, who lived in Chicago. The ladies who danced with Betty Taylor are now dancing in "Paradise Valley Revisited" under the direction of Bea Buck. The original members of the chorus line were Maybelle Moore, Mattie Gaither, Della Gross, and Frankie Wycke. We had a seating capacity of 750 people and had it elevated so that everyone was able to see over those seated in front of them. We had the best acoustics in the city, and it was known as the finest club in the country.

The building was originally built for a dance hall, and adjacent to the Club Three 666 was the Paradise Bowl. Many people thought the Paradise Bowl was first, but the Club Three 666 was first, because Jap Sneed was able to help the Paradise Bowl get the material to build the place. Remember, that was in 1941 and 1942, during the time of World War II, and materials were hard to get.

I was the manager, and when we first opened we only had one service bar. We eliminated some of the seating area and made a private dining area and served lunches daily. The bar was open all day. The bar was constructed of glass brick and was in the middle of the lobby. We served terrific food, and our customers were a wonderful group of people who worked in the downtown area. During this time, blacks couldn't eat just anyplace. People who went to the YWCA, or some of the other businesses on St. Antoine, usually came to the Club Three 666 for lunch. Our club was first class all the way, and our clientele was well dressed at all times.

The Club Three 666 was beautifully decorated. We had to pass fire inspections, so our walls were aluminum. The lighting on the walls was attractive and decorative. We had a doorman and a large parking lot. Our clientele was mannerly. We never had any trouble.

Mr. Sneed had two partners, and he was the boss. Mr. Sneed suffered with arthritis. He would sit down in a chair; some days he was unable to get up. Many people would ask, "Why does Jap Sneed walk all day?"

I said, "to keep his muscles from stiffening."

We were open seven nights and seven days. We opened at 10:00 in the morning and closed at 2:00 A.M. the following morning. Because we opened at 10:00 A.M., we had a good breakfast trade from the neighborhood. We opened with the following employees: a cook, barmaid, a waiter, and waitress. At noon every day we had two young women waiting tables. We could seat forty people in that room for food. During the week we'd average two hundred people per night, and on Saturday we'd have a complete turnover.

I didn't let too many people go. In fact, I fired about four people all the time I was there as manager. I had the misfortune of having to let a bartender go on a Thanksgiving night. This bartender was one of the best mixologists that I ever met. He would never take a drink unless someone ordered a stinger; and then he would always make the stinger long, for himself, and consequently he got drunk. He then began cursing the waiters, and I called up from behind the bar, and he said, "That goes for you, too."

I said, "And you have just lost your job."

165

When Mr. Sneed came in, he said, "What happened to your bartender?"

I said, "I had to let him go."

He then asked, "Who's going to do the work?"

I said, "I am, but please don't bother me."

We had 756 customers that night, and I got a man to open the beer and wash glasses for me. When I got through that night, I could hardly move, but I never took him back. The interesting thing is the bartender and I didn't ever lose friendship, because he knew he was wrong. He was just weak for stingers, and they were so potent for they were made with rum and gin.

One day Mr. Sneed said, "I'm going to bring Buddy Fields in because he's the person in charge of the union, and the person you will have to deal with". Buddy Fields and I met, and we had an excellent relationship. He was head of the Musicians Union, and if I had any problems with the musicians, I would call Buddy. At that time the Musicians Union was one of the strongest unions in existence, and they could stop your show at any time. Buddy taught me how to buy acts and stay in good with the agents.

We had the following black booking agents: Rollo Vest, Stutz Anderson, and Chester Renny. There were several independents, and everybody had something to sell. They had singers, dancers, along with their own bag of tricks. At that time most of the booking agencies were in New York City, but Mr. Sneed supported every black agent by buying from them so they could get their commission. The William Morris Agency and Gail were the two largest white agencies, and we wouldn't let them take all the money. We would tell them, you're going to have to give something to Renny and to Vest.

The biggest attraction we ever had at the Club Three 666 was Marva Louis. We made more money with her appearance than we made with any of the other performers. We had a cocktail show on Sunday and one on Monday. The person who handled our advertising was a Jewish person whose name was Harold Bird. He had contacts with all the newspapers. When he interviewed Marva she told him, "I will never wear the same gown twice." And she didn't. She was there for three weeks, and we carried a packed house during her entire engagement. Many women came to see what she was wearing. The funny thing about it was we were paying her eight hundred dollars a week, but she made enough for the three weeks her first week there. We also had a big band in at that time.

It was on a Sunday night in June 1943 before 12:00 P.M. when we were told that a black baby had been thrown in the river at Belle Isle. There were 350 people in the club, and fifty of them were black. The others were white. We were getting a dollar twenty per person; twenty cents was tax, and the dollar went to the house.

We had done the cocktail show and the evening show when the inspector in that precinct called. We had an excellent relationship with him, and he said, "Sergeant Chester is on his way over there."

I said, "He's standing in the office now."

He said: "We have a disturbance in the city of Detroit, and I am closing all bars in the city, immediately. Do not open until further notice."

We made an announcement that there was a racial problem and we had been asked to close. We had three men working in the parking lot. We had a front door and two back doors. They brought their cars around from the lot, and the patrons were calm and took it in stride. It was done orderly and we had no problem evacuating the premises. I thought this would soon blow over. The next day I went to the Club and called the inspector. He informed me that no place would open until further notice. However, it was straightened out by the end of the following week. We didn't lose our business nor any of our people.

I had a friend that was stationed at Selfridge Field, and they had a show at the Club Congo (formerly the Plantation) and had promised to take it to Selfridge Field. I received a call from a general at Selfridge Field, and he asked me, "Do you have a friend by the name of Sergeant Perkins?"

I replied, "Yes."

He said, "Your friend told me that you were rehearsing a show today."

"We are," I replied.

He said: "We need a show. In five minutes you are going to hear all the noise in the world." We did, for they sent a group of soldiers down with their sirens going on their cars, and we stopped the rehearsal.

The chorus girls said, "Let's go," and we went to Selfridge Field. One day the general called me from Selfridge Field and said, "From now on, when our men are out, they have been instructed to frequent your place." The 99th had come in from Tuskegee, and we had soldiers every night. We did two or three shows at Selfridge Field and were surprised what it did for our business. The girls would meet the boys in the afternoons and evening, so we always had a crowd. We never regretted it, for it was a terrific experience for all of us.

BIOGRAPHY

Richard L. King was born on March 25, 1909, in Thomaston, Georgia. He graduated from Eastern High School and Detroit Institute of Techology. He worked at the St. Antoine YMCA while attending school. He managed Club Three 666 from 1942–49. He was later a salesman for Hiram Walker.

❦

MARGARET McCALL THOMAS WARD

My dad and my mother were publishing a newspaper in Montgomery, and it was at that time that the Klan was rising. It was because of that and the fact that he was very, very outspoken in his editorials that made them decide that it was time to leave Alabama. They moved to Detroit with his mother, my grandmother. My mother always worked with my father because my father was blind. He was not born blind. He had studied and had been accepted at Howard University, and he was in medical school at Howard when he lost his eyesight; and it was a result of scarlet fever.

I was going to give you the lineage of the *Tribune*. The one in the 1800s was a white paper. He came here and worked for the *Detroit Independent*. That closed and there was a hiatus. Then he was employed by a man named William Peck to work for him and begin a new newspaper. That was around 1930. He worked for Mr. Peck, my parents did. Mr. Peck had a printing office; Peck Printing was located at 2146 St. Antoine. That printing plant finally, I guess after about two or three years, was bought by another group and then by my parents. The printing establishment grew into the *Detroit Tribune*.

The *Tribune* started in 1933. I wasn't working at it because I was in junior high then, although my sister and I spent time there. The paper had to be mailed, and we had a large mailing; so we would go there for the mailings. It was a subscription newspaper, but it was also sold on the street. We would go there often if my parents were there late; and they did work awfully long hours, late into the night, sometimes, in order to get the paper out.

The paper was actually composed in the editorial office space, and then we had linotypists who set the print, then did the lock up of the forms; and the paper was published right there on the premises. Later, we would make the forms, set all the type, and then transport it over to the *Abend Post*, where they had the large, large presses where they would do the mat, and then from the mat they would print the paper. That was the next step. But the paper was always published and printed here in Detroit. That was always one of our features; and a selling point was the fact that it was truly a native effort.

We had a full staff. A sports writer. My dad wrote all of the editorials, but we had reporters. We had the whole *Independent* business office. We had photographers, many of the photographers who made their mark.

What they would do very often, the photographers and some of the writers and even the salespersons would start out with us and then move out into other papers. Some went to the *Pittsburgh Courier*, having left Detroit. Some went to the *Chronicle*. Some went to the *Chicago Defender*. The *Tribune* by and large was a training ground to people like Bill Patrick who was the first Detroit councilperson of color. He was a protege of my dad, and many of the people who became well known later in the community were proteges of my mother and my father. Ulysses Boykin was one of their proteges and later bought the paper when they decided to sell.

The original *Tribune*, which was the white paper, had been out at around 1900 or possibly even earlier than that. That *Tribune*, as I recall the evolution of the mainstream papers in Detroit, somewhere was the parent of the *Detroit News*. There is a whole sequence of the *News* and the *Free Press* of how they evolved. They became what they are and where by buying out other papers or by new ownership. So that *Tribune* no longer existed for a long, long time.

You can get a good record on the 1943 riot by reading the *Detroit Tribune*. You can get a record of civil rights in Detroit by reading the *Detroit Tribune*. Some things which they fostered were for everyone to vote; for a black councilperson, which came to pass; for blacks on the Board of Education. Striving for the NAACP, for the Urban League.

Another thing that you might like to know is that the Detroit Urban League office was on Vernor, which was right down from the

Detroit Tribune. The *Tribune's* office was also a stopping off point for everybody who was either en route to the Urban League, to or fro, or to the YWCA, which was a meeting place for everyone. Francis Kornegay will tell you even to this day that my mother was the person who convinced him to stay at the Urban League and ultimately to become the leader for the Urban League. When he first came, he was in the shadow of John Dancy. John Dancy was a very longtime, close friend of the McCalls', and of the *Tribune,* and the *Tribune* of John Dancy, so that we were very, very useful for the Urban League.

Another thing that the *Tribune* did that I think gave it a special place was the fact that it catered to the black churches in the community and gave a lot of space to church goings-on. Churches had a very strong role in the community; it was a symbiotic kind of thing, because the churches also gave support to the newspaper, so that it worked both ways. We had a large portion of our news that had to do with church news. Also, in those days the white newspapers printed no social news of blacks, so that black society, as you would call it, really found their voices in the black press; and the *Detroit Tribune,* of course, was foremost among those.

The *Tribune* developed a reputation for being factual and for printing the news in an unbiased way. Even long after my father died, people have gone back to him and reminded themselves of him as a person who was of great integrity, so that there was never a buy off, or a silencing, or a cover-up of anything.

I would like to speak to that because we're talking about Paradise Valley, the lower end of town. St. Antoine was the street that ran the gamut of businesses, from legal to illegal. My sister and I would take the streetcar and get off at Gratiot and walk through St. Antoine Street to Columbia, which was just south of Vernor Highway. We had never been treated in any way but with great respect. No one bothered anybody, and we were very safe and very, very secure.

BIOGRAPHY

Margaret McCall Thomas Ward was born in Montgomery, Alabama. She is librarian/archivist of the Louise Wright Research Library of Detroit's Museum of African American History. In 1979, as field archivist of the Burton Historical Collection of the Detroit Public Library, she organized the Fred Hart Williams Genealogical Society. From 1939–45 she was writer and office assistant for the *Detroit Tribune,* a family-owned and -operated weekly newspaper dedicated to providing communication to the black community.

EDWARD DAVIS*

My first big break in the automobile business came after I had worked at Dodge Brothers' for eleven months. This was early 1936, and Mr. Lampkins was my benefactor. He had just arranged to put his son, Merton L. Lampkins, into a Chrysler-Plymouth dealership. . . . Lampkins asked me if I would like to try selling cars for his son on a part-time basis. I said yes, but at first I kept my ten-hour-per-day Dodge job, spending a few hours nightly and all of my weekend working for the Lampkins dealership at 16330 Woodward Avenue, in a high income area of Highland Park. . . . I was the only black there . . . who had a white collar job. It wasn't really all that prestigious to begin with, but as time went on I built up a large clientele among the black community. Most of my prospects were gleaned from the workers at Dodge and their friends. Word got around that there was a black car salesman who was watching out for the interests of his buyers.

I "banked" my experience of nearly a year working both at Dodge Brothers and at the Lampkins agency. That was time enough, I felt, and I could risk quitting my Dodge job to sell cars full–time. . . . Lampkins

*Excerpted from *One Man's Way*, by Edward Davis, pp. 18–25.

171

made one condition that I had to live up to. I could not work on the showroom floor with white salesmen. I was told that if I worked on the floor, I would be seen by prospective white buyers, and that would be bad for business. He gave me working space in the stockroom, tucked behind his office on the second floor. His office looked out over the showroom from a balcony so that he could survey his domain. You had to climb a stairway to get there, and you had to pass his office to get to mine. I purchased and brought in some office furnishings and my prospect card files. . . .

Most blacks in Detroit lived in a small enclave during the years from 1930 to 1943, and, if they could spend money with other blacks, spend it they did. It was relatively easy for me to work this small area drumming up business. As long as I was not selling too many cars, my efforts didn't make much difference to the white salesmen. As my business grew, however, it began to rankle them. I knew Merton Lampkins really didn't mean many of the things he said, but he began making cracks about the amount of money I was making on commissions from my sales. His salary was about $500 per month, and he kept moaning about how Ed Davis, a black salesman, was racking up more than that! One day, while I was in my office and he was on the phone, I heard him ask, "What color do you want? Black? We have them—black as a nigger's heel." That remark bothered me, and several days later I asked him about it. He just laughed it off and said he hadn't meant anything by it. Still, his cracks, intentionally malicious or not, had an effect on the others in his agency. . . .

In 1937 I read that bonus checks would be issued to veterans of World War I. I thought this would mean that a lot of people who earlier could not afford a car would now have a few hundred dollars extra which they could invest in one. After talking over my idea with Mert Lampkins and settling on the dealership profit he would accept, I sold twenty to twenty-five cars to veterans. In some cases the veteran had not received his bonus check by the time the deal was closed and we were ready to make delivery. In such instances I sometimes underwrote the down payment myself, paying the dealership out of my savings. This sometimes amounted to as much as $150 on a car. When the bonus check arrived and the owner paid the dealership, I would be reimbursed.

By this time the agency's service manager, a southern-born, hard-drinking man named Hurley, couldn't stand me anymore. He had never liked me, perhaps because of his ingrained southern prejudice against all blacks. I used to come down to the service department before breakfast and talk to the customers bringing in their cars for service, trying to interest them in a new car. Sometimes I'd drive them to work. This really annoyed Hurley. Until that time the agency's business hadn't been all that great, so he kept his hostility in check, but now that I was bringing in more sales he had to work harder. The additional cars I was selling to veterans didn't help matters; Hurley was under pressure to get even more cars ready for delivery to my customers.

Things came to a head one Friday when I got a check for my sales plus reimbursement on the down payments I had underwritten. It totaled more than $1,800, a big sum in those days. Word spread throughout the dealership. To make matters worse, the rumor had it that the amount was $3,000. It was more than a "cracker" like Hurley could take. His red nose and red neck glowed with anger.

I was not very sensitive to the tensions in the dealership. There was a reason: I felt good inside that all those veterans whose down payments I had underwritten out of my pocket had repaid me. It wasn't just the money—I was also glad that my judgment and faith in them had been vindicated. On that particular day I had some customers waiting for service, so I went to Hurley and asked when the cars would be ready. He was alone when I walked in. "Will that delivery for Thompson be ready this afternoon?" I asked. Hurley had told me before not to talk to him; I had been warned, but I was not prepared for what came next. He swung, hitting me in the mouth. He didn't knock me down, but I was stunned. I retaliated in the only way that I then knew. I groped for a hunk of metal nearby and I knocked him to the floor.

Lampkins ran down from his office and took control. After the many remarks he had made to help stir up things, he let his better judgment prevail. There was no probing the open wound of antagonism, no immediate condemnation of one or the other of us, no rush to judgment. The following week he called the two of us in and explained his position. "I will not tolerate any more of what happened between the two of you last week."

Hurley spoke up. "I will not work here with this guy."

"When are you leaving?" asked Lampkins.

"Now!" said Hurley.

"Your paycheck will be ready tomorrow morning."

I never expected to see Hurley again after this incident, but he came to see me when I opened my own company. As a result of our fight and the fact that he drank too much, Hurley had been fired, was blackballed, and couldn't find another job. He asked me for work! I expressed regret that I had nothing open.

The events of these few years with Merton Lampkins had taught me some important lessons. You must fight for what you want, but honestly and forthrightly. You must overcome disadvantages by turning them to your advantage. You must learn to live with yourself and then learn to live with your fellow man. I didn't ask for the fight, and I was more embarrassed than anything else when it happened, but it worked to my advantage in the long run. Until then, nobody in the dealership respected me much; from then on they had plenty of respect. . . .

BIOGRAPHY

Edward Davis was the first black franchised automobile dealer in the United States—from 1940–71. He served as general manager of Detroit's Department of Street Railways under Mayor Gribbs. He received the United Foundation Leadership Award in 1949, the National Business League Award in 1964, the Small Business Administration's Businessman of the Year Award in 1966, the Booker T. Washington Business Award in 1969, the *Time Magazine* Quality Dealer Award in 1969, and the Greater Detroit Chamber of Commerce Award in 1972. He has served on many local and national boards of directors.

KERMIT G. BAILER

I was born on 4–17–21 at my home on the west side of Detroit. My parents were Lloyd E. Bailer, M.D., and my mother was Mabel E. Bailer. I was the youngest of three boys, the oldest being seven years older than I and the next one being five years older than I. Their names were Harold and Lloyd. I lived at the same address on 30th Street for thirty years, going to Sampson Elementary, McMichael Middle School, and Northwestern High School.

My parents were very well educated, my father being a doctor and my mother a voice major and University of Chicago graduate. We did a lot of cultural things like go to the Art Institute and go to see the Detroit Symphony. My mother was a Christian Scientist, so we were members of the Christian Scientist Church, and we attended the First Church of Christ Scientist, which is right across the street from Old Main at Wayne State University. My mother was quite religious, and we lived in a strict Christian Science atmosphere, even though my father was a doctor.

In high school at Northwestern, because of race we were not permitted to participate in many sports; we were not permitted to come to the school dances; we were not permitted to belong to many of the academic clubs; nor were we permitted to be on the student council or participate in

175

high school plays. Other than the fact that we could go to school with whites, we were as rigidly segregated as were blacks in the South. A friend of mine and I happened to be the first blacks to become a part of the high school tennis team. Up until this year, 1937, no black had ever played on the tennis team. No black had ever played on the basketball team. All we were permitted to do in athletics was to run track and play football.

I finished high school in 1938 and went to the University of Michigan, where I was in the class of 1942. I found Ann Arbor and the University of Michigan to be as rigidly segregated as Detroit and its schools.

Before I went away to the service in January of 1943, I had a lot of interesting experiences in Paradise Valley, the exciting area at Adams and St. Antoine. Two things were dominant about it. First of all, there was first-class entertainment and food throughout the area. At the Club Plantation, which was in the old Norwood Hotel, you saw such famous stars as Louis Armstrong, Earl Hines, and their orchestras. You also saw the famous tap dancers of the period including Bill "Bojangles" Robinson. The establishments also had marvelous food, where I often used to eat my dinner while watching the entertainment and having a few drinks. They had the Club Three 666, which was another fabulous night club that was owned by a dear friend of mine, "Jap" Sneed. In the Valley you saw first-rate entertainment. The entertainment was comparable to that appearing in New York, Chicago, or anywhere in the country. Of course, we were also extremely proud that blacks owned these entertainment spots.

There was also gambling in the Valley, and I would often sit next to people like Bojangles and other famous entertainers playing poker. All the well-known dancers, singers, musicians, and professional boxers came to the Valley for its entertainment. Joe Louis was there whenever he was in town. It was a very exciting and thrilling place to be in the late 1930s and early 1940s. I remember the businessmen who owned the places as being businesslike, efficient, and prominent in the community. Like most of my contemporaries and friends, I used to go down there as a high school and a college student. From 1940 through 1943 I went to school part-time and worked full-time so I could afford to eat and be entertained there.

During World War II I was in the all-black U.S. Army Air Force unit known as the Tuskegee Airmen. I spent a year at Tuskegee where I was in pilot training. I was in several serious accidents and was ultimately "washed out" or "eliminated" from pilot training, but was sent immediately to aerial navigation school. That first extended trip into the South at Tuskegee, Alabama, was a shocking experience. In earlier years I had been South on a couple of short trips, but I had never spent any time in the South. At Tuskegee I was shocked at hearing whites call blacks "nigger" to their faces and at the rigorously enforced segregation laws and customs.

The aerial navigation school to which I was assigned was located at Hondo, Texas. I went there in November of 1943 and graduated in February of 1944, getting my wings and my second lieutenant bars. I went from there to Roswell, New Mexico, where I spent three months in the aerial bombardier school. I was then sent to Yuma, Arizona, where I spent two months in aerial gunnery school, ending up as a well-trained high level navigator, bombardier, and gunner, after which I was sent to an Army Air Force base at Godman Field, Kentucky, where I was assigned to the all-black 616th Bomb Squadron of the 477th Composite Bomb Group. Soon afterward we were joined by another Detroiter, Coleman Young. Thirty years later, he became Detroit's mayor, and in 1975 he hired me as Detroit corporation counsel.

In 1944 the group was briefly moved to Freeman Field, Indiana, where there was a historic mutiny of 103 black officers, who insisted on being admitted to the all-white officers club from which they were barred by the commanding officer. When they were rejected, the 103 were confined to quarters; and much later on we were quickly moved back to our original base at Godman Field. Later on only three officers ended up getting court martialled for this uprising, and all were acquitted. The group never went overseas because the war ended while we were in training.

The Tuskegee Airmen were trained in stages, the Air Force first experimenting to learn whether "blacks could fly single-engine fighter aircraft." Once the fighter pilots went over to Africa and Italy and demonstrated that they were first-rate pilots, the Air Force decided to train us in multi-engine bombardment planes. I was part of that second wave, although I was at Tuskegee when most of the early fighter pilots were trained. While we were training in bombers, the fighter groups who had gone over and flown their missions came back to the states to join us, so that by the time I got out we were no longer the 477th Bombardment Squad, but were the 477th Composite Group which was composed of P-47 fighter pilots returned from Europe and we, the bomber group. We were trained to attack the beaches of Japan before invasion by U.S. ground forces. In fact, I think our orders were to leave for Japan on a date two weeks after V-J day. So we were all highly trained and skilled in our business but never fought in the Pacific.

I left the service as a first lieutenant making four hundred to five hundred dollars a month and came back to the city of Detroit to a thirty-dollar-a-week clerk's job. I was married by then with one child, so I had to figure out how to make more money. I knew the only avenue was school, so that's why I quickly got into law school. At that time you could get into law school with less than a bachelor's degree. Since I had about three-quarters of a bachelor's degree, I was admitted to the Wayne State University Law School in 1946. I finished in February of

1949 and immediately entered private practice with a fellow named William Patrick, Jr., who had been a long-time friend of mine through elementary and high school. In 1955, I became an assistant prosecuting attorney in Recorder's Court. That lasted three years, and I came back and continued in private practice.

Blacks began coming to Detroit in great numbers when Henry Ford announced the five-dollar-a-day wage in 1921. When I grew up, blacks were sprinkled throughout the city, and they lived peaceably in many predominently white neighborhoods. But even in the '20s and '30s, whites were fleeing from the west side where I lived whenever they had the money to get out and buy better, more spacious homes. I don't think it was race that they were fleeing from. They were upwardly mobile and wanted more space and more attractive properties. Detroit homes, particularly in the area where I lived, were mainly frame structures on thirty-foot-wide lots. They were beginning to develop and sell homes out at Six and Seven Mile roads and the Livernois area, all of which were on larger lots. Whites moved to obtain brick homes and bigger lots and more space and more beauty. And they could afford it. In that day many Eastern Europeans, but especially Poles, lived on Detroit's west side in my neighborhood. While Hamtramck was full of Poles, many blacks lived there as well; and few blacks lived in Highland Park, which was primarily white.

In the postwar years of 1946 and 1947, housing patterns were dramatically altered as a result of massive displacement and relocation. The State was building and expanding the freeway system, which displaced many low-income or poor blacks in the central city. They were forced to find replacement housing in previously all-white neighborhoods. Real estate brokers began opening up housing opportunities for blacks in areas such as the LaSalle Boulevard area, Boston-Edison, Arden Park, Chicago Boulevard, and adjacent areas.

This massive displacement by the building of the highway system and by the commencement of the so-called urban renewal and clearance at other Detroit location served to provide new neighborhoods for blacks, but many could not afford to maintain the more expensive housing units. This led to overcrowding in these new areas and overpopulation of schools and other public facilities. The more affluent blacks moved into the Boston-Edison area. The less affluent moved into homes south of these areas while others moved into white areas on Detroit's east side. Prior to that, except along Hastings Street from Gratiot north, there were very few heavy concentrations of blacks in Detroit and no so-called ghettos. Many blacks did live in integrated neighborhoods; but once this postwar crush began, whites began fleeing in even greater numbers to the suburbs. That's when the Southfields, Troys and similar suburbs began to build up and the city began to empty. Almost overnight the city became practically all black in many areas inside of Grand Boulevard and, to some extent, outside the Boulevard. I moved to the Boston-Edison area in 1951. Today's neighborhood blight commenced right after World War II and was not the result of the riots of 1967.

Night life moved out of the Valley in the late '40s and went uptown to locations centered around John R and Canfield. The Flame Show Bar and the Frolic Show Bar, and then Randolph Wallace's Waha Room caught on, but blacks no longer controlled entertainment at most of these new locations. The two show bars were owned by whites, who began to bring in even more prominent entertainers than had the entrepreneurs in the Valley. They began to bring in many who became legends, such as Sarah Vaughn, Harry Belafonte, Errol Garner, Billie Holiday, and George Shearing. The major black proprietor was Randolph Wallace, who owned both the Waha Room and the Randora Hotel. Two doors away from the Randora, another black businessman, Sunnie Wilson, also owned a popular hotel and lounge. There were other black businessmen opening up businesses in the John R and Canfield area, but whites had more money and were bringing in bigger acts and were thriving to a greater extent.

In the same period the Gotham Hotel was owned and operated by blacks who reportedly were in the "numbers" business. It was a first-rate hotel and was where everyone who was anyone in the black community went, since it was first-class, and we couldn't go to the white hotels. It was also a place where all visiting black celebrities stayed while visiting Detroit. In the hotel there was a marvelous restaurant called the Ebony Room. It had great food and had a first-rate chef, who prepared an elegant menu comparable to any of the white restaurants. This wonderful, well-maintained hotel was the scene of most prominent social gatherings. If one did not wish to entertain in their home, the Gotham was the place to go and was the major social meeting place for most of Detroit's citizens of color.

Not only were neighborhoods deteriorating in this 1940 to 1970 period, blacks were having a terrible time with the administration of justice. The city had an all-white police department, all-white prosecutors, all-white judges, and all-white everything. Then Soapy Williams came along in 1948, was elected governor, and he and the UAW began to open things up a bit and bring a few black appointments to the bench and use black voting power to change things.

In the early 1950s Soapy appointed several black judges, including Elvin Davenport, Charlie Jones, and Wade McCree to the Recorder's and Wayne County Circuit courts. This action broke up the all-white law enforcement system and gave blacks an understanding of their real political power as an important voting block in the Democratic party. Black candidates soon began running for public office in Detroit and for state legislative offices, quickly electing candidates to the Detroit City Council and the Detroit Board of Education.

In the 1950s and thereafter blacks became the most politically potent body of urban minorities anywhere in the nation. Soon blacks had more elected officials representing Wayne County than was the case in other states throughout the nation, and that power was strong enough to ultimately unseat a white Detroit mayor and lead to the election of Coleman Young, formerly a state senator. That period was revolutionary. At the time, many other cities had a proportionately larger black population, but very few elected black officials. Elsewhere minorities seemed slow to discover how powerful their vote was and how to change their life by using the vote, especially in the North, where there were no voting restrictions.

In the 1950s the Cotillion Club, of which I was a founding member, spent a lot of time emphasizing these issues as well as attacking police brutality and discrimination in the hiring and utilization of minority policemen. We had a variety of programs, first trying to increase voter registrations and, at the same time, trying to break down the police department's pattern of discrimination against black applicants and members of the department. When the club became involved, there were no more than eight black policemen on a five-thousand-member police force. We were very active in that effort and ultimately integrated scout cars and increased the number of black members of the force.

To demonstrate the depth of racism in the department, the club engaged in an experiment by first trying to give an award to the white policeman who had done the most for community relations in black areas. We found that the policemen weren't flattered, because no white policeman wanted to be known as being friendly to blacks. We finally began meeting with the mayor and telling him that he had a rigidly segregated and discriminatory police force and he should institute change. The Cotillion Club was instrumental in defeating that mayor, mainly because of his rigid attitude against integration of the police department or an increase in its minority makeup.

In those days life was dominated by racial discrimination, and it played an enormous role in my life and the lives of my friends. We were so limited in so many ways. I don't know how any black could discuss life in Detroit in the 1930 to 1960 period without describing the expansive level of racial discrimination here.

It hit me probably as soon as I began to understand conversations around me. It hit me when I was six or seven as I listened to my older brothers talk about limitations in their careers, even if they finished college. It hit me when I listened to my mother argue with my brothers that in spite of the fact that blacks were unwelcome in the Christian Science Church, that we should go there anyhow and just ignore the racism. It was a daily subject.

What I am talking about is living a very narrow life in a large, dynamic city with a host of opportunities but for "whites only." There's almost nothing you can ask me about the first fifty or sixty years of my life that was not controlled by matters of race. From my perspective, although I had an excellent potential and got a good education, I led a very narrow existence. For example, why would I tell you about being on the corner of Hastings and Adams or Beaubien and Adams? It's only significant because if you go there today, you'll see it's an empty, ugly space. What was I doing there? I was there because I couldn't go downtown to more pleasant surroundings.

I'm relating these stories, not necessarily to make segregation and discrimination a huge focus, but to explain how burdened our formative years were with the disease of racism. If you ask a white lawyer my age what he did as he matured into adulthood, he'd say he went to the University of Michigan Law School, graduated, and went and got an office in the National Bank Building and prospered thereafter. From my point of view, race required that I spend most of my formative years struggling to survive and succeed in a very hostile and confining environment in which I was forced almost daily to do battle with the white establishment.

What I'm really telling you is how a I coped with racism twenty-four hours a day, seven days a week, thirty days a month, and three hundred and sixty-five days a year. Everything that I've told you is all tied into that subject, because I would have lived a very different existence if racism had not so dominated my life in Detroit for so many years.

BIOGRAPHY

Kermit G. Bailer was born on April 17, 1921, in Detroit. He attended Detroit Public Schools, the University of Michigan, and Wayne State University. He served in the U.S. Army Air Force in 1943 as First lieutenant aerial nagivator bombardier gunner with the 616th Squadron of the 477th Composite Bomb Group as a Tuskegee Airman. He was a practicing attorney and a trial lawyer with the Wayne County Prosecutor's Office. In 1961 he joined the Kennedy administration as attorney-advisor to the U.S. Commission on Civil Rights. He then served as corporation counsel, City of Detroit, under Mayor Coleman A. Young. He is retired from Ford Motor Company. Kermit and his wife, Penny, are parents of Kelly and Ryan.

*Norman McRae is a well-known chronicler of Detroit's
black history. McRae and his wife, Shirley, enjoyed many
evenings out at Detroit's favorite night spots where the
great entertainers performed.*

NORMAN McRAE

I was born on September 25, 1925, in Detroit at Herman Kiefer Hospital. My father was a waiter. He died in 1930 of TB. I still remember playing on the street, and my mother came from the Hastings streetcar line. When I ran up to her, she was crying. She said my father was dead.

My father was from the rural part of Georgia. I found out that he ran away from home when he was about twelve years old. My mother used to nose around in his drawers, and she found out that he had a family in Georgia. She took him home to bury him. We had to change trains a lot. Then we'd have to wait for the casket to be taken off and transferred. I can remember standing on the platform someplace in the South. It was about five in the morning. It was jet black. As we stood there, I saw the dawn come up. We buried him and came back to Detroit.

My mother worked in Grosse Pointe as a maid, and we stayed with relatives. I was such a problem kid. The summer of 1934 my mother sent me down to Birmingham, Alabama, where she was born, to stay with my aunts and uncle. When I was there, I received a letter that I was going to have a stepfather. So I came back, and we moved to Saginaw in September of 1934. We stayed there ten years.

I would come back to Detroit to visit relatives. I have an aunt, Mrs. Etta Morris, who was very instrumental in my life. She would buy me back-to-school stuff, and I would go back to Saginaw with part of Hudson's. She lived at 411 King. That was in the heart of the "black gold coast" in the '40s. The Bledsoe family were very dear friends of ours. They lived two doors from us. Mrs. Bledsoe had grown up with Paul Robeson, and she never lost faith in him like some people did. I can remember the only time I met him was when his star began to descend. There was a concert at the Detroit Institute of Arts, and Mrs. Bledsoe took me backstage to meet him. As a young man my only black heroes were Joe Louis and Paul Robeson.

I was in the Navy. I did my basic training at Great Lakes in Camp Lawrence. After that, because I scored high on the test, I went to Naval Training School at Hampton Institute. Once you walked out of those gates you were slapped in the face by the segregation laws of Virginia. That's what got you. You had to ride in the back of the streetcar. We used to go to a place called the Lee Theatre in Phoebus. We had to sit in the balcony. Some guys refused to do it. It was worse in the army in the South. Any number of men were beaten up because they wouldn't go to the back of the bus or because they talked back to a sheriff.

One of the great ironies of World War II is that when we started taking German and Italian prisoners and bringing them to this country and putting them in various places, the prisoners had more rights than the black guys guarding them. They could go to the white PX. They could go to the white base movies. The Armed Forces is much different now because Truman enforced the desegregation of the branches of service.

The thing I remember about Detroit at that time in the '40s, I remember taking the Woodward streetcar. It was a big deal to go downtown to the Fox, the Michigan, the United Artists, and all of the theaters. Basically, I'm a loner. I have a lot of friends and a lot of people care about me and I care about them, but I tend to be reclusive at certain times. Then the action moved north on John R. When I was in college, I became a member of Alpha Phi Alpha Fraternity. That was the number one social thing for black kids in college, and we used to have our big dances at the Labor Temple. The Labor Temple was on the corner of Elizabeth and Park. It was the nicest place for blacks to have dances.

I can remember one of the things that titillated the audience was innuendo. Bowser and his partner were two different kinds of black comedians. They were very clean-cut, more of the Bill Cosby type. They were the precursors of Bill Cosby. One was a straight man, the other guy set up the jokes. He would say: "We represent the National Brassiere Company. What nature has forgotten, we fix with cotton!"

There was a scene where this guy with a black face, it was makeup, had this very light-skinned wife. The only props on the stage were a bed, a table, and two chairs. He said to his wife: "I'm going to work to-day. Don't you be holding that little baby boy, 'cause he knows what it's all about. He's getting grown up too fast"; then he leaves.

Then she says: "Hot dog! I'm glad he's gone. Now I can let my back-door man, 'Sweet Papa' Tim, come in."

So Sweet Papa Tim comes in, and he says, "You know, baby, me and a couple other Jew boys were on the train going to Pontiac the other day, and I didn't know that there were two parts of the chicken."

She said, "Baby there's the dark meat for the thighs and the white meat for the breasts."

Then he said, "Well, baby, come on and sit down on my dark meat, and put your head up on my white meat."

So it goes on like this for awhile. Then the husband slips back in and says, "I caught you. I caught you!"

And then Sweet Papa Tim gets down on his knees and says, "Please don't shoot me, 'cause I come from Pontiac." And then the husband lets him go.

And his wife starts running around the bed and he chases her with a gun, and she faints and falls on the bed, and her dress comes up to just above her knees. The husband looks at her and puts his gun down and starts taking off his coat and shirt and says, "You know, baby, one of these days I'm gonna hurt you."

Then there was great laughter, and the lights would go out on the stage.

On Mondays we used to go to a place called Lee's Sensation that was on the north end. They used to have great blues singers like Alberta Adams. She'd sing this song, the punch line of them used to crack everybody up, "What makes my grandma love my grandpa so?" And she would repeat the line several times. Then the punch line would be, "He's got the same old stroke he had fifty years ago."

I remember going to the Valley, especially after I got out of the service. They had the Club Three 666, Sportree's, Lark's, 606, and others. Let me tell you something that happened to me back in 1948 when I went to the El Sino. A guy came up to me and said, "Sir, could I get you some weed?"

I said, "No, man, I never use the stuff."

He goes away and returns later, "Say, man you know I have some girls that you. . . ."

I said, "No, thanks."

He said, "Shit! I can't do nothing for you, can I?" You always had those guys who were trying to make a dishonest buck, and you had some working girls working in places.

I can remember going to Sportree's to see the female impersonators. Lark's was more of a bar. Lark's Bar and Grill. Some of them served food. I didn't get any food at the times I went. I was only interested in drinking beer.

When most people went down to the Valley, they dressed to the nines. They were sharp.

In the 1950s, when Jersey Joe Walcott was a world champion heavyweight boxer, he was refused admission to Carl's Chop House. You couldn't go to a lot of the restaurants around town. For instance, if liberal whites and blacks had a meeting somewhere and they went someplace to have a drink afterwards, it was always a hassle because they didn't want to serve the blacks. One of the places where blacks, during the '35, '45 period, when the Sojourner Truth scene was going and demonstrations were being planned, used to meet was at the YWCA. The cafeteria there had great food. The Lucy Thurman and the men's Y were next to each other.

One of the funniest stories I heard—it didn't happen to me—but there was this black woman who was extremely fair; she could pass if she wanted to. And she and her boyfriend or husband were on the Woodward streetcar going down Woodward to the Fox—that was a big deal on a Friday or Saturday night, to go to the Fox or the Michigan or United Artist Theatre—and there was this white woman who kept looking at them. Finally he looked back and said: "Yes, she's not white, she's colored just like me. The only reason she doesn't look like me is your old granddaddy was tiptoeing around the slave cabins." And the white woman's husband said, "I told you to mind your own . . . business."

One of the nice things about Detroit was that a man with no skills and a strong back could come here and work. Many guys my age worked their way through college by working at Ford or other plants in the summer. Eventually, if he got seniority, he could count on a pretty decent income. If he didn't blow his money, he could have a home; and his kids could go to Wayne University and get a college education.

BIOGRAPHY

Norman McRae, historian, was born in Detroit on September 25, 1925, and educated in Saginaw, Michigan from fourth grade through high school. He served in the U.S. Navy during the last months of World War II. He graduated with an A.B. and M.A. from Wayne State University and earned a doctorate from the University of Michigan. He has taught in the Detroit Public Schools and was head of the Social Studies Department when he retired in 1991. He has researched and written widely in the area of the black presence in the United States and is the author and co-author of several history textbooks.

I was born in Detroit and lived on the east side in Black Bottom. I remember going to Duffield School. We lived on Mullett between Elmwood and McDougall; and, of course, I remember Joe Louis's mother living down the street on McDougall. I remember the two stores, one on the corner, the southeast corner. There was another one catty-corner across the street from it. It was on the northwest corner. I remember going to those stores. There used to be big jars of pickles, and they would just reach their hand in there for people who wanted to buy sour pickles. I remember the Carver Theater which was up on Chene which was where we went. I guess it was about Chene and Chestnut.

I remember hearing stories about the cemetery. Kids would like to slip in Elmwood Cemetery from time to time, and there were all kind of stories about Elmwood Cemetery. They claimed there were ghosts there, and certain people would say they could see blood when it rained. It still didn't keep us from occasionally slipping in the cemetery, so that I guess mainly we screamed and hollered. I never saw a thing in there.

My family was never rich, but we were never poor in the sense of the other people there. I did not even realize this until I was an adult. Everybody practically in our block received something from the Good-

186

fellows, and the Goodfellows never brought us a box. This disturbed me, hurt my feelings. I can even remember crying about it.

There was a family that lived next door to us on Mullet where there were eight or nine children in that family—the Ambrose's. There was one of the Ambrose girls that was my age. We would sit down; and we would daydream about things to come and what have you. We were dreaming about what we were going to get for Christmas. I loved dolls. Christmas wasn't Christmas if I didn't receive a doll. I was saying that Santa Claus is going to bring me some kind of doll, and she said: "Santa Claus is going to bring me a doll! I hope I don't have to share it. But in case I do, the Goodfellows will bring me a doll." They had it down pat, exactly what was going to be in the Goodfellow package.

I kept waiting, and the police officers and whoever would bring the Goodfellows baskets kept bringing the baskets, and we never got one. I remember even asking one day, and they said, "Were you on the list?"

I said, "I don't know, but I know everybody got something and we didn't."

He told me, "Well, ask your mother to call your school."

I was out of high school when it dawned on me, it took me this long to figure out why the Goodfellows never brought us anything. I can remember around September or October, we'd be in school in Duffield, and they'd say "How many of you in here have a working father?" My hand always went up. Most of the time they said, "How many of you in here mother's working?" They didn't give us anything because we didn't need it. It was for those who were in need. How in the heck was I supposed to know this? All I knew was it was like discrimination. We didn't get anything. That was something that always disturbed me. I wondered, well, why don't they leave me something? But they didn't.

I had to go to Northeastern, and I hated Northeastern. Northeastern at that time was very prejudiced. I remember having an English Literature teacher there, she had four rows. All the black girls were in one row. All the black boys were in another row. All the white girls were in one row, and all the white boys were in another row.

I started going to the Paradise Theater when I was about nine years old. I was fascinated ever since that time with the music, the lights, like my Christmas tree lights and the shiny instruments, and the gowns that they wore. We loved to go to the Paradise. I remember someone discovered that you could stand outside the stage door and get autographs. To see these people and to see that they were real human beings that were made of flesh, this was fascinating.

I started Fan Clubs, Inc., when I was eleven or twelve years old. There was some teen magazine that I wrote to, and that was the first time my name was in print, national print, too. They wrote about Fan Clubs, Inc., and it was for Count Basie, Buddy Johnson, Billy Eckstein.

In fact, I started Billy Eckstein's first fan club. Arthur Prysock, Illinois Jaquet, there were about seven of them. This was my first time of having a brand new idea to offer to the public. Nobody else had done a Fan Club, Inc., so I guess that was why they wrote about me in this national magazine.

I went to Chicago in 1949 because I couldn't find a job in Detroit with just a high school education and because I was black.

Then I came back to Detroit in 1951, and I got a job at the Gotham Hotel. I was the secretary to John White. John White taught me half of everything I know, especially about black pride. John White paid my tuition for me to go to Lewis Business College. There are a lot of things about him that I should never forget. In order to work for the Gotham Hotel there were a lot of principles. One was you must belong to the NAACP. Number two, you had to be a registered voter.

John White was a cousin of Coleman Young. He told me some things that I did not understand then. There were a few of them that I got very angry about. He told me that integration was going to hurt the black businessman as much as it was going to help him, maybe even more, which I did not understand at that time. I do now understand what he meant, because he meant that when the white hotels opened up, the blacks just flocked to them and they have been doing it ever since. I worked at the Gotham from 1951–1955.

I left there for awhile. I had an application in with the City of Detroit, and I went on the road with the Reverend C. L. Franklin, which was by far the most exciting job I ever had. He was preaching as an evangelist, but they had a complete "show," if you will: the Clara Ward Singers, and the Bradford Singers, and Sammy Bryant, who came out of his church, a little gospel singer. We traveled all through here and went to Washington, D.C., and Baltimore, Louisville, Kentucky. In Louisville, Kentucky, for instance, as we were checking in—it wasn't a hotel that you stayed in, it was like a boarding house—Joe Louis was leaving. He had been a guest there. These are just memories that I have. That was in 1956.

John White had a love for black people, and he had a direction in which he thought they should go. The Gotham Hotel was known as the finest hotel anywhere in the world, not just in the country, in the world. Mr. White had paintings. I met anybody who was anybody there, including Coleman Young. I met Dr. W. E. B. DuBois there. I met Adam Clayton Powell, a very regular guest. John H. Johnson was from Johnson Publishing, publisher of *Ebony* and *Jet*. I met Roy Wilkins, Marian Anderson, anybody who was anybody in Detroit. Sammy Davis, you name it. They all stayed in the Gotham. Mr. White had beautiful suites. The "Errol Garner Suite," "the Duke Elington Suite," the "Count Basie Suite." He had gorgeous paintings in there. J. Edward Bailey, the photographer who made it and just died a few years ago, was around the hotel almost daily. It was like a melting pot. It was a place where everybody who was anybody that was black, that's where they stayed. In the lobby, anybody who was anybody like John Roxborough, the baseball players, Larry Doby, Luke Easter. All of the early ball players would come up there. I remember one day the game was rained out, and because the white players didn't want that much to do with them, here come Larry Doby and Luke Easter and the whole bunch.

I knew about the numbers, and I saw them play the numbers. We had honest numbers men. If you played your number today, number one you had a carbon; you had a copy and they had a copy. They had rules. You couldn't have what they called a short ticket. You had to add it correctly; and if you didn't add well, you best ask your pick-up man to add it for you. If it went in and your number hit, that afternoon whenever the horses finished, which is where they got the numbers from, they would pay you for it. It came out at 6:00 P.M., and by 8:00 P.M., you had your money. It was just as honest as the lottery.

I guess my love for Paradise Valley came because I was angry. I was angry after having waited all of those years to go to Paradise Valley and the Club Three 666. I never got a chance to go there, because when I got old enough it was gone.

BIOGRAPHY

Beatrice M. Buck grew up in Detroit and graduated from Northwestern High School. She attended the Detroit Institute of Technology and Lewis Business College. She worked at the Gotham Hotel in the 1950s and traveled with Reverend C. L. Franklin for a year as a staff member. In 1957 she was employed by the City of Detroit, where she worked for the Detroit Police Department. She is now retired but active in writing plays and songs as well as producing musical shows, such as "Paradise Valley Revisited."

African Americans
in Detroit and the United States,
1938–1947

1938	Michigan Equal Accommodations Act passed.
1941	Ford Motor Company strike and start of Local 600 (April).
	United States declared war on Japan (December 8). Detroit becomes known as the Arsenal of Democracy.
	President Franklin D. Roosevelt issues Executive Order 8802 establishing Fair Employment Practice Commission to prohibit discrimination in defense industries.
1942	Sojourner Truth Homes completed. Negroes and whites clash as result of tension created by severe housing shortage (February 27).
1943	Race riot in Detroit, 34 people killed (June 20-21).
1945	World War II ended (August 14).
1946	In previous three decades 200,000 southern Negroes moved to Detroit.

MARCENA W. TAYLOR

In 1938 I was working at the post office; and Snow Grigsby, head of the Detroit Civil Right's Committee, was working there. Previous to this time they wouldn't even give a black guy an application blank for the fire department, and he opened that up. I understand about five thousand took the examination. They were from around the Gratiot area. They called about sixty out of there, and I was one of those. In fact, there were four or five blacks in that first sixty of the five thousand that took the examination. Most of the blacks that took it graduated from the University of Michigan; the rest of them graduated from the southern college. But the rest of them failed, all but one of them, Arnold White.

An officer at training school talked about "an explosion that was so powerful it knocked a nigger wench down a block away." All that time I stayed cool.

That first day we got to the station the white boys had been notified to come early, so, Marvin and I weren't there. When we got there the people in the neighborhood all gathered around the station, and they kept coming; blacks would drive by. Oh, the police were there, and they wouldn't let the blacks get out of the car. So, we stood out there, and I know at one point a lady said: "You niggers stay here, you're dead. In their contracts [it said] no niggers for nine years."

So, finally this one black guy came walking by; and I told him, "Call Snow Grigsby;" and he did. Grigsby got in touch with the police commissioner and got in touch with the mayor.

The union fought my becoming a firefighter. At that time we worked twenty-four hours with twenty-four off. There was an article in the paper that said, "Negroes are being placed in the Detroit Fire Department where they have to eat and sleep with white men in the manner of real family life. Please help us to right this inhuman. . . ."

In the dormitory it was unheard of for the blacks to stay with whites. The captain moved out of his room and moved the other black and I to his room. We couldn't eat with the rest of the people. In the kitchen we had to use our own plates and utensils. We had to wait till the other officers finished eating. They would sit and start smoking. Then I would go in and make my food.

We had toilets in the basement and on the first floor and third floor. My assignment at Warren was working in the basement. We had different assignments. And if I decided I had to use the restroom, I had to go to the top floor. I refused to go. The boss said he's going to take me down. I said, "You take me down."

They wouldn't speak to me for several months when I first started. I got books from the public library and would sit and read. Youngsters from the neighborhood would sit and talk with me and go to the store for me.

Once, when we were at a fire, a policeman was taking a report and said to a black woman, "What's your name?"

She said, "Mary Smith," and he started calling her Mary.

I said, "You must be a relative. Don't you ever call anyone by their first name." I was a different type of character. They referred to me as the "bad one."

BIOGRAPHY

Marcena W. Taylor was born on January 25, 1911, in Chattanooga, Tennessee, and moved to Detroit in March 1927. He attended Miller Middle School, Northeastern High School, and graduated in 1928 with honors. He attended Livingston College from 1929–1933. In 1932 he was counselor at the Detroit Urban League's Green Pastures Camp. He rose to the rank of battalion chief in the Detroit Fire Department.

ERMA HENDERSON

Long before I met the famous artist Paul Robeson and the renowned educator and author, Dr. W. E. B. DuBois, I had worked for a long period as a volunteer supporter of the Council on African Affairs, a New York-based organization formed by DuBois and Robeson and directed by Dr. Alpheus Hunton. The literature published and distributed by that organization sought to educate Americans, particularly African Americans, on the truth of life in Africa. I recall distinctly organizing young people in baptist churches to help me distribute and sell booklets to various missionary societies so that the horrible working and living conditions of the African people in the Belgian Congo and South Africa might become well known.

Both Paul Robeson and Dr. DuBois were well known for their lectures on Africa, but Paul chose also to use every opportunity to speak out about the terrible conditions which African Americans were subjected to in the United States, and he lent his time and talents to fight injustice in many American cities, including Detroit.

Detroit, in the early '40s, was having a terrible struggle over who would occupy the last permanent housing project to be built for the duration of World War II. Federal housing was segregated. African Americans had been promised the housing. The location of the project was in the midst of an all-white community and six blocks from the closest African American neighborhood. Public rallies were called. Speakers from across the country came in support of African American factory workers who sorely needed the housing.

The Honorable Hopson R. Reynolds, who then headed the Civil Rights Department of the International Brotherhood Improved Benevolent Protective Order Elks of the World was joined by the distinguished artist and speaker Paul Robeson at one of those rallies, adding significant potency to the protest. The African Americans won and were permitted to move into the Sojourner Truth Homes, even though the federal decision was the catalyst accelerating the 1943 race riot.

I recall many occasions when Paul came to Detroit to support the labor movement—marching and singing on the picket lines. So in addition to the concert stage, where he captured the hearts, minds and imaginations of many people, Paul Robeson became equally famous for his role in speaking out boldly against injustice everywhere. This great man, in size, in voice, in determination, and in leadership, was as much at home as a lawyer, athlete, and actor as he was on the concert stage. He seemed to gather strength as he walked and talked with the poor, the disenfranchised, the laborers and the children.

Although I had enjoyed a working relationship with Paul, it was only after my mother and I attended *Othello* at the Shubert Lafayette Theatre that I got to know him personally. We were invited to an after-theater party, where for the first part of the evening everyone was so overwhelmed by his outstanding performance that it was difficult to quiet down. As the evening grew late, those of us who could, sat entranced by the stories of his travels and the folk songs he sang from around the world. I can only vaguely describe the joy of that once-in-a-lifetime experience.

It was shortly after his now famous Peekskill speech that Paul Robeson was banned from the concert stage. His speaking out politically was not accepted by those in the concert arena or political power circles.

He came to Detroit immediately following Peekskill and was denied housing accommodations by the management of Detroit's world-famous Book Cadillac Hotel. People who knew and loved Paul rallied in picket lines to protest. Rental halls, for public appearances, were closed to him. When the anxiety and fear became so prevailing, a committee was formed to find a suitable place where Paul could sing and speak out. We visited my dear friend, Sunnie Wilson, who owned the famous Forest Club on the corner of Hastings and Forest Avenue. It had a bar, a lounge, and a large hall occasionally used for meetings, a skating rink, or a dance hall. Although Sunnie Wilson was young, he was one of the most influential and successful African American business leaders in the city of Detroit and state of Michigan. He agreed to allow Paul Robeson to be scheduled at the Forest Club.

When Paul arrived, he was pleased not only to see a packed hall, but long lines of people wrapped around the building trying to get inside. Many police had been assigned to keep tabs, but they were not counted on for protection. Instead, the trusted citizens who prepared for Robeson's appearance provided a dignified entourage of protection and support. The predicted riot never happened. An enthusiastic crowd of well-wishers, supporters, and curiousity seekers stood in awe as Paul Robeson sang song after song and spoke elegantly about his tragic experiences which subsequently led to his banishment from the concert stage.

Paul Robeson was the son of an A.M.E. Zion minister who had once pastored at the famous Mother Zion Church, so it wasn't unusual for him to want to return to his church roots for spiritual support. He was so warmly received at Mother Zion that he began to travel to churches of all denominations around the country.

My own church then, Calvary Baptist Church, hosted a major Paul Robeson concert with Roberta Smith Barrow and I as co-chairs. The supper was tremendous, and the concert was a hugh success.

Having been born in April himself, Paul thought it a good idea to celebrate his birthday with Arthur M. Carter, my godson, and his brother, Raymond, who were also born in April. Joined by my children, Patrya and Phillip, and a few neighbors and friends, it took only a matter of minutes to demolish a twenty-one-pound rib roast before polishing off all the ice cream, cake, and candies in the house. But it was a very good party. And in Paul's own words, he often referred to it as his "Special Birthday Party."

Detroit and Paul Robeson were inseparable during a perilous time in our history. We shall always cherish and never, ever forget that extraordinary journey through pain and despair, courage and victory—with Paul!

BIOGRAPHY

Erma Henderson was born in 1917 and came to Detroit one year later. She was port secretary for the National Maritime Union and initiated the picketing of the Barlum Hotel to break down its racial barriers. In 1957 she managed William Patrick's successful campaign for Detroit Common Council. In 1968 she became executive director of the Equal Justice Council. Henderson won a seat on the Detroit City Council in 1972, and in 1977 she became its first black president. President Jimmy Carter appointed her to represent the United States at the International Women's Year Conference in Mexico City. Ms. Henderson organized a forty-person delegation to Africa in 1984. She is retired from the Detroit City Council and is proprietor of a health food store in Detroit.

Thornton G. Jackson grew up in the closely knit Sojourner Truth community in the 1940s.

DISCUSSION ON SOJOURNER TRUTH HOMES
GERALD V. BLAKELY,
KENNETH G. BOOKER,
ROBERT BYNUM, JR.,
THORNTON G. JACKSON,
AND ADAM SHAKOOR

ROBERT BYNUM, JR.: I guess it was on a weekend. I had never seen black people ice skate. It was cold. It was 1942. I sat there watching them skate. The gentleman whose skates I used has passed since then, and we had the same size foot. He said, "Do you want to ice skate?" I said I had never done it before. He said to put on his skates. I put on his skates, and he put on my rubbers and whatnot, and I tried to skate. All the rest of the guys were skating. That always stuck in my mind.

Of course, there was the gentleman in the summer who we all knew as Dad Newcomb. He used to sit on the steps of the administration building and lie to us about when he was young. He was a very tall, good-looking man. Every morning everyone would jump up and run over to the administration building and sit around. He would tell us stories. He was very influential and a fine man. They were stories for young boys and young men to hear.

I lived over on 4623, being ten or eleven years old. We came in right after the disturbance.

KENNETH G. BOOKER: When we moved in the state troopers and the National Guard were here. I was about three or four when we moved in. I remember the state troopers were all over. The building we lived in was their headquarters. When we got in here, I got into it with my father. As a little kid, I broke and ran to keep from getting whooped. There was a big square behind the administration building. All the state troopers were marching in that particular area. I was trying to get through them. They kept pushing me out. All I could think of was this big gentleman coming after me, and I knew what to expect because I was going to get a whooping. They kept pushing me out of the way, and I was so mad at them.

We used to play behind the building. We called it a hole, but it was down in the ground. The basement windows were in that spot, but they had a big rail around it. We used to jump down there and hide if we played war.

A lot of this area over this way used to be a farm area. They had an old abandoned farm building over where the park is now. That was when they first built. The farm building was on the edge of the project. We used to play in the building when it was abandoned.

Across the street used to be the woods. There were two hills over there. We used to camp out and take corn with us and put it underneath the sand and build fires on top of it and eat the corn after it was cooked. We'd play over there in the 1940s and the early 1950s. We improvised a toboggan from a car hood and would go down the hills. There were rabbits and pheasants, snakes, everything.

My mother used to have to take us over to a friend's house. When my father was working, we stayed over there together so we would be in one house and not be spread out. That was during the riots in 1943. The reason why they had that other thing was that the people in Conant Gardens didn't want us out here as well as the whites didn't want us to be a project either.

GERALD V. BLAKELY: After looking into it, it wasn't everybody in Conant Gardens. What happened was that during that particular period that was the only area that blacks could get FHA loans. They were more concerned about the property values going down. It was the idea that it was a project and would take the property values down. The only thing that disturbed me was that, during that particular period, it seemed like they were siding with the whites to keep us out. Basically, nobody knew what the real reason was. This didn't come out for many years.

ROBERT BYNUM, JR.: Conant Gardens at that time was really the only black-owned area in the city. These people had a relatively high standard of living, I would imagine, as opposed to the people moving in the projects which were off Hastings Street and down Livernois. Basically hoodlums—this was the attitude that they had. The blacks that would come here would be beneath them. Therefore, they didn't want this.

THORNTON G. JACKSON: They were schoolteachers and postal workers. Back in that time you were big folk if you were a schoolteacher or postal worker. Factory workers were looked down upon.

Then with the white population, on the other hand, it seemed as though Conant Gardens sided wholeheartedly with them. They had meetings on who was going to come in here and who wasn't.

It was like we were scum. How many times were you told you were a project boy? When you mentioned where you came from, they would look down on you. Everybody who didn't live in the project called us that.

At Pershing we made sure we got their respect. You had to show that you were from the territory and that you could take care of your territory.

ADAM SHAKOOR: In later years there developed a division even within the Sojourner Truth project from those who had lived in the project on Eight Mile Road and then moved to Sojourner Truth. The administration building was the dividing line. On one side of the project were the thugs, and on the other side were the nonthreatening folk.

GERALD V. BLAKELY: Seemingly people from all over the world were moving in—Alabama, Georgia, Mississippi. I was only nine. This appeared to me to be people from all over. We were a city within a city. We were an island. It was very rare that we would play with old friends. Everything was new, even the air. The surrounding neighborhood was foreign and hostile. The parents were unaware that the children had made the administration building the dividing line. We set our own standards.

ROBERT BYNUM, JR.: I remember my own mother and some other mothers, they used to play bridge. The living room wasn't that large. When they had bridge, it was like they were out in Bloomfield Hills; they had drinks and the whole shebang. We'd come on this side of the park, and they'd have poker and blackjack.

GERALD V. BLAKELY: I remember when my mother said we were moving, I asked if were were going to have an upstairs and downstairs, because I loved stairs. She said yes, and I felt very good about that. When I came out, there was no grass. It seemed so country to me at the time. It was so overwhelming, so new, so clean.

The relationships that grew out of this were so fantastic, because most of us are still friends. It was necessary for us to unite, because we had a feeling that everyone was against us. It was just a feeling. It drew us together.

ROBERT BYNUM, JR.: It was very necessary. When a man would come and drop a ton of coal, you had to get someone to help. If they would help me with my ton of coal, then I would help them put in theirs. Things like that drew us together. My dad would tell us that the coal man would come tomorrow and drop a ton of coal while he was at work. When he came home, he would expect that coal to be in the coal bin. I would go out and get someone to give me a hand. My dad was working fourteen to fifteen hours a day during the war.

GERALD V. BLAKELY: Another thing that was very important, our neighborhood store was five blocks away. We didn't go to the store alone. We would go in pairs for safety. We rectified that though. It wasn't the kind of violence you see today. But, in order to gain respect, we did okay for ourselves.

ROBERT BYNUM, JR.: I don't know if Mrs. Booker remembers this, but where I really gained respect for her was when some teacher hit a child at Atkinson School. This was the only time that I ever saw a black parent challenge the system. She went over there and said, "You don't be hitting."

THORNTON G. JACKSON: You talk about people. I guess I ate at her house just as much as I ate at home.

ROBERT BYNUM, JR.: You talk about eating! We'd have Sunday dinner. Mr. Booker would cook the best beef roast in the city. When we finished eating, I'd tell my mother, "I'm going down to George's for awhile." She said okay.

When I'd get down there, Mr. Booker would say, "Bobby, tell that boy to cut you a piece of meat." Then Otis would come down to my house, and we'd have crackers and milk.

The concoctions we made up! When the ice man would come around, we'd get a piece of newspaper and tell the ice man to chip us off a piece. That was our popsicle.

GERALD V. BLAKELY: When they had the co-op store here, Mrs. Williams was one of the store clerks. I didn't know how to read the scale. I was a kid. I loved windmill cookies, so she gave me a bag of windmill cookies. She gave me almost a pound, and I was only spending about fifteen cents. She filled the bag up. No, she didn't weigh it. I said, "Mrs. Williams, put them on the scale and weigh them." She put her hands in and started taking them out. I said, "Thank you." I felt so dumb. I started learning how to use the scale.

THORNTON G. JACKSON: Everybody in the project went to one of those two stores. You would pay by the end of the week on Friday. That's when your father got paid. A lot of them would let you go. I know of instances when my father didn't have all the money at the same time, and he said, "Go up there and give so-and-so so much on the bill."

GERALD V. BLAKELY: See where that fence is? We used to climb that fence. Remember the milkman and the Awrey's man who used to deliver? They would leave coffee cakes in the people's doorway. In the summertime, as kids, we used to get up real early. We'd get a quart of milk and the rolls and go up by that fence and go down the other side. The bad part was when the man came to collect money. "We didn't get no. . . ."

"What are you talking about?"

That, I believe, stopped them from coming out here. They figured the people just didn't want to pay.

THORNTON G. JACKSON: When World War II broke out, each one had a victory garden. When the tomatoes got half-way big, the kids would come over and have tomato wars. You'd look around at the project, and you saw tomatoes everywhere. There were always a few left for the people to eat. That was one side of the project against the other.

GERALD V. BLAKELY: I remember my literature teacher named Mrs. Hawkins. One thing she didn't like—chewing gum. She considered that collecting garbage. She used to tell all the kids, "Don't collect garbage in your mouth; spit it out." One day I insisted on popping my bubble gum. You're supposed to go to the principal's office to take a kid home. I kept popping it until she caught me. She was at the blackboard. She grabbed me by my hand out of the seat and walked me home. She didn't stop to ask the principal nothing. She grabbed me by my hand and told my mother. She was so mad. That was the most expensive piece of bubble gum I ever had.

ROBERT BYNUM, JR.: We did a lot of stuff. But as far as our parents were concerned, we respected them impeccably. If we were smoking and we saw Mrs. Booker, hey, the cigarette was gone and she would never know it.

I turned the corner one day coming out of the store. I was smoking. When I turned the corner I almost ran into Mr. McTweet. I took the cigarette out of my mouth and put it into my pocket. I knew he had just left my father. He said, "How's your father?"

"He's fine." So we stood there talking and talking. I guess he knew he was about to set me on fire. He never said anything to my parents, never said anything to me. When I came home from the service and had Vickey, my oldest girl, I came out one day. They were playing ball out here. I came to watch the game.

He said, "How you doing, Bobby? You still smoking?"

THORNTON G. JACKSON: I remember so many things. Some of the best years of my life were spent in this project. As we got older, we were running with each other. Bobby went in the service. Gerald went in the service. I think I was the oldest thing around.

ROBERT BYNUM, JR.: A guy came to the door and asked for Thornton Jackson, Jr. At that time I thought his father was the biggest man I knew. He was huge. He said, "What do you want?"

They said, "We've come to get Thornton, to join the army."

His dad said: "My son, Thornton? He belongs to me. He don't belong to no army."

ADAM SHAKOOR: The families that were the first families in the project had to fight in order to be here. They would talk about how lights had to be put out, and they were all crouched down, standing guard in their homes. They were ready to give their lives.

People came from all over to make sure that this project stayed a project for African Americans. It was something that was seen as a very big step, because this was the first project of brick row houses. When this one was built, that was when whites decided they wanted it, because it looked better than what they had perceived it to be.

I was a little bit after that time. My parents had moved here during the 1942–43 period of time. I was born here in 1947, grew up here the first eight to ten years of my life. I have very good and vivid memories of a very formative period in my life. In the early '50s it was pretty much like the early '40s. We traveled in groups. Three or four of us would go to the store. It was a home, a community for all of us. Just about everything that we needed was basically within the confines of this project area. If someone was sick, people came and inquired about their health.

My generation hadn't been born in the South, but most of our parents were born there. We learned a lot of things that would have been learned had we been born in the South. For example, the various types of card games—"Georgia Skin," "Coon Land," and this type of thing—were regularly played.

We learned various aspects of hunting, how to identify certain kinds of sounds in the woods. My father would take me across the road into the woods, the place where they are building the prison today. I might be out there with him for hours. He would tell me things as we went through the woods. It was a very formative period in my life and one that I think instilled in me the beginning stages of a desire to make things better.

I knew about the social struggle early on. I knew that conditions weren't always going to be right. I knew that there would be things given to you and then taken back from you and that you'd have to fight to get them.

I think that's true of a lot of people who came through during that period of time, understanding the struggle and what had to be done. We do have some very strong success stories. But tears well up in my eyes when I think about some of those who had greater potential than myself, but the discipline was missing. It was basically that they got into illegal activities. The quick money was made early with skills that they had, but after a few years, it caused them to be in prison or to their demise.

ROBERT BYNUM, JR.: We policed our generation. Some of the older fellows, if they would see us on a certain corner, which was about as far as you could see at a certain time of night, they would say, "Hey, go home." They were three or four years older than us.

We said, "You're not my daddy."

"Go home, or else you'll think I'm your daddy." That in itself kept us in line, along with our peers.

If he was a troublemaker and always starting something, you'd say, "Hey man, don't start that. We're going home." That broke up a lot of stuff. A lot of guys who wanted to do drugs were stopped by their peers.

When I got out of the hospital, they gave me a surprise party in the old administration building. I was sitting around the house. My dad said, "Why don't you get dressed? They're having a party over in the administration building."

I said, "No," but he kept on, so I said, "All right." So I put on my uniform.

I was walking over there, and I passed this guy who said, "Hey, soldier, where are you going?" He said, "They're having a party over at the administration building." He said, "They're giving a party for some dude named Robert Bynum." I said I was him, and he said, "You're kidding." So we both went over to the party. I guess everybody in Detroit was there and their kids. They were all in there. I came home in 1951. There was a lot of cute little kids I showed how to ice skate and play ping pong.

ADAM SHAKOOR: Sojourner Truth is unique in terms of people that I've known who have grown up in a project area in Detroit. I haven't heard any of them talk with any of the good feeling and the closeness that this community had. I guess it was born out of the struggle that we had in order to have this as our own. People really had difficulty moving away.

BIOGRAPHIES

Gerald V. Blakely was born on June 8, 1932 in Detroit and has two brothers. The family has lived in various Detroit neighborhoods, including the Sojourner Truth Homes. He has compiled a history of this important neighborhood.

Kenneth G. Booker was born on September 15, 1937, in Detroit and was raised in the Sojourner Truth Homes. As a child he was a champion speed skater. After serving in the armed forces he worked at the Veterans Administration Hospital and at the Cadillac Motor Car Company. He enjoys working at electronics and carpentry and is a portrait artist.

Robert Bynum, Jr., was born on July 3, 1931, and raised in Detroit, where he spent the first sixteen years of his life. At age sixteen he went into the military, where he spent nearly five years. Upon discharge he returned home to a "loving wife and to raise a family of three lovely daughters and three fine grandsons."

Thornton G. Jackson was born in 1932 in Detroit and grew up in Sojourner Truth Homes. He graduated from Pershing High School.

Adam Shakoor was a part of the Sojourner Truth community. He graduated from Salesian High School. He worked at the Ford Rouge plant for a short time. From 1981–89 he was a judge in the 36th District Court. He is currently deputy mayor for the City of Detroit. Mr. Shakoor and his wife, Nikki, are parents of eight children.

WINSTON E. LANG

My mother was a widow with six kids during the depression. We didn't know one day of hunger. But my sister's husband remembers his father going out and catching pigeons and squirrels in order to have something to eat. We never went through that, because at that time they had mother's pension, the forerunner of Aid to Dependent Children.

Mother was on the mother's pension and was working. The social worker told her she couldn't work. The worker visited one evening and said, "Mrs. Lang, I came by earlier and you weren't here. Where were you?" Mother said she was at work. The worker said, "Mrs. Lang, the reason we're giving you this money is so that you won't have to go out and work."

Mother said: "If I don't go out and work, my kids will not have the same things other kids have, and I want to see to it that they have as much as I can possibly give them." The social worker just sort of turned her head and pretended that mother wasn't working. We were fortunate; but when you talk to other people and they said they almost starved and they had both the father and mother in the house, you can see the picture. There was no work available, and they weren't going to give families anything as long as there was a man in the house. The social system added to the disintegration process in many cases.

1943 in my own personal experience was very disheartening. We did go to school with all ethnic groups. We did choose our friends on the basis of who's a good guy and who's a bad guy, and many of my friends were nonblack. To see a riot happen and to see people attack my friends, that was a very disheartening experience. There is one thing that makes me remember. I was graduating from the eighth grade, and the law was put into effect that there could be no large gathering of any group for any reason. This was during the riot. Therefore, my mother couldn't come see me graduate from the eighth grade.

In the middle '60s I worked with a street gang. I remember taking one of the gang member's mother somewhere. She told me: "Mr. Lang I appreciate what you are trying to do for my boys. They are not bad boys, really. They were doing fairly well in school; but their father and I broke up, and I had to go on welfare, and I haven't been able to really buy them the kind of things that they should have. They had holes in their shoes and their pants; other kids laughed at them. They just simply told me, 'Mother, we are not going to school to be laughed at.' It was just so embarrassing."

The son of this same woman said that one time his mother was cooking, and she realized she didn't have any salt. She told him to run down to the corner store and get a box of salt, something that should have taken five to ten minutes at the most. What happened was that he had food stamps with which to pay. He would go and get the salt, and one of his friends would come in, and he didn't want the friend to know that the family was on food stamps. He would put the salt down and pretend he was looking for something else. That friend would go out, and he was about ready to pay for it, and here comes another friend. It happened maybe two or three times in a row. What should have been a ten-minute journey at the most, turned out to be a half hour. Finally, the store cleared, and he paid for the salt with stamps and got home and then got a whipping, because his mother thought he had been goofing off.

Our drug problem in Detroit started, I would think, during the '60s. You have a lot of ideas coming to the forefront. Black pride was coming to the forefront. With these ideas came a kind of liberal outlook on most things that had been sort of frowned upon before, drugs being one of them. As long as someone is doing something in their own place, it doesn't hurt anybody. Then the sexual expression, as well. People started living together, wanting to see if they could get along with one another; and if they couldn't get along with one another, they moved on and lived with someone else. It was that kind of attitude toward family relationships, stable relationships, that emerged, a more liberal attitude toward any kind of a social behavior. As long as you were doing it and not hurting anybody. Then the liberal attitude toward morals became progressively worse. Individual or couple's actions began hurting other people.

When you talk about the destruction of the families and the role that having a job or not having a job played, two instances come to mind in terms of the way I've heard it described. One is that now you have the Aid to Dependent Children, welfare, whatever, that more or less caused the family to break up. The attitude used to be—if there's a man in the house, you get nothing. If he isn't there, you get something. That was a wrong approach, if true.

In more recent years, when the attitudes seem to have changed somewhat, they have again said to the fourteen-or-fifteen year-old girl, maybe it starts at eighteen or nineteen; but when she comes up pregnant and the whole family is suffering from the lack of income, then she needs additional income to help feed the baby. They are just barely getting breakfast on the table for the household, and a baby comes along that needs diapers and formula. Here again you have money, or lack of it, entering the picture. It used to be that as long as you live with your parents, you are not going to get any money. So the girl would move out. This is idiotic, because when they move out into apartments of their own, it is going to cost the system more to pay for her living alone than it would to pay for the formula and the baby and everything else at home. And then it becomes an awful temptation for the guy that did the impregnating to fall right back into the scene where she is now living alone, and you've got the whole pattern repeated.

Our so-called sociological answers to the use of government money have been a miserable failure in this particular area. Those are actual forces that helped to disintegrate the family.

In terms of a guy walking out because they didn't want the responsibility, I think it is a misnomer. I think they may have walked out ostensibly under certain circumstances, where they knew the family could get more money.

BIOGRAPHY

Winston E. Lang was born on December 20, 1929 in Detroit. He earned an M.S.W. in social work from Wayne State University. He served as assistant director of the Detroit Urban League from 1969 to 1978, executive director of the Detroit Branch of the NAACP from 1978 to 1987, and is currently director, City of Detroit Human Rights Department. He is married to Lois Lee Lang and the father of three children.

208

JAMES T. JENKINS

In 1941 I started work as a bus driver and a streetcar operator. I went all over this town. I remember driving a bus on West Seven Mile Road when it was a two-lane road. The big migration didn't cross Six Mile Road until World War II. When you went out Six Mile Road, after you crossed Wyoming, you were in the country. You could see nothing but pheasants and rabbits running across the fields.

When I started driving the bus, you had very few blacks driving the bus at that time, and mostly all those were carryovers from World War I. Most of them worked for the old Detroit Interurban Railroad.

You drove up to a corner on the bus and opened your doors, and they would turn their backs and say, "I don't ride with niggers." We used to laugh about it.

We used to pull up in front of the Fisher Building on the Dexter bus going to Fullerton or Fenkell and open the doors, and they'd turn their back on you. Me and a guy would holler out: "Well, you better come on and ride with me. The one behind me is blacker than I am."

The fare was six cents, one penny for a transfer. People used to get on, and we had to make change. They used to take their money and hold it in a way that they wouldn't have to touch your hand.

In 1943 I was walking on Waterloo across Vernor Highway, just east of Waterloo Cemetery. I was on vacation. I went out to the little confectionery at night to get my *Free Press* and ice cream. I saw the Grand Belt streetcar packed with people. That was a typical Sunday evening about nine or ten o'clock. Everybody was leaving Belle Isle Park. It was very hot. We didn't have a radio on; television had not come into being at that time.

Monday morning I got up and turned the radio on. The first thing I heard was, "rioting in Detroit." I thought, what are they talking about? Everybody had their radios on, and people were calling people up. I was going out to the north end, and I caught the Fort streetcar. The guy told me: "You be careful when you get off downtown there on Monroe. Those fools down there have paper bags, and they got a brick in the paper bags. If you see somebody coming toward you with that bag in their hand swinging, you run away from them, because they get right next to you, those white people would hit you upside the head."

When the Fort streetcar came off of Clinton onto Gratiot, it went around by Sam's and then down Monroe. When we turned on Randolph, here comes a little black boy coming up Monroe by Sam's. I bet you there were two hundred whites behind him. I said, "Oh, my God."

The Eastern Market was a great place. You'd go over there; and all the stuff that people sell you now, they'd give it to you. I know when Joe Muer had his place started, there on St. Aubin and Gratiot. You couldn't go in, but I enjoyed a lot of that pickerel and walleye and red snapper. We are a group of people that got by on what people thought was nothing but trash. They threw it out. I was living on Elmwood in 1937, between Macomb and Clinton. We used to go over to Joe Muer's restaurant. They would just fillet the fish. They threw all the rest in the trash. All of that meat up there and all of the bone and all the tail. We used to go over there with a dishpan on Friday. If you'd give those guys who was parking cars a quarter, they'd give it all to you. You'd get a dishpan full of fresh pickerel, fresh fish. You'd take it home and clean it up, and wash it up, and you had a feast.

Senator Diggs broke the color barrier at Eastern Market. You know the restaurants inside the market there? They wouldn't serve blacks, so he broke that up.

I really couldn't see much difference in living in North Carolina, where I came from, or living in Detroit. You just had certain places down on Monroe, "greasy spoons" that would serve you. This was on Monroe and Randolph down to the Family Theater. You had three or four little restaurants that you could go into and get a hot dog or hamburger or whatever. But if you went up to Hudson's or to Frame's Tea Room on Farmer Street or any of those places, even Kresge's on Woodward and State, they didn't serve you. People used to walk in and buy a cup of coffee, and they had a special little chair to sit in with a little desk, like a school desk. Cunningham Drugstore, Kinsel's Drugstores, you couldn't eat in any of those places.

BIOGRAPHY

James T. Jenkins was born On October 16, 1916, in Laurens County, South Carolina. He graduated from high school on August 11, 1936, and came to Detroit. He worked at Henry's Swing Club in Black Bottom. In 1941 he began driving a bus for the City of Detroit. As a member of Men Who Dare he worked on the Scholarship Committee and became chair of the Entertainment Committee, which booked events and raised money. He retired in 1973 and in 1974 founded the Graystone International Jazz Museum.

Francis A. Kornegay, Ph.D., in the center of the back row, is president emeritus of the Detroit Urban League.

FRANCIS A. KORNEGAY, Ph.D.

I came here to work at the Detroit Urban League, June 1, 1944. We moved into the present building, July 1, 1944.

My title here was vocational secretary. My job was to find day work for women and day-labor work for men. And for day work they got six dollars a day, carfare, and perhaps lunch. I served in that capacity for one month. Then I went into Mr. Dancy and said: "Mr. Dancy, I'm here with a master's degree, and all I'm doing is sending Negroes on menial jobs which could be done by a secretary. There's nothing wrong with that, but my feeling is that we ought to do more. I have six hundred young Negroes, men and women with degrees, who have registered with the Urban League, and there isn't any place to send them." We sent them to the factory, and occasionally we sent one as a secretary; but that was few and far between.

I had two networking sources. One was a board member whose wife was very fair and passed for white. The other was a very fair Negro who also passed and worked at J. L. Hudson's. She was the secretary to a top official at Hudson's. They knew me very well, and they would pipeline things to me in terms of asking their bosses for breakthroughs. This was under the table talk, but it backed up my conversation with Mr. Dancy. He agreed that I should undertake this new approach.

When I went to talk to the top officials of companies, I knew what I could ask for, because I knew what they were doing. I was very bold and very frank, and said, "Why can't we put Negro boys and Negro girls who are out of school to work on part-time jobs like you are hiring white youth." Most of the companies then had work study programs, and they would accept white boys and girls from the Board of Education but they would not accept Negro boys and girls, because the Board of Education would not send them.

John Dancy said, "I'll have you see U.S. Senator Prentice Brown, because he's on the board of the Detroit Edison Company." He said, "I'll call Prentice Brown now and set up an appointment." Mr. Parker was president, and Mr. Dancy said he was a very fine man.

I went to see Mr. Arthur Dondineau, who was superintendent of schools. He said he could not have the Board of Education send Negro boys and girls to the Detroit Edison Company because he didn't know whether they would accept them, and that would give us kind of a negative reputation. He said, "If you can make it straight with the Detroit Edison Company, we'd be glad to do it."

So Prentice Brown set up the conference for me with Mr. Parker. I went to see Mr. Parker, and I told him the story about the Edison Company accepting white boys and girls from the school system and that they would not accept young Negroes. He was dumbfounded. He called in Mr. Sullivan, who was on our board. When Sullivan walked in and saw me, he was really surprised. Parker said, "Joe, do you know Mr. Kornegay?"

"Yes, I serve on the board of the League."

"He's telling me that you do not accept Negro boys and girls into our work study program. Is that right?"

Sullivan said, "Yes, it is."

Parker said, "As of this moment I want you to call Mr. Dondineau, superintendent of schools, and tell him that our policy is to accept Negro boys and girls the same as whites." That was our first breakthrough at a utility. That was one of the most important breakthroughs that we ever had, because it involved the Board of Education and a utility. From the work-study program many Negroes were hired at the Detroit Edison Company.

I got into only one argument, a big argument with [the] president of the Bank of the Commonwealth. He said, "We don't want any Negroes here because they might marry the white girls."

I said, "Then you don't want any more money from Negroes, do you?"

"Oh, yes, we want your money."

I talked with him at least several months, and finally I found out that he was a deacon at his church in Grosse Pointe. I said, I'm going to throw the book at him today because he's supposed to be a Christian. I went up to him and said, "I understand you're a deacon in your church."

He said, "I am, and I'm very proud of it."

I said: "That's fine. I'm not a deacon in my church, but I'm a good Christian. You know what? If I were you, I would be afraid to go to sleep at night because you are dishonest to yourself, to this bank, to this community. You will not take Negro boys and girls, and you know that the National Bank has done it, the Detroit Bank has done it, and Industrial National. Now why do you hold out to those people? I'd be afraid to go to sleep at night because I'd be afraid I might not wake up." In less than a minute the man began shedding tears and shaking. I said: "Great Lakes Insurance Company has $50,000 in checking at your bank. Mr. Charles Mahoney is on the board of the Urban League, and I'm going back and tell him to take the money out."

I went back and told Mahoney. He called up [this bank president]. He said: "Mr. Kornegay has told me your story. Three banks have taken Negroes in as tellers under Mr. Kornegay's direction. If you don't do that, I will take our $50,000 out and put it in the National Bank of Detroit which is one block up from your bank."

He said, "Tell Mr. Kornegay to come in tomorrow." I went back the next morning and he gave in. He said: "Mr. Kornegay, send me Negroes. We are ready."

Lou Franks was the manager of Lane Bryant, and he had heard about us putting on salespersons at Hudson's, Sam's, and Crowley's, and said, "Francis, I want you to send me a bookkeeper, and I want her to be a light-skinned Negress."

I said, "Just a minute," and I called Hilda Watkins, who was my secretary and said: "You pick up the phone before I go back. I want you to record everything we say." We must have talked almost an hour. I said: "Lou, as well as you know me, are you asking me to discriminate against my people? What is a light-skinned Negress?"

He said, "Anyone who is almost white."

I said: "I can't do this. If I would report this to the NAACP, they would sue you."

After talking about an hour, he said, "Francis, send me a good one."

I had many professional people on file. I did not do this purposely. I picked out a bookkeeper's application that was very good and called the lady in. She was almost as black as coal, but she had a charming personality. I called Lou and said, "I have a fine lady I'm sending." He interviewed her and hired her. She retired from that company thirty years later.

John Dancy would say: "Give them hell, Francis. If they call me up, I may tell them that I'm going to put it on the carpet, but I'm not going to call you on the carpet because you're doing things that I could never do at this time in my career."

John Dancy did everything he could do in his time, and he did it well. He could not do in his time what I did because they would have run him out of this town. But he knew how to handle the people in his time.

Henry Ford II was one of my closest friends and best resource persons. He'd tell me about his family and white people in Grosse Pointe, and I'd tell him about black people. When Henry had social affairs, my wife and I were invited to many of them. Christina Ford had a big party at the Whittier. She entertained the ambassador to the United States from Italy. My wife and I were the only blacks invited. Christina called and said, "Francis, you have to come."

I said, "Our son gets his master's degree at Howard University the same evening of the party, and we are going down a day early so we can take him around and reward him for having done a good job."

She said, "Tell Geraldine that one of you has to be there."

My wife said: "I don't dance as well as you do. You go."

I took my tuxedo with me to Washington. When I got on the plane, I went into a little restroom and put on the tuxedo. Can you imagine a big man squirming into a tuxedo in a plane's little restroom?

I got in my car and drove over to the Whittier.

They had over two hundred couples as guests. Henry and Christina had a table all by themselves. She sat in the middle, and Henry was to the right, and I was to the left. I danced all night, and some of the women came up and said, "Francis, I'd like to have a dance with you."

I said, "Ask Christina."

BIOGRAPHY

Francis A. Kornegay, Ph.D., is president emeritus of the Detroit Urban League. He was born on September 14, 1913, in Mt. Olive, North Carolina. He has worked as a dishwasher, janitor, dean of boys, and head of science and mathematics at Dowmingtown Agricultural and Industrial School. In 1944 he became vocational secretary at the Detroit Urban League; he was promoted to assistant executive director in 1960 and executive director in 1960, and served as president from 1977-78. He was responsible for convincing utilities, banks, department stores, and unions to hire blacks. Dr. Kornegay is now special assistant to the president, Omnicare Health Plan.

When I was thirteen I decided I wanted to be a model. So I starved myself, exercised a lot, and I never weighed over ninety pounds. And I looked through all the magazines, and I tried to convince my family to pay for my classes, and they said, "No." So they said, "I will pay for you going to college," and at that particular time I decided I would go to a business college, because I love math, I love accounting; and I enrolled in Detroit Institute of Commerce.

I was there a year, and Mrs. Gromes was the owner and founder of the Detroit Institute of Commerce. One day she came into the class, and she asked me and another friend of mine to step outside in her office. She wanted us to meet Mr. Kornegay. So I said, "Fine," and we met Mr. Kornegay, and he told us what he had in mind was for us to take an exam at the bank; and the bank was going to hire one of us. There was another school involved, and I don't know which school it was; but the idea was, they were only going to hire one person, one of us. And at the time I thought, "Why do you need so many people just to hire one person?" But I went to the bank. We all were tested, and about a week later the bank—it was Detroit Bank and Trust at that particular time—they got in touch with Mr. Kornegay, and he got in touch with the school, and they wanted to interview me in the personnel department. So I said, "Fine."

So I went and had the interview, and I came back to school, and about a week later I got the message that they decided to hire me. It was kind of unusual for me because I did not think about taking the job. I did not want the job, because my uncle was a friend of Richard Austin, and Richard Austin had told me that when I graduate I could come and work in his office because he had a CPA office at the time. That was what I was looking forward to. This was the field I wanted to be in. This was the direction that I wanted my life to go, and then this comes along—totally not planned. So I decided, well, let me think about it. So he said okay.

I went home. I talked to my family—my mother and father—and said, "What do you think?" You know I didn't think anything, because that is why I was asking them. I wanted to continue doing what I was doing because I was comfortable doing it, and I had a future that I believed in, and I had someone that believed in me.

So I asked Mr. Kornegay, "Is it possible for you to take the second girl or the next best or whatever it was they were looking for?" And he said, "No, they will take you or they won't take anybody."

I thought that was kind of wrong. I said, "Okay, what do I have to do?"

He said: "Well, they want you to start working today. I mean next week, you start next Friday. And you have to finish school at night."

To me it was out of the question, you know. Why should I turn my life around? But after talking to him telling me how important this particular project was to him, how he had been working on it, how he was talking to people, and if I didn't do it he didn't know what other time he could present it or someone else could present it, I said, okay.

I started, and I went to school at night. I completed my education, and I wasn't very happy doing this. I guess I am a selfish person. When I make up my mind that this is what I want to do, that is all I want to do. Even when he pointed out the importance of me doing it, I was not caught up in a lot of breaking down barriers, because I came from a family who told us that we can do anything that we wanted to do. That we had the same opportunity. That they believed in us. I had not experienced a lot of racial incidents, because when I went to the South to visit my grandparents, my best friend was a little white girl.

So I couldn't understand when I went in to the bank why I was not treated as nice or as friendly as I thought that I should have been. That was not a big problem, because I was there to learn. That was my goal, that was why I was there—not to make friends, not to socialize. So that is what I attempted to do. I decided that I was going to be the best clerk. I was going to be the best bookkeeper. I was going to be the best teller that they ever had; and I succeeded in doing those things because I didn't spend a lot of time in those areas. I moved right along.

I had a manager who was very supportive. He would always sit me down every week and say, "Are you having any problems?" The problems that I did experience there was nothing he could do about: the things that might have been said, or people who would not talk to you, or people who would not go to lunch when you went to lunch. I want to tell you everybody in that office was Polish. So I was the only black person there.

There was one male teller. If I answered the phone and he had to use the phone, he would always proceed to wipe it off; and I saw him do it, and I was kind of wondering why was he doing that. Then I said, if I say something about it, he'll probably say he has a cold and he didn't want anybody else to be exposed to his germs, and I would look like a fool. So I said, well, if he wants to wipe off the phone every time I can't do anything about this. This has nothing to do with my learning, but it is an experience, and let me see how I can overcome this.

There were incidents where tellers would not allow me to go in their windows and pick up the work, the checks. So I would just not go in there, and eventually the manager would want to know why is the work piled up so high in this teller's area, and it is getting late in the day, and you have to run the machine. I would say, "Oh! I must have forgotten to pick it up," because I didn't know how to complain because nothing physically was done to me.

There were little incidents that happened, and I feel that—and I have to attribute my background—I never felt inferior. I don't feel inferior now. And I guess it's what you think about yourself; and I thought about those little incidents and I felt like—now, if I buy into that, I am as bad as they are. So I am not going to do that. They'll have to create something else, because I know that every time that I went home on Friday, they did not expect me to show up Monday; but I said, that's what they want. I would cry a lot because my feelings were hurt; but I said, if I don't go back, that is exactly what they want me to do. But I am going back and I would show up.

At my retirement party I said to the person who hired me—Mr. Jack Talbot—"I don't think you guys expected me to be around for forty-two years, did you?"

He said, "No." So it was quite an experience for me. After awhile I guess they were convinced that I wasn't going to steal, that I was going to show up on time, that I wasn't lazy. Consequently they hired other blacks into the organization.

I feel like my career was hampered because I was the first. I feel like I was like a test person. There are other people who came in after me who have attained levels of vice president, senior vice president, and I am very happy for them. I am glad that nobody else had to experience what I experienced. Today when I tell people the story, they tell me, "Oh God, I couldn't have done that!" That is why sometimes I think I was the only person who could have done it, because there are a lot of little things that do annoy you. Even today there are certain things that are said, and you think about them and you say, "I wonder why they said that?" Because in my mind racism is still alive and well. The struggle is still going on. There is never a time that you let up and feel like everything is okay, because it isn't. It isn't okay.

I realized where I had to go to start this job; and I realized that of all the branches that Detroit Bank and Trust had, there was only one manager who would allow me to come in the office and train. I prayed very long and very hard, and I asked God to be with me at all times, and He has not left me alone. So it's easy when you take Him with you. It makes everything else so much easier.

BIOGRAPHY

Annie Ruth Cartwright Williams was born on March 28, 1929, in Birmingham, Alabama. She was one of seven children, the third child of Luther and Mary Cartwright. She was raised by her grandmother, Annie Patton, and came to Detroit at the age of nine. She attended Durfee Junior High, Northern High School, Detroit Institute of Commerce, and Wayne State University. She became the first black employee of Detroit Bank and Trust in January 1949 and retired in March of 1992. She is the mother of three.

Nancy Ann Green Allen grew up on Detroit's west side, where her parents, Hattie P. and Pressley Green, were community leaders and proprietors of a neighborhood business.

NANCY ANN GREEN ALLEN

It seems like the thing I remember about the city is that it was really clean. And it wasn't clean so much because it was the responsibility of the city to keep it clean, but the people who lived in the city helped to keep it clean. I can remember when you cut the lawn, you'd wash the sidewalk and the curbs with soap and water and sweep it with a broom and then rinse it down.

I lived in the city of Detroit on the west side. We lived on 23rd Street, right across the street from Ira Wilson's Dairy. The dairy, of course, was part of the community and always furnished the community with ice cream, etc.

The other part of Detroit was that it was really kind of rural. Where we lived we raised chickens in our backyard. We had a full garden in the yard. All the fruit trees had fruit. I guess the life of the fruit tree is just so long. As the city was built, when they moved out, they probably planted real fruit trees so they matured at different times. I can remember we had a sweet cherry tree and a sour cherry tree. And I love cherries!

I played primarily with boys all the time. I think I still get along better with men. I have three sons. Not that I was a tomboy. I played with them because I liked being the lady, the one that they had to watch out for, take care of.

Daddy was involved in politics and involved in getting the unions organized. He worked at Ford Motor Company for awhile, and I have never seen the time when they weren't trying to organize the unions. I can remember being on that bridge, the famous overpass bridge in the early '40s, just as a little kid, because daddy took me every place.

I was the first-born, so he didn't have a son to take. All he had was this little scared daughter. I was scared of everything. But I was with my dad so you wouldn't be that scared. I had my little placards, and we marched across the bridge. I had my little union hat on, with all my little buttons and things. I didn't dodge any bullets, but we did treat people at our house that had been wounded because of the strikes.

Dad was not a person that belonged to any of the organizations in the community. He never belonged to the Cotillion Club, although many of his friends did; nor was he part of the Nacirema Club. The only thing he ever joined was when they were putting forth the effort to get the unions organized. He would belong to things like that if they had a goal like fighting for civil rights, that kind of thing. But he would not belong to any of the other elite organizations.

He was really interested in kids, especially young men. He never had a son, but he kind of adopted the young men in the neighborhood and not only provided a father figure for some of them, he also helped finance their education to college. In fact, a scholarship fund has grown out of it since his death.

Daddy's ideas were always the kind that you kind of twist up your face at because they were not what everyone was doing at the time. And then a couple years later everybody was doing that. He was always just a little bit ahead of his time. Later, mom and dad went into business for themselves. My mother was in the grocery store, my dad would be in the pool room, and we usually had somebody at the house. So, my parents were right there at our fingertips.

I remember as a child, my aunt lived on West Grand Boulevard. In the summer we would sleep out there on the island in the middle of the Boulevard. Nobody had air conditioning back in those days. When we spent the night with her in the summer, we used to stay out on the island. We had cots. I can remember the little cot that I had.

I can remember the war. Everything was rationed. I can remember some little brown stamps. You'd have to have so many stamps for sugar, bread, butter. And I can remember the blackouts. You were supposed to turn out your lights; but instead we had those real heavy dark shades that you'd pull down.

I decided I would be a dietitian. And that's what I studied to be at Wayne State University. I took up nutrition and dietetics, and I got my degree in dietetics. That's when I ran into my first experience with any kind of racial prejudice. This was just before Dr. Martin Luther King and his civil rights movement. After I graduated from college and I'm ready to go get a job as a dietitian, I went to Wayne's placement center, and my counselor gave my credentials over the telephone. That was to a hospital in Detroit, and they said: "Oh wow! Perfect! Just what we're looking for! We want somebody just out of school." They said, "Send her over."

I walked in, and I said, "I'm Mrs. Allen from Wayne State University." People would come and look at me and then they would go back. Others would come and look and then they would go back. So finally this lady came, and she sat and she looked me and she never said anything. Then she got up and she went and got another lady. So finally they said that they thought they had something, a position, but it just so happens that the position they thought they were going to have was not going to materialize. The person was going to stay on at the hospital that they thought was going to be leaving and, "Thank you for coming." That was experience number one.

The next place I went was an industrial complex, and the lady came out and she told me that I was just too young, that I had to supervise older women and at my age I just couldn't handle it; I was just too young.

Then I got hired at another hospital. The lady who interviewed me was real impressed and gave me all the papers and things to fill out and said the only thing I had to do was take my physical, and she would call me the next day and give me a date for my physical. Then she didn't call. Then she didn't call the next day. I said, "Well, I'll call her." So I called her, and she apologized and told me that even though she had hired me, her hires had to be approved by the board and that when she presented it to the board that they didn't accept me.

BIOGRAPHY

Nancy Ann Green Allen was born on September 12, 1937, in Detroit. She graduated from Northwestern High School and Wayne State University. She is an administrator for the Detroit Historical District Commission and former director of the Museum of African American History. She is a member of Alpha Kappa Alpha Sorority. Mrs. Allen has been married to Judge Alex J. Allen, Jr., for thirty-four years, and they have three sons—Alex James Allen III, Michael Pressley Allen, and Derek Jerome Allen. Mrs. Allen and her family attend Mayflower United Church of Christ.

Ret. Lt. Col. Alexander Jefferson (left) and Richard D. Macon were prisoners together during World War II. They have been close friends since that time.

DISCUSSION ON WORLD WAR II WITH TUSKEGEE AIRMEN

RET. LT. COL. ALEXANDER JEFFERSON, U.S.A.F. AND RICHARD D. MACON

RICHARD D. MACON: Let me tell you how I met Alexander Jefferson. When we became cadets, we ended up at Walterboro Air Base for basic training. We were called dummies. I was called into a room one day, and a little fellow called me "Dummy Macon" after I had told him my name. He said, "Dummy Macon, here's what I want you to do."

I said, "Yes sir, Mr. Jefferson." That's how I met him. It was the beginning of a very good friendship, even though we were hazed. He was a gentleman, a very fine guy. He hazed, but with a human spirit. Some hazed like demons.

To give you an idea, one night one of our upperclassmen came into the dummy barracks. Some dummy brother saw him and yelled, "Attention!"

This night we were having a discussion about shotgun shells. He said: "He said there were two hammers that hit the shell, and I said there was only one. We want you dummies to solve this problem for us." He sent us all the way out to the range where they shot guns and skeets.

It was about twelve at night, and we had to go out there and find some shotgun shells to prove that he was right. Of course, there was only one stroke on the shells, but we had to look all over trying to find some shells with two. We had to come back and have no excuse for not being able to find them. We were braced after that. Bracing means he may say, "Dummy, hit the dew point." That means sit with your back up against the wall and nothing up under you. The only thing that is holding you up is the muscles in your legs pushing your back against the wall.

RET. LT. COL. ALEXANDER JEFFERSON, U.S.A.F.: It's been a very long and enduring friendship that has lasted about forty-seven years. I finished in January 1944 and he finished in February 1944, and we have been together ever since.

I left Walterboro the first of June, 1944. You must have left about the first of July. Consequently, I started flying combat the middle of July, and he started the first of August. We both were blown away on the twelfth of August. I had eighteen missions. He had six.

We were in Ramitelli, Italy. There are sixty-four airplanes and four squadrons, sixteen airplanes to a squadron. Each squadron has approximately twenty-five pilots plus a hoard of enlisted personnel and other complementary officers. There were four of us in a tent. A tent is approximately ten feet by ten feet, a wooden floor or metal grating floor with four cots. You wake up at approximately 5:30 A.M.; get washed up; get dressed; put on your flying togs, helmet, goggles, flight suit, big boots, large gloves. First thing you do is go to eat. Never drink too much coffee, because the missions are usually five to six hours long. You are sitting in an airplane which is about that wide. Of course, there's a relief tube which runs from here down to there, but try to get to that relief tube with a parachute on with straps across the legs and shoulders. Therefore, never drink coffee in the morning.

After breakfast you go to the briefing room, where all these sixty-four pilots are sitting watching a huge screen. Gleed would walk in. He was the captain at that time. Everyone was smoking, a lot of horseplay going on. Waiting. Nervousness. Gleed would walk in; he was our operations officer. He would walk up and say, "Gentlemen, this is the mission." And he would pull the curtain back. You'd see the red line running from Ramitelli going up into Germany, and everybody would say, "Ohhhhh!" Of course, I wasn't nervous. I was never nervous. There would be take-off times for each squadron. Each would take off at a different time in order to take off on this one strip.

224

RICHARD D. MACON: The bombers were usually flying from other fields. The one that was closest was at Foggia, Italy. They had a schedule. They would take off at about 4:30 in the morning. We had a little radar then so they could track us just a little bit. They would not fly straight to the target. They would fly with a heading like this and turn on the heading and turn on the heading again. If the Germans could anticipate where they were going, they would have the full force to meet them there. If they were kept guessing, they would have to keep all of the bases covered.

We knew where to pick them up. All the bombers wouldn't be together. They'd be coming from many different directions. The fighters would take off three or four hours later, and we'd do the same kind of manuevering. My first mission, I thought, now how in the hell can they have us twisting all over the world and end up together? He said, "Rendevous time is 10:17."

RET. LT. COL. ALEXANDER JEFFERSON, U.S.A.F.: You'd look at your watch, and it would be 10:15:30, and you'd look over at about three o'clock about two miles away, and there the bombers would be. We'd meet them right on time. There would be another squadron of P-51s from another group who had been with the bombers for an hour and a half or two hours. Then they are low on fuel, so those P-51s would have to go back. We'd take over and escort those bombers from point B to point C. When our fuel was up, another group of P-51 fighters were taking off three hours later and would take over from where we had them and escort them on. The bombers would just keep right on going to the target.

Each squadron took off at the end of the runway. Remember now, you had four machine guns loaded with fifty calibers, five hundred rounds per gun, ninety two gallons of fuel in each wing, forty-five gallons sitting behind you in a tank. Underneath each wing there is a drop tank of one hundred and ten gallons. You're sitting there just like a flying gasoline tank. You're sixteen airplanes parked at the end of the runway. Your wing is tucked into another guy's wing. You're all sitting there, and these props are moving, and you've got your feet on the rudder holding the brakes because this big prop up ahead wants to pull you ahead. Meanwhile, down at the other end of the runway, one squadron starts taking off. They take off. These sixteen airplanes take off. Then it's your chance to take off. Then the other 332nd would take off, and finally the fourth. It was exhilarating. Sixty-four airplanes with all the noise and the fervor and excitement. You'd take off, rendevous, and fly in formation.

The first time I ever got sick inside of an oxygen mask. . . . We were at 32,000 feet so you had to have an oxygen mask. We escorted B-17s to Romania over oil fields. The B-17s would get to the initial point, and they would turn and fly straight to a huge black cloud right over the oil fields. The black cloud started at approximately twenty thousand feet and went to twenty-five thousand feet. It was five or six miles in diameter, just like a huge hockey puck. They would fly straight into the black cloud. It was anti-aircraft. The Germans would fire the shells up, and they would explode. We would take off and go over and sit on the other side of the black cloud and wait for these B-17s to come out. As we sat there, we looked back. The B-17s go into the black cloud, and then after a while you'd see one come out of the bottom of the cloud with a wing gone and fire coming out. You'd hear someone on the radio: "Okay you guys, bang it off! Bang it off! Bang it off!" You'd see one parachute come out and a second parachute come out, and then the whole damn thing would explode.

Then all of a sudden it struck me. There were ten men on the plane. Two got out. Eight men died right in front of your eyes. I got sick inside the oxygen mask at thirty-two thousand feet. So you take it, and you shake it out, and put it back on real quick. But I had to sit there for two-and-a-half hours back with a stinking mask. It's frightening. They tell you that war is glamorous. We never saw anyone get hurt in an airplane unless it's your own blood, because we were in the ship by ourselves. But war is hell. This glamour that we often see is for the birds. Except when I saw Macon. His eyes were red; that's another story.

We escorted B-17s and B-24s from Italy up to Romania, from Italy to Poland, from Italy to Berlin, from Italy to Munich, from Italy to France. We escorted B-17s and prevented the German fighters from shooting them down. Our unit has a war record of never losing a bomber that we were escorting. Escorting means simply sitting there like a mother hen hovering over her chicks. You hover around and when the Germans came in, we would fight them off. Many times the Germans wouldn't even come in, because they saw us there. There were other times when you would go on fighter sweeps, and you could shoot anything. Those were opportunity times, when the guys in our group really did get some victories.

RICHARD D. MACON: Different fighter squadrons would be assigned to escort different squadrons of bombers. Your job would be to know where your bombers were. Many times planes would be straggling out of formation or having some other kind of difficulty.

The Germans were something like a wolf pack. They stood and watched. Wolves catch the stray that falls behind the farthest. They would pounce on that plane and shoot it down. Or they would send seven, eight, or ten aircraft off to the side, menacingly, acting as if they might come into the squadron. Many times some of the white fighter pilots would think: "This is the time for me to get a kill. I'll go out there and shoot them down." They would take off going out there to at-

tack instead of defend, not realizing that they were leaving their bombers unprotected. There would be fifteen to twenty other planes up there
waiting for that to happen, and they would come in and shoot down
some of the bombers. The bombers were well-protected with their own
firepower, but it wasn't enough. They couldn't maneuver the way
fighter planes could to get into position to shoot. We were more agile.
They used to call us the "Red Tail Angels," because we stayed right
there and saw to it that nobody came from up here to attack them and
shoot them down. We never lost a bomber, because we stayed in one
place.

My first flight I was flying up from Ramitelli. The Norden bomb-
sight was a brand new, state-of-the-art device at that time. The only
shortcoming, as we look back, was, from the initial point of the bomb
run until the bombs were dropped, the bombardier was in charge of the
airplane. That smoke that he was talking about, they didn't deliberately
fly through that smoke. The smoke just happened to be where the Germans sighted and shot at most of the planes, and that's where it accumulated. That's where our planes had to go in order to drop the bombs.

The bombardiers were pretty good with the bombs, but they were
sitting ducks on that bomb run, because they couldn't fly but about one
hundred forty miles per hour and straight. The Germans knew this, so
all they had to do was aim the guns to hit something going one hundred
forty miles per hour, and they could shoot them off like that. We
couldn't do anything about blocking the flak from coming up. All we
could do was sit there and hope they got through so we could escort
them back home. When we got over the target, we went around to the
other end and waited for them to come out.

I'm flying along here with my squadron leader and enjoying the
trip. This is my first trip. I was looking around. I saw these clouds and
thought this is pretty high for clouds—thirty thousand feet. I didn't
think there was too much weather up there. Here is another cloud.
That's flak! When I realized that they were shooting at us, too, I tucked
in under my flight leader, and from then on I flew some very tight formation, because Bill Campbell had a reputation for knowing when to
move because he could see the guns go off. I didn't know how to do
that. He could see the guns go off, and he assumed that they were pretty
accurate, so he would just turn at about the time the flak would get up
that high.

Historically, in the northern part of France, the allied troops were
stalemated with the Germans, and they wanted to have some kind of
pressure relief or diversionary action in the south so that the Germans
would have to start looking that way, and hopefully the allied troops
could start moving. This was only supposed to be a diversion. The Germans, according to the intelligence that we got at this briefing, did not

have it well protected with guns. But they had radar all up and down the coast, so that if they saw something coming they could call; and the planes could get there soon enough to probably avert it and attack from that side. It was absolutely stupid to attack from that side, so the Germans didn't pay it any attention. The Americans had chosen a general who didn't follow orders too well. George Patton did what he wanted to. They had chosen him to open up this diversion in the south. We had to shoot up the radar to keep them from catching him coming in to land the troops.

RET. LT. COL. ALEXANDER JEFFERSON, U.S.A.F.: I was tailing Charlie on my target, which meant I was on the last plane. We shot up radar stations. As I went across the target at about fifty feet, I heard this big BOOM! A hole came up through the floor, and when I looked up, there was a hole atop the canopy. I surmised afterward a gunshell came up and exploded, so I pulled up in a half-loop and fire came up, and I bailed out at about eight hundred feet. My buddies, all fifteen, went ahead of me. They saw the airplane go in, but they didn't see me get out of it. (A KIA was sent home to my mother.) I remember seeing the tail go by. I pulled the ripcord. I pulled it out and looked at it; and just at that time she opened, and I hit the ground. Intelligence had told us to roll over, dig a hole, and hide your chute and get to the free French, because this was southern France. I hit the ground and rolled over, and I looked up, and a German said, "Ya." I landed in the middle of the guys who shot me down. They treated me with all the respect of an officer.

RICHARD D. MACON: Mine was in Montpellier. My target was there. The strategy was to fly over the target at a high altitude, and then after you got far enough inland so that the mountains half-blurred you out, we were supposed to drop down so that the radar couldn't pick you up, and then come in and jump over the mountains. It looked good on paper.

I was one of the spares that day. They have sixteen planes in a squadron and two spares. When you get ready to do some maneuvers, you have to get rid of the external tanks, because the plane does not maneuver with those tanks on. You just pull a lever; and that releases the catch, and they fall off. Sometimes they don't fall right off, and you have to shake it a little bit to make it fall off. This guy didn't know how to do it, so I was trying to help him so we could hurry up and hit the target. We came in over the target a little later than the rest of them did.

Usually what they did was have the guns shooting up, not at any target, but just shooting out here like a spray of water. If you fly through water, you get wet. If you fly through the bullets, some of them will hit you. Nobody is shooting at you particularly. Joe had a direct hit, and his plane blew up. BOOM! I knew there was nothing left of him.

228

But at the same time there were holes I saw in my wing. I knew I had been hit. I tried to maneuver away, and the plane wouldn't maneuver away, and then I knew that my controls had been shot out. The plane flipped over upside down, and I was headed straight for the ground. I knew I was a dead duck. So having nothing else to do, I went through the procedures they taught us to go through in emergencies. Get off the oxygen mask and release your safety belt, and dump yourself out. I knew I couldn't do any of that, but you might as well do something and not go down like this. Then everything went red. I "redded out."

When you're going down . . . everything is going in the same direction. When the plane goes up . . . your body has a tendency, according to Newton's law, to keep going straight. That means that your body is stuck to the plane, and it keeps going up with the plane, but your blood isn't. Blood keeps going down until it hits rock bottom. That means that all the blood drains out of your head and you can't see anything. That's called blacking out. If it is upside down and you're going down, the same thing happens but in reverse. Then all the blood keeps going down toward your head, and all that blood in your head makes you see red, and you can't stand but just so much of that before your eyes start popping out more, or you're bleeding from the head and it kills you.

I tell people my eyes popped out. They didn't, but I was happy that the weakest vessels in my head were in my eyes, because if they had been in my head, I would have been dead. I regained consciousness about forty-five minutes later. I tried to get up and get rid of my parachute. I didn't know that my neck was broken and my shoulder was broken. It was then that I saw these legs, three sets of them very close to me. When I looked up, these Germans were saying, "Ya, ya, heraus mit sie" telling me to get up, I guess. I tried to get up, and they saw that I couldn't, and they helped me up. I was paralyzed from the waist down. They dragged me to the car and took me to one of the field hospitals. That's where they reset my shoulder.

We had heard all of the things about the tortures that the Germans do, and that included castration. They had shown us instances where they had done that, and I knew this was going to happen to me at the time. As soon as I got there, and they put the pad on my nose, I was fighting, saying, "No, no, no!" When I regained consciousness the first thing I did was check to see if I was all still there. I was surprised to find out they hadn't done it yet. But I knew they were going to do it sooner or later.

My plane had crashed into a farmhouse they had commandeered for a headquarters. It had exploded with the airplane and killed some German soldiers. They were bitter about that. They had come to shoot me to avenge for their death. The next morning they took me to a farmhouse. They took me over the stone wall so they could shoot me. They wanted to do it in style so the men could see it. Now I didn't have to worry about all these torture things they were going to do to me. They were going to kill me. I was going to die anyway, so this would speed it up. They finally got me propped up there on the wall so they could do their thing. They put some blindfolds on me, and then I heard soldiers coming out. I could imagine that they were counting cadence, and then they stopped, and you could hear them make a right-face. An order was given, and they put one in the chamber. Click. Click. You could hear all this. Another order was given, and I figured that was aim. Then this big gate opened. Someone yelled "ACHTUNG." I heard a voice say, "Lieutenant Macon," so I figured he was looking for me. Then somebody came and took the blindfolds off. This officer, who was a Captain Hauttman, took me out and told me that he was taking me to Frankfurt because they wanted to interrogate me to find out what was going on. That saved my life.

They took me over to the bottom of the Rhine Valley. It's the last stop coming down the Rhine before you get to the channel. In this barn they have a round manger where they feed the animals. They put some straw in there and put me in there. About two o'clock that morning I'm finally getting comfortable. I heard somebody messing with the lock. They got around me and held a light on me like this. I couldn't see anything past the light. Somebody on the other side of the light said, "It's a spook." (This is our own private joke. We call each other spooks because the Germans said they couldn't see us at night.) Somebody said, "It's a spook," and I knew they were friends. It was this dude here.

RET. LT. COL. ALEXANDER JEFFERSON, U.S.A.F.: That's how I found him. I landed right in the middle of the guys who shot me down. They took me immediately to the officer who was in charge of the coast artillery. They took me about two or three miles down the beach to a little house sitting right on the water. Out on the porch was a glass table, and sitting at the table was a German officer. I saluted, and he said in perfect English, "Have a seat, lieutenant." I was scared. I sat down. The porch went right down about one hundred yards to the ocean. Beautiful white sand. He said, "Have a cigarette." My own cigarettes, by the way. The first thing they did was take your cigarettes, and take your watch and your Parker fountain pen, and your eyeglasses. We had Ray-Bans. It turns out the guy was a German who had gone to the United States to the University of Michigan for a doctorate in political science and had gone back to Germany, and they put him in the Army. He asked if I'd been to Washington. I went to Howard University, but quite naturally I said no. He described Washington, the black area, Howard University, the night clubs, the crystal caverns.

"You ever been to Detroit?" He described the Valley—the Three 666 nightclub on Adams Street, the little joint across the street where the girls were. He described how to get the Oakman streetcar downtown around the library, how it would turn and go north on Hastings. He described Sunnie Wilson's bar. He described the hotels on John R, the Gotham. He had been there.

That's the night I met Macon, where we saw him at two o'clock in the morning in the straw. From there we were taken up the Rhone Valley to Wexlar, Germany for interrogation.

RICHARD D. MACON: We went by wagon with hay on the top. They didn't know my neck was broken. They just knew I was blacking out every time I moved my head. When we finally got to Frankfurt three or four days later, they thought my neck muscles were hurt so they put a mustard plaster on. I didn't get any attention for the broken neck until more than a month later. Somebody was always with me, so if my head moved, they would catch me if I blacked out. I had to walk very carefully.

One of the POWs had been in medical school. He said: "Dick, something else is wrong with your neck besides strained muscles. I'm going to see if I can get them to do something about that." Two or three days later they arranged for me to go to a hospital. When the Germans pulled out of France, they commandeered this hospital and brought the whole staff as prisoners to staff the hospital for prisoners of war. These were French prisoners, but they were almost a complete staff. They didn't have any x-rays. The Germans finally gave them one x-ray film. They said, "That's it. If it doesn't work, that's all we have."

There was a little break, and four vertebrae were crumbled up in a lot of little pieces. They put me in traction for about twenty-four hours. They took the straw off the bunk, and then the bunk was just wood. I had to lay on the wood with my head over the edge. One of the French boys went and stole two bricks out of the hospital wall, and they made a strap and tied it under my chin to hold my head back, and I was like that for about thirty hours. By this time I knew I was among friends. We could talk, and we kidded each other a little bit. It wasn't too bad.

RET. LT. COL. ALEXANDER JEFFERSON, U.S.A.F.: They knew more about us than we knew about ourselves. They had a large book, about two feet long and a foot wide. Across the front it said "332nd Fighter Group, Negroes, Red Tails." When the guy opened it up, he thumbed through all the pages and finally stopped. He said, "Lieutenant, isn't that you?" It was my class picture. They knew your father's social security number, how much money he made, how much he paid in taxes on his house, where he went to high school.

RICHARD D. MACON: I got married just before I went overseas. This guy showed me the picture that was in the newspaper of me and my wife.

RET. LT. COL. ALEXANDER JEFFERSON, U.S.A.F.: They were all listed—all the generals, the colonels, the lieutenant colonels, the majors, the captains, all the enlisted personnel.

I enjoyed sitting there because I hadn't had a cigarette in three, four, five, six days.

RICHARD D. MACON: When they interrogated me, we were at the same place the second time. It was in Frankfurt, and we were separated then. I was in a cell all by myself with only one little window which was too high for me to escape. The morning of my interrogation the guard had come around serving breakfast. Breakfast was a slice of black bread with some ersatz margarine. It was white. It wasn't yellow like butter at all. You spread it on that black bread. That was my breakfast. I didn't want to put it down because in my particular cell I had a stone bed and no bedclothes, just a stone bed and a blanket. The other animals—body lice, fleas—they were all over what was there, including me. You learned how to deal with them. But I didn't want them to eat my bread.

Before I could eat, another guy opened the door and said, "Come with me!"

I said, "I haven't eaten my breakfast yet." But he didn't understand what I was saying. He took me down for interrogation, and I had a piece of bread in my hand.

The lieutenant who was in charge down there said, "Lieutenant, are you coming down here for an interview and you're going to bring food to eat?" I was embarrassed. I said I didn't want to leave it back in the room. He said, "Let me get a piece of paper so that you can put it down over here." He was condescending, trying to make me feel bad. But I didn't want him to bother my piece of bread, because it was all I had to eat that day.

There were two German SS men in the room. He sat at the desk, and I sat like I was being interviewed for a job, facing him. He asked me all these questions, but it was just like Jefferson said. I knew absolutely nothing.

He said, "We are not trying to get information from you. We are just trying to make sure that you are not an imposter. We don't want to send somebody else to camp for officers. I'll give you one last chance. You had a code name when you were flying that nobody knew. If I give you half of that name and you can supply the other half, then I'll know you are Lieutenant Macon." He looked me right in the eye, and he said, "Sub." My name was "Subsoil Sixteen."

I said, "soil."

He said, "That's right. You were 'Subsoil Sixteen.' " That ended my interview.

RET. LT. COL. ALEXANDER JEFFERSON, U.S.A.F.: We both ended up at Stalag 3, eighty miles east of Berlin.

RICHARD D. MACON: We were on the same train.

RET. LT. COL. ALEXANDER JEFFERSON, U.S.A.F.: So all in all we spent nine months in Germany.

BIOGRAPHIES

Ret. Lt. Colonel Alexander Jefferson, U.S.A.F., was born on November 15, 1921, in Detroit. He is a graduate of Chadsey High School and earned a B.S. from Clark College in Atlanta, Georgia. In 1942 he joined the Air Force and served with the 15th Air Force, 332nd Fighter Group in Italy. His awards include Air Medal, A.F. Achievement Medal, A.F. Presidential Unit Citation Medal, American Defense Service Medal, European-African-Middle Eastern Campaign Medal, American Campaign Medal, Prisoner of War Medal, World War II Victory Medal, Armed Forces Reserve Medal, National Defense Service Medal. He retired from the Air Force Reserves in 1969 and from his position as assistant principal with the Detroit Board of Education in 1979. He is a founder of the Detroit Chapter of the Tuskegee Airmen. He is a life member of the Silver Falcons Association and serves as an Admissions Counselor for the U.S.A.F. Academy and U.S.A.F. ROTC.

Richard D. Macon was born on August 21, 1921 in Birmingham, Alabama. After completing studies at Miles College in 1942, he volunteered for pilot training. While a Tuskegee Airman he served as a P-51 pilot with the 99th Fighter Squadron in Ramitelli, Italy. After discharge he organized a flying school in Birmingham, Alabama. He then earned advanced degrees in mathematics at Indiana University and taught at Miles College in Birmingham and Southern University in Louisiana. He was a teacher and administrator in the Detroit Public Schools from 1954 to 1989. Mr. Macon is a founder of the National Tuskegee Airmen. He is vice president of the National Museum and vice president of the Detroit Chapter, Tuskegee Airmen. He belongs to the Military Order of the Purple Heart, American Former Prisoners of War at Stalag Luft III, Veterans of Foreign Wars, and Disabled American Veterans.

Herschel L. Richey has been active in the Virginia Park community for many years. He has served as president and chairman of the board of the Virginia Park Community Investment Associates.

HERSCHEL L. RICHEY *

I am an American, too—despite the fact that my skin is dark, despite the fact that my forefathers were slaves who came over in chains sweltering in the stifling, musty hold of some ship.

Out of the hate of bondage; out of the bravest acts and words of my people of past generations; out of the necessities of a new and competing world; out of the desire for freedom, security, peace and tolerance I have tried to create and adjust my life.

In my struggle with the intolerance inflicted upon my people, out of my griefs, out of my sins, I have laid by a great store of memories. They are a part of my being—no mere gushing of words can tell of them. They are too deeply hidden for words.

I have read of many great men of my race and of many great deeds. But I also know of many great men and of many great deeds unsung and unrecorded. . . . .

I remember the black sharecropper kissing his wife and babies as he comes in from his fields, fields so vital, for producing the needs of all mankind, black and white, in peace time as well as in war time.

*"I Am an American Too," excerpted from *Racial Digest*. Detroit: Community Publishing Company, May–June 1943, pp. 21–23.

I remember the tired and grimy factory worker falling asleep on the streetcar as he rides home from his work, work that is so essential to the maintaining of American industries in peace time and war.

I remember the young black youth in Mississippi or Michigan kissing his gray-haired mother good-bye as he goes to enlist for the purpose of preserving the American way of life.

I remember the same mother grief stricken and tearful as they bring her son home, his body torn and mangled, not the victim of the Japanese marauder, not the victim of the German storm trooper, but the victim of a bestial, blood thirsty malignant southern, American mob.

I remember a raving, fanatical mob, not in the South, but in Michigan, the heart of the American war industry, abetted by biased policemen, trying to prevent Negroes from moving into homes built for them, homes which were to house them while they labored to produce materials for the protection of all American mankind.

I remember the worker in the street making a song as he plies his drill or electric hammer to the pavement while the steam of black tar floats up and fills my nostrils.

I remember black mothers bending over hot, steaming washtubs, slaving, sacrificing in order to make life easier for their children.

All manner of men and women, planning, working and saving in order to give their children a better schooling than they had received. Reformers crying out against police brutality, against high rents, against discrimination in industry, against segregation in the navy and army, against inequalities in our school system; dreamers battling against the full tide of materialism.

I remember all these things and many more. They help to steady me when I lie awake at night or when I walk the streets in the dark nights of injustice and violence that have come over my people. I stand up straight when I walk. These are my people who have suffered but whose spirit has not been broken. Because they are Americans, too, and have faith in this land. They are of one race and of all races. They are free yet bound to the wheel of intolerance.

I turn and look at the faces around me, the black faces and the white faces. Are they not all my people? Are they not all Americans? Have they forgotten so soon the great principles laid down in the Declaration of Independence—"We hold these truths to be self-evident, that all men are created equal, that they are endowed by their Creator with certain inalienable Rights, that among these are Life, Liberty and the pursuit of Happiness."

Have we advanced so far, accomplished so much, suffered so much, hoped for so much, all in vain? Is this new civilization to become an old civilization, where man has no regard for another man's life, liberty or happiness?

Have all our brave deeds and acts been in vain? Shall men remain civilized, justful and intolerant for so short a time? Is freedom a lie? Is brotherhood of man a lie?

What was won by courage and bravery must be retained by courage and bravery. Neither can I rest on my memories. I must make new memories for my children and my children's children.

However, through it all I can see a vision. Over vast prairies, beyond highest mountain tops and across the great ocean expanses, I see white men fighting side by side with me, in the air, on the seas, on the land, fighting for liberty and freedom, for they have realized at last that I am an American, too.

BIOGRAPHY

Herschel L. Richey was born on July 18, 1905, in Columbus, Indiana, and moved to Detroit in 1926. He attended Indiana University. He worked for the U. S. Post Office for thirty years and was president of the National Alliance of Postal Employees. He fought to see that black clerks had the opportunity to enter all areas of the postal service. He has been active in the Virginia Park community for many years, serving as president of the Hutchins School PTA, participating in Citizens for Better Schools, the Citizens District Council, and the Virginia Park Community Investment Associates.

Earl F. Van Dyke was a great jazz musician whose imprint can be found on virtually all Detroit Motown productions.

DISCUSSION ON LIFE AND MUSIC
THOMAS H. "DR. BEANS" BOWLES, SR., AND EARL F. VAN DYKE

THOMAS H. "DR. BEANS" BOWLES, SR.: Sometimes by the time you get to what you want to do, you've been filtered down so much, usually you're too old. You don't have that kind of energy anymore. So you have a new thing, and you do the best that you can with what you've got, and you keep working, and you're leaning toward everything that you want to do. I guess it's called the wisdom because it filters down, and you come out with something that's probably more compatible.

But after you get to a certain level, after you see that you've reached a level and find out that you haven't done anything; and then you keep striving or you quit. You're at the twilight of your mediocre career, and you still don't know anything. I had dreams of retiring at thirty-five, retiring from making money and just being a recluse and playing music.

I was drafted in 1943. I was in Great Lakes for boot training, and I don't guess I was the best sailor. Every time they got ready to send me to another duty station, I'd go off AWOL. They gave me a chance to come home, and I never did come back in time. The guy finally told me, "If you don't come back in time this time you're going straight to the Pacific." This was in the '40s and the war had started.

I was being taught to be a sonar operator. The reason I got into sonar was, being a musician, I had pitch. I could listen and tell which way the pitch was. Sonar is the underwater detection of submarines, and they used the same thing as the antenna for radar. The same thing underwater is sonar. They send out the sound, and when it comes back, if it's higher the object is coming toward you. If it's lower, it's going away. You have these controls where you can measure the size of an object, and you can tell which way it's going—if it's in a turn, how fast it's going. That was the first cathode ray tube; that's the first time I had seen that. They had television, they said then, but I didn't know anything about that. That's where I went to school.

In fact, I was one of the first enlisted blacks in anything other than the mess boys or steward's mate. Every pilot or every officer had a steward's mate to make up his bed; he was a slave. In the Navy, he had a steward's mate to take care of his things. He made his bed, took care of his clothes, polished his shoes, brought him his food. This was for every commissioned officer. Some of them had several. So when I went to the Navy, I didn't want that. You either became a cook, a baker, or a steward's mate.

When I got there, they had a little window with a hole in it that big; and I stuck my papers under there and bang, bang, it had Navy all over it. I said, "No, No, man, I can't go to the Navy." I pushed them back and the guy just kicked me in the buns and said move on. So I was in the Navy.

We had a hard time in the Navy because we were the first group that had a chance to do anything else besides those three offices. We weren't integrated. Then Joe Louis donated the proceeds from a fight. It was over a million dollars. Then somebody else had something to do with it, put in some kind of legislation to allow us to do other things. You had a black chief petty officer. You had a warrant officer, and you had doctors. Those were the only black officers you had in the Navy. Then after this, everything started to happen. Before I got out of the war which was, less than two years, they had a captain, they had a command, he had a couple of ships. I was a seaman. You couldn't even be a seaman. You had the rank of seaman first class, but you were still a steward's mate. They also had musicians, and it was a very select group to get into the music thing.

In the sonar class there were ten of us, and I was pretty good, so I graduated at the top of the class. We had a chance to practice in the night. At that time the "Wolfpack" was out there from Germany the "U-Boat Wolfpack." They were patrolling that area along the New Jersey coast, Cape May, Atlantic City but they were outside the two-hundred mile limit. We would go out maybe ten miles. There were also whales out there that we had runs on. I hit something. It was coming toward us. I was in a little sub chaser. I broke out in a cold sweat. The guy was over and he told me what to do. I was measuring the thing, and it was the size of a submarine. I had control of the ship, and he said, "You've got to make a run." I made the run and made two depth charges on the side. I killed the biggest whale you ever wanted to see!

When they got ready to ship me out, we were getting ready to leave, and I asked for my books, my notes. I didn't get my notes. They said:' "Don't worry about it, we're going to ship them to you the next day. This is classified information. The next place you'll have them. They'll be there when you get there." I have yet to see them, so they had no intention of me serving as a sonar operator. I couldn't operate without them.

EARL F. VAN DYKE: When I went in the service I was fortunate, because I got put right into the division band. We were only supposed to have so many men in the band, like thirty-eight. We had one hundred and eight men in that band. The band was so large, but it was all black because it was still discrimination. They used to send us out, break us up in like four bands. We were like the division band, and we would go out and play at parades.

I know where "Beans" is talking about jumping ship, I used to jump the ship every time. Our plan was, when the ship got into a port, we were trying to wait till we got to Manila or China before we would let them see us. They got John Bird and Dwight Mitchell in Guam. I heard them call my number. I never will forget that, because my number was two-six-two. I was on the ship hiding; I wouldn't come out. When they call your number you have to get off the ship. Guys were going to be stationed when their name was called. And the next stop was the Johnstons, so I hid. Somewhere I messed up. The next stop was Okinawa. How they found me, when it came time for Okinawa, they found me so I guess somebody told them.

In a transport there are a lot of places to hide; you'd be surprised how many floors they had up under them. They knew that people were hiding, but as long as they had the strength, a certain amount of men, if they called your number and you didn't answer, they'd call somebody else. They'd get you sooner or later. But they called me at Okinawa! Geez! I got dumped there.

When the war broke out, I never will forget, because across the street from me, there were two little girls who lived there and they were of German descent. Maybe it was 1942. We looked out one day and all these government vehicles were out in the street. My father was out there talking to the man that lived over there. They were kind of crying. When my father came back, I asked what was happening. He said, "The government is moving them out of the neighborhood because they are Germans, and we are at war with Germany." That's what was happening. Same thing with the Italians; they moved them out.

239

When I was about four years old my mother used to sing and play the piano. My father worked afternoons, and my mother wanted me to stay up with her. She would stay up late and practice, and I would come along and pick up tunes behind her. I would pick up the same notes. So one night she got me to stay up. She said, "I want you to play for your father what you just played for me."

So I said, "Okay," and I stayed up.

Right away, he came over and closed the piano down. He told my mother: "Mary, we don't want him to learn how to play by ear. We want him to learn how to play correctly, to learn how to read his music." So he took me and found me a tutor, and that's when I started, in 1935.

By 1943 they used to have amateur shows in the Paradise Theater, and I won the first prize there. There was a man named Rollo Vest who was the booking agent. He was the one who had the amateur shows. At the time I was in there, Lionel Hampton was in there with his band, and that's how I more or less got a break. I was about fourteen. From then on I started playing around town with the local bands until I went to service. When I went to service I finished my education.

THOMAS H. "DR. BEANS" BOWLES, SR.: When I got to Detroit in 1940, I was a real country boy. I didn't know anything. They used to pick on me. I had real funny, country-style clothes and like the haircuts the guys got today, that's what I was wearing. The guys pay twenty-five or thirty dollars to get it today, and mamma used to give it to me with a bowl. That's why I laugh at them. I used to say to mama, "Please let me go to the barber shop. Please don't cut my hair." They didn't have electric clippers. They used those hand clippers, and you got to cut them before you pull them up and they never did. OUCH!!!

As a child I played the clarinet. I was a horrible musician. Living in Indiana and being the best guy in the city, in the black community I should say, you thought you could play well until I got here. My teacher was a violin teacher who read the book the day before I got there and then would teach me what he read. He knew music but he didn't know anything about the instrument. He could teach me enough so that I could play with a group and look good with the community. Fifty cents for a lesson. He was a violin teacher, and I was learning the clarinet.

Earl and I bumped into each other all those years. We really met in 1961. I worked at the Flame for six years as a saxophone player. I raised my family at the Flame. I had two boys while I was there. "Maurice King and the Wolverines." I can't get it together, but I know I went from Sunnie Wilson's to the Flame. Sunnie still is mad at me about that, because we had a thing going over there with Yusef and a Barry Horten from New York who played the piano, Mack McCrary. It was the "McCrary Allstars," that was the name of the band. It was his band

240

and he hired me. Either Candy or Yusef and me. Dagwood was the drummer. I don't think we had a trumpet.

EARL F. VAN DYKE: One of the first jobs when I came home, we were working at a club out on Mack called the J & B Bar. We got twelve dollars and fifty cents a night to split between us. We ended up with two dollars and fifty cents apiece.

THOMAS H. "DR. BEANS" BOWLES, SR.: We didn't teach in those days. Seven dollars a night was a lot of money compared to what other people were getting. You could buy a loaf of bread for a nickel. I got two cigarettes for a penny.

EARL F.VAN DYKE: We used to go up to Silvercup and get two loaves of day-old bread for a nickel.

In Black Bottom there was quite a bit going on, because when I came back home, over there on Adams where they had Paradise Valley, Paradise Bowl, Three 666, 606, Stan's, Turf, the El Sino, and that hotel, the Avalon was across the street from the bowling alley. Stutz had his office in there. Then down here they had Henry's Swing Club. They had a lot of acts in there. Then that one place called the Long Bar. There was a club on Hancock and Hastings.

We used to always meet up on the corner at Canfield and John R. There was a guy down there, Mr. Kennedy, who used to sell hot sausages, tamales, outside on the corner. We used to stand out there and talk. All the musicians used to stand out there and meet and talk all night about our gigs. Right now it's a parking lot for the medical center. That's where we'd always meet up to swap gigs or whatever.

THOMAS H. "DR. BEANS" BOWLES, SR.: We'd talk lies, and when it got to be early in the morning we'd go over to Maxie's and eat some "cat heads" and biscuits. Maxie's was a barbecue place. Shorty Long was working in there. A one-man act playing drums.

The ambience of the '50s was the greatest thing in my life as far as music is concerned, because we had brotherhood, we had respect. Didn't make much money. You never make a lot of money in this business unless you get to be that one person out of a million that goes to the top. You get a chance to build your confidence. You live a good life. You enjoy your life, and there's places for you to work. Now there's no place to work. There's no place for a young musician to even hone his wares so that he's competent. We used to go to the West End. They used to come to my house on a Friday night.

At the Flame we had a battle of the bands. Maurice King the house band, Billy Gohlson was playing with the alto player, Earl Bostic, and Bill Doggett. Three bands. Friday, Saturday, and Sunday I'd have a jam session at my house. That started after we got off work. We'd play from Friday until Sunday night or Monday. We used to bring a "Texas Fifth" in; everybody would drink, and then my wife would fix pies and cakes and food. Those were good times. We developed our music.

EARL F. VAN DYKE: I'll tell you what really happened. At the time Detroit was like a mecca for good musicians. And I never will forget, when I first came home from the service, Jackie Gleason came here, and he raped the city of good white musicians. He picked up his musicians very easily. Then you had people like Duke Ellington, Count Basie, Andy Kirk; everybody was coming through here taking musicians out of here. By 1955 everybody was gone.

In order to protect jobs for a select few, they created a union and made it difficult for you to get in it. Most of the musicians didn't have enough money to pay the initiation fee. The guys would come in and take you off the band staff. You were blackballed. If you played good enough, then they'd let you come in, but you had to play at certain places then. You didn't really make that much money.

The other thing was the way the big bands came here and took the musicians. We were working with Lloyd Price, and Ray Charles had a seven- or eight-piece band. It happened one time that we were on the same show. Ray was a hot item. He was really the star. That was in Atlanta, Georgia, and James Brown was there, too. We played the show. Ray was the hot item, but we had the smoking band. We burned them up. I never will forget that. The manager came around to the hotel and was trying to hire guys out of Lloyd's band. He wasn't successful in Atlanta. When we come back to New York, soon as the bus pulled up to the hotel, who's standing out there but Ray's manager, and he was offering guys money, so that started breaking that band up. That's how Ray formed his large band. Lionel Hampton, same thing.

THOMAS H. "DR. BEANS" BOWLES, SR.: When we first started going out with Lloyd's band, they would have a white dance and the black dance. The white ones would come in first, and the blacks would come in later, and we would play the longest part for them. Then they got to having black and white, and they'd have a string down the middle of the floor; and the white guy would stand there with the flashlight, don't let nobody cross that string. We got to swinging one night and the string broke, and it was over.

EARL F. VAN DYKE: I was working with Chris Columbo and Jackie Wilson, and we'd come into town and we were lost. Chris always said, if you were lost, the best thing to do was go to the police station. We went to the police station and the sheriff told us, Chris talked to him, he said, "Oh yeah, you going to do that dance down there with Jackie Wilson." We said, yes, and he told us where to go and everything. He told us he was coming to the dance.

Chris said, "Great, we'll play a selection for you." He said okay. Number one was, when we got to where we were having the dance, it was a great big tobacco barn. Nobody was in there. We went in, and they had this little stage set up. Chris went around there and said, "Who's the manager, and where's the so-and-so."

The guy came out and said, "I'm the manager, and you set up right there boy."

He said, "Who are we going to play for?"

He said, "You just set up. They'll be here."

After we set up, maybe about half an hour or forty-five minutes, these great big doors to the tobacco barn opened up. These six-by-sixes came in loaded with black people on the back. Trucks, six-by-sixes, eighteen-wheelers. They had them loaded up in the back. Everybody was standing up. I don't know how many there were; I'll just say six. They made them get off and lined up next to the trucks. The white man said: "I will be back at 11:00 P.M. to pick you all up. I want you all to be lined up here ready to go." We looked at one another, because we're not used to no shit like that. Our contract had said from like 9:00 P.M. until 1:00 A.M.

Chris panicked. He run to the manager and said, "Our contract says from 9:00 P.M. until 1:00 A.M."

He said, "Boy, you just play until we tell you to stop."

Chris said: "Okay." and said, "It looks like we'll get away early." At 10:30 P.M. he told us to stop. We stopped, and everybody started getting in this line for the trucks. They opened up the doors and the trucks came.

Now the sheriff hadn't come yet. He comes in with the trucks. When they loaded up the trucks and everybody was pulling out, he told us, "Now I want to hear that damn song." Ain't nobody in there but us and this here sheriff, and we had to play this damn song. He had gotten violent.

Chris said: "The job is over. We have to go to the next town."

He said, "Not before you play this tune." The tune was "Your Cheating Heart."

When ["Beans"] was talking about how they put the ropes down with the white on one side and the black on the other side: Jackie Wilson had a bad habit of jumping off the stage. What happened was, they had told him, "Don't jump off the stage."

He said, "Okay."

We were playing a place like the Joe Louis Arena where they played hockey games where they put the floor on top. The floor started sweating. Jackie jumped off the stage and started sliding. I'll never forget. Chris said, "Oh my God." There was a little white girl sitting right up here. He slid right up to where the girl was. He looked up and he saw her, but he just kept on singing. It was all right until she put her hands on his head. She got to feel his head. She was laughing.

The police came from everywhere and said, "The concert is over." We stopped playing, and they just got so aggravated because the response was not fast enough so they started whopping our ass. That was in New Orleans in 1959. We come out and we went sixty miles the wrong way, just trying to get out of town.

We just got paid. We had a pocket full of money, and we were hungry. We couldn't find a place to eat, and we stopped on the road. Chuck Berry said, "I'll go in here and ask them," because white people in the south loved Chuck.

The guy said, "Yeah, we'll feed them." He brought us in and paraded us through the restaurant in the back with the garbage cans and told us we had to eat back there.

THOMAS H. "DR. BEANS" BOWLES, SR.: I remember Mobile because I never wanted to go back there no more in life. We played on the pier. It was like an island across the bridge, and you get to this place where we had to play. Me and Sam walked back across the bridge and went to a little restaurant. We walked in, and the first thing the guy said, "We don't serve no niggers in here." I was smoking, man! This guy was a bum, a white man, who came up to me and asked me for some money to get something to eat.

I went off. I said, "Man you got a chance to be president of the United States." I pulled out my money and said: "Just look at that. You know I just went in there, and I couldn't get nothing to eat, and you go beg me for something to eat. Man, you better get out of my face." I put the money back in my pocket. He looked at me and looked at the place. We didn't have nothing but peanuts and candy. They didn't even have any hot dogs we could eat out there.

EARL F. VAN DYKE: Remember when we were playing with Lloyd and we pulled the bus up? We stopped to get some gas, and all the white people started coming up and standing in the doorways with shot guns and shit. All we were doing was, the bus driver stopped to get some gas. They came out and stood in the doors. When the man stopped the bus, we all jumped off the bus to stretch your legs, go to the john. When the people saw us come off the bus, the rifles and shotguns and things came out. We said, "Oh, oh!"

BIOGRAPHIES

Thomas H. "Dr. Beans" Bowles, Sr., was born on May 7, 1926, and moved to Detroit in 1944. He is a professional musician and has performed for audiences around the country. He is a thirty-second degree Mason; a member of Kappa Alpha Psi Alumni; a board member of the Detroit Council of the Arts and Graystone International Jazz Museum; a member of Jazz Alliance of Michigan; Imperial Deputy of Music, Imperial Council of Shrine, Prince Hall Affiliate. He is owner of the Three Bee's Production Company and Har-Den Music Company.

Earl F. Van Dyke was born on July 8, 1930, in Detroit. He was taking music lessons by age five and began earning money as a musician at age fourteen. He was a studio musician for Motown and played for many artists, such as Stevie Wonder, Aretha Franklin, and others. In the 1970s he began teaching music at Osborn High School, and he retired in 1991. Throughout his adult life he performed in clubs in Detroit and across the country. He died on September 19, 1992.

Frances Quock's mother was strict and would not allow
her daughter to date men who lived in the boarding house she ran.

FRANCES QUOCK

Going to the Graystone Ballroom in the late '40s was a wonderful thing. We would get all dressed up. This particular night Duke Ellington was playing, and no one would dance with me, so I was standing there as a wallflower.

I became very insulted, and I said, I'm going to go up to Duke Ellington and ask for his autograph. Instead of giving me an autograph he gave me a telephone number where there was going to be a party. My mother said: "Don't go with musicians. They're bad."

I'm sorry I didn't. I was invited to go to the J Hop at the University of Michigan. They were playing there. But what I learned from that was that Duke Ellington speaking with me and talking to me made me feel that I was such a wonderful woman, and that changed me, giving me a lot of self-esteem.

Every time that he would come to Detroit, he and Al Hibbler, they would call me up, and we would go out and have lunch. That is what I remember about my first visit to Detroit.

BIOGRAPHY

Frances Quock was born on September 25, 1922, and moved to Detroit in December 1945. She first worked as a cosmetologist. At the age of fifty-three she enrolled at Marygrove College and received a degree in gerontology in 1978. Continuing her education at Wayne State University, she earned a B.A. degree in sociology in 1981 and is currently a candidate for the master's program. She is recipient of awards from the National Political Congress of Black Women and was on the board of directors from 1985–90. She is married to Tom Quock and is mother to Andre Bowman, Tom Quock, and Kim Young Quock.

*Roberta McGuire Pickett,
Ph.D., was co-founder of both
the Detroit chapter of the
National Council of Negro
Women and the first
international chapter of Delta
Sigma Theta.*

DISCUSSION WITH MEMBERS OF DELTA SIGMA THETA SORORITY

JERRYLEE JOHNSON,
CECIL WHITTAKER McFADDEN,
ROBERTA McGUIRE PICKETT, Ph.D.,
CAROL A. SAYERS PURYEAR, Ph.D., AND
ROSE MARIE DICKENS SWANSON

CECIL WHITTAKER McFADDEN: When I became president, I was elected in '41 and served on the the planning committee for the convention, but actually took office in January the following year of '42. Those were the war years. And we started doing things that were very important to the war. We contributed money to the USO to entertain soldiers and sent gifts to soldiers so they would get things at Christmas and on holidays.

We also gave scholarships to other young women. We gave a play, or it was a series of acts and plays, to raise money called the "Jabberwock," taken from the word in *Alice in Wonderland*. And all these different clubs would participate and compete. The "Jabberwock" raised money to give scholarships to high school students and girls who wanted to go to college.

Then the war years had sororities doing even more things. I looked to the presidents coming behind me to deal with the Delta Home for Girls and things like that. So the graduate chapter was engaged in civic responsibility. Sometimes it was difficult during the war years because you had to contend with gas shortages, being rationed, and had to go to meetings and double-up in cars and things. You had to deal with the

248

blackouts. If you met at someone's house you had to draw the drapes. We still carried on the services of a community organization. We considered ourselves as leaders in the community, setting the tone.

The opportunities for black women college graduates were limited, but we did have social workers. We had nurses. We had a lot of teachers, because that was one of the opportunities.

They discouraged you in school from taking anything that they felt you could not get a job as. There were many jobs because I remember. . . . I was a business administration major. And I tried to get a job at Hudson's in the office, in advertising, and was told very bluntly the only openings were either a maid in the lavatories or elevator operator, which I thought was an insult to somebody with a college degree because of the color of their skin. We all had that problem.

CAROL A. SAYERS PURYEAR, Ph.D.: We started off with twenty-two founders and one chapter. We now have eight hundred chapters. We are international and have 185,000 women. In Detroit we have approximately sixteen hundred with a financial roster of about seven hundred. So that tells you how we have grown.

JERRYLEE JOHNSON: Of course, I was one of the first ones when they had us all drive out for voter registration. I came here and registered because they asked us to register at the Urban League.

We worked in the rain. We drove people to the polls; we picked them up and took them back and forth. We had our cars and we furnished them to drive to the polls, and we babysat for the mothers so they could vote. That was one of the things we did. We didn't worry about it.

I have been chairman of "Jabberwock" and worked with it for many years. When we had our golden anniversary celebration in Washington, I was one of the persons who did attend. And we had an audience with President Kennedy, Lyndon Johnson, and Lady Bird.

We had a luncheon where President John Kennedy spoke, and they said, "No one touches him," as he went out. I just stuck my hand through the crowd, and he shook my hand.

CECIL WHITTAKER McFADDEN: We had many fund-raisers trying to raise enough money to get the down payment and also furnishings for the Delta Home for Girls. And someone came up with the idea of having a poker party.

It was supposed to be people that you knew and what they contributed was to go to the home. You served food and drinks that were complimentary. It was at a very prominent lawyer's home. And someone, we suspected it was someone who was having some problems with someone else, had tipped off the police that there was going to be an illegal gambling session. And plainclothesmen entered. And the people on the door assumed that they were guests because they were in plainclothes.

I remember I was busy playing cards and gambling. The pot was in the middle. And they positioned themselves, one behind each table. And all of a sudden they said: "Freeze! This is a raid!" And they reached for the money. And insensibly I reached for my money; nobody was supposed to grab my money. When they said, "This is a raid," I backed off. And they started taking names and said they were going to call for the patrol wagon.

And the attorney whose home it was in said: "No. This is a private home. There's no law being broken here. The people can't go down."

But the thing that really saved us, one of the plainclothesmen had attempted to buy a drink at the bar. And the person behind the bar said: "We're not selling any drinks. This is a private party, and if you'd like a drink you can have one, or if you'd like some food, here's some food." Now if we had been selling it, it would have really gone hard, selling the liquor unauthorized, after hours, without a license. But we did not sell any liquor. So some people were very upset when they started taking names, because they could just see the headlines, "Delta hit!"

I thought I saw God. I'm going downtown in the patrol wagon. But the lawyer, whose home it was in, convinced them that they did not have a case. So, they said, "Well, okay, we won't take you down; but everybody go on home."

He [the lawyer] said: "No. They don't have to go home. This is a private home, these are my guests, and will stay." So, they left, and the party continued.

But I remember a couple of people, who shall remain nameless, went upstairs. They refused to play any more cards because it made them kind of nervous, and they had lost. And as the party went on, I don't know how much we made, but we did make some. That was for the Delta Home.

ROBERTA McGUIRE PICKETT, Ph.D.: Another project that we had to raise money for the Delta Home was having "chitlin" dinners. We sold "chitlin" dinners and sweet potato pies and made quite a lot of money.

ROSE MARIE DICKENS SWANSON: I'd like to mention my undergraduate activities. I remember the sorority as a base, a hub of the black social life on campus. It really provided that kind of platform for us, and I think it enabled us to grow as young people, mingling with others.

I believe it was 1956 when our sorority won first place in the Panhellenic Sing. And that was with all the groups, black and white, fraternities and sororities. We were putting together these makeshift outfits, and I remember that for costuming they gave us one-hundred-percent-plus. We were talking about Delta Chi, this very wealthy, white female sorority, and we said: "Oh, we know they're gonna be decked-out. They've got money, they've got this. . . ."

The sorors who were shorter were the little girls in this skit, so they made the pink pinafores and they wore the socks. Those who were tall, like myself, were like the college students, and then we had a high school group. And it was really something. We got a hundred-plus straight down for everything. We didn't win first again, but we placed for the rest of my college years. We placed in the Panhellenic Sing because we really did have good voices.

We had many public service projects we did as undergraduates. We serviced the Delta Home for Girls. I remember when we did the hygiene packs we gave out at Christmastime. We had parties for Children's Hospital, and we'd give food baskets for the needy.

JERRYLEE JOHNSON: I remember that we had a Delta Choir. We used to go to the hospitals and sing Christmas carols. We had many performances, and choral groups appearing at various churches.

BIOGRAPHIES

Jerrylee Johnson was born on September 21, 1910 in Natchitoches, Louisiana. She has lived in Detroit since 1932. Mrs. Johnson retired from teaching in 1977 and has devoted her energy to volunteer activities for several organizations, including the Michigan Cancer Foundation since the 1970s, Urban League Guild, United Negro College Fund, United Way, and YWCA.

Cecil Whittaker McFadden: See p. 147–48.

Dr. Roberta McGuire Pickett was born on August 14, 1916 in Detroit. She attended Fisk University and earned her doctorate degree in educational leadership from Wayne State University. She has been an elementary school teacher, principal, college instructor, and writer. With a scholarship from the NAACP and Detroit Round Table of Catholics, Protestants and Jews, she studied intercultural relations at Harvard University and developed a project for use in the schools. She co-founded the local chapter, National Council of Negro Women, and first international chapter Delta Sigma Theta Sorority. A straight "A" student she was awarded a graduate professional scholarship and fellowship to Wayne State University to complete studies for a doctorate in educational leadership. Dr. Pickett is a charter member and vice president of the Detroit Chapter of Top Ladies of Distinction. In 1980 she received the Spirit of Detroit Award.

Carol A. Sayers Puryear, Ph.D., was born on January 20, 1937, in Detroit. She is the daughter of Leon R. and Reber Lillian Sayers. She was educated in Detroit Public Schools and earned B.S. and M.Ed. from Wayne State University and a Ph.D. in curriculum instruction from the University of Michigan in 1985. A retired administrator of Detroit Public Schools, she is presently an instructor at Wayne State University. She has been a member of Delta Sigma Theta Sorority since 1956 and is past president of the Detroit alumnae chapter. She is active in many social and civic organizations. She married Hermon Puryear in 1959; her children are Kimberly Anne and Hermon Sayers.

Rose Marie Dickens Swanson was born on August 23, 1937, in Detroit. She attended Detroit schools and received degrees from Wayne State University, University of Detroit, and University of Michigan. A retired school administrator, Ms. Dickens Swanson is a college supervisor for Eastern Michigan University. She is past president of the Detroit alumnae chapter of Delta Sigma Theta Sorority and serves on the Delta National Executive Board as chair, Program Planning and Development Committee. She is a member of Metropolitan United Methodist Church.

AUSTIN W. CURTIS, D.S.C.

I think it becomes important to find out the problems that existed in terms of discrimination and the barriers that existed. What happened as far as black people coming to Detroit, leaving the South, and of course coming here and making more money than they'd ever made. At the same time they were not prepared for urban living, which compounded the problem. A city can be very cold. When I came here in 1945, there were the pockets where blacks could live. On the west side, just west of West Grand Boulevard, south of Tireman. Further west out to American, that was a pocket. There was the area between John R and Hastings. The other area was Conant Gardens.

There were things that you wouldn't think would prevail from a business standpoint. As one example, Avon would have separate sales meetings. The blacks couldn't meet with the whites. It was very interesting to me how they can talk about reverse discrimination and forget all about those things. All of these major companies now take the approach that there was no discrimination, now that they are recognizing that there are dollars available from the black community.

Black people tend to accept what whites say without any question. I guess that had been passed on through the generations. If you went

South, most blacks used just their initials, because the southern whites wanted to find out what your first name was so they could just call you by your first name. So you used your initials so that they couldn't find out what your first name was. That was true when I went to Tuskegee. They didn't want to call you Mister. Those are all the things that were humiliating. Regardless of what your background or your preparations, that wasn't respected.

I went to Tuskegee in 1935, on a fellowship, to serve as George Washington Carver's assistant; and during that time there were three hundred to four hundred lynchings a year. There was a department of lynch research and they kept a record of lynchings.

After Carver died, I came here to Detroit in 1945. Detroit had the reputation of being the leading city in the nation for black businesses development and progress. Now, with integration and the openings of opportunities to go elsewhere, a lot of those businesses don't exist any longer. This is a thing that is so very important, that we as a people have had to cope with—controlling more of the dollars that we earn. Until we get to the point that we do that, we are still in danger. We have made progress individually, but as far as I'm concerned, as a group we have retrogressed.

When I started in business, there was no competition from the major companies. The black market was totally ignored. Now our problem is with the majority companies.

The Housewives League was successful in promoting black businesses. That was started by Reverend Peck. He was the minister of Bethel A.M.E. Church. His wife organized the Housewives League. That was an auxiliary of the Booker T. Washington Business Association. These women would go to the merchants and ask for black products that were produced by blacks. If they wouldn't carry them, then they would see that people wouldn't buy there any longer. It was effective.

As people feel that they are secure and they are satisfied with what they are, they gain insight of these other problems that exist. In the beginning there was recognition that something needed to be done. The movement of Dr. King focused attention on the problems that existed for blacks. So many of the things that were happening to blacks weren't recognizable because they were not publicized. I think television played an important role in making known the conditions that prevailed. Where people are secure in their own little circle, they don't have that added concern of the total problem. There are all those factors that come into play.

Much of that blame can be placed on us not recognizing what was necessary and essential.

BIOGRAPHY

Austin W. Curtis, D.S.C., was born on July 28, 1911, in Institute, West Virginia. He graduated from Cornell University in 1932. Two years later he moved to Greensboro, North Carolina, and joined the teaching staff at the Agriculture and Technology College. In 1935 Dr. Curtis became the assistant of Dr. George Washington Carver at the Tuskegee Institute. After Carver's death, Dr. Curtis succeeded him as director of research at the George Washington Carver Foundation. He moved to Detroit in 1945 and established the Austin W. Curtis Laboratories. Dr. Curtis has been active in the Detroit community and received awards from many organizations, including the Booker T. Washington Business Association, NAACP, Sigma Pi Phi Fraternity, and St. Cyprian's Episcopal Church.

Left: *Richard V. Marks was director of the Mayor's Interracial Committee from 1954–68.* **Right:** *Ernest Goodman (in shirtsleeves) was at home with other activists. After a concert, he visits with singers Roberta Barrow and Paul Robeson, and friends in the home of Reverend Charles Hill.*

DISCUSSION ON CIVIL RIGHTS
ARTHUR MICHAEL CARTER III, ERNEST GOODMAN, ALMA THOMAS HALL, RICHARD V. MARKS, AND JOHN J. "JACK" WHITE

ERNEST GOODMAN: The Thirteenth, Fourteenth, and Fifteenth Amendments were added to the Constitution following the Civil War. The clear purpose was to guarantee equality to black people. While I was aware that slavery had been abolished, what I saw and took for granted was that blacks were not equal to whites. The modern notion of civil rights occurred for me as an individual in the early 1930s during the depression. Following that, when I began to read more widely and to participate in community activities, it developed rapidly.

ARTHUR MICHAEL CARTER III: I think the beginning of my awareness of the civil rights movement was with the election of William Patrick to the City Council. I remember, as a kid, I participated in handing out flyers for William Patrick. Before that, Reverend Charles Hill of Hartford Baptist Church was one of the first African Americans to run for City Council in modern times.

ALMA THOMAS HALL: We lived in a Polish neighborhood. Being Catholic, we tried to go to the local church. St. Josephat's was two blocks from us. My mother went and they said: "No, you can't attend church here. You don't speak Polish." This is when my mother turned her religion around. She got mad at the church. But we went to St. Peter Claver.

We lived a kind of conservative life. Moving here, the main thing my parents were concerned about was education. That was the most important thing that they thought that we could get in Detroit, because they had lived down South. I graduated from Northeastern High School in 1933. When you went to high school, you took a college course or a general course or a commercial course. So I took a general course because they told me, "Missy, you won't go to college." It included chemistry, biology. I went to summer school. I took just about everything. There were no jobs. I went to Cass to summer school because then I wouldn't have much else to do but sit on the porch, and I didn't like that.

When I finished high school, I took a postgraduate course. I passed all the civil service examinations—the federal, the state, the city, the Board of Education. When I showed up, I didn't get hired because they found I was black. I never got a reply of why they turned me down. My mother was wondering why, because I'd get an eighty-five or eighty-nine, and I'd take the test over. Once I got a ninety-two. But they would offer me a job in the kitchen or cafeteria. I went to the Polish people that had a store on Hastings Street where they sold milk. I was hired there to work.

RICHARD V. MARKS: One of the more important assignments I had in the military, I got a break because I left an infantry position and a bunch of us were sent to school. At that school, which was in Clinton, New York we studied French and German language. We were all destined to become interpreters after we graduated and be seated throughout the service and then go overseas and be positioned as an interpreter.

In that unit, out of two hundred, a good fifty of the soldiers in the unit were black. That was the first time that I had any living experience with blacks. We were completely segregated. We lived in dormitories but on a segregated basis. I didn't even realize it. It was just so neatly arranged, and no one ever talked about it. The experiences were very interesting because soldiers had been assigned to this unit regardless of their rank or background. So you would sometimes have drill sergeants who were black leading this two-hundred-man complement in military exercises and drills.

Our classes were not segregated in any way. We were completely integrated, and some of the blacks and whites were native-speaking Germans and French. Others were trained linguists. Some had taught in colleges and things like that. I came to the unit claiming only one language, which was Spanish, and they weren't teaching it there. That was the first real contact I had on a living basis. We played poker together. We surfed together. We went to school together. We went into town together. That was in 1944.

257

When I went overseas, I went over with an all-white unit. We got overseas about the time of the Battle of the Bulge. Our unit was assisted by a segregated black tank battalion. As it happened, in service there were lots of feelings about race, particularly with a segregated army which we had. Blacks were usually in a quartermaster corps, in the support units. Most of the fellows who were assigned to infantry positions, where life was at risk, always felt that was pretty cushy back there. There was a lot of hostility of a racial sort. Our unit, when this black tank battalion was assigned to us, they proved to be such courageous soldiers and did so many really heroic things in relationship to our men that attitudes in our position changed almost completely.

I was in a position to observe that because I was in a military police unit. Whenever we pulled duty, when we would have to patrol towns and that sort of thing, when our soldiers if they were black got into trouble, in this particular unit, we didn't have any problems. We could solve the problems. Whereas we would have fights going on constantly between the American soldiers and the British soldiers. The Americans would call them "Limeys", and the British would fight back. You just had a hullabaloo on your hands. That was sort of the genesis of my own, the basis of which I really got straight on the subject of race. The subject of how you measure a human being.

When I came back from service, we came back to the city that Dr. Carter has described. It was a thoroughly segregated city. You couldn't go to a major hotel downtown and have a cup of coffee with a colleague. I couldn't. When I joined the staff of the Mayor's Interracial Committee in July 1947, one of the first things we discovered was the fact that we had to take advantage of the Diggs Act, which theoretically guaranteed the right of people to eat in public places without discrimination. We discovered that we ourselves had to be forcing that issue.

We became a city overwhelmed by the issues of racial hostility in the war years. The riot was really an outgrowth of people registering on the problems and the feeling that nobody was prepared to help out, to do anything. So, when I went to work for the agency, it was very clear that the first thing we had to do was to get people together to the point where we kept the peace. You can't keep the peace unless you do justice.

I did a study of racial factors in Detroit hospitals. We found out that while some of the hospitals were beginning to hire black nurses that were trained, none of the hospitals in Detroit had, at that point, ever trained a black young woman in their nursing school. At Mercy College, when I went out there with my research materials, and I asked, the sister said, "Well, when a black girl comes we just tell them they can't enroll." I knew that the minute we put that in a report and published that report, that the reactions in this city from the good people, white and black, Catholic as well as non-Catholic, would not let them continue that, and that's exactly what happened.

We also took a look at the hospitals. At that time no other hospital except Receiving Hospital, a public hospital, had ever trained a black man or woman as a doctor, as an intern, or a resident. Harper Hospital, a hundred years in existence, never had a black doctor on its staff. We said, that has got to change. We got lots of agreement that these things had to happen, but still nothing much was happening. Then they decided they wanted to clear all the area and expand those hospitals, and the black community took the position that there was going to be no movement, no clearance. They were going to oppose it right on up to the Supreme Court, if necessary, unless there was agreement that those hospitals would open up their training facilities for nurses, for doctors, open up their hospital staffs, and open up their hospital rooms.

I served under three mayors. Under Mr. Cobo who was a Republican. I was a Democrat. He didn't want me, but my best friend was the editor of the *Michigan Chronicle*, and the mayor knew that and so did the business community. It was tired of all this race baiting and hostility. They wanted somebody in there that would get the job done. So I got appointed even though Cobo didn't like me. Cobo was the darling of the property improvement associations. All those groups that were always out there fighting the movement of any black person into decent, safe, and open housing.

But I got appointed and, as I say, I served under Cobo. He died several months after I was appointed, and I served under Mr. Miriani, and we did the public housing issue, and we solved the hospital issue under his administration. But at the end of his administration he got kind of wild. He decided that there was too much crime in the city and that they had to crack down on criminals. The way the police department defined criminals was, literally anybody that was black that wasn't where they were supposed to be was subject to arrest. I took the position that the crackdown was immoral and unworthy of a city, so I knew I was going to be out if Miriani got elected, and damned if Cavanaugh didn't get elected. Saved my neck.

In government you don't survive forever. In my later years we worked on problems like the police Department. It was the primary problem because it was a department that refused to hire on an open basis. It did take until the administration of Coleman Young to complete the opening up of the job of police officer in the community so that whites and blacks can share in the opportunities for jobs and in the responsibility for maintaining a lawful and orderly community. But I got ahead of them because I made a statement at the time when they told me I should shut up. They said, "You be quiet," and I just couldn't conceive of myself giving leadership to a community and just putting tape over my mouth; and I didn't want to fight them. But nevertheless some reporter asked me a question, and darned if he didn't use it, and darned if I didn't get fired.

ERNEST GOODMAN: About 1947–48 George Crockett—my legal associate at that time—and Judge Elvin Davenport—he had not yet been elected—and myself represented the family of Leon Mosley, a four-teen-year-old black who had been shot in the back by police. We pushed hard for a coroner's jury, after the prosecutor had refused to issue a warrant, to conduct an inquest into the cause of death. Public outcry was so strong that this seldom-used procedure was granted. After a highly publicized hearing, the citizens' jury recommended the issuance of a warrant. The prosecutor reluctantly issued the warrant.

Under the law at that time, the defendant could waive a jury. The law now requires the consent of the prosecutor to the waiver. The police then made sure that the case was assigned to a judge who would be understanding of their point of view. That was Judge Gordon. After a rather short trial, with the prosecutor presenting a lackluster case and the judge showing his deep-seated prejudice, he found the defendants not guilty in a long written statement, in which he blasted the NAACP for having been guilty of conspiring with myself and Maurice Sugar's law office in which I was then an associate, of causing the defendant policeman to be so unjustly accused of a crime of which he was totally innocent. In those days only rarely was a policeman ever accused of brutality and never charged, as far as I can remember, if the injured or dead civilian was black.

JOHN J. "JACK" WHITE: I worked in a factory at General Motors where there were twelve thousand workers, and, to the best of my recollection, before the war there were three blacks. Two of them worked on the bailing machine that bailed the cardboard and scrap metal. The other one that I remember worked in the garage of the executives, washing their cars. Those were the only three in that number of people.

I was fired in 1929 for participating in a work stoppage that was encouraged by some of the people. I was fired again in 1934. All of these were before the union. With each one of the experiences, you encountered people that altered your attitudes and questions. This was a process of divesting myself of all the racist ideology that I had been exposed to. And also anti-semitism and anti-foreigner.

I often think of my father, who was a trade unionist, who once saw me as a kid and said, "Who's that girl you were with?" I told him it was an Irish girl. He asked what parish she was in. He said, "Why don't you find a nice Irish girl in your own parish?" That's how provincial they were. That was not uncommon. That was true of Italian, Polish, and Hungarian, and all the ethnic cultures. There were enclaves in this state that were pretty tight.

Black Bottom and those blocks down St. Antoine, you would go there on Saturday for cheap whiskey and entertainment at the blind pigs, which was considered the "up" thing to do among the whites.

Many of them were clubs with very few blacks. They were mostly whites with black entertainers and black ownership.

ERNEST GOODMAN: In all this discussion, one person's name has not been mentioned—Reverend Charles R. Hill, pastor of the Hartford Avenue Baptist Church. Reverend Hill was a great and courageous leader in the black community in many different ways. Yet, today, few people remember his name and the important role he played. His life's work was vital to the development of civil rights in this community.

I have here some pictures that we took during the Progressive party campaign in 1948. This one was in Reverend Hill's basement. Paul Robeson had just finished a concert at Reverend Hill's church. In those days Robeson was no longer permitted to give his concerts in a public auditorium. Usually in Detroit he was at the Masonic Temple, which was usually filled with five thousand listeners. Now, nobody would have him except Reverend Hill and the Hartford Avenue Baptist Church. That night, after Paul had sung in the church, Reverend Hill invited some friends to join him at his house. The picture shows some of the guests.

The Progressive party was organized to support Henry Wallace, former vice president, in opposition to the cold war and supported complete equality of black and white.

In 1950 we decided to form an interracial partnership of lawyers, the first such interracial partnership that we knew of in this country. George Crockett, Mort Eden, Dean Robb, and myself were founding partners. Judge Claudia Morcum became an associate member in 1959. Bob Millender joined the firm in 1962 and became a full partner in 1966. We devoted a large part of our time to handling civil rights cases. We didn't make much of a living during the McCarthy period, but it was a hell of an interesting practice.

JOHN J. "JACK" WHITE: Reverend Hill had come to some of us in the labor movement and suggested that during the Korean War we organize a delegation. There was a rally in Chicago against the war. He suggested that we try to get a labor delegation. We were influential in getting seven hundred delegates from Detroit, a lot of them from Ford Local 600 and other UAW locals, to go to Chicago and attend the peace rally. While I was there with the delegation, Dr. DuBois was presiding over that, there were ten thousand people. He called me up from the audience. I went up there, and he introduced me to the audience and commended us for our large labor participation. I went to sit down, and I sat by Paul Robeson. We got to talking.

Subsequently he came to Detroit for a concert. I had fallen off a scaffold and was babysitting with the kids while my wife was working. I got a phone call one day and it was Paul Robeson. He asked me if I could come down to the Book Cadillac Hotel, he'd like to spend some time. I said I'd like to, but I was babysitting. He said, by all means, bring the children. So we went down to the Book and Brown, his accompanist, asked us if we'd wait until he got through with his concert. He knew my Irish background and he had spent a year in Dublin. He was tremendously impressed and he told me stories. He regaled us with some Irish songs. He was such a huge and gentle man.

ARTHUR MICHAEL CARTER III: During my high school days, I remember the "Big Four." I don't know what the formal name was, but we certainly recognized them riding in these big cars with four police officers coming out with rubber hoses and cracking kids across the back. Every police station had a "Big Four." They would stop people indiscriminately on the street corner as boys would be walking from school. At that time, I was sixteen or seventeen. I was a student at Eastern High School, between 1954–1958. That was the time of the reign of terror of the "Big Four." We were frightened. While I was not personally involved in any altercations, I do remember the fear.

I can remember during the late 1940s and probably through the 1950s, there were integrated groups of people meeting around the city. My reference point would be strictly with my parents, Arthur and Alberta Carter, and Erma Henderson, who would become City Council president in the 1970s. I remember as a child going with my parents to Erma Henderson's apartment on Canfield near Woodward. At those meetings I would sit and listen to people like Mr. Charles H. Mahoney who was president of the Great Lakes Insurance Company and who was very active in the community. I believe Coleman Young stopped by once or twice during that period of time.

There were strong coalitions at that time between black activists like Erma Henderson, Coleman Young, and activists in the Jewish community. I remember them talking about the lynchings in the South during discussions in Erma Henderson's apartment during the late '40s.

Harry Truman became president in 1945. I remember the friends of Erma Henderson sending telegrams protesting the lynchings in the South to the president at Blair House. They were renovating the White House at that time. I remember the "Blair House" being said over and over again. Of course, that impressed a seven- or eight-year-old.

I also remember the national convention of the Progressive party. The Progressive party was a party which was viewed as a party to the left of central political philosophy in the United States. Erma Henderson, my godmother, supported Henry Wallace of the Progressive party, for president in 1948. I can also remember the rumors about our phones being tapped as we moved from the '40s after the convention, into what I later learned was the Senator Joe McCarthy era. McCarthy was a U.S. Senator who ruined the lives of thousands of citizens by accusing them of being members of the Communist party. I remember discussions around the issue of our family phone being tapped because of family support for Henry Wallace.

The highlight of that period for me actually occurred in April of 1954, when I got a phone call at home one afternoon. It was raining that day. We lived at 3461 Holcomb near Mack. Erma Henderson lived on French Road near Canfield. She called me and said, "How would you like to celebrate your birthday today?"

I said, "Well, it's a little early," because my birthday was April 27, and this was somewhere around the 14th or 15th.

She said, "There's a real special man at my house, and I'd like for you to come over and meet him." I said okay. It was raining, so I got on my bike and rode in the rain. My mother was already over there.

I rode by bike from Holcomb and Mack to French Road and Canfield—about two miles. Erma Henderson met me at the door and introduced me to this very huge man with a very warm smile. It was Paul Robeson who often stayed with Erma during his visits to Detroit. There were many African Americans and whites and others who wouldn't be caught on the same block with Paul Robeson because of his political views. He later became a hero, but in those days you were subject to investigation by federal authorities for just communicating with Paul Robeson. I remember the roast beef Erma had cooked that day. It was the first time I had ever seen anyone eat rare meat. I was very impressed.

We must have stayed over there for four or five hours that evening. He talked a lot about his life and his singing. He told us a lot of stories. I don't remember the details, but I do remember us sitting at the table eating and doing a lot of laughing. He was a very kind and gentle person, and there were a number of other kids there that evening—black kids and white kids. We had a delightful time. Later on I learned much, much more about that era and what was going on at the time. For me, that is a very important memory—that one evening with Paul Robeson, my mother Alberta, and Erma Henderson.

Everyone remembers the march down Woodward when Martin Luther King was here in Detroit and the march on Washington, but there was another march right here in this area. It was in 1962 or 1963. It was down Michigan Avenue in Dearborn. The issues centered around housing. I do remember being extremely frightened. I remember marching down Michigan and eggs being thrown at us and fruit. "You niggers get out of here. We don't want you." I think the march started somewhere on Michigan Avenue near the Dearborn City Hall. Hubbard was still the reigning monarch mayor in Dearborn.

We knew about racism in Detroit. As a kid, we knew we couldn't go to this or that place, and there were restrictions as far as restaurants and hotels. During this march the name-calling, the physical contact, was just the epitome of racism in terms of the very aggressive and hostile behavior of the Dearborn whites. Some shoving and pushing occurred, but we were very well disciplined. My best friend, Leon Lucas, was with me, and we locked arms. I can remember getting home that night and breathing a sigh of relief, having survived that kind of experience.

The marchers had signs. I did not personally have one. There was the traditional song, "We shall overcome." That was a terrible sound to the ears of some of the folks who lined Michigan Avenue that day. The singing helped to keep us in line and gave us strength to endure all that. My personal attitude was to strike out and hit someone and really get into a street fight. That was not our purpose, however. That was not the issue that day.

It's interesting that I only encountered Orville Hubbard one other time, and that was at the funeral of a county commissioner about twenty years later when I served on the Wayne County Commission. By that time he was in a wheelchair and was unable to speak. Then, as history would have it, I ended up voting for his granddaughter, Susan Hubbard, to serve as a county commissioner nearly twenty-six years after that particular march.

The Joe Muer's restaurant right here in the city of Detroit would not serve African Americans. My father, during the '30s and 40's, could not go in and be served. The only way he could get a fish dinner was to have it wrapped up in newspaper and served out the back door. Every time I go into Joe Muer's today for a business meeting, that memory sticks vividly in my mind. I told one of the Muer family members some time ago, "You know, there was a time your family would not serve my family, unless it was wrapped up in newspaper."

The marches in the '60s and that whole era were, in part, I believe, precipitated by some other events. The African countries were being liberated. Ghana gained its freedom in the late '50s, and one African country after another became free of colonial rule. I believe that was a source of pride and inspiration to people here in this country and city where we had our own forms of apartheid, not only in the South, but also right here in Detroit. This point could be lost in history. We were every bit as segregated in the '40s and early '50s in Detroit as black Africans are in the Union of South Africa today in the 1990s.

Detroit was certainly not the "arsenal of democracy" that it was touted to be.

RICHARD V. MARKS: The significance of the period of marches was that a certain balance of power in the country was shifting. It was very clear that there was a common cause in the civil rights struggle. You had all the religious denominations that up to that point had never really joined the battle. They joined with King. You had major Catholic,

Protestant, Jewish, the union movement just involved up to its ears with money and personnel. It was a fantastic period because it represented a time when something changed in the country. All these battles that we were having individually with this restaurant and that restaurant. Can we cross Woodward Avenue for housing and that sort of thing. As the population changed, we finally began to get national legislation. Some forces in the country just realized that you cannot have a national transportation system and exclude some people. You just can't do that. You can't have a black child wanting a Coke and hamburger and he can't get it and his father can't get it. You can't have that kind of conflict going on all over the nation.

BIOGRAPHIES

Arthur Michael Carter III: See p. 98.

Ernest Goodman: See p. 66.

Alma Thomas Hall was born on May 16, 1912, in Arcola, Mississippi, and she moved to Detroit in 1927. Her father was an American Indian, a Creek from Alabama. She has worked for the federal government in the Department of Defense in civil service positions.

Richard V. Marks was born on March 10, 1922, in Beckmeyer, Illinois, and came to Detroit after World War II. He earned an M.A. in sociology and taught at Wayne State University for a short time. He was hired by the Mayor's Interracial Committee as a research assistant in 1947. He served as director from 1954–1968. He retired from the Human Rights Department in 1984.

John J. "Jack" White: See pp. 136–37.

Left: *Harry Bernard Boglin III (top) grew up in the Brewster Projects. During the 1940s he attended Sacred Heart School and Church, where he was an altar boy.* **Right:** *Mary Ann Humphries' family came here from the West Indies; she was born in Detroit and attended Sacred Heart School and Church.*

DISCUSSION WITH SACRED HEART CHURCH MEMBERS
HARRY BERNARD BOGLIN III, MARY ANN HUMPHRIES, EMMA JEAN JOHNSON, AND ANTHONY E. McCAULEY, SR.

HARRY BERNARD BOGLIN III: I was born on Farnsworth and Hastings. In 1947 we moved to the Brewster Projects, and I started coming to Sacred Heart around that time. My parents were from the West Indies.

The one thing interesting about the Brewster Projects, we were the first ones to live in government condominiums. There were doctors, lawyers. Jesse Steward was the first black sergeant on the police department. Many policemen lived there. Mr. Hamlin was an executive for Metropolitan Insurance. There were a great number of schoolteachers. There were a lot of doctors who had just started their residency. There were people who had private businesses. There was a guy who had a tow truck who lived there. A number of them worked at Hudson's downtown. A number of them were maids. A lot of them did day work in Grosse Pointe. It was housing for middle-income blacks.

I was an altar boy at Sacred Heart. At that particular time there were twenty-some altar boys, I believe. We were called at that time

Knights of the Altar. Most of the altar boys hung out with each other. We didn't play with the other boys in school or anywhere else. We'd get out of school for a funeral. We used to fight over 6:00 A.M. mass at the convent because after 6:00 A.M. mass the nuns would give you breakfast. It wasn't breakfast; it was more like a banquet. There were about eighteen nuns, and all of them wanted to serve you a plate.

MARY ANN HUMPHRIES: St. Peter Claver started in 1911. It had been a little Protestant church at Eliot and St. Antoine. That's where we went until 1938. This was a German parish. They gave us this church.

ANTHONY E. McCAULEY, SR.: I can remember about 1945. I started first grade in 1945. I had brothers and sisters who were ahead of me already going. I was supposed to go at six, but I remember my father telling me that they were going to start me at five. If I could keep up, then I could continue to go. So I did.

I can remember very clearly getting in trouble and having to do penance for being out of your seat or talking and turning around. One of their favorite penances was having you write "X" number of times, "I will not do whatever."

For instance, they might say, "Write this fifty times and bring it in tomorrow." If you didn't write it or bring it in, it doubled. It would behoove you to do it the first time. From that experience, I learned how to write with three pencils. You can put three together and write that way and get your stuff done much faster. They didn't say how small, large, whatever. You could arrange your pencils just right.

MARY ANN HUMPHRIES: Sometimes you would have it already done from the last time you got in trouble. You knew you would always get in trouble again so you wrote it down and you brought it in already written.

ANTHONY E. McCAULEY, SR.: I wasn't an altar boy. I tried out to be an altar boy, but I was just a little bit too rambunctious. You had to be quiet and learn your Latin. I learned Latin, but I wasn't quiet. Mr. Moore was the custodian here for years. He used to call me "Beans." He said: "You were never still. From the time I first saw you come in here, you were never still."

I can remember very clearly, when we had to go to the bathroom, they would line us all up and march us down the hall to the bathroom together. The girls went this way and the boys went that way. In the boys' bathroom, when you went down the steps, I would always try to see how many steps I could jump down to the bathroom. When I was mellow, I could maybe jump three or four. I would grab the banister. It was about fifteen steps. My goal was to try to jump all the way to the basement and not touch the other steps.

I was constantly moving. I used to run a lot, and you weren't supposed to run. You were supposed to be real pious.

267

When we were in class, I can remember very clearly getting caught doing something and having to go up to the front of the class and kneel down and face the blackboard. If you turned around, then you would get popped. I remember getting popped on more than one occasion. If I told my father, he'd pop me again. So I learned not to tell him.

I can remember my fourth-grade teacher, Sister Bernadette. I thought she was an angel. I really enjoyed her. All the nuns wore white.

At that time Wonder Bread and Silvercup used to put their bread in waxed paper. They asked us to collect that and bring it in. We would use those, take the blocks of wax, and chip it up real small. It was sprinkled throughout the entire building. Then you were given the assignment to put the waxed paper on your feet, and you would go out there and slide up and down the floor. And you would wax the floor like that. It was a combination of punishment and work. If you did it during the school day, then it was like a little reward. You got out of class, and you could be in the halls. If you stayed after school and did it, it was like punishment, because no one wanted to stay after.

Periodically, especially on the weekends, you could come into the nuns' house, the convent. You could work over there. A lot of the kids liked to get in there, I guess because of the mystique. Same thing in the father's house, the rectory. You just wanted to get in and kind of look around and just see what was going on. If you were good and you were chosen to be one of those who would help out, then you got a chance to come in. They would give you little treats. A lot of times it was a little sandwich or maybe some juice.

EMMA JEAN JOHNSON: Sacred Heart was very good to me. I joined in 1952. My kids were not going to Sacred Heart until a sister there sent me three cards—for the oldest girl and the oldest boy and the next oldest child. I asked her how much would I pay for their tuition, and she said that it would be half-payment for all of them—two hundred and fifty dollars. She said that she had seen in the project that kids were not in school. They were out in the neighborhood, and they were not going to school. They had a roundtable discussion. They read how many children people had that had joined the church. They voted on it, and they voted for the three oldest children I had.

Father Kirchbaum was a German priest. I told him I couldn't get them no stockings, no shoes. He said, "Well, I got a drawer here, and you've got a namesake, and every year they put money in that namesake." That's like a godmother and godfather. They put money in a drawer for their names, their Catholic names like Mary. The person who gave it had that name.

They would collect toys and clothing for the children, and one time a girls' school in Grosse Pointe would pick different children's names. The girls would come here and pick a name out of that box. That child would write down what they wanted for Christmas, and they would get that child what he wanted.

Father Kirchbaum went in there and got the namesake's money and gave it to me and told me to go downtown to get the things. I told him how I might never pay it back, and he said: "You're not supposed to. That's what they're there for, to help the poor people in the neighborhood." That's why the church was here, for low-income people that could not afford to get the things, like a confirmation dress. But he wouldn't tell me who was doing it. That was a secret.

My oldest son, Charles, was in the first grade. He didn't understand, because it was confining. Sister Anthony went and got a baseball bat. She got him a football, and she got him a basketball, and she went in the school yard and left her class and was playing in the school yard with him.

MARY ANN HUMPHRIES: Another thing I can remember about going to school at Sacred Heart is that we were led to believe that the only church was the Catholic Church, and if we went to a Baptist Church, we would be punished. If we did, we had to go to confession.

I feel personally there was prejudice right in the school. In all activities that I ever participated in, I was always put at the top of the class. I was not an A student, and I think that had a lot to do with my complexion. As I grew older, I realized it was wrong. Another time, when I was older, I went to Father Kirchbaum to confession, and the priest would not forgive me. I don't know why he wouldn't. I didn't kill anyone. I went to another priest and told him, and he forgave me and told me to forget about Father Kirchbaum.

HARRY BERNARD BOGLIN III: One of the principles that is needed for the black community and the blacks that live in the United States is extreme discipline. One of the reasons that I was made to go to Sacred Heart, even though I wanted to go, was extreme discipline. I was extremely rambunctious. My nickname is "Spanking," and that is because I got a lot of whippings every day. I was always doing something —breaking windows, shooting people with my BB gun.

I was made to go to Sacred Heart, and there was a change in me that my mother used to pray to God every day for. When the street lights came on, I was in the living room. Before Sacred Heart, God knows where I was.

Once when I was visiting my aunt who lived over on the West Side, I went over to a restricted area of the railroad tracks and was caught by the police. I was seven or eight. The police arrested me. My mother found out about it and called Father Kirchbaum. I was called out of class and had to report to the rectory. He said: "I understand you do not know what restrictions are. You don't know that you're not supposed to go in certain areas. I am shocked that an altar boy did these things. I don't want to hear about this again. You say the rosary."

MARY ANN HUMPHRIES: There was a policeman for the Brewster Project. His name was "Shorty" Black. That was what we called him. He looked out for all the kids in the neighborhood. And if you did anything mischievous or whatever, he made sure that your parents knew about it. That was in the late '40s and '50s.

EMMA JEAN JOHNSON: My son, before he was large enough to go to school, he was outside on his roller skates, and one of his skates came off, and he didn't know how to put it on. I saw the policeman bending down. He saw the policeman coming along and asked him to put on his skate for him. He was a white policeman.

BIOGRAPHIES

Harry Bernard Boglin III has lived in Detroit since birth on June 8, 1938, and grew up in the Brewster Projects. His mother was from Alabama and father from Trinidad; they met at the Graystone Ballroom. He learned tailoring from his father, owner of "Harry the Tailor." He was the first black tailor employed by Hudson's. When he was in the Navy from 1961–65, he worked in electronic counter-measure and traveled all over the world. He now works as "the last person to let you down," a grave digger.

Mary Ann Humphries was born January 9, 1932 in Detroit. She attended Sacred Heart Church and School and graduated from the school in 1950. She was married in 1952 and blessed with two boys. She worked for the Archdiocese of Detroit and has done work in the public relations field since then. She has also worked in the medical field. In retirement she continues to work part-time at Riverview Hospital.

Emma Jean Johnson was born on April 15, 1923, and lived on St. Antoine in Detroit. She worked at Providence Hospital. She joined Sacred Heart Catholic Church in 1952. Her children are Paulette Danzy, Sharleen Jefferson, and Charles Johnson.

Anthony E. McCauley, Sr., was born on June 4, 1940, at 3502 St. Antoine in Detroit. He was raised in the Brewster Projects. He is brother to Mary Cosey; their late father was Jesse L. McCauley, Sr.

Mary Clarice McCauley Cosey lived in the Brewster Projects from 1939 to 1962.

MARY CLARICE McCAULEY COSEY

My family moved in the Brewster Project in 1939. It was just built. And I was there till 1959 when I got married. The first house that we lived in was at 642 Mack. Almost across the street from Charles Diggs's Funeral Home. I was just three or four years old. But my most vivid memories come to the house that's 3502 St. Antoine. When our family increased, we moved across the court to a three-bedroom house. That was on the corner of St. Antoine and Eliot. That's where I spent most of my growing-up years.

I could go around and name every family that lived in every row house that surrounded this court where we played. And everybody looked out for one another's children. Our family was quite unique, because my mother died and left five small children ages four months to seven years of age. And that left my dad to raise us. My father wound up raising four of us, and his mother took the four-month-old to Kentucky. My father was left here with these four children, three boys and a girl. The neighbors seemed to take a great interest. And I can very well remember the different ladies combing my hair and getting me ready for school and that kind of thing. They really saw after us since there was no mother in the home.

271

Another one of the things was going to the Brewster Center and swimming. We loved that. We'd go down there for swimming, for skating, for just everything. We just went down to Brewster Center and played. Those were very, very pleasant memories.

At Christmastime, because my bedroom was on the front of the house, I could look out my front window; and when the Hudson's parade was going north on St. Antoine, there was this little me in the window looking out at the parade going up. But I should have been asleep getting ready to go to the parade the next day. So by the time the floats and things came down Woodward the next day, I had already seen them. They were going from the warehouse up to Frederick. And then I'd be in the window looking at 'em.

It was a highlight. My dad always made sure we went to the parade. I remember my dad with the stepladder so that we could see, so the younger children could stand on the stepladder. He would carry that for a long way.

One of the most pleasant memories that I have living in Brewster was being able to play outside in the court. In the wintertime there was plenty of snow and ice, and we played on the sleds and ice skated. The neighbor men would come out and push the snow back and put water in and make a little pond for us. There was a big sandbox where we would play marbles, shooting marbles into sand. The slide, the swings, and horseshoes. And to this day my brother's an excellent horseshoe player because he played out there—horseshoes every day.

When we would have court dances, they'd have all the lights on, and people would be blasting music, and the police would be out there. They had a project policeman. We called him "Shorty" Black. He would be out there and make sure everything was all right and everybody was okay.

BIOGRAPHY

Mary Clarice McCauley Cosey was born on August 12, 1936, in Detroit. She is the second oldest of five children. The family lived in the Brewster Projects from 1939 to 1962. She received an L.P.N. degree from Detroit Practical Nursing Center, a B.A. from the University of Detroit, and an M.A. from Wayne State University. She presently teaches in the Detroit Public Schools. She holds membership in the Detroit Federation of Teachers, Detroit Area Council for Teachers of Mathematics, and the Association for Supervision and Curriculum Development. Mrs. Cosey is married with three children and one grandson.

WILFRED E. LITTLE

I came to Detroit in 1940. I had never really intended to come to Detroit. I had never thought of Detroit as a place where I would end up living. Lansing was my hometown, but previous to coming here I had been in Ohio. I was teaching at Wilberforce University. Mary McLeod Bethune had convinced the Roosevelts to set up some training centers in some of the black colleges to train people with skills that they could use in the defense industry. I met fellows from Detroit while I was there who were teaching also. As a result, sometimes I would come with them on weekends when they would come home. I got involved with people in Detroit, and the first thing I knew I ended up staying here.

At first I worked with a fellow. We were taking subcontracts doing machining. We had been teaching that at Wilberforce. This was during the Second World War. We had a few machines we set up in a garage, and we would work with those. We did that for awhile until, as the war effort began to slow down, many of those jobs began to fade away.

Then, in 1941, I became employed with a company called Cut Rate Department Stores, which was over on Hastings and Livingstone in those days. This company mostly concentrated on the black neighborhoods. I sold furniture and household furnishings, then eventually became the manager.

Along Hastings, that was the most active of the streets, because there was so much going on over there, everything from A to Z, which created a lot of activity. At night there was a whole different population on the streets than there was in the daytime, because that was where a lot of the nightlife was and a lot of the activities that usually take place at night. They had a lot of prostitution. If you wanted . . . back in those days it was reefers . . . you could just go on Hastings Street and find it there. They had everything that the people wanted. But in the daytime it was the grocery stores and household furnishings stores, the cleaners. They did their business in the daytime. At night when they closed, the other places opened up. It was a whole different population, different people, everything.

At the place where I worked a truck driver there was a Muslim. One day he walked up to me and said, "You're a Muslim, aren't you?" I told him I didn't know what that was. He thought I was fooling and said, "I know you're a Muslim."

I said: "No, I don't know what that is. What is it about me that would make you think I'm a Muslim?"

"You don't smoke. You don't drink. You respect women. You don't let these people that we work for take advantage of us."

Many times the owners of the business, when time would come for employees to get their raises, they would begin to intimidate them. They'd find fault with everything they were doing and make them feel uneasy about their job, and they'd be afraid to ask for their raise. Or if they'd ask for their raise, they had intimidated them to a point where if they'd refuse to give it, they could get away with it.

I recognized what was going on; so whenever I would see them doing this, I would intercede. I would just say, "Look, it's time for him to get this raise, and you're trying to intimidate him and get him to the point where he won't ask for the raise; or if he does ask for it, you can put him off." They would think I was going to get fired for doing that. For some reason they never fired me. To me it didn't make any difference. I just didn't like to see injustice, and I would speak out in their behalf.

He said, "You make them respect our women when they come in here." For some reason these white men would feel like when a black woman would come in that was nice looking that they could just say and do whatever they want.

When I would see this happening, I would walk up to them and say, "Listen, if that was one of your women that came in here, and you saw me doing and saying what you were just saying and doing, I don't think you would want to see that happen, would you?"

When they'd write up their contract, they'd write an altogether different price. Sometimes they'd add as much as one hundred dollars or more to their bill, and the person wouldn't even know it. I said, "You have the stuff priced high enough that you make enough profit without cheating." You had people coming in from the South and other places. Some of them couldn't read too well. They hadn't gone to school. They were too busy trying to make a living. They'd get a job in the factory where they started making some decent money, and many of them couldn't even count their money too well. There were plenty of people here looking to help them out and take their money away from them. I'd let them know that it just wasn't right. People couldn't understand how they kept me because you'd think they'd want to fire me, but they didn't.

Finally I went to a Sunday meeting to hear a speaker. He related what he had to say to history, and when you listened to him, you had something that you could keep in your mind and relate to your experience in America. He would go to history and show how we ended up here in slavery. The same people that gave us the religion that we had, which was Christianity, were the same people that enslaved us. Those same Christians that enslaved us and gave us this religion were the ones who lynched us. Those same Christians were the ones who ran the government and were the ones who were exploiting us. Those same Christians were the policemen in our neighborhoods who had their foot up our behind and were misusing us. The police force in the black neighborhood was nothing but an army of occupation. They were just there to keep niggers in their place.

What he was going to do when he completed this was prove to you that the white man was the devil. They would also point out that because you know a few good ones, don't think that all of them are good, because those good ones are the ones that the bad ones used to get you in a position where they can take advantage of you. All of these things were pointed out; and when he would get through you'd say, "Well, maybe the white man is the devil." Everything that you were told that the devil would do to you, the white man has done it. You don't have to die to go to hell. You're already in hell if you're born black in America. Eventually I decided I would get involved in it.

After I got involved, my wife and I would write to my brother Malcolm—he was in prison at the time—and explain to him what we had gotten in and what we were finding out. When he got paroled—I got him paroled to me in 1952—I got him a job to work with me at the furniture store. That was part of the conditions of his parole. Anyway, we wrote to him, and he began to become interested in it. The only thing he said he couldn't understand was the part about the white man being the devil. I had a brother, Reginald, who had been on the street with Malcolm, so I sent Reginald out to talk to him.

What Malcolm really was, was a courier. He used to go south and come back with two of the biggest suitcases you ever saw. In those days they didn't have dogs to sniff that stuff. As long as a person wasn't afraid, they could walk right by them with it. He was a person that didn't have any fear. He had confidence in himself. He'd walk right up in front of them and right by them, and they'd look right at him and wouldn't realize what was going on. The people he worked for out of New York would pay him one thousand dollars a trip for that. He said, "I made good money."

The way Reginald made him see it, he said: "You thought they were your friend. You were the one taking the chance. If you had got caught, you were the one to end up in prison. The one thousand dollars that they paid you wasn't anything. What you were bringing back was probably three to four hundred thousand dollars. They just gave you a penny, and you were the one taking the chance." Then Malcolm began to realize that he was being exploited, too.

Back in those days a lot of the ones who had control of the entertainers would get them hooked on drugs, and this is how they controlled them. That way they could pay them what they wanted. Malcolm was one they used to go get the drugs. Name entertainers would be somewhere on the road, and they couldn't get what they needed. Malcolm would be the one they'd send to bring them their supply. This was controlled out of New York by the same people that were exploiting entertainers and doing a whole lot of other things. They were in legitimate businesses but were controlling a lot of these entertainers with drugs.

He used to tell me: "It can't happen without the complicity of the police. In order for the drug business to run, the police have to be involved in it also." He told me that many times when he would come back with his load, he'd see the police there at the airport, and they would never come to him. He recognized them in their plainclothes. These were officers who usually wore uniforms when they were on duty. They would be there and they would follow him until he got that stuff delivered where he was supposed to deliver it, to make sure that it got where it was supposed to go. They not only got a cut, they were part of the business. He found out that in most cities where it operated, the police were in on it as well as the Mafia. They worked together.

He turned to Islam after he realized that he was only part of the exploited group. He really hadn't gotten ahead like he thought. He realized he was just being used and exploited just like everyone else, just in a different way. Then he could see in the general sense that the white man was the devil. He's the one that has the control. He can bring this stuff into the country. He can make the arrangements through the Police Department to get their complicity. He began to realize that, "Hey, the white man must be the devil."

I got him paroled to me because I didn't want him to get loose again in Boston or New York. I had a job for him. I wanted to keep him away from people that were in the rackets, because if he got back out there with them he would be back in it again.

I had a hard time with him for awhile because every pay day he'd be mad. When he'd get his money and look at that money, he would be mad. In those days what he was getting was considered good pay for working people, but not for hustlers. He said: "Now, I worked all week, eight hours a day, six days for this. I'll tell you something. I could have breakfast with you. You bring me into the city and leave me off. I'll meet you for lunch, and I'll have more money than this."

Every week I had to deal with that. I'd tell him he'd end up in prison or end up dead if what you were doing was helping white folks to exploit our people. I was able to hold onto him because I stayed right with him. He worked with me. When he got off work, he had to ride with me because he didn't have a car. I took him straight home. This was in about 1953.

At that time I was up on Oakland Avenue at the north end store, but there was plenty going on around there, too. He was the kind of person who could spot it. I'd be driving, and he would look at a person and tell me the certain mannerisms they had that would give them away. He'd say, "Now that woman there is a prostitute." He'd tell you the guys that are hustling dope. He could spot a user. He could tell you a plainclothes cop as soon as he saw one. When they live on the street, they live by their wiles and something inside, an instinct that they follow. They get to the place where they are very alert.

I've known many alert people, but I've never met anybody as aware as Malcolm. I couldn't understand how he could keep up with what was going on all about him all the time. He'd keep up with what was in the immediate vicinity, and at the same time he was keeping up with everybody that moves. He's weighing them all the time while he was talking to you. He didn't miss anything. Anything that came within his vision or sight or sound he was aware of it.

Eventually I was able to get him to Chicago to meet Elijah Muhammad. I had already told him: "If we can get Malcolm involved in this some way, I don't think he'll get back out there on the street. But he's got to get involved. He's not the kind of person that can just be a believer. He's got to be active." So I got him to Chicago, and he liked what he saw and heard in Elijah Muhammad and decided that was what he was going to get involved in. From then on he never got involved in what was going on in the street. If he was out there, he was trying to get them out of it and into "Islamic," he called it at that time.

Among the siblings in a family you have some who pair off and are closer to each other and who you'll tell your secrets to. That's the way it was with me and Malcolm. I always knew where he was and what he was doing. I would never tell the rest of the family. He would come and tell me what was what, but he knew that I wouldn't say anything. It never went beyond me. I would try to get him out of some of the things he was doing, but if that was what he had his mind made up to, I knew I couldn't change it, but I would always be there for him when he needed me.

The time came when it became obvious that the stand he had taken could easily get him wiped out because he had stepped on everybody's toes. He was always pointing out how the police were involved. He was pointing out how the Mafia was operating because he knew all this. Every other organization, he was pointing out their weaknesses. He was the kind of person that ended up: whatever came up, came out. One white writer in New York said he was brutally honest. He would just tell it, and you couldn't do anything because it was the truth. He had a way of getting to the heart of whatever it was. He was always pointing out America's weaknesses when he'd go to Africa and Asia and even in Europe. He'd say: "I'm from America. I'm from a country that has no value at all on the life of a black man and who a black man cannot look to for justice and freedom and equality." He was telling the truth.

BIOGRAPHY

Wilfred E. Little was born on February 12, 1920, in Philadelphia. He was a machining instructor at Wilberforce University before he moved to Detroit in 1941. He was a salesman for Cut Rate Department Stores on Hastings from 1941–1945. Mr. Little also worked for Beneficial Finance Company, and he retired from Michigan Bell as a public relations specialist in February 1988.

Renowned percussionist Roy Brooks began to play the drums when he was three years old.

ROY BROOKS

I was born March 9, 1938, the year the planet Neptune was discovered and "Superman" was created. I was born in Receiving Hospital in downtown Detroit.

Being an only child, I had a lot of love and was always surrounded by this. I always had what I wanted and whatever, a lot of affection.

I discovered music when I was three years old. Music always intrigued me. I danced at this age. The music was there, so my parents bought me my first set of drums when I was seven years old. And to the assemblies I'd bring a snare drum, and I'd play. And the teacher would ask the kids in the class, "Children please express what you would like to be when you grow up."

So one kid said, "I'll be a policeman." And I never would participate because I was a drummer there and that's all I ever wanted to be. So I never would say, "I wanna be a drummer." I just kinda shyly wouldn't say these things. So drumming put me in another. . . . Kids looked at me as a real musician.

At age twelve I became interested in basketball, which took me away from the drums temporarily, and I went into high school playing basketball. And I was pretty good. But basketball is a very integral part

279

of my life. It's like an offensive concept or it's like a martial arts situation. There's so much to learn from it. I would spend hours in my basement dribbling. That was my forte, which is percussion, if you dig it, you see. It's like the idiom called jazz. It's improvised to a great degree. You have plays that you have to make up something.

The word jazz, in many African dialects, it means to hurry up. And that's what it is, it's quick. Music is an absolute concept. In other words, if you can't hear it, you can feel it. Deaf people can hear music through their spine; they can feel it. You can feel the tones, you can feel the rhythm through the spine, so to me that makes it an absolute concept; If you can't hear it, you can feel it. We don't think of music necessarily as a feeling; it seems to be secondary to talk about it as a feeling. People say, "Oh yeah, I heard that." But it's a feeling involved there, too. It comes from the musician himself.

I went into the jazz idiom. I got hooked onto Charles McPherson, Lonny Hillier, James Jameson. And these guys were prolific Charlie Parkerites. And they were under the tutelege of Barry Harris. So we would get together at my house, thirteen at this time, and we would practice these tunes. And we would practice the feeling and whatever it took for us to play. And we would play dances—we were in high school at this point—at the Urban League, Friday or Saturday night for our school chums. And they were dancing to our music. I mean, the floor was packed. There's a room there like a ballroom, and it used to be packed. And we used to play, not every week, but every month we would perform.

And we would emulate the records that we would get, but we tried our own improvisation. And the biggest compliment that a musician can have is if somebody dances to his music. That's gone now because musicians are in the clubs now, and people sit down and I suppose intellectualize what it is; but there should be dancing.

We were live guys, so when we were at the Urban League, everybody, the guys, were sharp with ties and suits of that day. In fact, the suits are coming back. So it was a whole social thing going on. It was male and female. It was real different. I haven't seen that since.

Music had a lot to do with it, because the girls would find out who were the best musicians on these records, and they would dance to these certain records, and they would try to be on the level of the guys who were supposed to be hip. So it was like a hip thing there, because they were gathering around the music. The social thing was gathered around the music and the fact that they could dance together; and that's another thing, people danced together, they touched.

Now, black people, at one time, could dance to anything. There didn't have to be one certain beat or one certain rhythm or rock. And go back to the jungle. If there was a drought there was a guy that came out and danced and made it rain, right? The Indians, it was the same thing. So the dance is a very integral part of our society, and we aren't dancing right at this time. You see the rappers? I say, wait a minute man, what is that? What are you doing? Ten years from now you won't be able to do that. It's all right, but there's no females. They put some females in the background, but there's not a hand touch, there's never nothing. The male or female never touch.

Now, my contingent is in the jazz dance. We touched, and to be close wasn't necessarily a sexual thing; the female was following the male, and it wasn't that he was dictating, it was just like jazz. Whatever he thought, that's where she was. If she stumbled, hey, she was probably ostracized. So there wasn't no stumble; she followed the guy wherever he thought that he wanted to go, she was right there with him.

I won an athletic scholarship playing basketball at the Detroit Institute of Technology. And at that time I didn't want to play basketball, because I had just started working for Yusef Lateef at an after hours place in Delray, Michigan, on Friday and Saturday. And I would practice eight hours a day. I was aspiring to really be something; this is where I wanted to go. I just kept doing what I was doing. I kept practicing and studying.

My first major road trip was to Las Vegas in January of 1959. This is before I went to New York with the Four Tops, Joe Henderson, Kirk Clancy, and Clarence Sherril. We were out there six weeks, and I saw another side of the entertainment world I've never forgotten, because they do everything that's big, grandiose. And Tony Bennett, he came and applauded the group, I mean stood up. I said, "Man, that's Tony Bennett!" And then I saw a lot of money, the most money I've ever seen in my life. In September of 1959 Horace Silver called me to come to perform with his group in New York, and I stayed with Horace Silver for four-and-a-half years. So, that was the acceleration of my career, and it's still accelerating, thankfully.

BIOGRAPHY

Roy Brooks was inspired to take up drums through listening to Elvin Jones at Bluebird when he was a teenager. He played with Yusef Lateef and Barry Harris at the El Sino. He worked with "Beans" Bowles at Lavert's Lounge. He played with Horace Silver from 1959–64 and with Yusef Lateef from 1967–70. He has also worked with Sonny Stitt, Dexter Gordon, and the Four Tops. He has performed for audiences around the world. He is a founder of MUSIC (Musicians United to Save Indigenous Culture). His own groups include the Artistic Truth and the Aboriginal Percussion Choir.

Wardell C. Croft has been chairman of the Wright Mutual Insurance Company since 1950.

WARDELL C. CROFT, FLMI

Wright Mutual Insurance Company was organized by an undertaker by the name of Arthur Garfield Wright. He was a very successful business-man and undertaker. In fact, it has been quoted that Mr. Wright was one of the first black millionaires in this town. He had, what we call, a burial association, and that was converted to Wright Mutual Insurance Company in 1942.

The first chartered organizational structure was classified as an assessment company, even though it was life insurance. The assessment company only provided a small amount of life insurance, with a maximum of five hundred dollars, when the company started. And finally it was increased to fifteen hundred dollars; that was only for the purpose of burial expenses.

At that time blacks had trouble getting life insurance, because of the fact the major white companies would not insure blacks because of the so-called high mortality. You could get a limited amount of insurance. The major white companies were classifying blacks in their high mortality category. They were limited as to the amount they would insure. There were many insurance companies that wouldn't insure blacks at all.

There was a high mortality rate simply because blacks did not have access to health facilities. Their income was very low, and they had the worst jobs in the world. Consequently, they had the worst pressure, a strain that affected their well-being. As a result, even hospitals discriminated to a degree. And so that caused a higher mark-up than the whites. Since that time the blacks have been catching up very fast, in longevity, with whites. There is a small difference now according to the actuary statistics.

At one time Detroit had more black businesses, I suppose, than any of the major cities. And that's because of the Booker T. Washington Business Association, organized in 1930. The Booker T. Washington Association at that time had their own display, where they would have a big exhibit fair where they would put wares on display once a year and then, I suppose, they exchanged ideas and experiences.

I think it's important to know that Detroit, starting with World War II, was a mobilized arsenal of war, the manufacturers of tanks, and pulling people together. It helped to mobilize people, and it created employment for a better quality of life. I suppose it was the first major city that had so many black homeowners, I mean of single homes. The large population of homeowners did a lot for Detroit and its people because they took pride in their homes. And people upgraded themselves into a better home and a better environment, and that kept the spirit and kept them ambitious, continuing to strive for higher accomplishments.

As Wright Mutual progressed, it had difficult problems with its operation. And so in 1950 I came to really run the company, because it was in the red with its operation.

Many of the leaders of Detroit served at one time as president of the Booker T. Washington Association. For instance, Secretary of State Richard Austin was president at one time. As I said, many blacks in high places today are people that have once served as president of the Booker T. Washington Association or are members.

At one time the Chamber of Commerce had no blacks as members, and as things began to change they began to open up. I remember a person coming right into my office before we expanded to recruit me into becoming a member of the Chamber of Commerce. And I recall when the YMCA just started to change. The chairman of the board of First Federal was chairman of the executive committee, like the chairman of the YMCA Board. And he drove to my door with his chauffeur and came in my office to recruit me to serve for the Metropolitan YMCA. That just goes to show things weren't open in 1967, and those blacks that they felt were successful, they would go out of their way to recruit them. That's why I say the chairman came to my door.

I really think that the mere fact that equal opportunity presented itself to blacks in this community has been a tremendous plus for Detroit, because many of them would not have had the opportunity in government, holding big positions or being exposed.

The mere fact that New Detroit was born in 1967. Just to give you a personal experience, I didn't know Henry Ford II, previously. But after becoming acquainted with him personally, I could call Mr. Ford if he was in his office or if he was in New York. He's one man that returned my call. If I hadn't been involved in New Detroit, I wouldn't have had the opportunity to meet Mr. Ford or get close to Mr. Ford.

And I remember another incident when the United Negro College Fund Alumni met in Detroit when Mr. Jim Roche was the chairman. And they wanted Mr. Roche as speaker, and most of the time those fellows are hard to get. By being affiliated with New Detroit, I was able to get Mr. Roche to be the luncheon speaker. And the same thing with Joe Hudson or Max Fisher. This exposure was beneficial to them and beneficial to the black community, because you moved the barriers when New Detroit was formed. And they sat down to talk with blacks because of the serious nature of the riot and decided that, "Looky here, the business community must do something to solve this racial problem." And they did. They put money in and they were involved personally, not at a distance, personally.

BIOGRAPHY

Wardell C. Croft, Fellow, Life Management Institute, was born in Gadsden, Alabama, and is the fifth child of eleven children. He is a graduate of Stillman College. He is chairman and chief executive officer of the Wright Mutual Insurance Company; board member of New Detroit and Detroit Renaissance as well as Stillman College; and chairman of the Trustee Board of Second Baptist Church. He has served as president, Booker T. Washington Business Association; National Insurance Association, U.S.A.; and Life Insurance Association of Michigan. He served as chairman and organizer of First Independence National Bank. He is past vice chairman of the National Business League. He is married to the former Theora Cunningham and is grandfather to three and great-grandfather to three children.

*Waldo Cain, M.D., struggled
for many years to achieve equal
status and privileges at Grace
Hospital.*

WALDO CAIN, M.D.

When I came out of high school I just knew I was going to go to college because everybody went to college, but I really didn't have any strong idea about what I wanted to do. I decided that maybe I'll be a teacher. I took one semester in the education program at Wayne and decided I didn't want to be a teacher. They sent me over to the Trowbridge School. My sister was the principal there. They sent me over there for what they called volunteer leadership of young boys. Those young boys drove me crazy. I was a freshman in college, and I said, "No, absolutely not, I can't stand these kids."

I decided at the end of my freshman year to switch to pre-law. The courses that I started taking for half of a year were so dull. They used to sit us down in alphabetical order in class which meant that with my name starting with "C," I was down front most of the time. I would sit there and I could not stay awake. I decided, if this is what it takes to be a lawyer, I don't want to be a lawyer.

I started taking pre-med courses and found them fascinating, and I enjoyed them. I said, this is really fun, and I think I'll do this. That's how I got into medical school, just sort of accidentally. I never had one of these childhood desires to be a doctor.

285

I went to Wayne for undergraduate school. Then the war started. This was World War II. At that time Wayne would take each year one black and maybe two Jews into their medical school. I didn't have an outstanding grade point; it was maybe 3.0, which was not good enough for me to have been accepted at Wayne. I would have to have damn near 4.0 in those days to get into medical school, because there was just one slot. Everybody knew that. I never even applied to Wayne.

I applied to Meharry because I had a lot of friends who went there, and it was an all black school. That's in Nashville. That's the only place I ever applied. I sent my application in the morning after Pearl Harbor. Pearl Harbor was on Sunday. I wrote for an application on Monday, because I knew that they were going to start this war and if I don't get into medical school, I'm going to go to war and I'll get killed. It was just that selfish.

I went to Meharry. As a senior student, I wrote to Receiving Hospital and to the then-St. Mary's Hospital, which later became Detroit Memorial, requesting an application for a position as intern. I indicated that I would graduate in the upper ten percent of my class and Detroit was my hometown. I never received an application from either hospital. Could it be that neither medical director received my letter, or could it have been that in those days they knew that if I was graduating from Meharry, I had to be black?

I stayed there in Nashville for six years after I graduated. We came back to Detroit because at that time Detroit had the highest per capita income for black people of any city in the U.S. That's why we came to Detroit.

One of the first things that I did when I came home was to call down to Wayne and make an appointment for an interview with the professor of surgery. I went down and had lunch with the vice chief of surgery, the associate professor. The professor was in Japan. The associate professor who was in charge was Nick Gimbel of the Macy's and Gimbel's Department store. I had lunch with him and made rounds, and I told him that I had passed my boards and would like to become affiliated with the university. I'm just beginning, but I have plenty of time to do work in the clinic. So he said, "sure. You will be appointed as instructor of surgery, and we'll give you two mornings a week in the clinic at Receiving. I'll let you know when you start." I thought that was great.

About ten days later I got a phone call from him, and he was very apologetic. He said the professor was back. He was the chief of surgery at Receiving. He said, "The professor says no." He had never met me; he had never seen me, but he just knew I was black. He had never trained a black resident in his life. At that time they had one black resident in surgery, but we didn't count him because he wasn't American.

He had never trained a black American. All black Americans know that foreign-born blacks are treated differently than native-born blacks in this country. They are perceived differently. So that was the end of that appointment.

I owe my appointment at Grace Hospital to a great part to Dr. Dewitt T. Burton, because he knew the doctor who was medical director at that time at Grace, named Warren Babcock. He literally took me by the hand into Dr. Babcock's office. They were on a first-name basis, apparently old colleagues. He said: "This is my boy. I want you to make sure he gets on the staff." At that time Grace had one black surgeon, who didn't operate there very much—Remus Robinson. Remus Robinson was doing most of his surgery at Providence Hospital because he had gotten disenchanted with the system at Grace.

I got appointed to the staff at Grace at the bottom of the totem pole, what they call volunteer assistant. This is in about December or January. I never got a patient in the hospital. That's the lowest rung in terms of seniority. You're a volunteer assistant, then assistant, then associate, and then you get to be senior. Volunteer assistant is the bottom of the ladder when you are board certified. You have to be a board certified surgeon in order to get a teaching appointment.

From the time I was appointed until I had to go into the army in the Korean War, I never got a patient in the hospital. Beds were always full. I didn't have a lot of patients; just starting out I would have not even had one patient a week to be admitted to the hospital. I also had applied to Harper. They answered my application and gave me an interview with the chief of surgery at Harper. I had an interview with the chief of surgery at Grace which went well.

I went down to the David Whitney Building to interview with the chief of surgery at Harper. Apparently he hadn't looked at my application, because everybody had their picture on there. He was a big, ruddy-complexioned guy. When his receptionist told him I was there, he, in a very pleasant voice said: "Sure, take him in my office and have him sit down and give him a cup of coffee." I went in and sat down; and when he finished with his patient, he came in. I'll always remember that he had on a white shirt and red tie and this white lab coat. When he walked in and saw me, he turned just as red as a beet. His manner was very cordial, very affable; but you could see that his whole face turned the same color as his tie. He was very cordial and read my application but said: "We just don't have any vacancies on the staff now. We have a long waiting list."

By this time I had my orders to report for the army, so I told him: "Doctor, I'm going into the Army for at least two years, and all I ask you is to put my name on the list now. I know that in two years somebody's going to die, somebody's going to retire or move away; and by the time I get back I ought to be at the top of the list." I never heard from Harper.

In order for a black physician in Detroit to become a surgeon prior to the mid-1950s, he became a resident at one of the small proprietary black hospitals that were created because the doors of the major hospitals were closed. Despite very limited resources, these pioneers rendered services and acquired skills that were unknown outside the community of black professionals. These hospitals were usually fashioned from pre-existing structures. Sometimes a simple four-family flat was rearranged internally to accommodate fifteen or twenty patients.

Trinity Hospital had an arrangement with the City of Detroit so that patients who were not selected by the ER resident to be admitted to Receiving as teaching cases might be transferred to Trinity or other similar hospitals. All of the patients transferred to Trinity were, of course, black. This arrangement resulted in a large patient load of severely ill people that tested the skill and ingenuity of these doctors with very, very limited resources.

In addition to the in-house care patients, the residents and their preceptors frequently visited as observers famous American clinics and attended the Wednesday morning conferences at the University of Michigan. These hospitals each produced physicians recognized as surgeons by their colleagues although they all did general practice as well as surgery. This was not unusual for that time. Two of the hospitals that are affiliated with the medical center now, to my knowledge, had general practitioner surgeons as late as the early 1970s, but none of them were black. For in those days to be black was to be labeled automatically, "Not qualified."

Before blacks were admitted to mainstream hospitals, medical care was primitive. The caliber of the physician really didn't change, but they just didn't have anything to work with. They had no place to work. We had a hospital that was right across the street from Harper called Parkside. Parkside was an old, two-family flat. The operating room was on the first floor and they had patients on the first and second floor. When the patient came from the second floor to the operating room, they carried them downstairs on an army-type litter.

A high percentage of patients did not have Blue Cross. You were taking care of people whose hospital bill would be paid by the county at a very meager rate, or they had no insurance at all. I can recall seeing a patient with intestinal obstruction at old Kirwood Hospital, and we didn't have a suction machine. Even at Meharry we could hook them up to wall suction. They had these little portable suctions at Kirwood, but the thing didn't work. It's 3:00 A.M., and I have this tube down this patient, and the wall suction won't work. They only had one. What I had to do was tell a nursing supervisor to give me an aide and let the aide sit

288

there with a big syringe and just syringe all night long. But it worked. It was the most primitive kind of thing, but they worked. People got well. It took a lot of imagination on the part of the surgeon.

My white friends who practiced in the suburbs would never let me see their Blue Cross vouchers. Dr. Carter had two offices—one in Troy and one in the Fisher Building. He got paid more for doing the same operation if his patient came from his office in Troy than in the Fisher Building. When some official at Blue Shield found out that this Dr. Carter in Troy and this Dr. Carter in the Fisher Building were the same, they demanded that they get the differential in money back from him, because they had paid him too much out in Troy.

One of the ways that they put the black hospitals out of business was, in the first place, these were proprietary hospitals. These were not public, nonprofit hospitals: they were for profit. The doctor who owns them has got to make some money, and in order to pay his employees and make some money himself, they put as many beds in as they could comfortably fit. What happens is that the board of health or the state licensing committee comes around and says, "You've got three beds in this room, and you can only have one." They just cut the lifeblood out of them, and they couldn't maintain the hospital population enough to make ends meet, so they had to fold.

I went into the army and came back, and I was on the staff at Grace. The first time I had a patient to put in the hospital at Grace when I came home from the army was a woman with cancer of the breast. By this time the medical director had changed. I called for a bed for a patient with cancer of the breast, and they told me that there were no beds. I said okay and waited a couple of days, and again there were no beds. I went to the medical director and said I was on the hospital staff for about three months before I went into the army two years ago and never got a patient in the hospital. I've been in the war for two years, and now I've got my first patient; and they keep telling me they don't have any beds, and I can't believe it. He picked up the phone, and I had a bed just like that. He said, "If you ever have any trouble getting a bed, you let me know."

At that time Grace Hospital and all the hospitals in Detroit were rigidly segregated. They would just ask you on the phone, "Is your patient colored or white?" It was insulting, but what could you do? In order to fight this whole thing, there were a total of about fifteen black physicians on the staff at Grace. I was walking around with a chip on both of my shoulders. They made me chairman of the committee to document the racism at Grace. The only black people who worked at Grace were nurses—R.N.'s. There were no black nursing students, no black orderlies, no black residents or interns. None. Nurses were in such a short supply that they had black R.N.'s. This was in 1955 or 1956.

We organized this committee, and I assigned everybody a geographic area in the hospital, and on a daily basis they were to go and document the race of people in every bed. We did that for about six months. Then I asked that we have a meeting with the chairman of the board of trustees. We had a meeting with the vice chairman, the chairman sent his vice chair. He wouldn't come. I thought we were going to have a meeting one-on-one with one guy.

When we got into that meeting room, it was the whole executive committee of the hospital. It was the chief of every service and the chief of staff. I was still a volunteer assistant on the surgeon service, and here's my chief of surgery in there. We gave them the documentation of the segregation of patients in the hospital where we were being told that there was no similar private room available and there were rooms with one white person in the bed and the other bed was empty. All of our patients went to big open wards or they went to a room that had a black patient in it already. If the rooms had two black patients and there was no empty bed where one black patient was, you didn't get a bed. There might be a totally empty room, but you didn't get that bed.

We documented all this for the vice chairman of the board. I was sitting right next to the guy who was the chief of surgery. He's the top and I'm the bottom in the surgical hierarchy. He, in the presence of the vice chairman of the board, told me that my patient didn't belong in the room with his patients. The vice chairman of the board sat there and said: "Yes, we're going to see to it. We're going to take care of it." They didn't take care of a damn thing. The room clerk still had the power to segregate, to assign all the patients. The major reason that it was stopped was that this medical center was a germ in somebody's brain.

We were going to have the big Detroit Medical Center, and they needed to have property condemned around it to build these hospitals. In order to condemn the property, it had to be done with City Council approval. We got to Bill Patrick. Lawrence Lackey was president of the Detroit Medical Society at that time. Lawrence Lackey went down before the City Council, and the Council passed a resolution to the effect that Harper and Grace would not be allowed to condemn property for expansion in the medical center unless they showed positive signs of integration at all levels in the hospital. That's how we broke up the segregation.

At Grace Hospital I was appointed to the teaching staff, which meant that I was supposed to have an intern and a resident assigned to me. The intern and the residents are supposed to do the paper work, and the history, and the physical on the patients; and when you operate, they come and scrub with you. I was never assigned an intern or a resident. When I operated, I had to call somebody that I knew who was most often somebody in gynecology, like Charlie Wright, to come and scrub with me because I didn't have anybody to help me.

Here again, the whole thing revolves around money. Blue Cross/ Blue Shield came out with a new kind of policy about a year later. The initial policy was that they had a fee for surgeons but no fee for a surgical assistant. They came out with a new policy that paid for the surgeon and his assistant. But they would not pay a doctor a fee to assist in surgery in any hospital that had an organized training program, because the residents are supposed to do the assisting. Blue Cross pays the hospital on the basis of their cost, and part of the cost of the hospital doing business was the residents' salaries. They said they were not going to pay for somebody to assist when you have a resident.

When this policy became effective, again I went down to the directors and said: "Doctor, I can't get an assistant in the O.R., and my patients are paying the same premium as everybody else. Blue Cross says that I'm entitled to have an assistant for this patient's premium. If you don't see that I get an assistant, I will have my patient sue you, and I will sue myself, because I have to have an assistant to do an operation. I'm not going to call my friends, because they have to work for nothing." I got assistance from that day forward, just like that.

Everything in those days was done by seniority. I could never start an operation at 8:00 A.M., because I was at the bottom of the totem pole. I had to wait until everybody who outranked me had boarded their cases, then I could start operating at about 2:00 P.M. in the afternoon. I became known as the troublemaker, and I was. I never got promoted. Never. From that time until the time that Harper and Grace merged, I was still a volunteer assistant. Guys who came along who were interns and who were residents in Grace's surgical residency program, they finished their residency, got out into private practice, came on the staff as volunteer assistant, then they got promoted and promoted. I stayed a volunteer assistant for fifteen years.

It bothered me a lot, but what it really bothered was I guess my ego more than anything else. I was able to do my work, but it made me angry, and I stayed angry all the time. I still get angry when I think about it. My white colleagues said, "Waldo, you're bitter."

I said, "You're damn right."

Prior to the affiliation of Hutzel, Grace, and Harper hospitals with the university surgical program, there was not a single black surgical resident trained in either of the three hospitals. I know that at Grace and Hutzel we had residents from Germany, Ethiopia, India, South America, China, the Philippines, Canada, and perhaps many other nationalities that I did not recognize, but not one black American resident.

It is an historical truth that the philosophy and the behavior of the person at the top determines to a large extent the behavior of those lower down in the hierarchy. The leader may not be able to modify the belief of his subordinates, but he certainly can modify their behavior. A rather dramatic increase in the numbers of black trainees in the Wayne State University program began with the coming of Dr. Alexander Walt.

When Alex Walt came to town, the surgical residents from the medical school were rotating through Hutzel. I taught a lot of them, a lot of surgery. He heard about me from his residents. He called me and asked me to have lunch. I went down to his office, this is about twenty or twenty-five years ago. He asked me, "Why aren't you on my faculty." I told him why. He asked if I would like to have an appointment now. I said, "Sure," and he said, "It's done." He appointed me to the faculty of the medical school right there and then in 1968 or 1969. He had been a professor for two or three years before my appointment. He was a South African.

It's a nice little aside that an American WASP . . . refused to have me; and Alex Walt is a South African Jew, and he invited me onto his faculty. I always had bad thoughts about South Africans just because of the way they treat blacks in South Africa, but for the past twenty years he has been as fair with me as I could want him to be. He has given me every opportunity that I could hope to have. I have a very warm spot in my heart for Alex Walt and for John Reid Brown.

One of our greatest faults as a race is, I call it self-hatred. It permeates our whole society. We don't believe in ourselves. I think it's because of the white man's brainwashing. As a race in this country, we have only recently gotten to the place that we believe that we are the white man's equal in anything. I hate to say that but it's true.

BIOGRAPHY

Waldo Cain, M.D., was born on September 29, 1921, in Gadsden, Alabama. He moved to Detroit in 1936. He attended Wayne State University and Meharry Medical College. He is a Diplomate of the American Board of Surgery and a Fellow of the American College of Surgeons. He is on the staff of Harper-Grace hospitals in Detroit. Dr. Cain is married to Natalia Tanner Cain, M.D., and is father of Sheila Cain, J.D., and Anita Cain Longs, M.D., who is married to Curtis Longs. He is grandfather to Tanner Longs.

Mackie C. Johnson joined the Detroit Police Department in 1952 and was a founding member of the Guardians, an organization formed to combat problems in the black community. Mary Upshaw McClendon founded the Household Workers Organization to upgrade the skills and wages of domestic employees.

DISCUSSION ON CRIME AND LAW ENFORCEMENT

MACKIE C. JOHNSON, WINSTON E. LANG, MARY UPSHAW McCLENDON, AND FRANCES QUOCK

WINSTON E. LANG: You will hear it said very often that things are very different today than they were. We used to leave our doors unlocked. We used to sleep out on the front porch in the summertime because you didn't have air conditioning in the houses, and you wouldn't be afraid to sleep out on the front porch.

There was very little in the way of muggings. But I do recall in the late '30s my sister's Easter dress being snatched from my brother's hands as we walked back from the seamstress's after picking them up. Two fellows came out of the alley and snatched them. I don't know if they knew what was in the package or not.

Those kind of things were few and far between in reference to the black community. I'd be somewhat skeptical as far as news coverage of crime in the black community, largely because the policeman's word was law, and whatever he said happened. Whatever a police officer said happened against a black person, that was law.

293

FRANCES QUOCK: We had a saying that they shoot first and ask questions later.

WINSTON E. LANG: In terms of crime I guess the biggest crime going on on a regular basis in the black community, which most people didn't view as crime, was the numbers. We used to have policy as well as the regular numbers. The regular numbers sort of resembled the lottery of today. Policy, I guess you could play one number at a time. They paid off, to my understanding, a lot better than the lottery paid off. I think you got five dollars per penny.

MARY UPSHAW McCLENDON: In a single action people would be moving. They'd get their pay and zip, they would be gone. Until the next one came. They paid off right there.

WINSTON E. LANG: That was against the law, and you might call it criminal, but it was an accepted kind of thing in the black neighborhood. I never found anybody who would turn a numbers person in. Everybody knew who the number man was. Everybody gave the number man respect like they gave any other business person respect.

MARY UPSHAW McCLENDON: Another thing is that the police weren't so holy. If they should happen to catch you, you'd have to pay them off. When we were living on Raphael, right off of Russell, we'd see them get this pickup man. They picked him up and put him in the car and drove him around. "We can't get any today. They done took Steve." After awhile Steve would come back down the street whistling. Steve said, "I had to pay them off."

FRANCES QUOCK: My mother won enough money to pay down on this house. Later on, when things were getting very tight for her, she rented the basement out. This is where the numbers men were. Then the police would come and collect there. So it's true about the policemen collecting their monthly bribe. That was at 93 Adelaide between John R and Woodward. The house is still there. In fact, Danny Thomas lived here before my mother purchased it. There is a church, St. Patrick's, across the street, where he went to pray that if he became popular, famous, he would establish the St. Jude Hospital.

MARY UPSHAW McCLENDON: Also, during the numbers game, when police were hot on their trail, they would move from house to house as their headquarters. If they didn't have enough money to put in their own phone, you couldn't use your phone, because that was their phone up until they'd leave.

They'd give you a certain number of dollars per week to let them operate from your house. If they got real hot on their trail, they'd have to move on to somewhere else. They'd have to move on at 4:00 A.M. in the morning. They didn't have too much to move. They had telephones and the slips.

If you pay off one or two police, they're going to tell the rest of them, and they're going to want a payoff. Before you know it, you're paying off five or six policemen, so you don't have no profit. If they get on your trail, you just go.

WINSTON E. LANG: The numbers would be calculated from a race track, I think it was out of New York. If you knew how to add them and get the averages, that would be the number for the day. Where I was working, this fellow knew how to get the numbers. He was doing the cleaning and pressing, but when the race results came over the air, he would stop and get out a big piece of cardboard and chart them. Then he would get the number for the day.

One of the numbers that everybody used to hit on when they got hot was Joe Louis's weight. Whenever Joe Louis was fighting, whether he was at 215, or 200 or 190, that was the number people would play. If it looked like that was going to come out, then there'd be some shenanigans to change that number.

MARY UPSHAW McCLENDON: They also had what was known as, "house rent parties," with gambling such as punk and blackjack. That was a way that the house made money. Plus they would be selling drinks.

FRANCES QUOCK: Many of your elitists, when they didn't want to be known, they'd come to this house.

MARY UPSHAW McCLENDON: If you don't have any other means of making money from your roomers, you have your friends come in and they buy drinks or maybe they use a room. You charge them for that instead of going to a hotel. It's a way of making money.

Some fellows would come there from all walks of life. One white fellow, he didn't want to carry the woman in the bedroom and pay the fee for the room. They was on the outside. This colored fellow was drinking. He didn't mean to shoot nobody. He didn't know they was in the close corner up there. He thought he was shooting up against an old tin building. He thought there was nobody around, until Mr. Jones hollered, "Ed, you shot me." He couldn't press no charges and told them who he was with. You know, when everybody ran out, they saw who he was with.

WINSTON E. LANG: Even though these kinds of things were going on, they attempted to shield it. There was not openness about it. If a kid was to run into a place where this was going on, he'd be shooed out of there right away. He'd come to ask somebody to cut the grass or sweep the porch. "Get out of here, kid." They wouldn't let you hang around. They kept the children away; that's the big difference.

FRANCES QUOCK: On John R, where we had the different night clubs, they would go around at Christmastime to get their bottles of whiskey that the owners would give them. Just to hear them speak, you'd think they never did that. By the time two or four scout cars pull up and three or four men get out, and you give each one a bottle of whiskey, that's a lot of whiskey. That was after Prohibition.

MARY UPSHAW McCLENDON: Another thing they used to do to the small store owners, they'd go in there and pick up what they want, and the store owner was afraid to say anything. I saw them tell the boy working in there to get some liquor, and he handed it to them and they walked out. They were bad. Cafés the same thing. Fix them some food and then walk out. In a café on Hastings Street one young man said to me, "If they can come in here every morning and eat free, every morning before you go to work, you come in here and I'm going to feed you free."

WINSTON E. LANG: A friend of mine worked on the milk wagon. These were not police officers, just common gangs around the neighborhood. If he'd see them coming, he'd just get off the wagon until they took what they wanted and left. Then he'd get back on. This was in the late '30s, early '40s.

MARY UPSHAW McCLENDON: I had a terrible experience back in the '60s. Right across the street from 1155 Collingwood was a tall building. The school children knew it. "Don't walk on that side. That's a drug building." They were operating from that building.

I decided that somebody had to say something about it, so I called down there to the police. I told them what I suspected. I told them my name and my phone number, not where I lived. Then I got suspicious. I said, "You're concerned more about that than you are about catching them." Shortly after that I was coming out of the Wayne Market on the corner of Collingwood and Hamilton. A police officer in uniform walked up to me and asked my name. I told him.

He said: "Come down here to the corner. You see that building over there? Don't you so-and-so as long as you live call downtown and talk about what you suspect." I was so flabbergasted and surprised. I imagine I was looking at him like a fool. He said, "Go ahead and take my badge number down and turn me in if you want to."

I said: "Officer, I wasn't trying to get your badge number. I'm just so surprised and shocked. That's why I'm looking at you like that."

He told me my "black so-and-so would be dead," if I turned him in.

I was angry myself and upset when he said, "Go on."

When I got in the house, I called Ms. Crowley and told her what happened. She said: "You should have known better than that. Walk up here one afternoon, and we'll walk you back home. I want to show you how they're lined up in the back of that building, different police cars." Sure enough, I called and walked up there one afternoon. We turned out the lights and watched them. The string would go up, the string would go down. Dope going up, money coming down. Sometime the cars were right close together. They had to come out across that old A & P parking lot, five or six cars.

She said that wasn't one night; that was every night. They got to pay them off. They got so bold they'd go in with brown paper sacks. I knew the boys were selling in the sheds. They would get on the corner and sell theirs and wrap it like it was a lunch and put grease on it to make you think it's a lunch. She said: "We got to pay them. They know me in here."

One day a man was beating up a woman in there and I called. They didn't bother to come. That's the reason I won't tell them. I don't care what happens. I saw many times how money transferred. Where drugs is concerned I wouldn't tell them nothing. Because he told me in the profane way, you'll get killed.

MACKIE C. JOHNSON: During the police crackdown in 1960–1961, any police officer who had any personal whims, any attitudes about black people, he could inflict it upon them. As a young police officer, I could see this. Some police officers, especially those who had a dislike for blacks, if they had a tie and suit on they would be subject to a lot of degrading. This was all for the simple reason that there's an opportunity to do it.

A lot of southerners were here. When they started integrating the police department, racism flared up. That kind of attitude is prevalent even today, where racism is ingrained.

From a historical background, when the five-dollar-a day started right after World War I, after the Model A Ford, the police officers of the metropolitan cities were more or less oriented to ethnicity. The behavior of blacks was seemingly so much different. So the first thing they did was go to the South to recruit police officers who "understood them" as they called it. This is the vernacular of police thinking at the time. The South had a different value system.

The southern policeman's method of operation was explained very explicitly by W.E.B. DuBois in *The Soul of Black Folks*. He said the southern police system was set up to replace slavery. It was to control blacks. It had nothing to do with justice. As black people we often looked at anyone who had been in the criminal justice system as somewhat of a martyr. It shouldn't be that way. But overt and brazen examples of injustices by the criminal justice system created the climate where police officers are not respected because of the history of the past.

Up until 1916 there had been seven black police officers hired by the City of Detroit. The quota of five percent was established in 1890 when the black population was five percent. But no matter how many the police department recruited, they made sure that as many as came in the front door, just as many went out the back door.

WINSTON E. LANG: I have a buddy whose father was on the police force. Back then black people were not supposed to buy a Packard car. It was sort of like the Italian car that Sammy Davis allegedly couldn't buy in recent years. With my friend's father being on the police force, he bought a Packard and drove it to work. This was in the late 40's. From that point on there was a whole lot of commotion about him and the way he was doing his job. They finagled him around until they got him off the job long enough to lose that Packard. After that they said there must have been a mistake, and they brought him back on. The Packard was an elite car in terms of the white establishment.

MACKIE C. JOHNSON: When I came to the Detroit Police Academy in 1952 the instructors let us know that the 13th Precinct was one mile square, and that there was a crime happening every minute. The newspapers did not tell you anything about the crime situation. The attitude was that for black people it doesn't matter.

FRANCES QUOCK: I remember between 1952–1954 I was living on Adelaide. I think I was pregnant at the time. This policeman drove up in his car and stopped right in our driveway. He asked me to come over to him. I would not go because I had fear. I didn't know what he wanted with me. I had not done anything wrong. I don't know whether he's going to get me in the car and take me off or what. I did not go. I went right into the house.

MACKIE C. JOHNSON: That was my area. I worked the street there. At that time the Detroit Police Department had an unofficial policy which is known as disorderly person investigation. Every police officer working could use his judgment to determine who to arrest.

I worked the 13th Precinct scout cars and the Disorderly Person Investigation cars. Sometimes the prostitutes' insights into their roles and the police roles were illuminating. I recall one making a remark which helped me better understand the perception some have of the police role back in the 1950s and 1960s. She remarked to me: "You know what you are? You are just a police pimp for a John."

"What do you mean?"

She replied, "You lock me up and take me downtown to be examined for any sexual diseases. If I am clean, I'm back on the streets in a few hours, in the same location. The johns want clean street prostitutes, so they come down here [Woodward and John R, Adelaide, Watson, Erskine, Willis, and Canfield] where the clean street prostitutes are, and the police help make this possible."

Like I said, I worked the cars. My job was to lock them up.

When Jerry Cavanaugh got elected, he appointed a former supreme court justice, George Edwards, as a commissioner. Consequently any kind of police action that formerly had been taken for granted was examined and changed. If you wanted to lock a prostitute up, you had to show that she hailed somebody. You just couldn't see them and say: "Girl, I know you're a prostitute. I'm going to lock you up."

Sometimes I would be fascinated by what I would see on the street. There would be a woman between sixty-five and seventy years old every Sunday morning. We decided to wait and see what happened. It seemed to be too early to go to church, but she looked like she was going to church. Sure enough she was picked up. It was a young guy, a professional man. We asked her, "This is really amazing at your age and everything. . . ."

She said: "That's what's interesting about our society. Sometimes people are attracted to the older folks."

I got some insight into some things that ordinarily I wouldn't get, the fact that a person at a very young age can be attracted to certain things and when they grow up they don't lose it. They still have that attraction.

Well, I used to have to lock up a thousand a month.

FRANCES QUOCK: Many of the women, they couldn't get jobs. Rather than go to some suburban white woman's kitchen and get on her knees and scrub, they found it easier to make money in that way.

We used to have girls. You keep a book, and the lady of the house would be the madam. You would call up certain girls. You get the nice ones, the very attractive ones, and they would come to the house.

WINSTON E. LANG: When I was about ten or twelve my brother was working at a store called the John R Palmer Market. They had me come down to work as the delivery boy. This call came from one of the apartment buildings for some groceries to be delivered. I think all the people in the store knew what kind of place it was. They sent me with the box of groceries. When I got inside, there was this lady who must have weighed three hundred pounds. She was standing there with nothing but her panties on, breasts exposed; and she was smoking a cigar. Girls were sitting all around the wall. When I got back to the store, everybody was laughing. I imagine that was a house where you could get a little bit of everything.

BIOGRAPHIES

Mackie C. Johnson was born on May 17, 1930, in Berwyn, Oklahoma. He graduated from Lincoln Consolidated High School, in Gene Autry, Oklahoma, in 1947. He joined the U. S. Army in 1948. He became a member of the Detroit Police Department in March 1952 and retired in March 1990. He was a founding member of the Guardians. He earned a B.S. degree from Wayne State University in philosophy. He married Pearl Davis and is the father of four—Duane, Debra, Derek, Darren—and grandfather of five—Monique, Candace, Courtney, Connor, and Dommnick.

Winston E. Lang: See p. 208.

Mary Upshaw McClendon was born on October 3, 1923, in Red Level, Alabama, and moved to Detroit in 1955. Throughout her life she has been active in human and civil rights issues. She worked as a household technician and has been founder and president of several organizations. The Household Workers Organization was founded in 1969 for the purpose of upgrading the skills and wages of household technicians and those in related fields of employment. The People's Convert was established in 1982. She has received numerous awards, including being included on the Silver Scroll for the 25th Anniversary of the United Nations Declaration of Human Rights.

Frances Quock: See p. 247.

ROBERT "BOB" L. CUNNINGHAM

My mother and father didn't tell me that I was different than anybody else in the world until I raised the question to them. The first time that I realized that I was different, when I found out that I was black, stemmed from one of those first experiences catching the streetcar. It was the Woodward Avenue line, and I must have been about four. I was with my parents, and my parents were visiting a relative over on Trowbridge. We caught the Woodward streetcar, and I was sitting in a seat in the back of the streetcar. I used to love to go to the back to watch the cable that kept the arc on the pole. I finally sat in an empty seat. Before Trowbridge, the streetcar had filled up, and there was a white woman that came back. She said to me, "Move out of the seat." My parents were up further. She said, "Boy don't you see that I want that seat. Move out of the seat."

I said, "I'm not going to move out of the seat." She asked why. I looked around and there were other seats available.

She said, "Look nigger. . . ." I didn't even know what the word meant. I just got out of the seat, and I went up and told my mother.

I said, "Mom, that woman took my seat."

She said, "What do you mean, took your seat?"

I said, "I was sitting over there and she made me get up."

She said, "That's all right just sit down." I was too embarrassed to tell my mother what she had said to me, because I didn't know exactly what was going on.

Later on, when I got to the house I said, "Mom, what did she mean that I was black, what did she mean by nigger?"

She said, "She said that to you?"

I said, "Yes." I asked: "What does that mean? Am I different? Why did she call me that?" I asked her what does the word nigger mean? When she told me where she was coming from, tears came down my eyes because then I knew that the world from that point on would look at me differently. I understood, in essence, that if you were black, you were marked for the rest of your life in American society.

BIOGRAPHY

Robert "Bob" L. Cunningham was educated in Detroit Public Schools and graduated from Northwestern High School in 1961. After serving in the Armed Forces from 1963–1964 during the Vietnam War, he was employed by Ford Motor Company in 1965 and was an active member of UAW Local 900, where he served on many committees. In 1973 he was hired by Wayne State University as a labor program specialist in the Labor Studies Center, where he has been instrumental in providing computer assistance in data management. Mr. Cunningham has a bachelor's degree in general studies and a master's degree in education.

African Americans
in Detroit and the United States,
1948–1957

1948	Orsel McGhee purchased a home on Seebaldt in an all-white neighborhood of Detroit. In an appeal which reached the United States Supreme Court restrictive covenants in property deeds were ruled unenforceable.
	President Harry S. Truman issued Executive Order 9981 establishing for the armed forces equality of treatment and opportunity for all persons, without regard to race, color, or national origin.
1954	Charles Diggs, Jr., elected Michigan's first black congressman (November).
1955	Emmett Till, a black fourteen-year old, was murdered in Money, Mississippi, for speaking to a white woman (August 28).
	Rosa Parks refused to give up her seat in the colored section of a Montgomery, Alabama, bus for a white man and was arrested (December 1).
	Montgomery Bus Boycott began (December 5).
1956	Martin Luther King home bombed (January 30).
	Federal troops ordered to Little Rock, Arkansas, to prevent interference with school integration at Central High School (August).

1957	Nation's first civil rights bill since 1825 passed (August 29).
	William Patrick elected first black councilman for the City of Detroit (November).
1950s	First blacks hired at Michigan Bell, Sanders, National Bank of Detroit, Detroit Free Press. Montgomery Ward, and Burroughs.

*Nina Mack Lester, H.H.D.,
rose from secretary to managing
editor of the* Pittsburgh
Courier *in Detroit. She is
pictured with staff members
Isabel Defkin (left) and Mabel
Alexander (right).*

NINA MACK LESTER, H.H.D.

The *Pittsburgh Courier* was the largest weekly newspaper in America. It was black-owned. They had eleven branches throughout the United States, from coast to coast. In Detroit it was called the Detroit edition of the *Pittsburgh Courier*. At that time it was the largest of all of their branches in the U.S. and the only one eventually headed by a woman. And I was the only woman.

John R. Williams was the editor of the *Courier*, in the 1940s, and he asked me to come and serve as his secretary. So that's how I got my start with the *Pittsburgh Courier* right out of high school. They said he had difficulty keeping a secretary. He had a new secretary every week. I said, "Well, he won't chase me away."

I got my break when he was out of town once and a big story broke, and they needed someone to write that story. So the Pittsburgh office called, and I told them that he was out of the city. They said, "You think you could write it?"

I said, "Oh yes." So I wrote the story.

I did go to Washington, D.C., once after that. I wasn't expected to write a story. I was just going as a guest of the president of the United States. The reporter who was supposed to cover President Johnson's inauguration didn't show up, and they called me in Washington and asked me, "You're the only one with credentials there, so could you write the story for all eleven of the *Pittsburgh Courier* editions throughout the United States?" So I did the headline story for all eleven of the papers for that event. That was the inauguration of Lyndon Baines Johnson.

During the '50s people were complaining to the newspaper that the tests that they gave them were unrelated to the job that they were asked to do. Federal Department Stores were giving difficult exams for the prospective employees, exams that were way out of line. So we worked with them and got them to change the type of exams that they gave individuals because people were failing the exams; but they really could succeed on the job.

In 1967 they closed the *Pittsburgh Courier* Detroit office. There was a man at the MESC [Michigan Employment Security Commission] who was a friend of one of the executives out at the Ford Motor Company. He said, "I've got a lady that you ought to have on your staff because you don't have any blacks." And they were trying to get them to hire a black person because they'd never had a black person work before for a Ford publication. And he said, "She was general manager and editor, and she's a charming young lady." So he said, "Send her out to see me. When can she come?"

And he said: "Well, she's sitting here in my office right now. We were just talking, and it was just a coincidence that you called at this time."

And he said, "Ask her can she come in tomorrow?"

I went in the next day, and he said, "You know, we have five applicants for this opening." This was on a Friday. So, he said, "We'll let you know on Monday as to the person we select for the position." And I wasn't dressed for the job because I was dressed to go out to a social function. I had on my fur coat and after-five attire.

So when I walked in, I apologized. I told him: "That was the only way I could accept the appointment, because I already had a previous commitment. I hope you'll accept me this way, but I don't dress this way for the office." I said, "I always stress that my staff dress for the occasion and not overdress or underdress." And I showed him a scrapbook that I'd done for the YWCA because I served as their public relations chairman for nine years, and I wrote all the stories that were in there.

I handed him that scrapbook, and they looked at it, and they said to me: "We're going to make our decision on Monday. We do appreciate your coming." And we just chatted awhile.

So, on Monday at 3:45 P.M. they called me. They said, "We arrived at our decision."

I said, "Oh, thank you so very much for calling; that's very kind of you to keep your commitment to call me."

"And we've decided that you're the lady that we'd like to have work for us."

Ford went on strike, and I was the last hired. As a settlement in their strike they decided to close down all of their publications except for two. They had a lot of people with much more seniority than I had. And they explained this to me. They said: "We're not going to fire you, but we just want to keep your name on our payroll. And you don't have to come to work, but when there's an event going on where they need someone to represent the Ford Motor Company, we'd like you to attend. You'll still get your paycheck. And when Henry Ford returns to the country"—he was out of the city—"I'm sure he'll find something for you to do because I know he wouldn't want us to let you go."

When I got married I had the largest wedding that Detroit had ever had. I had twenty-four attendants. An all-velvet wedding. A fifteen-foot train. I had a perfume shower. It lasted me from 1948 till twenty years ago. I got married at Metropolitan Baptist Church. The church held a thousand people, and the people were lined up around down to the corner four deep in both directions. They couldn't get into the church. Nobody believed everybody would come who was invited, but I guess they all did.

BIOGRAPHY

Nina Mack Lester, H.H.D., has worked as a newspaper editor, television hostess, community relations consultant, and business owner. She was the youngest general manager of a major publication and the first black to work for *Ford World* in Dearborn. She owns her own business, L & T Advertising Specialties.

Along with other members of the NAACP, Ofield Dukes picketed Crowley-Milner's, a downtown Detroit department store, in 1962 for refusing to hire black salespersons.

OFIELD DUKES

I came to Detroit at the age of six from Laverne, Alabama, with my mother and three sisters. We came to join my father, who was up several years before to work at the Ford Motor Company. He came and lived with a younger brother. That was about 1941.

I attended Duffield Elementary. I then went on to Miller High School, where I worked on the school paper as a sports reporter. I was the president of the 12-B class; the vice president of the senior class, and served as student manager of the basketball team, from which I became a fan and protégé of Will Robinson, who was a coach. Will at that time was the most successful basketball coach in the state.

Miller, from 1946 to 1950 when I was there, was the only all-black high school in the city of Detroit, and he [Robinson] often talked to the players about demonstrating not only the capability on the court, but their citizenship, because the lower east side had a reputation of being violent and unruly. So he spoke to the players about playing like champions and thinking like champions. In order to be first class on the basketball floor, you had to work hard, you had to practice, and that was only part of it. You had to be good students; you shouldn't smoke; you shouldn't curse; you need to be courteous to people; you need to be real disciplined. During the basketball season the players were prohibited from staying out late and messing around with ladies. So in order to be first class, it was also an attitudinal thing; and he indicated that as blacks, you had two strikes against you. Number one, you were black, and two, you went to a school that was not academically the best in the city; and the question was what would you do with that third strike. He was very philosophical.

Miller won the city championship for four years straight when I was student manager, and I gained so much from the philosophy of Will Robinson, who influenced so many of his players to move from the ghetto through education on to college. He had a tremendous record for that.

After graduation I tried to enter Wayne State University but failed the entrance exam not only once, but twice. I had to go in as a nonmatriculated student while working at Sears as a porter. At that time Sears was not hiring blacks in sales. Sears was not even hiring blacks as so-called "grease monkeys." The only position that blacks could qualify for at Sears was in maintenance. So I worked there for three years while attending Wayne part-time.

I was drafted in 1952 into the military and went to Fort Bliss for training, then to Korea for thirteen months. Although I was sort of a playboy in high school and wrote a lot of love letters, which provided early experience in writing, in Korea for nine months I didn't see a woman at all. I spent time on a lonely hill overlooking Chowan Valley about five miles from the front doing a lot of reading. One of the books I read was William James's book on pragmatism. Life has certain essential functions and the theory of utility. If something is functional, meaningful to you, use it. If smoking and drinking were functional social roles, then fine. If they didn't have any meaning to your life, then there was no need for them.

When I got out, I went to Wayne, passed the exam, and was a B student, graduating with a degree in journalism; was vice president of the MacKenzie Union; chairman of the music committee for the Union organizing jazz concerts. I was the only black in a journalism class of nine persons.

A few weeks before graduation Sprague Holden came to me with his head down and said, "we've been able to place the other eight members of the class at the *Detroit Times*, the *Detroit News*, the *Detroit Free Press*, but we can't do anything for you." At that time, in June 1958, the *News*, *Free Press*, and *Times*, were not hiring black reporters. Not even black copyboys. I was never discouraged by that. I just remembered what Will Robinson said: "You always have two strikes, and it's just a question of what you're going to do with the remaining strike." So I graduated with a degree in journalism without a job.

In 1961 I moved to become an assistant editor of the *Michigan Chronicle* under Longworth Quinn. I did all of the editorials. Mr. Quinn had so much faith in my judgment, all he would do is come in and say, "Okay, what are the editorials for the week?" He was one of the black pioneers. Nothing happened in this city, politically, without people coming by the *Michigan Chronicle*.

Now, the founder of the *Michigan Chronicle* was a guy named Louie Martin, who founded the paper in the '30s. Louie was a political genius. He left the Chronicle and went to Chicago. From there Joseph Kennedy, and Sargent Shriver tapped Louie Martin in 1960 to come to Washington to help develop a strategy for John Kennedy's presidential campaign.

After Kennedy was elected, Louie became a vice chairman of the Democratic National Committee and became a key mover and shaker when Kennedy was killed. The person greeting Mrs. Kennedy at the airport in Washington [when she returned from Dallas] was Louie Martin, and a few of the other inner circle people. After Johnson took over, Louie Martin became a very close friend and advisor. It was Martin who advised Lyndon Johnson to appoint Thurgood Marshall. When that appointment was made, Lyndon Johnson held up the ceremony for an hour to find Louie Martin who was on the golf course because he would not have the ceremony until Louie Martin showed up.

The latter part of March 1964, Longworth Quinn, the general manager, came to my desk with his head down. Louis Martin still owned the *Chronicle* and was in Washington, vice chairman of the Democratic National Committee. He says: "Louie. . . ." (He calls Louie the Leader.) "The leader has called and says they need you in Washington."

I said, "Mr. Quinn, I'm not going."

He said: "I'm sorry, but you don't have a choice; and if I have to fire you for you to go, I just have to do that. You don't have a job here anymore. The leader wants you in Washington." So I packed my bags, and the first Sunday in April I was driving to Washington. I became deputy director of the President's Committee on equal opportunity, and all the meetings were held at the White House, chaired by Lyndon Johnson. We had regional meetings, so it was a tremendous exposure to a president who was the greatest civil rights president in the history of the American republic.

In 1968 the liberal democratic senators warned the president: "Don't do anything on open housing because it would be fatal. Mr. President, you've done all of this. You've passed the Voting Rights Act. You have done what John Kennedy never dreamed he could do." Senator Hart and the others just thought it would be disastrous for the Democratic party in 1968 to push fair housing because the party was divided on that. Lyndon Johnson went down to Georgia one Sunday to see the

82nd Airborne off to Vietnam. Things were going bad. He went up to a group of black soldiers and said to one, "Why are you in this volunteer group?"

The soldier looked at Johnson and said, "Mr. President, for the first time I'm a part of a group that respects my dignity; and I feel like a first-class citizen." Lyndon Johnson went back and he said his prayers that night, and he thought that if these black soldiers who feel like first-class citizens can go to Vietnam and fight from an integrated bunker, then I'm going to go to hell and back in fighting for this Fair Housing Bill so that when they return, they can live in an integrated community. He went against the grain of his own politics, and he knew that in part it would be fatal.

Somehow blacks had faith in Lyndon Johnson. He spent time just talking to them about his life, and the pain, and how he became committed to civil rights as a kid. He talked about pragmatic politics and just told the blacks that you've got to be involved in both parties because people are people, Catholics are Catholics, whites are whites, and you have to play both sides of the street. He said, "Don't tell anybody I ever told you this." He said that he would want to go down in history, not as the war president, but he knew that people would always remember because of Vietnam. Deep down, he said, the greatest accomplishment is doing something to provide opportunities for Negro Americans.

People who were part of Washington understand and appreciate a man who remained himself and was committed to the forgotten people. When you look at Medicare and Medicaid, scholarship aid, Title VII, Title VI, all of those programs that benefit people, Lyndon Johnson set them in motion.

BIOGRAPHY

Ofield Dukes was born on August 8, 1932, in Luverne, Alabama, and moved to Detroit in 1939. He graduated with a B.A. from Wayne State University. He was founder and president of the Young Adult Division of the NAACP. He became assistant editor of the *Michigan Chronicle* in 1961, where he won three national writing awards in 1964. That year he moved to Washington to join the administration of President Lyndon Johnson and the staff of Vice President Hubert Humphrey. He later established a public relations firm, Ofield Dukes & Associates.

LIONEL F. SWAN, M.D.

I came to Detroit in 1951. Before I came to Detroit, I lived eight years in Alabama. For an individual who was born in the West Indies, Alabama was one of those places that it never dawned on me to go. So why did I go? While I was doing my second year as a resident in the hospital in St. Louis (I finished medicine in 1939), there were very, very few places that allowed blacks to do any hospital training. One had a hell of a time getting an internship, let alone a residency. The only places that one could get this type of training in 1939 were a few in Howard University, one or two at Harlem Hospital, about two in Baltimore, one or two in Chicago, and St. Louis.

I did a year at St. Louis, and I was entering my second year when I was called up for the draft in 1941. I applied for a commission. At that time I was informed that the Army was not giving commissions to black doctors. Many of the men were drafted as privates. The only way one could avoid being drafted as a private was to join either the Veterans Administration or the Public Health Service. I joined the Veterans Administration. The only place you could serve in the Veterans Administration was in Tuskegee. I lived in Tuskegee, Alabama, from 1941 to 1943.

I went to Birmingham in 1943, and I lived there from 1943 to 1951. In Birmingham black doctors had no major hospitals where they could hospitalize their patients. If one had seriously ill patients, one had to get one of his white colleagues to put them into the hospital.

That policy sometimes had serious consequences. I had called a white colleague who agreed to hospitalize a woman who I diagnosed as possible kidney failure. When she reached the hospital and her husband, not knowing the name of the white doctor, stated her doctor was Dr. Swan, the admitting clerk recognizing the name as that of a black doctor obviously not on the hospital staff, refused to admit the patient. She died shortly thereafter on the same day. There was a universal outcry of condemnation of the clerk's action, but nothing was done except possibly a promise to use better discretion in the future.

In Detroit the situation was not much better. The difference was that a few enterprising black doctors had opened private hospitals. There were Kirwood, Edyth K. Thomas, Trinity, Burton Mercy, and about three or four others. Black doctors worked in these hospitals and also a few white doctors. A handful of doctors were on the staff of Grace Hospital, but most of the other hospitals refused black doctors. Here and there a few black doctors got on the staff of white hospitals; I got on the staff of Blain Hospital.

Some time in 1968, when the city was receiving federal funds to build the present medical complex including the medical school, it was noted that one of the involved hospitals had consistently refused to train black interns or residents or to admit a black doctor to its staff. Realizing that the use of federal funds for a discriminatory project was not legal, the president of the Detroit Medical Society, Dr. Lawrence Lackey, and I, at that time past president, protested to the City Council against this project until this particular hospital would end its policy of discrimination. Dr. Charles Wright was also involved in this protest. The involved hospital promptly admitted four black doctors to its staff, and the medical center was built; and overt discrimination against black doctors was ended.

In 1956 a boy by the name of Emmett Till had been lynched in Mississippi, I guess for looking at a white girl or whistling or something. The next year a Dr. Brewer was killed in Columbus, Georgia. The members of the Detroit Medical Society felt that we should support the NAACP more liberally to enable it to fight these evidences of injustice. Accordingly, as president of the Detroit Medical Society, I wrote summoning all our members to a meeting to bring one hundred dollars each as a significant contribution to the NAACP.

It was the biggest meeting we had ever had. Fifty-nine doctors were present, including the owners of the black hospitals. We met in the Holiday Room of the Gotham Hotel, a black-owned hotel on John R.

Each of the doctors brought and contributed their one hundred dollars. After the money had been collected, Dr. Alfred Thomas suggested that we use the money as a basis for an NAACP dinner. The idea was accepted by the NAACP leaders who had been invited to the meeting. The community responded enthusiastically to the dinner, which raised $27,000.

BIOGRAPHY

Lionel F. Swan, M.D., was born on April 1, 1906, in Trinidad. He came to the United States in 1923 and to Detroit in 1951. He received his M.D. degree in 1939 from Howard University. He is in private practice in Detroit. He has been president of the Detroit Medical Society and president of the National Medical Association, the first from Michigan. In the mid-60s he led a delegation to meet with President Lyndon Johnson to discuss health problems of black Americans. He was a co-founder of the NAACP Fight for Freedom Dinner in 1956. As an NAACP board member he collaborated to end discrimination against black doctors. He has received honors from several community organizations: Detroit NAACP, Michigan Senate, Detroit Urban League Distinguished Warrior, and many others.

DAVID S. HOLMES

When I went to work in the plants you worked an eight-hour day, and you had ten minutes off for a relief before lunch and ten minutes off after lunch. Lunch was a half hour; and that was it, twenty minutes during the whole day. The rest of the time you were tied to the assembly line. You did whatever job you were assigned to the whole time. Looking back at it now, I sometimes wonder how the men stood it.

I became a committeeman in the plant after about four months. A committeeman was what you'd call a plant lawyer. He took the grievances of the employees to the employer. From there I went to the UAW Political Action Committee.

I became a precinct delegate while I was still in the plants. My next step up the ladder was ward captain. I had several precincts in that ward. And from ward captain I ran for state representative, my first public office in 1954. I lost.

In 1958 I ran again and lost. And then a young lady named Charlene White, one of our first women state representatives, died. And I ran in a special election in 1959 and won that seat; and I've been a legislator ever since, representing basically the near east and east side of the city of Detroit from the river up to Highland Park and Hamtramck.

My second term in the House of Representatives I won by seven votes. That was a battle that was fought all the way to the Supreme Court. It was a battle between myself and a Polish fellow. Polish people just had a little better voting pattern than blacks, although the district was two-thirds black; it was only one-third Polish. I just won by seven votes.

From an overall picture, I was respected cautiously, basically through ignorance, because some of them had never even seen a black until they got to Lansing. I got along with the more liberal-thinking whites. With the more conservative-thinking whites the feeling toward me as a black and the other blacks wasn't necessarily racism. We had one or two. The feeling, as a whole, was a cautious standoffishness, because they just didn't understand us. As a whole, in my thirty years serving in Lansing, I've grown to respect all my colleagues, and I have a feeling they respect me too.

When I was first elected, there was a young man who campaigned in my election very hard. After the election, Fred sat down and told me how he got a civil service job here with the State of Michigan, and he'd lost it because he falsified his record. He was in prison in Chicago, Illinois; and he didn't put that down. In an investigation they found out he was in prison, so he lost his job. That's where I got my idea. (When he was in prison he was a wild young buck. I think he was seventeen, eighteen years old.)

One of my jewels as a lawyer, here in this state, and named after me is the Holmes Youthful Offender Act. That was the law that said that if the judicial system felt that a young person, regardless of race, creed, or color, but mainly black, was found guilty of violation of the law, that the judge could put him under the Holmes Youthful Offender Act from eighteen to twenty-one. And if he made it to twenty-one without getting in any more trouble, they would expunge his record. And the judges are still using that law.

BIOGRAPHY

Senator David S. Holmes was born on August 11, 1914, in Covington, Kentucky, and moved to Detroit in 1940. He received a B.S. degree and honorary doctorate from Virginia State University and did graduate study at the University of Michigan. Before his legislative career he was employed as a UAW-AFL-CIO aide. In 1959 he was elected to the Michigan House of Representatives and in 1974 elected to the Michigan State Senate for the 4th District. In 1974 he was a delegate to the Democratic Charter Conference. He holds membership in the Masons, Alpha Phi Alpha Fraternity, 13th District Business and Professional Men and Women's Club, and Trade Union Leadership Council. His family includes wife Avis E. Green and daughter Patricia

Ann. In the legislature he is chairman of the Senate Democratic Caucus. On the national level he is an executive board member, National Black Caucus of State Legislators; National Conference of State Legislatures; and National Conference of Insurance Legislators.

DISCUSSION ON LIFE AND MUSIC
WENDELL R. HARRISON AND
DONALD WALDEN

WENDELL R. HARRISON: When I was five years old, my mother made me play the piano, to give me some kind of cultural awareness or discipline or whatever. The bottom line was to keep me out of the street so she could watch me. When I went to grade school, I couldn't play the piano, so I started the clarinet.

DONALD WALDEN: That's when I started trying music, when I was in the third grade.

WENDELL R. HARRISON: Then I went to high school and ran into Charles McPherson, Roy Brooks, and James Jamison; and that's when I ran into Donald. All of a sudden they started talking about Donald Walden. I was getting reports and thought, "Who is this guy?"

When we were in high school we used to play at the Urban League, Nacirema Club, also the Ferry Center. These places were actually a good basic foundation for playing jazz. Also the student center over at Wayne, Mackenzie Hall.

DONALD WALDEN: I actually started playing in the eighth grade at McMichael's. Charles McPherson and I had a metal shop class together and neither of us wanted to be there, so we went up and talked to Mr. Banta. He gave us a test to tap on the table and you could tap back. If you'd do that, he'd give you an instrument. That's how I started.

318

The downside of that is my family moved to the east side shortly after that. I went to Barbour on the east side, and the closest thing they had to a saxophone was a mellophone. Since I couldn't get a saxophone, I took it. But I never really learned how to play a scale on it. I started at Chadsey in the ninth grade, and that's when I really started playing.

I guess I was performing by the time I was in the eleventh grade. Eleventh or twelfth grade was the time when I used to get these house-party gigs. We'd get about fifteen dollars.

WENDELL R. HARRISON: I got paid more in one night than I would bring in on a paper route so I was big stuff then. We got ten dollars a gig, then it went up to twelve dollars and fifty cents, and then fifteen dollars. That was big money. In some cases I made more in a weekend than my stepfather was making in a week. Before that I had a paper route, and I had a little grocery store job on Linwood at Meatland making thirteen dollars a week, and I worked seven days.

When I could make twenty-five dollars in two days and doing what I wanted to do, I was in heaven. I would just picture myself playing on the bandstand, somewhere in New York, making my living playing music as opposed to being in a factory or whatever. My stepfather said, "If you're not going to go to school, you're going to have to go out to the plant and get a job."

I said, "I'm going to school, but here I am making as much as you're making in three days in three or four hours a night."

He said, "Let me see how long this is going to last."

I was really trying to prove that I could make money playing jazz.

DONALD WALDEN: I earned my first horn working in a barber shop up the street on John R and Canfield. There used to be a beauty shop and a barber shop owned by a husband and wife team called the House of Joy. I used to clean the place up three days a week. I was offered my first horn working up there, cleaning this place up, when I'd make about fifteen dollars a week.

WENDELL R. HARRISON: There were so many clubs that had jazz, especially on the weekends, from Thursday through Sunday; and they had Monday night jam sessions. Flame Show Bar on John R; Chitchat Lounge on 12th Street; Eagle Show Bar; Spot Bar; Kline's Show Bar; and several others between Grand Boulevard and Clairmount. Between these blocks was just like being on Broadway. Also we used to jam in Delray. I had to sneak into these places because I was too young. I had to go out there because I heard so much about these guys playing jazz. These guys were serious. The word was serious.

DONALD WALDEN: I heard some of the most intense music I have ever heard in my life out there. Yusef Lateef worked there for about two to three years at the West End Hotel. Every saxophone player that came to Detroit was compelled to go out there and have a battle on the saxophones with Yusef. They would stay there until six or seven o'clock in the morning. Serious, stomp down playing.

The level of music in Detroit in the '50s, after Charlie Parker died, was higher than it was in New York. Guys would come here from New York, and they had to practice to come to Detroit. These were master musicians from Abe Woodley to Yusef Lateef.

WENDELL R. HARRISON: There was a certain segment of the community that learned how to play in the penitentiary—federal institutions. They might have got caught with a joint. They had the concentration and solitude to play and to really get it together in jail. People like Charlie Parker were idolized. Their students would be able to come out and get work. Some are famous today.

Some people thought they had to do drugs to play well. They would say: "They're using drugs. Maybe that's why they are playing like that." But it wasn't true. They had put sober hours into their craft; and if they still played well when they were high, it was because they were on automatic.

DONALD WALDEN: Reefer was a lot more serious then than now. Now you might get stopped with a bag of weed in your car, and the police officers don't even pay attention. Thirty years ago you might go to jail. The jazz community and the art community were always twenty-five years ahead of everybody else, so you know they sampled it.

There are very few jazz musicians that have serious drug problems. It was a fad. You could make a case for Charlie Parker being the father of the drug culture because he actually was the one who popularized, brought drugs to the street level. Many musicians followed along in his footsteps, but it's something you don't see that much of anymore.

Back then a movie star would say, "I'll do a role for two or three kilos of cocaine."

Today the audience isn't there. We lost one generation to the Motown explosion and another generation of jazz musicians to the drug culture of the '60s and '70s. Before the Motown era, rhythm and blues was primarily played by unskilled musicians that didn't have a lot of knowledge for the most part. It only generates a certain element of population acceptance. The difference that the Motown era made was that the music was created by jazz musicians and was polished and made sophisticated enough that it was able to be marketed to a much wider audience. In effect we kind of shot ourselves in the foot. All of that music was created by jazz musicians.

WENDELL R. HARRISON: When I was in New York in the '60s, Jamison was a bass player and was here in Detroit playing electric bass. I couldn't believe it, because I remember Jamison playing upright bass and having a concert sound. But he was the guy that really made the electric bass popular. He was a legend.

There's another guy, Earl Van Dyke, piano player, composer and arranger and jazz bebopper, that made a lot of hits for Motown. I did a session with him for Barry Gordy before I left.

When you were asking why have things changed, it has been the factory that was primarily responsible for a lot of the change, because in the '40s and '50s and '60s the industry was hot. Detroit had Ford and Chrysler as well as Studebaker and Packard plants. Everybody was making some money. Black folks was coming up from the South and got hired and were making a lot of money in these factories. Motown hired a lot of folks. Folks would work in the factory but would go and record for Barry Gordy.

Back in those days I remember when I would go up to Lionel King's, a little coffee shop. In his shop they had bohemians, these beatniks, kind of intellectual. You just don't have that nowadays.

DONALD WALDEN: Those same types are into rock and roll. The intellectuals would compare with the population of bohemians and beatniks. Also, the college campus was a great place for jazz artists. There was a big group of intellectuals that don't necessarily let outside forces determine their thoughts. But at the colleges they are the most conservative people in the world now. It doesn't look real good. The clubs are gone.

WENDELL R. HARRISON: In one aspect that might be good because jazz is concertized, which it should be.

DONALD WALDEN: The only thing bad about that to me is the concert stage is really for a working band. On a concert stage you've got one time to get it right. But in a club, if the first set is bad, you still have a shot on the second or third set.

WENDELL R. HARRISON: The club thing was like the English pub. They would come to the club on Saturday night just for information, just to see what the latest gossip was, to meet your friends, and to hang out and laugh.

DONALD WALDEN: We used to do a lot of parties here at the Urban League for a group of coeds. We could do a Friday night in here, a Saturday night at the Ferry Center, an early Sunday morning at the Elks up on Warren. They'd have these little Sunday morning breakfasts and might have a gambling party.

WENDELL R. HARRISON: Then in the church you could perform—like St. Stephen's, Hartford Baptist, and so on. You could work there on Friday and Saturday night for some type of birthday party or a wedding. The churches would really support this music just as much as the clubs. We would play at night what we had heard on the radio. We would hear "Bye, Bye, Blackbird," or C. C. Ryder, the Four Freshman, or Glen Miller; and we would play the same music with a jazz concept.

The record companies encouraged creativity, whereas today, if you can do something, develop something for a couple of months, "We'll put you out all over the world, son."

That's one of the reasons I started out playing the clarinet. It took me actually twenty years to learn the instrument. Everybody was really studying to master their craft. Record companies would encourage this. Everybody was into the creative thing. That's not encouraged today. Illusions are encouraged, for some kind of strange reason.

BIOGRAPHIES

Wendell R. Harrison was born on October 1, 1942. He has worked as a performing musician since he was a teenager. He moved to New York when he was eighteen years old and performed with many musicians and entertainers, including Lou Rawls, Ella Fitzgerald, Sarah Vaughn, Woody Shaw, and others. He presents workshops and classes throughout the United States and Europe. He has recorded extensively and written instructional material. He is principal of Rebirth and Wenha Productions. In 1992 he received grants from the Arts Foundation of Michigan to compose two suites for his clarinet ensemble.

Saxophonist/composer Donald Walden was born on July 12, 1928, in St. Louis, Missouri. He is a graduate of Chadsey High School and studied with Larry Teal and Barry Harris. He began his professional career in 1956 performing at local dances and social events. He worked for a time at clubs in New York City. From 1966-70 he was an accompanist for the Aretha Franklin Orchestra, as well as Motown artists Stevie Wonder, the Four Tops and others. He has performed with Tommy Flanagan, Barry Harris, Gerald Wilson, and Dizzy Gillespie. Donald Walden formed the Detroit Jazz Orchestra in 1982 and the New World Stage in 1986. In 1985 he received the First Annual Governor's Arts Award.

DISCUSSION ON LIFE IN THE BREWSTER HOUSING PROJECTS
GLORIA MANLOVE HUNTER AND
ELEANOR MANLOVE

ELEANOR MANLOVE: The first part of the project that was built was on Benton and Erskine. Then later on we lived on Watson. We didn't get in when it was first built because that was when my father was living, and he didn't want to move down there. Shiloh was right in there—Mack and Wilkins. It was built a little different. The floors were cement, and they just left the bare cement showing. The whole place was cement—the walls, the floors. They were sort of like a gray. You had to have rugs.

GLORIA MANLOVE HUNTER: St. Peter Claver was on Beaubien and Eliot on the south side, and then as you go back I think there was just the Center, and then there was Louie's. Louie was an ex-Navy man. After Louie's, there was Mr. Dotty's grocery store, where mother ran a tab for years and years. It was like in the middle ages, with the wooden counter and the potbellied stove and the peanuts. They lived behind the store. Mr. Dotty was black, and so was Louie. Naturally Mr. Dotty and his wife and daughters, they were upper crust. Their father owned the store.

It was horrible when you think about it now. I remember the food at Dotty's would be spoiled. By the end of the month, the hot sausages would be like little knots. But you bought it anyway. He didn't put any

323

more out until he sold the last one. I don't think he'd ever stock the shelves, because he would buy ten of everything until it was gone.

As we got older and we moved down on Eliot between Hastings and St. Antoine, we were about seven or eight, it was easier for us to go to the store; and mother would give us this note saying what she wanted. I would alter the note. She would put down potato chips, and I would put down four bags. I loved windmill cookies; and she'd put down two, and I'd change it to a twelve. I could do her handwriting better than she could. I'd make her give me a long piece of paper so I had plenty of room to put down the rest of what I wanted. I would eat all the potato chips and so on.

Now, you remember Jack's right there on the corner of Hastings and Eliot? Jack's Drugstore is where you guys would go and put in your numbers. I remember because Miss May would send me up there. He was a white man. I remember the floors were tiled, and that's when they still had the fountains and the bar stools, and they sat so high. And then there was a little grocery store, and then a restaurant, and then the alley where the prostitutes hung out. They would pay us a quarter to watch for the police. When "Shorty" Black would come, you'd holler. We thought it was fun. We didn't realize there was anything bad.

ELEANOR MANLOVE: We used to go to the Castle Show. You'd go there, and there'd be so many people; and everybody would be talking out loud and everything, but you all looked forward to that. You'd get your plates. You'd get a whole set of plates. This was after the war.

GLORIA MANLOVE HUNTER: You got a plate, and you'd get the bowl. Some people would get their whole set of dishes from there. On Saturday from 12:00 P.M. to 6:00 P.M. it was kids there. From 6:00 P.M., on it was for the adults. Some tried to double back and get two plates. It was the flowered stuff. For the poor, it was your finest china. You'd get the bowl, the salad bowl, and saucers.

We lived on the third floor, and right up over our apartment was the roof, which we made our private domain. We had our club up there. The roof was a world in its own. You traveled by roof. In the three-story apartment buildings the kids knew we could travel all through the court by roof, because if you went in somebody else's court, you could get beat up; that was enemy territory. You jumped from one roof to another. Mom didn't know. Kids had a world of their own. We would climb around the walls. Sometimes if she wasn't home, we could monkey-climb from the first floor all the way up to the third floor and get the window open and come in the apartment.

Sometimes we had to almost do it for survival. If we stayed out on the weekends until it was dark, the prostitutes and the pimps would be pulling the "Murphy" on the white man. These men would tell white men that would come into the area that there were prostitutes in these apartments, and they would take the money. The guy would say, "Okay, you give me twenty-five dollars, and you go up to apartment

675; and in that apartment there's a woman there for sex." When these white men would get there, sometimes they would be drunk or they would be angry. And the doors were steel, so the men would be hollering and beating on the door. They would try to set a fire; they tried to burn the place.

Whoever thought that using cement and steel wasn't a bad idea was correct, because when Mom and her neighbors would finish with the paper, they'd put it outside the door. We kids would collect it for sale or the papers went to the incinerator. These guys got together one night, and they decided they were going to burn the door down to get to this woman. And had it been wood, it would have burned. But since the whole building was brick and steel, it wouldn't even burn. They would try to kick the door down or take the handles off the door.

The kids had a signal. When we would go to the Castle and stay past 6:00 P.M. to see Buster Crabbe and Flash Gordon, you'd catch some grown-up coming into the movie, and you'd walk next to them so the usher would think he was your parent; and then you'd stay in there or you'd crawl up under the seat. When you'd come out, it would be after 6:00 P.M., and it would be dark. Sometimes when we got home, the lights would be off in the hall. If a light was out, you didn't know if one of the junkies had screwed the light bulb out because he was out there shooting up. You didn't know if it was a prostitute turning tricks in the hall. You didn't know if it was a setup.

So you would stand there and holler, "Hey, Ma." She would come to the window and tell us to come in the building or not to come in the building. If she told us to come in the building, it was just that the light had gone out. If she said don't come in the building, you couldn't go in because you were afraid someone would harm you. So you learned to walk the walls. We'd start at the first-floor window ledge. Somebody would boost you up, or you would stand on something like a rock; or you could jump and grab the ledge. And you could go from the first floor to the second floor. Then we'd get to the third floor, and we'd crawl in the window, and we'd be in the house. It really worked well when you were supposed to be in bed. In our court, remember the tree that was outside the kitchen window? Our mother knew some of it. We'd go out the kitchen window and jump to the tree. As I got to be an adult I would drive through there and look at the tree, how far it was away from the window, and say I don't believe that I used to do that. It was just as natural as rain.

Downstairs Mom and her friends had a bench that they would sit on. The ladies would sit on the bench [in the summer] and talk all night and barbecue. They'd make a pit.

ELEANOR MANLOVE: We'd stay out all night in the summer, come in at 5:00 A.M. or 6:00 A.M. when it got light.

GLORIA MANLOVE HUNTER: Sometimes I was on punishment; maybe we had been told we had to stay in the apartment. I'd go to the kitchen window and go down the tree or come out of the apartment and go up on the roof and walk the roofs. You'd go from building to building. If I wanted to go over to my girlfriend's, I'd be on top of the roof. When I got to her building, I would simply lower myself down on a window sill and just go on around to her place. It was a whole network, and you knew Mom and her friends were going to be down there all night.

Every once in awhile you'd go back home; or you'd have a kid that could come out, go peek, and see if your mother was still on the front bench. Sometimes we'd be playing right behind. They'd be sitting on the bench talking, and we'd be playing right behind the apartment listening for them. So as soon as Mother said, "Wait a minute, Hattie, let me go upstairs and get so and so," I knew it was time to skinny back up that tree and get in the apartment. Then we could stay out all night because they were out, if you weren't on punishment.

ELEANOR MANLOVE: Sometimes I'd be mad, and I made them stay up there; and it would be so hot.

GLORIA MANLOVE HUNTER: We wouldn't be in there! We would do different things when we could stay out. All the kids would get together; and we'd make french fries, bags of french fries. And then we would make peanut brittle, because you'd go to the store and get three cents worth of peanuts. You'd use five pounds of sugar, which wasn't anything, because they were commodities. We would make french fries. And then you'd sit down on the front step and you'd play "That's My Car," while they were barbecuing or when the old ladies would sit out. We'd sit there sometimes all evening long and play, "That's my Car." A car would come down the street, and if you could name the car and the model, that was your car. But you had to call it out first. Or we'd play "Pony Express."

If somebody really owned a bike, it was generally put together by parts. I don't think anybody ever had a new bike in their life. Well, a few of our friends did. That was a big thing in a kid's world, because some of my girlfriends, like Dorothy, had a different father every week, so she always had new clothes and treats and things like that. And we didn't have but one father, even though he wasn't there. We were kind of different, so we were always on the tail end. I don't think I ever had a bike. A lot of my friends did because of those new daddies, if she got him around the kid's birthday, I guess.

We'd have the bikes and play "Pony Express." To play, there were two groups. You'd just ride all night long and see which bike got back first. We could stay out real late because your parents told you, "Don't leave the front of the house." When the street lights came on, you had to be in front of the house; and you were, and you'd just ride around the block. They'd be talking. They would pay attention, but they knew. With Benson and I, you could see one or the other. That's the way we lived, especially at night.

Remember when they had the fire over at the barn? All the horses were running. I'll never forget that. There used to be a stable over there. Over there on Beaubien between Eliot and Mack. All the junk men used to stable their horses there. One night it caught fire. I'll never forget it, because there were horses on fire running down the street, and they were screaming. I'll never forget that, because I was a little kid, and we lived right there on Beaubien between Eliot and Mack. You could smell it, and I had never smelled burning flesh. They were hollering and screaming; and the men themselves, some of them were just crying like babies. They had to shoot the horses in the street. It was frightening, but it was fascinating.

One of the junk men, when they shot his horse, he just laid there on that horse, he just cried. They told me that the horses were like brothers or sons to the sheenies and the junk men. The police were out there, and they were running all over. They had to rope off the area because the horses were going wild. They tried to save some, but they were running into the houses and running into cars and into the projects. So they had to shoot them.

Mr. Brown was the vegetable man, and he came every single day. He had a wagon, like "Tony the Italian," but this was Mr. Brown. He had a horse, and the horse's name was George. We would lay in waiting for George, and we'd take our pea shooters. George would hit Eliot and Hastings, and he would trot around just as nice. The first eight or ten units were row houses before you got to the three-story apartment buildings. He would trot, but when he got to our unit he'd take off. Mr. Brown would be yelling, "Ho, George, Ho!"

But, see, George knew we were lying in wait with those pea shooters; and we would aim for his balls or his butt. Especially on Saturday. During the week you'd be in school, and it was kind of hard to get George. George knew Saturday very well. Mr. Brown would be waiting on my mother or something; and all of a sudden he'd take off, and Mr. Brown would throw his hat like that. George would take off. I didn't know if George could smell us or somebody would land one. You waited for that.

The other thing was if you could distract Mr. Brown, you'd steal everything—the apples and the oranges—while he was waiting on one of the parents or while he was watching George, because he knew George was getting antsy.

That was like Dotty's. Mr. Dotty knew when we came in the store that kids were going to take certain things like the peppermints and penny candy. I'd put down "twenty-five cents penny candy" over Mother's shopping list. You know how much candy you could get for twenty-five cents? You get three Mary Janes, oh, God, along with four bags of chips and about fifty windmills. I'd eat the chips before I got home, and I buried the rest of it on me. Then you'd come in the apartment, and I'd say, "I got to go to the bathroom," and I'd run and put it in my stash. Or I would get a great big box of HiHo crackers.

Remember the Bookmobile? I always read a lot. Every Monday and Wednesday the Bookmobile would come. I think I had a library card when I was five years old. Because at Lincoln, when you went to the first grade, your first big trip after you painted the picket fence was to go to the Bookmobile. That to me was my make believe world. I could get books. The librarians could depend on me. They'd let you take two books. But I was there every Wednesday and Monday faithfully. The librarian started letting me take out as many books as I wanted because she knew that I would bring them back. If you went to the Bookmobile today, you would be considered a wimp. The kid's a real nerd. I was real nerdy.

Then the Bookmobile was run by all white people, but they would take the time because they were there from three o'clock, as soon as you got out of school, until about 6:00 P.M. Sometimes they'd have books waiting for me because they knew I was coming. They'd sit there and read them to me or help me learn to read. Basically that's how I learned to read and love books. They would say, "Okay, here she comes," and they'd have my little stack. Everything from the *Red Pony*; and as I got older they had me reading good literature. I was reading Steinbeck when I was quite young. But it was only because those people cared. Sometimes there would be a line. They only let two kids in at a time, and I thought that Bookmobile was such a big building to me as a little kid. Now when I see one, I realize how small it was.

Mom, remember on Sundays and on the weekends when you would put Pat in the stroller and we would walk up to the Main Library? They had a children's reading hour. Mother would leave us there. We were poor as church mice, but we could go to the children's reading hour. If Pat was one, Ben was seven, and I was eight. We'd walk up there from the Brewster Projects because you couldn't always afford the bus; and we would push my sister in the stroller. Then we'd go by the bakery and smell all the goodies. It was Wonder Bread, and you could get a free sample. Then you'd go up to Vernor's, and Vernor's used to give the free floats on Sundays and the Vernor's pop. You could go down there and get a sample.

We'd go to the library, and I remember when there would be ballets at the Art Institute. We would sit there, and I guess we just looked so poor and bedraggled that they would open the door and let us in. My mother, and Ben, and my baby sister. We would just be sitting there on the lawn because it was just so nice to have all that green grass. She would let us play right there at the Art Institute, on the steps. The ushers, I guess, would feel so sorry for the little black lady and her little black children, and they would let us in. That's where I saw my first ballet. I saw "Sleeping Beauty." At intermission they would put us back out. It was marvelous to us because we were black. It was like a dream world to see all the ladies dressed up.

Diana Ross grew up in the projects. When Ben went to Cass, he never rode the bus. Sometimes it would be cold or snowing, and I'd say, "Why don't you take the bus?"

He said, "Oh, I go down and pick up some girls that go to Cass." I never knew and he didn't say who they were. He said, "They've got a quartet."

Remember the penny-candy store next door to Friendship Church? The way they got the kids to come to church was get in a bus and round you up. If you went to church, they'd promise you that you could go to the penny-candy store and get ice cream. Some Sundays we would go to three or four churches. You'd start at Sacred Heart because it was quiet. You'd go over to Friendship, and you'd bet on whose mother's panties you were going to see. Then you get down in the seat. We were always afraid, but you knew that there was a penny- candy store next door. Then another bus would get you and take you to a sanctified church. You could dance. To us their way of celebrating their religion was doing the chicken dance. You could make almost a quarter just going to churches, because if you went to the sanctified church, they would give a kid a quarter and an ice cream. It was in Paradise Valley.

On Saturday nights you knew when the Shakers and the Kingsmen were going to fight. The word would come down by Wednesday—big rumble on the street. Grown-ups knew. By sundown, everybody would be off the street. It was just like "High Noon." It was like an underground society. Did they have any mothers? Nobody talked about it. Everybody knew who they were, but the parents were separate from the kids.

See, a mother could have a son in the Shakers. Nobody messed with her, but she still was not looked at as evil. Her son was a bad boy; it wasn't her fault. She was always pitied. She was well taken care of. The women folk, remember there were very few men, just those weekend fathers. The women were a separate society.

Women were treated different. They weren't looked at as being vulgar, even the women who were prostitutes. They made money; so in a way they were respectable. Like my best friend, we knew what her mother did, but it was all right because she could give her nice things. Now all the women might gab. My mother and Miss Hattie would sit there and talk about Miss Sadie and a couple of the others; but to kids they were fine. They had stuff. They were almost like the elite of the neighborhood.

So when there would be the Friday and Saturday night fight, by sundown, unless you were sick, everybody stayed in or you'd do your network around the buildings. You'd go up on the roof. Sometimes you couldn't go on the roof because they would fight on the roof. The battlefield was the roofs as well as the streets.

You'd get stabbed to death, shot, but not anything like it is today. A knife was the weapon of choice back then. You would live to brag about it. Adhesions from the knife were like a badge of courage. If somebody was killed, it was a rarity.

Mother would take us shopping, and we would take the streetcar to Belle Isle. That was the biggest trip. I remember it ran on Beaubien and then Jefferson. I think it went across, and it was such a long ride. For a special treat we'd just ride from one end of the line to the other. That would be our treat on Sunday. Mother would say, "Now if you are good, we'll go for a streetcar ride." So all week that meant we didn't burn down the house.

Mother would make us go to bed at seven o'clock, even in the summer. We would go into the bedroom and make a tent and get some matches and cook. You see, in the projects you had radiators; so we'd play house, and I'd have to cook on the radiators. You'd go get a couple strings of spaghetti or macaroni, and then we'd turn the radiator up. Since it didn't work in the summer, you had to cook dinner for your husband, so we'd get matches.

So one night mother was having a party, the "blue light specials" you had; and we were in there playing house, in the bedroom. It was early; every other kid is outside. But we were in the bed and had made a tent, and I got a match . . . the covers started burning. I told Benson I had to go to the bathroom. I wasn't going to get in any trouble. The covers started burning, and I left him in there. I know eventually Eleanor was going to start smelling the smoke. Sure enough, that's what she did.

Mother was clean. At night, if you got up and you wanted a glass of water, you would go in the kitchen and turn on the light, and you would jump back 'cause the roaches would just scatter. And you would be stepping on them, and they would be bopping, and they would be flying out of cabinets. Everything mother had, and she still does it, was wrapped in bags with a tie on it because everything would have roaches in it. It wasn't so much that we didn't keep our unit clean; but they would travel from one unit to the other, just marching up the stairs. Mother would never let us spend the night with too many friends because of bedbugs. The big thing was to take a bar of soap and smash them.

Mother was always referred to as Miss Manlove. Now some of our friends had mothers. . . . When I make reference to Miss Sadie, you know what kind of woman Miss Sadie was. But Mom, she was always Miss Manlove. She was always the lady that set table napkins on the table when we would be having grits and bologna for dinner. We always set the table. We were kind of different. Mother always reminds me of her family, reminds me of people from "Gone with the Wind," that at one time had money and became the genteel poor. Mother didn't even cook like the other black mothers. She doesn't realize that now. We were setting the table when there wasn't anything to eat. Most of our friends didn't know the proper way to set a table.

But the older people that lived in the project or who were there from the inception of the project were different. Even the kids that we hung with, when they did really bad things, generally I was not included; neither was Benson, because Miss Manlove was different. The only thing they ever let us in on was when they knocked over the Polar Bear truck. All they did then was let me have a whole container of ice cream. But when they did things like drugs, Ben and I never got into drugs—the weed or the heroin. God knows it was prevalent enough. It's just that we were kind of different.

We'd roam. We'd go all the way downtown. We'd walk through the project, a whole band. Ben was stuck with me because he was my brother; and if he didn't let me go, I was going to tell. "Fruity" was stuck with Peggy. There might be four little girls in the bunch with each ten little boys, and we would start in the project and walk through the project all the way downtown, all the way to the river. This means we'd go through Black Bottom. We had an uncle that ran a numbers shop. We were big shots. We'd stop at uncle's place and he'd give us fifty cents, and he gave all the other kids maybe a nickel or a quarter. Then you would go to every gas station, and you'd turn on the water and you'd drink the water. You hit every pear tree, every apple tree. You would go to a gas station and steal a couple of tires. You roll those tires until you roll them into the street or try to roll them into a car. Nobody thought about causing an accident. We'd go downtown, and we'd walk around. We're kids, seven, eight, nine, ten, eleven years old. We did it year after year. That was our fun.

We'd go to Belle Isle, walk all the way down to the river, throw rocks at the fish, scare all the little animals, do whatever kids did. Then we'd go down to Hudson's and look in the windows. A bunch of little bedraggled kids. Then you'd walk back to the project. Nobody bothered you, and you didn't bother anybody. If you were lucky, it might be a weekend when they were having the union parades. If you saw a parade coming, you'd say your father worked for Ford's. Then they would give you a hot dog or lemonade or whatever. You'd go down to the railroad tracks and pick at the bums, but they'd make sure that the girls stayed away because they'd say that the bums would steal your clothes and your shoes.

331

By then they were building the Douglas Projects. They had these big sand dunes. There's not a kid in the world that could get around playing in these big sand dunes. They were as tall as the Douglas Projects, some of them. Mother knew when we had been down there, because you'd have sand in your clothes and in your shoes. We'd take off our shoes and leave them way over there so they wouldn't get sand in them. We'd take our dresses and put them in our panties and play on the sand. These were mountains. Believe me, when you think that some of them had to be three- and four-stories high, they were just mounds of sand that they were going to use to construct those fourteen units.

We had a couple of friends that were killed. One boy, he was smothered in the sand. That's why they didn't want us to play over there. It was dangerous. Kids didn't understand that. We just knew that it was fun. Sometimes when they quit work they'd leave those great big caterpillars and things; and so you'd climb on them, not realizing that you were two- and three-stories high.

I could be up on Wilkins, and the jungle drums would say, "Miss Manlove is looking for Sissy." And they'd say, "Miss Manlove is on Benton." So we'd be walking up Hastings. The jungle drums would tell me to come through the court, and they would tell me don't go that way because your mother. . . . This was the way we lived. The jungle drums, every kid along the way would tell you, "Miss Manlove was at such and such a place. Cut over on Shiloh; go this way." When she'd come back, I'd be sitting on the front steps of the apartment building.

We could walk to Diggs's Funeral Home. Remember when we used to sneak in there in the funeral home? If you really wanted to have a gas, you'd go into the back. Them old dopey girls, they would get up under the casket. Did Ben tell you about the time, I guess they were having a family viewing, and they didn't realize we were in there peeking around; and all of a sudden we realized there were people in there, and we crawled up under the caskets and just lay there. I don't know what made us do that. We put our hands under that lady's skirt. It was shameless. They had slumber rooms where the bodies were. It was a dare that you stick your head out and yell, "Boo!" They would be chasing us all through the funeral home, and you'd get caught in a room with those bodies, and you'd jump in the casket.

But then we'd scare ourselves. Living on the third floor, those lights from the Metropolitan House of Diggs flashed red. Mother would stand there and to make us go to sleep she would say, "Woo, woooo." The closets didn't have doors; they had a curtain. She knew when the wind was going to blow out of that bedroom window and hit that curtain, because she'd say, "If you don't go to sleep, they're coming to get you," and she'd go, "Woooo." The wind would blow. We knew, because we had been over at the funeral home, everybody's coming to get us. We had seen enough bodies that day to scare anybody.

We only had one bedroom. Benson slept on a cot next to the wall. Pat as a little baby slept in a dresser drawer until she moved up to the bed with my mother and I. The three of us slept in the bed. We would say, "Pull down the shades," because we knew that undoubtedly one of the bodies was after us.

Hastings was just fascinating. Peoples Bar, you could go up there and work the street as kids; and you could make pretty good, because you knew that everybody's weekend father or the real father went in there on the weekend; and they were going to get drunk, and the average drunk was going to see his kid and give his kid a quarter. While he was reaching in his pocket to get that, he was going to spill all of his other change; or he'd give money to every kid that was with his kid.

The pimps and the prostitutes, they had nice cars and nice clothes, and they were nice to children. If you got a favorite prostitute that you'd work for, in the winters you'd do her hot bricks for her. You'd give her bricks so she could stand in the alley. They'd warm bricks. You'd pick up a few bricks, and she'd make like a stand. That way she wouldn't be down on the ground where it was cold, and you just might make like a platform for her. Or they would just warm bricks, put them next to the gallon drums, and you'd bring them to her, and she'd stand there. Sometimes you could get one who would give you a dollar or whatever; then you'd go up to the ten-cent store, keep your dollar, and steal everything in the ten-cent store.

ELEANOR MANLOVE: I never sat and wondered when my children were coming home. After they'd be gone too long, I'd get out and go look for them. One of the reasons why I think that a lot of children are like they are, maybe they were out in the street and you would say to the mother, "Where's so and so?" She would say, "I don't know." After they were gone so long, I'd go look for them.

BIOGRAPHIES

Gloria Manlove Hunter was born on October 3, 1942. Her family originated in the Virgin Islands. She graduated from Central High School and earned a B.A. in business from Central Michigan University. She has worked for the Chrysler Corporation for twenty-five years. She is married and the mother of a daughter and son and has one grandchild.

Eleanor Manlove was born on November 1, 1920, in Detroit. She is the mother of three—Gloria Manlove Hunter, Benson Manlove, and Sheila Manlove.

MEL RAVITZ

My obligation has been to the whole Detroit community, and I certainly have been aware, since I've been a very young person, of serious discrimination against African Americans in our country and in our city. I have chosen, on as many occasions as possible, to join with the African American community in its efforts to fight against discrimination, prejudice. I've done this both as a teacher, as a citizen of the city, and in my professional roles as City Council member, director of the Mental Health Board, and in all of the nonpaying roles that I had. If that gets me viewed positively by some members of the black community, that's fine. I've done essentially, however, what I felt was right to do.

My upbringing, my reading, my professional training, for example, in anthropology and sociology, have conditioned me to view people as people, period, absent any other consideration. With that as a kind of basic background, I was quite active during the period of the '50s in working for open occupancy housing. I remember working with such people as the late Monsignor Kern; Beulah Whitby, who was then deputy director of the Community Relations Department; Richard Marks; and Arthur Johnson. A number of us would be involved in these panels that were set up primarily through the Catholic Archdiocese. We would go out to different parishes and draw a crowd and controversy and respond to questions.

When the notice was sent out in that general parish that we were having a discussion on open occupancy housing, there would be critical people, hostile people coming, too. This, I remind you, was almost thirty to forty years ago, so that the attitude was extremely hostile.

We had opposition here in the city of Detroit, too, and certainly in the suburbs from such groups for instance, the Northwest Federated Civic Association, which was an organization of home-owner organizations which up until 1962 was very powerful. In conjunction with a good number of real estate brokers, they were involved in keeping neighborhoods closed not only to African Americans but also to Jews, Italians, etc. This was somewhat around the time, maybe a little before, the infamous Grosse Pointe "point system" came to public attention.

We thought that a pretty fundamental solution to problems of education, to problems of family development, etc., would be for people to be allowed to live where they wished to live.

I went to work for the Detroit City Plan Commission in 1953 as a staff sociologist. I was asked to go out and organize block clubs as part of the federal program of neighborhood conservation. The federal legislation had been adopted, I believe, in 1952. About a year later I was out trying to organize block clubs in our so-called pilot neighborhood, which was on Detroit's east side, in the area north of Mack, east of Bellevue up to Van Dyke, and as far north as Warren, a thirty-five block-area which I then proceeded to organize, block by block. This was a racially changing neighborhood. It had been principally a German and Italian area before.

Black people were new in the area, were hesitant and unsure of their place with regard to the older white residents. And the effort to organize block clubs was a fascinating thing. I got black and white people to come together into each others' homes for the first time ever. We'd call a block club meeting and we'd get them to sit down, and they began to see that their problems were the same. For example, alley problems. We had many barn-like structures in the backyards that had been left over from an earlier era, structures that needed to be torn down. Some were falling apart. And so we made the alley the focus of our first action efforts to consolidate the thinking of the people of the neighborhood. And the block club as an instrument for racial integration was an interesting device. The focus on common problems worked.

They [white people] were just fearful. They had grown up, you see they'd been socialized to believe that black people meant trouble, meant crime. Particularly, their concern was property values. Now, whether that was a smoke screen or what, that was a concern.

335

The next phase of my involvement had to do with the Patrick-Ravitz Open Occupancy Ordinance. Now with Bill and myself on the council, we put together this open housing ordinance. So big was the public hearing on that ordinance, so vigorous was the opposition, we couldn't hold it in the City-County building. It was too small. We went across to Ford Auditorium for an unprecedented public hearing. This was about 1963. Patrick was still around. The new term had begun in 1962. It could have been late 1962.

We lost, seven to two. Even the so-called liberals on the council that were elected with us would not go along with an ordinance that opened the city to people without regard to race.

There were all sorts of other devices that could be used: steering people by real estate brokers, or just refusing to show people. There were no penalties even. An ordinance provides penalties. So we wanted the law to say that this is the way in which Detroit, policywise, was going to behave.

And it wasn't until much later that the City Council finally adopted an open occupancy ordinance. It was rather meaningless then because African Americans had moved to all parts of the city. But in 1963 it was very much of a problem. All sorts of threats, violence. We had tires slashed. I did. Bomb threats, all kinds of things. Police in front of my house, protecting my family and so on. I'll never forget the hearing over at the Ford Auditorium. We were booed and booed and booed.

It was also during this time, it was 1963, when Dr. King was in town and marched here in Detroit. I was involved in that march. Later that year Bill Patrick and I flew off to be in the Washington march.

BIOGRAPHY

Mel Ravitz was born on January 7, 1924, in New York City and moved to Detroit in 1928. He attended Detroit Public Schools, graduating from Central High School. He has earned a B.A in history from Wayne State University, an M.A. in sociology from the New School for Social Research in New York, and a Ph.D. in sociology from the University of Michigan. He was a professor of sociology at Wayne State University from 1949–87. He has been a Detroit City Council member from 1962–74 and 1982–present. Mr. Ravitz has served on the boards of many community organizations and currently is staff director of the Detroit-Wayne County Community Mental Health Services Board. He is married and the father of six children.

Lamar N. Richardson, Jr. (left)
poses with Aunt Martha
(center) and sister Sally (right)
in the yard of their home on
Leland Street.

LAMAR N. RICHARDSON, JR.

In the 1950s we lived on Leland Street between Chene and DuBois. My grandfather had a very large house. There was a vacant lot, and my father's house next to that. They were all fenced together. It was a wooden fence, with about six-to-eight inch boards eight-feet-high all the way across the back. Across the front was the wire fence. It was somewhat like a compound. The back gates were always open between the two yards and the lot, so there was a lot of exchange. No one locked his doors then. None of the children had keys because you didn't need a key.

In our house there were six people—my mother and father, and four children: two older sisters, myself, and a younger sister. In my grandfather's house there were quite a few people. My mother was the oldest of nine children. At one point all eight of her brothers and sisters lived in that house, along with the older brothers' and sisters' spouses and their children. My earliest memory of growing up has in one house the six of us and in the other house my grandfather, my grandmother; my Uncle Clarence, his wife Fannie, and their son Michael; my Aunt Ruth, her husband Napoleon, their son Garland; my Aunt Gloria, her husband Charles, their son Gregory; my Uncle Oscar, my Aunt Colleen, my Uncle Philip, and my Aunt Martha.

My grandfather was the head of the house. Every Saturday, early in the morning, it was market time, and the family would go to the Eastern Market. It was a great treat to go to Eastern Market. They would buy live chickens, eggs, gobs of meat and vegetables. Everything was fresh. They would bring them home by 9:00 or 10:00 A.M. in the morning. Chickens were running all over the backyard. Groceries were being put away. There was quite a bit of hustle and bustle.

People would be organized for the killing of the chickens. My uncles would wring the chickens' necks. The women would dip chicken in hot water on the stove. Then they would bring them to us children on the porch who had to pull the scalding hot feathers off. After the feathers were pulled off; they would take them in and singe the final feathers off, and then they would gut them, right there on the kitchen table. Everyone participated. All my uncles were the gutters. I was so happy when I graduated to that point, because the feathers were too hot. I quickly learned how to put my hand in there and pull that stuff out, because that was better than trying to pull the hot feathers. Everyone participated.

Certain days were set aside for washing. That poor backyard would just be filled with sheets and clothes and everything that had been washed.

My grandfather always kept a garden. He would rotate his crops every year. One year he would grow potatoes and beans, cantaloupes, things of that nature. Another year he would grow tomatoes. We had lots of fruit trees in the back—peach, cherry, apple trees.

The family used to hunt a lot, so every winter they would go hunting and bring in a catch of deer. The deer was also butchered the same as the chickens, there on that huge kitchen table. Once they caught three bears. That was the most exciting thing in the neighborhood—this car driving up with one huge bear on top of the car and two bear cubs on the fenders. That was a big thing.

Times were quite different. Everyone knew all the neighbors. The neighborhood was quite mixed, in that it was black and white with various ethnic groupings. There were, within our block of about twenty families, about six Polish families, a couple of Italian families. The rest would be black families. The kids all played together. We would play baseball and basketball in the alleys behind the house.

For recreation most of our activities were limited to playing in the alleys, but the alleys were quite clean. In fact, we had to keep them clean so that we could play. Later, we could go into vacant lots; but with all the freedom that we had on the block, as a rule you didn't go much beyond the block. You were free to roam on the block, but you could never cross the street. We had to stay on our side of the street, and sometimes they would give us parameters of houses: "Don't go beyond that house. Don't go past Mrs. Green's house. Don't go past the alley."

Church was a must. We grew up at Second Baptist Church. Every Sunday my grandfather would go around early in the morning. He would come to make sure everybody was getting ready for church. We would go to church. The church had a section that was called Youth Church, for the young people, on the fourth floor. Our instructor was a woman named Miss Reid who was an African missionary. She herself was from one of the Caribbean Islands, but she often traveled into Africa. She taught Junior Church.

Going to church was actually a big treat, because Miss Reid told fabulous stories. If you weren't at church, my grandfather would come by to visit that day to find out why. After church it was almost a ritual that he would stand in front of church until he had seen certain key family members just to say hello.

Both my parents were very good-looking outgoing, popular, and well-dressed. They took good care of us. My father used to sell cars also, as a sideline. He sold cars for Harry Newman Lincoln-Mercury. Every year or two we would get a new car. In those days I guess they were demos. He was not a showroom salesman; they didn't have black showroom salesmen in those days. The black salesmen had to go and find their customers and bring them to the showroom to write the deal. They couldn't be in the showroom and have someone walk in and buy a car. You had to go out and find someone who wanted to buy a car, bring them to the showroom and sell. For that you were allowed to purchase a demo at a reduced rate. He was still buying the car but it was less than if he was not a salesman.

It was always a treat. Sometimes when my father got a new car he would come to school to pick us up. You'd see this beautiful car parked out in front of school and you'd come out, and everyone is saying, "WOW," and who should step out but your father. It happened more than once, totally unexpected. My father was very supportive of all of us, any of our activities. If there was an assembly or meeting at school, my father would be there. If there was a baseball game or soccer game, he would be there.

I went to Cass for only a year, then went to Northeastern, really feeling my oats, and I didn't think it was necessary to be in school every day. I was a naughty boy. I skipped school a lot, and I got caught a lot. The last time I got caught I was told that I was not Cass Tech material. "Next semester you go to your neighborhood high school, if they will have you." Actually it did give me great awakening, whereas I had a ball at Cass playing around, hanging out in the Bungalow. The Bungalow Grill was the hangout. It was the classic sweet or soda shop—hamburgers, sodas, and soft drinks. Any black person who went to Cass hung out at the Bungalow, if they could. The place would get so crowded; and seniors, of course, were the big people. So freshman had to really know somebody even to get in the door. I had friends who were older. Also I skipped school, so I was there early. I'd get there before other kids.

When they gave me my walking papers I transferred to Northeastern. I never thought someone could kick you out of school. It was something that you heard about, but it never happened, especially if you were passing your subjects. Well, they did. When I got to Northeastern, I made a major turnaround; and I was very serious about school then. Although not an overly serious person, I became involved in extracurricular activities, became a member of the Honor Society. Eventually I was president of my graduation class. I attempted people-organization a lot, because we had a lot of problems.

Northeastern had a majority black student population, but the administration was white, with a lot of the old bias or prejudice notions that they held onto. Many opportunities that were available to young people growing up were not available to us for the simple reason that the administration didn't feel that we needed these things or didn't think we were interested. It used to bother me. I played in the band at Northeastern, and it bothered me that when they told us we were receiving new instruments, they were instruments that were stamped with another school's name on them. They were instruments that another school had gotten rid of, and we were getting them. Stands to hold the sheet music would come with "Denby" silk-screened on them. Denby got new stuff, and we got their old stuff. That just wasn't right.

I graduated in 1963, January. One of the issues at Northeastern, whose school colors were gold and green, was: why can't we wear green robes for graduation? The answer was always: black is the color of graduation robes, except for Cass Tech, who wore green, and Commerce, who wore purple robes.

We said: "How can you have exceptions for some and not for others? Why can't we wear green robes?"

"It just can't be done," we were told.

We organized a petition drive from the parents. We asked all the seniors to get their parents to write a letter that said they would like to see you in a green cap and gown. The principal called me into his office for a consultation, and what he told me was that one of the main reasons that he didn't want to push the green was that a large percentage of our student population were black and that the green robe contrasted too much with the skin color. That was his argument.

After football games there were lots of dances and things like that and teenagers used to fight. They weren't fight-to-the-death fights; generally it was well organized and well orchestrated. If we lose the game, we're beating you up, so you better not try to win. If you were going to win in somebody else's court, you better have a lot of support to help you fight your way home. That was just the way it was. Nobody looked forward to it, but it was understood on your home field they better not win. They had to be tougher than you on and off the field to win. There were teams who were rough. This was basically football. Not so much basketball. After the football game, if the opposing team won, there was going to be a fight. Seldom did the opposing team win! It was the same for us when we went out.

There were rivalries. Northeastern and Eastern were sharp rivals, and that was tough. They were close to each other. Northeastern is Warren and Grandy, and Eastern is Mack and Grand Boulevard. We had the overlap. A lot of the kids who had gone to the same junior high schools would go to one of those two. Also, when they changed Miller from high school to junior high, the kids who would have gone to Miller went to those two high schools. There were other rivalries, too. Most of the schools had sharp rivalries.

These weren't really rabble-rousing days; they were fighting for our rights. We picketed once. We had a picket over the green caps and dances. This is 1963 now. Even before then, 1961–1963; that was the start-up of publicizing the civil rights movement. A lot of that was just an energy that was in the air. We weren't imitating anyone, because there was no one to imitate. It was just energy in the air if you protested something that was right. One of the things we protested was the history books we had to read. In 1963 they brought out a new American history book that had about two pages on blacks; a paragraph on Martin Luther King. He was still alive at that point, but by that time had gained a lot of respect. About two pages total on blacks in America. We felt that was wrong. How can this be a black school and you give us a history book that doesn't say a thing about black people? The teacher's response was, "Black people didn't do anything."

I married in June of 1967; the rebellion was in July of 1967. Shortly before I was married I received my draft notice to go into the army. I went and talked to them, and they gave me a delay because I could prove this wedding was already planned. We went ahead with the marriage in June, with the understanding that I had to leave for the army in August. My wife and I had an apartment on Martindale and Boston.

That Sunday morning her family was having their family reunion picnic in Canada. My mother called that Sunday morning, asked if we were going to church. (We were attending Fort Street Presbyterian Church.) She said, "Don't go. There's a race riot going on." There was lots of fighting, and it might not be safe to go there. Understand that my mother could see two fellows on the street fighting and report it as the start of the war. I took it with a grain of salt. I didn't hear anything on the radio about it.

When my father-in-law came to pick us up for the picnic, we drove out Grand River for a ways and didn't see any type of disturbance. We took the bridge. We had a wonderful time at the picnic. We were playing cards and winning. Suddenly I heard on the radio that they were going to close the bridge at a certain time because of this disturbance going on in Detroit. Everyone turned their radios up. Yeah, there was fighting going on in Detroit, started at a blind pig. It is so bad now that the bridge to Canada is going to be closed at a certain time.

Quickly everybody started scrambling for their things and getting them in the car and getting back to Detroit before the bridge closed. There was such a traffic jam to get to the bridge. On the bridge, a jam. There is a high point on the bridge where you really have a panoramic view of the city. Never in my life have I seen anything like it. It was as if some Cecil B. DeMille had created a scene of Rome burning. Nothing but flames. The whole city was in flames. You could see it from that high point very well. Huge flames. Everywhere you looked things were burning.

We came through, and by the time we cleared customs and made our way to Longfellow, fire engines were wailing all around us. You could hear the shooting. Even as we were driving down the street, the Boulevard, windows were breaking. All the alarms were going off. It was just getting dark.

BIOGRAPHY

Lamar N. Richardson, Jr., was born on March 8, 1945, in Detroit. He attended Campbell Elementary, Miller Middle School, Northwestern High School, and Michigan State University. He is a Vietnam vet. He has worked for his father in the Lamar Modernization Company, for the City of Detroit, and the governor's office, State of Michigan. He is married to a Ghanian princess, and with his wife owned and operated Gye Nyame, a West African restaurant. He now has his own business, conducts tours of West Africa, and markets African products.

DISCUSSION ON 12TH STREET BUSINESSES

BERNARD ODELL AND ODIS RENCHER

BERNARD ODELL: One incident I'll always remember, when I first came. I was about nine when I came here. My brother was making so much money he gave me five dollars. I thought that was the "Bank of Detroit." I couldn't spend it because everything was penny candy. I gave him back four dollars and seventy-five cents and told him to give me a quarter a week. That was 1917–1918.

I started working for the City of Detroit Recreation Department in 1929. I led physical education. I stayed there thirteen years until 1943. The city went broke in 1929. I was laid off.

ODIS RENCHER: I came to Detroit in 1935. I went to McMichael and Northwestern. I lived on the west side, where, at that time, we only had a small area. Nobody lived north of Tireman. I went to Northwestern High. There were many discriminatory practices. We were not allowed to use the YMCA pool across the street. You were not allowed in the Y at all to use the facilities. Our swimming had to be at the school pool.

BERNARD ODELL: I might go back to say that blacks weren't very welcomed in any athletics back in the 1920s. There were one or two, but I guess their prowess got them to the forefront.

ODIS RENCHER: In 1951 I got married and opened my store. When I first went to 12th Street, there were very few blacks in business at the time. I had moved next door to a Jewish fellow who owned a restaurant. Greenberg's Restaurant. It was he who kind of went to the forefront for me, because they made a survey of all the business owners in the area: "Would it be all right if we rent a store to this man?"

Greenberg said, "Sure, let him come in."

He was a very nice and fair man. The building was owned by a doctor. It was mostly Jewish. He leased it. In a few years I bought the place. Greenberg became a tenant, and a clothing store moved in next door. I rented to him. They were somewhat shocked that I was owner of the building, but we never had any problems. We always got along real well.

I went to National Wholesale Drugs. I had about one thousand dollars to spend on merchandise. They said, "Go ahead and spend what you have in cash, and we'll match it with merchandise, and you can pay us on a regular basis." I did, and what I got was all backroom stuff, something that you couldn't sell for prescriptions. I had to get a prescription to use the medicine, balances, and things you use in the pharmacy department. I waited two or three days for him to send a man out to take the order. He didn't, so I went down. He said: "Well, you haven't been in business before, so we can't let you have anything. We'll have to wait until you are established." Then I went to McKesson. They let me have a couple-thousand-dollars-worth of merchandise. Each time I got an order, I paid ten or fifteen dollars toward the bill.

They only gave me backroom stuff. That's what you had to have in order to pass inspection, to get a license for pharmacy. These things had to be in place. There was nothing you could do until you got a prescription for it. McKesson allowed me credit so I could get whatever I needed to operate. That's how I got started.

The neighborhood was more than fifty percent Jewish, and I sold three-cent and six-cent items. That's what kept me going. I sold ice cream, everything with the fountain: chocolate malts, and banana splits, and hot fudge sundaes. A banana split was thirty-five cents. Seltzer was three cents and five cents. Coke was five cents. A double dip was fifteen cents. Every day the Jewish people, in particular, would go out for a walk and stop by and get a seltzer, maybe an ice cream. Those that had more money to spend would get maybe a hot fudge sundae.

I didn't have enough money to really stock my shelves like they should. They would say, "I'm going to have to have a permanent, so you have it in for me Friday, and I'll come and get it." I would order it Thursday, and they would be there Friday to come pick it up. I'd make fifty cents or a dollar on that. There wasn't a lot of money tied up.

I had a salesman who was very nice, and he would come in and more or less coach me as to what to buy, "Get three of this, one of this. . . ." I was able to stock my shelves. The next time I was able to buy a dozen Alka-Seltzers. That's how I more or less got started.

I was above Clairmount, which was a totally different community. There was a migration of home buyers in the late 1940s. When I went to Florida in 1944, there were no blacks living west of Woodward. When I came back to Detroit in 1951, it was primarily black, particularly where we were. There was a drastic change in those six or seven years.

There were less whites in your community than mine, because I assumed there were thirty-five to forty percent whites in my community. The change kept increasing as you went along. I stayed there thirteen or fourteen years.

I saw drastic change coming early in the 1960s. I was broken into three times. A little prostitution. You could see the change coming. So really, I wasn't interested in staying.

The way I feel about it, migration is an economic thing. You're seeking jobs. Jobs were the answer. Detroit was a job city, where the factories hired anybody and everybody. Actually, when a city starts growing like that you have internal problems. These internal problems went with migration. As a result, you get conditions you may not want to live next door to.

At that time 12th Street was very commercial—with bars, drugstores, grocery stores, everything. But it brings all the bad habits along with it.

ODIS RENCHER: Just before the riots, business was as usual when I went home Saturday night. We took the kids and were going to Canada. We had two girls. We took them down Sunday morning to the Y, where they got the bus. On the way back we saw this smoke. Then the police were around. We didn't go down 12th Street. We went down Woodward. I didn't know what was going on. Of course, the radio was on, and we found out later what was going on.

I couldn't even go over there. If you can imagine what kind of feeling I had. I had all my life's savings, everything there. We were finally able to get over there. They claim the reason why they burned my store was that the clothing store was in my building. They went in and pillaged the clothing store and set fire to the clothing store and took everything. The clothing store was owned by someone else. From my store they took what they wanted. They only respected what they wanted to.

I didn't know any of the people who were looting. Some of the people I had seen in the neighborhood. When I was able to get over there, I saw them walking with things on their arms, carrying a couch, things like that. I didn't know any especially very well. Many of them who

345

lived in the neighborhood participated, too, but many were not from the neighborhood.

It was all lost. If it wasn't stolen, there was water damage or smoke damage. I had to pay five thousand dollars for the demolition. The city didn't arrange for my demolition. They would have. They would arrange for it and bill you whatever they wanted to. So I figured if I go ahead and pay the five thousand dollars, that would be it.

I've seen incidents on 12th Street at the time. It was the "Big Four." Four big burly policemen rode down the street in a Lincoln, rode up and down. There was a man I saw one time out in front. He was just drunk and trying to get home. He wasn't bothering anyone. One decided he wanted to get out. One got out and beat and kicked him just because he was a little inebriated. He hadn't said a thing; he wasn't bothering anybody. That was the attitude. That had been building up, too.

When this happened, it was a hot summer night. Everybody was out. It had happened in other cities—Watts, New York. I think perhaps it could have just been a spark that ignited and was just slashing through from city to city. It was an opportune time to get started.

BERNARD ODELL: The "Big Four" operated citywide, just plainclothed; but you recognized them when they arrived. You knew it. They were law enforcement officers. They stopped for anything they felt like challenging.

ODIS RENCHER: I know when I first came here, to this city, I was living on 30th Street, so I walked up to the ice cream parlor one Sunday evening after coming from church. There were boys shooting craps on the corner. I walked up there to get a sundae. Just as I got to the door, these boys started to scatter. I heard brakes screeching from a police car. "What are you doing here?"

I said, "I'm up here to get a sundae".

"Get in the car." They pushed me right in the car and took me about seven or eight blocks away. They asked again what was I doing there.

"I'm just here to get a sundae."

"Do you think you can go straight home?" They let me out six or seven blocks away and said, "Take off for home." They didn't abuse me, but those are the things that happened. They had no reason. This wasn't the "Big Four." It was the regular police.

BERNARD ODELL: I never had it happen, but I remember when we lived on Scotten on the west side. One night when my dad was coming in, he put the key in the door. Two policemen accosted him and accused him of being drunk. My dad never drank a drop of whiskey in his life. We all came to the door. I remember that as a kid. He was just putting the key in the door, getting ready to come in the house shortly after dark. The policemen were drunk. I was ten or eleven.

BIOGRAPHIES

Bernard Odell was born on May 13, 1908, in Topeka, Kansas; he moved to Detroit in 1917 and lived at 221 Maple. Mr. Odell graduated from Northwestern High School and attended Wayne State University. He worked for the City of Detroit Recreation Department. He owned businesses in Florida and in the early 1960s became owner of a drugstore on 12th Street and Atkinson. He is now retired and lives in Florida.

Odis Rencher was born on September 18, 1917, in Scooba, Mississippi, and moved to Detroit in August 1935. He attended Northwestern High School, graduating in 1939. He served four and one-half years in the U. S. Army. He graduated from Wayne State University in 1950 with a B.S. in pharmacy. He operated a drugstore on 12th Street from 1951–1967. He currently has a drugstore on West Davison in Detroit.

MINISTER WILLIAM T. HOWARD

I was born in Florida and came to Detroit in approximately 1946. I was a kid. My father was a barber. He worked down on Chene, Hastings, or somewhere up around there. We came home one night from the movies, and all of our stuff had been set outside. My mother and the landlord got into it over something, and the landlord kicked us out.

In about 1947 we moved to Willow Run, and my father opened up a little barber shop, where he started working with another barber at first. Eventually he bought the barber shop. My mother went to beauty school and became a beautician. She did hair, and he cut hair at the barber shop.

I graduated from high school. I was in the bottom twenty percent of my class. The only thing I wanted to do when I was in high school—I didn't want to be a doctor or lawyer, social worker or teacher—I just wanted to be a pimp or a player, having a bunch of women, having them work for me and make me some money. That's all I wanted to do, so having a vocabulary, math, all that stuff wasn't important. After I graduated, I had a little job working at St. Joseph Hospital washing dishes.

348

A guy ran the "Murphy" on me for three hundred dollars. The "Murphy" is a con game. I always was the kind of person that would try to help somebody. A guy came along with a situation. It looked like I was going to get something, and I ended up getting got. It took my life savings—three hundred dollars.

Then I was determined to learn everything about the streets there was to learn. I hooked up with another guy, and we started going around places. We went to Chicago, Cleveland, Philadelphia, city to city, shooting pool, after-hours joints, hooking up with a woman here and there, and making a little change here and there.

I had one bad weekend. We were in Chicago, and we had won a little money. One guy went in his pocket and pulled out a knife, and he made it go all around his hand in a fancy type of manner. Another guy pulled out a knife and started sticking it in the floor. I was checking out the whole ordeal and said to myself, if the guy who owns the poolroom will allow this guy to stick his knife in the floor, when these guys get ready to stick us, nobody's going to call the police. Nobody's going to say anything. Maybe a couple of hundred dollars is not worth getting stuck, especially since there was like six of them, and I didn't figure we could make these guys eat enough pool balls. We lost that money. My partner was getting ready to sink the nine ball and I told him not to sink it. If he sinks it, we'll never get out of the pool room. He had to let the other guy make the nine ball, and we lost our money.

We left there, and we went to Cleveland, went to a club, hooked up with a few women. Found an after-hours joint. At the after-hours joint a guy came up and asked for some ID. I said: "I'm not giving you nothing. In fact, get out of my face before I knock you out."

The guy said, "You better show me something."

I said, "I'm not showing you nothing." I went back to the table and picked up the dice. "Hey, mamma got the blues, baby needs shoes, seven come eleven, seven make it to heaven." The guy came back and asks for some ID. I said, "What did I tell you man?"

So the guy took a thirty-eight out and stuck it in my mouth; and he pulled the hammer back; and he said, "You're going to show me something."

One guy said, "Man, he's the policeman, shoot that nigger." So we was street hustling. You can never be afraid. I pushed the guy's hand out.

I said: "Look, man, I leave my ID in the car so if I'm busted, I don't have nothing on me. I'm not the police. I came here to win a little money, have a little fun, and that's it. I'm not the police."

The other guy said: "Man, that nigger's lying. Shoot both of them." The hammer said click.

So I said: "Look, I'll tell you what I'm going to do. I'm going over there, and I'm going to take the bolt off the door. But I want you to have this in your mind." When the hammer went click, anything anybody said to me for twenty years flashed through my head in fifteen seconds. I saw my whole life go by in fifteen seconds. I said, "I'm going over there, and I'm going to unbolt the door. I'm not the police. Me and my partner, we are either going out standing up or laying down. Before you make the decision, I'm not the police."

I opened the door, and the guy was still pointing the gun. I put one foot outside the door, and the guy didn't shoot. Once I put one foot outside the door and he didn't shoot, I knew he wasn't going to shoot, 'cause he took too long. In the street, if a guy took a long time, that meant he wasn't going to do anything. We got outside the door. I almost fell down the steps running. Got in the car, got back to Ypsilanti.

On the way back home I thought about my situation and thought about my life. I said, well, the only way I'm going to do anything, I have to go to school. So I went up to the high school, and a counselor pulled my records out. He said: "Look, I don't think I can get you in a school. You didn't have a 2.0." I said I had to go to school. He said he would send me up to Eastern Michigan to take the entrance examination.

I said, "That's fine."

I went up to Eastern Michigan. They gave me the entrance exam. When I looked at the vocabulary section, they might as well have said, "Bill Howard, build the Challenger space shuttle," because I didn't know a word on the sheet. I just laid the sheet on the table and took me a nap, guessed on the other stuff.

The test scores came back to the high school. He said: "These are some of the worst scores that I've ever seen. The only way that you are going to be able to go to college, you're going to have to come back to high school for a half year."

I said: "Back to high school! Everybody's going to be cracking up laughing." He said that was the only way. I went back to high school. I took geometry, algebra. I got an A in geometry, a B in algebra. That brought me up to a 2.0. Then I went off to Jackson Community College. I had enough money to pay a first-month's rent. I was twenty at that time.

I told my father I wanted to go to college. He told me Uncle Sam needed some good boys, and they were hiring at Ford Motor Company. I said no, I'm going to school. I started at Jackson Community College.

A bunch of days went by. I was eating popcorn and Kool-Aid. Got myself a bunch of girlfriends so I could go over their house and eat, because their mothers would always say, "Would you care for something to eat, Bill?" I'd say no. "Well, come on and have some."

I said, "Since you insist" knowing I was hungry all the time.

The first-floor bathroom was my office because a lot of days I'd go in there, and I had got to the point where tossing those fifty-cent pieces to the line, I could almost get on the line every time. I'd win five or ten dollars. Miss a class, get myself a little food money. Then I had myself a few little "Murphy" tricks that I'd run on the white boys.

One of them was, I'd go to a white guy and say: "Look, John, you redneck peckerwood. I ought to knock one of you honkeys out."

Then the white boy would say, "You nigger man."

I said: "Hold it right there. Come to think of it, I don't even have to go through any physical confrontation with you, because my mental ability is far superior than your physical, because you're just a redneck, low-lying, peckerwood." By that time the white boy would be furious. One thing about con games, a person has to not think. If a person would think, nobody would ever get a con game ran on them. So they'd be so mad, they wouldn't think.

I said: "I'll tell you what I'll do. I'll take a piece of newspaper, and I'll set it out here on the floor. To show you that I'm mentally superior to you, I'll bet you five dollars that I'll walk around you three times and you'll get off after I walk around you three times. Give my man here the money." I put up my five dollars, and they put up their five dollars. I never let the rest of the white boys see the whole process.

He said, "You're not going to touch me, not going to push me?"

"No way, no way." I'd walk around them three times, and I'd put them in the middle of the floor where they can't lean on anything, can't sit down. "All I said was that I'd walk around you three times and you would get off. I never said when you would get off or how long it would take you to get off." Sooner or later, it dawned on them that they had to get off. Many times I had the five dollars in my pocket.

After I got a 2.0 at Jackson, my money ran out so I had to work some. My aunt got me a job at Ford's. So then I had to drive up to Jackson and drive back to work at Ford's. After one semester of that, I transferred to Eastern. Then I was working at the factory and going to Eastern. Ultimately, I quit the factory.

I had been six years at the factory, going to school and working. So when I told the foreman I was going to quit the factory, he said, "When you colored boys come in here and you get one of them cars and some of those suits, you not going to ever quit."

I said, "I'll tell you what, you redneck peckerwood, you just be at the gate on my last day when the whistle blows so you can see if I quit or not, because I'm going to knock your. . . ." I quit, and finally I went on and graduated from college. I graduated in 1968, Eastern Michigan. One of the tragic aspects of college life: when I got to Eastern, I was not prepared. My vocabulary was inadequate; it was not up to par, and my communication skills were very shallow.

I had to give a report one day in an education class on Socrates, and the instructor asked if I was ready to give my report. I said, "Yeah, man, ain't nothing." I put my paper down. I was the only African American in the class. I started out saying: "This dude, you dig, like Socrates, he's a cool dude, you understand? He's here coming out of this bag with this concept, you dig, called cognition, which was a real cool thing during that day. You understand what I'm talking about? Like it was a mellow thing. The whole philosophical framework here, you dig, was something about the whole process of learning and the knowledge base of mankind." Everybody was scratching their heads and stuff.

The instructor got up and said: "By 'dig,' he means this. By 'throwing down,' he means this. By 'cool' thing, he means this." I said to myself, here I am in the United States of America, and theoretically I'm speaking the English language, and I have to have an interpreter. Never in my life will I be inferior academically to any man black, white, Chinese, Indian, or anybody else. So when the library opened up on Saturday in the morning, I was at the door. When it closed, I was leaving. So I got my vocabulary to the point that I could communicate with anybody. If I had to stay up all night to beat a white person on a test, I would stay up all night long, until four or five in the morning, just to be number one.

When I went to the employment office in 1968, I was able to say to the lady: "Look, this is the kind of job I want. I want a job working in the community, working with people, and don't call me until you get what I want."

I left the MESC and went home, and she called me a week later and said: "Mr. Howard, I have a job for you. I got a job working for Wayne County Hospital working with TB patients for the Department of Social Services."

I said, "Ma'am, how long was I in your office?"

"About twenty-five minutes."

"Did I say anything about TB patients? Did I? What type of employment did I tell you that I want?"

"Doing community service."

"Correct. Don't call my house again until you get what I want."

"Okay, Mr. Howard." She called me a week later and said, "We have a job on 12th Street for the Detroit Urban League, a street worker. You recruit people for an education program and do some community organization."

I said, "That sounds like my type of job." I came down, and Roy Williams and Dr. Kornegay was here. I came down to the Urban League. I had on my loud blue suit, my white Stetson's on, my white necktie. I was super sharp. I came down, and Roy said, "This is the kind of guy we need."

Kornegay said, "We don't need no guy like that." I got hired. I became known as one of the best street workers in the country.

When you look at the African American, the portion of history where he went wrong or he developed his neurosis was back during slavery. During slavery, the slave masters implemented some programs. One of the things that he did when he brought the black man over on the ship and put him in a situation where they were all piled up on top of one another, defecating on one another, throwing up on one another, not being able to wash up or take a bath, and just not being able to wash up alone, and being smelly and being dirty, that has something to do with the development and the depleting of his self-esteem. Another thing that he did was separate the child from the mother, because he knew that the mother would give the kid a sense of worth. He knew that by doing that he would be able to separate him from his history and his culture and program him as being a breeder, as being a worker, a provider of labor in this country for the capitalistic gain of the few. A bunch of white folks didn't have no slaves and no property, and they were sharecroppers and going through the same kind of process the black folks was going through.

Then what he did was have sex with anybody he wanted to, and every now and then the white woman would sneak out and have herself some sex. Some of the kids came out different shades. He had some kind of commitment for them, so he put some of them in the house. He took some more out of the field and put them in the house. Once he created the house Negro from the field Negro, he instilled in the house Negro that he was better than the one in the field because he was in the house. That led to a degree of separation.

If you look at history during Reconstruction, whites and blacks were intermingling with one another in and out of marriage, in and out of wedlock. The white man saw this, those that were in power, and had to do something to keep this situation from happening, because he needed that labor and wanted that free labor. He passed laws to keep the white woman from being with the black man. Rutherford B. Hayes and this other white boy that was running on the Republican ticket in the South, they pulled all of the soldiers out of the South. They pulled the black troops and sent them out West to fight the Indian. That's how they became known as the buffalo soldiers.

Then that paved the way for the KKK and the white supremacists to go and do whatever they wanted to do, because the greatest period of time in America for the black man from a political and economic standpoint was during Reconstruction from 1867–1877. When the KKK and the rest of them got to do their thing, and the KKK fostered the whole concept of racism and black inferiority, the ruling class or the economic few in this country could concentrate once again on their economic growth, because they had the people, the working class and poor folks, fighting against one another. They were dealing with the issues of black and white instead of dealing with the issues of how come one man can spend forty million dollars on a painting and another man can't spend forty cents on a can of beans. Those were the real issues then and today. People just don't deal with the real issues. They've got all these facades—drugs, crime. If you get the economic perspective in the right place, all of these other things will fall into place.

BIOGRAPHY

Minister William T. Howard was born on November 11, 1941, in Panama City, Florida, and moved to Detroit in 1945. He graduated from Eastern Michigan University in 1968. He then joined the staff of the Detroit Urban League as street worker for the 12th Street Academy and is currently director of the Joy Middle School Project. He is married and the father of three daughters and one son.

African Americans
in Detroit and the United States,
1958–1967

1960	Civil Rights Act signed (May 6).
	Election of President John F. Kennedy and Vice President Lyndon B. Johnson (November).
1962	James Meredith was admitted to the University of Mississippi (September).
	President Kennedy federalized Mississippi National Guard (September 29).
1963	Medgar Evers, field secretary for NAACP in Mississippi, was shot and killed (June 12).
	President Kennedy met with civil rights leaders (June 20).
	More than 125,000 people marched down Woodward Avenue in Detroit singing, "We Shall Overcome" and "Battle Hymn of the Republic." March led by Martin Luther King, Jr., Mayor Jerome P. Cavanaugh, Governor John B. Swainson, Police Commissioner George Edwards, and Walter P. Reuther (June 23).
	March on Washington, D.C., for jobs and freedom. More than 200,000 marched, sang, and prayed, demanding passage of civil rights legislation, integration of public schools, a federal program to train and place all

unemployed workers, and a federal fair employment practices law barring all job discrimination (June 28, 1963).

Bombing of Birmingham, Alabama, church resulted in the deaths of four young girls (September 15).

President John F. Kennedy assassinated (November 22).

1964	The bodies of three civil rights workers—Andrew Goodman, Michael Scherner, and James Chaney—were found in Philadelphia, Mississippi; the men were killed while working on voter registration and implementation of the Civil Rights Act (June 21).
1965	Martin Luther King Jr., led more than 3,000 people in a 54-mile march from Selma to Montgomery, Alabama (January).
	Viola Liuzzo of Detroit shot and killed after Selma March.
1965	Malcolm X assassinated (February 21)
	Voting Rights Act signed (August 6).
1967	Civil disturbance begins at site of blind pig on 12th Street near Clairmount in Detroit. Damages of $50 million, 44 deaths, 7,331 arrests (July 23).
	New Detroit formed (August 1).
1968	Martin Luther King, Jr., assassinated (April 4).

Harold Norris has been a long-time fighter against racial discrimination. This picture was taken during the 1963 march down Woodward Avenue led by Martin Luther King, Jr.

HAROLD NORRIS

I'm a teacher and advocate of constitutional rights. For the last thirty years I've been a member of the faculty at the Detroit College of Law. Some five thousand lawyers have gone through my class.

After four years in the army and graduating from Columbia Law School in 1946, I came back to Detroit, my hometown, to practice. I was engaged in a large volume of constitutional law cases and helped re-constitute the American Civil Liberties Union in the city. I became chairman in 1959. After forty years on the executive board, I am board member emeritus.

One of the continuous problems associated with the Detroit Police Department and citizens generally was the practice of arrest for investigation. I wrote an article called "Arrest Without Warrant" which was published in the *Michigan Chronicle* and the NAACP's *Crisis* magazine. The statistical table that I had in that article indicated the number of arrests for investigation over a ten-year period. In 1947 it was eighteen thousand. In 1956 it was more than twenty-six thousand. An arrest is a taking into custody in answer for a crime. In law, arrests for investigation alone have questionable legal basis. What the police did was take people into custody and then try to find a reason for keeping them.

I tried to challenge that practice. First of all I had the statistics from the Detroit Police Department itself to establish what they were doing. When you have that many—we're talking about a third of all arrests—that meant that thousands of black people, working people, poor people were the subject of those arrests. Hundreds of black people in this city have arrest records as a result of that activity, which meant that they had problems with jobs—getting jobs, keeping jobs.

When persons are arrested for investigation, they also become subject to protracted questioning, perhaps the use of force, certainly psychological coercion. When you're in police custody, you're in a coerced situation. You're being compelled to be a witness against yourself, a violation of the Fifth Amendment. Arrests for investigation and its associated practices became the basis for a great deal of strain and stress between the black community and the police department. Such strain discouraged the community cooperation necessary for effective law enforcement.

The police department is supposed to serve everybody in the community and protect them and follow the Constitution. Certainly those who enforce the law are not supposed to break the law. But when you have abuse of authority, which arrest for investigation reflected, you have a large number of people getting the idea that police are not their friends. Citizens are discouraged by police wrongdoing from helping the law. People help the law by reporting crime, coming forward as witnesses, being jurors, and assisting police in distress. Indeed police engaged in illegal law enforcement are looked upon as an occupying power, not a protecting power.

So those of us who were seeking to protect the constitutional rights of everybody in every section of the city regardless of race, gender, income, were really trying to promote effective law enforcement by securing citizen cooperation. Protection and cooperation are reciprocal. When people are protected by the police, they will help the police.

Some people feel that if you protect constitutional rights, you impede law enforcement. The only way, it is argued, that law enforcement can be effective is to not protect rights but "short cuts and full steam ahead." It's called "alley court." In other words, get somebody in custody, beat the hell out of him, instill fear. Obviously, for an officer to hurt a citizen, to administer "alley court" justice, harms the law and is an abuse of the separation of powers doctrine. Police officers are a part of the executive department and are not supposed to administer punishment. Judges do. Police are supposed to apprehend persons who are engaged in wrongful conduct, to investigate and bring the people to the court, to the judicial department, for the administration of justice.

The conviction I have is that we're all responsible for the society in which we live. We're all responsible for the Constitution. Democracy is not self-executing. The law is not self-executing. The Constitution is not self-executing. We the people must be vigilant and hold all authority and power accountable and responsible.

We had an episode in our city, not far from here, in 1960. Several nurses working at Grace and Harper hospitals were the subject of homicide. A terrible thing. How do you deal with a problem like that? The police are not going to solve it without the community feeling that they should report information and help the police apprehend the people who committed this terrible thing. What did the police do, however? They engaged in what was known as a dragnet operation—taking hundreds of people, almost exclusively black, into custody, including Judge Elvin Davenport, Arthur Johnson, and a number of prominent people. I'm talking about fifteen hundred little people as well. A dragnet operation primarily against black people does not win community cooperation with police, but integration of the police department and lawful law enforcement do, we argued.

According to the *Detroit Free Press* on December 29, 1960, the mayor said, "The police should be able to go into places where they believe are suspicious persons and make searches on suspicion, then let the courts decide whether they did right or not." "Officers," said the mayor, "are to alert themselves to those persons who were in odd places at odd hours without reasonable explanation." I believed that the law's view is that a citizen has a constitutional right to be in odd places at odd hours if he is not committing any crime. I thought the mayor's statement an odd, indeed illegal, explanation of the Constitution.

We did have a rather effective political and community challenge to these practices as well as court challenges. We challenged them because the NAACP was active, the Detroit Urban League was active, the American Civil Liberties Union was active, the Democratic party became alerted, and because we won an election. We challenged a mayor who had been a prominent representative of the establishment, educated the community, and defeated him with a thirty-five-year old lawyer who never ran for political office in his life.

The night of the dragnet, Arthur Johnson, director of the Detroit NAACP, called me. I was then chairman of the American Civil Liberties Union. He said, "I'd like you to come down to St. Paul's Episcopal Church and explain to about a hundred community people the law of arrest, because we have to do something about this dragnet business." I came down and talked about it. Then we had a protest against Mayor Miriani's action. Then we had a big protest meeting at Ford Auditorium. It was January 16, 1961; the meeting was sponsored by the NAACP and the Interdenominational Ministerial Alliance. I was one of the persons who addressed some twenty-five hundred people.

At that point Jerry Cavanaugh decided to run for mayor against Miriani, the author of the dragnet. Horace Sheffield and a group of broad-based citizens organizations encouraged this decision. Cavanaugh won and became mayor of this town. He appointed a new commissioner and a lot of other things happened. The new mayor said it was his policy to enforce the Constitution.

When black people or Jewish people or women or minorities or majorities are doing battle for the Constitution, they're not only helping themselves, they're giving integrity to what this country is all about and protecting the rights and security of all. A lot of people say to me, "You do this because you like black people." Why, sure, I like black people; but that isn't the main idea. The main idea is that everybody has equal and effective access to these rights we're talking about; we give vitality and credibility to [everybody] in the United States of America. We're helping everybody in this country. Every time a citizen exercises a constitutional right and wins recognition of the propriety of that exercise, that citizen makes it possible for all people to have a sense of counting, of allegiance, of empowerment. We can change things. We ought to take confidence from what black and white people and all devotees of the Constitution can accomplish working together.

In my generation an effective working slogan was "Black and White Unite and Fight." I commend it to the next generation.

BIOGRAPHY

Harold Norris has been a professor at the Detroit College of Law for thirty years. He has been a member of the Detroit American Civil Liberties Union (ACLU) executive board for forty years. He was elected from Detroit to write the Michigan Bill of Rights and Constitution 1961–62 and wrote the provision prohibiting racial discrimination. He was one of the authors of the provision creating the Michigan Civil Rights Commission. In 1988 he was honored as a Distinguished Warrior by the Detroit Urban League. In 1991 the State Bar of Michigan named him Champion of Justice.

MARSHA L. MICKENS

My first memory of Hastings was that my father took me to a place near where his record shop had been. I was a little girl, about three or four. He walked me across the street from the place where we were standing over to this gigantic dirt pit that was in the ground. It looked like a canyon to me. He looked at me and said, "Ling Ting Tong," which was my nickname, "This is where Hastings used to be." All my life, as a little girl, I didn't know what that was. I just had this memory of this pit. As I got older, I realized that it was the initial diggings for the I-75 freeway. What my father so graphically understood and expressed with that sentence was that a way of life had been totally destroyed by the Chrysler Freeway. The street of Hastings just no longer existed.

I was born in 1954. My father had a record shop at Mack and Hastings. He was a man by the name of Joe Von Battle. My father was a brilliant person and extremely flamboyant. There weren't many places where you could buy black music in Detroit. He opened the shop selling black music—rock and roll, rhythm and blues. He was also very interested in the production of music.

He began to record in his shop. Hastings was always a place where there were a lot of entertainers, singers that came through the bars and the clubs. My father was the first person to record a lot of people because there was nowhere else they could be recorded. This was in the early 1950s. This was pre-Motown. It would be a big deal to go to Joe's record shop and have your voice recorded. He was open almost all night long. He always played records out of the loud speaker of the record shop so you could hear music as things went on.

Reverend C. L. Franklin had a church in the area and was already known for his extraordinary preaching skills. People would just flock to his church to hear him preach. My father had heard about Reverend Franklin—they were all in the same neighborhood—and asked if he could record these sermons. They would play these sermons on the large speakers outside, and more than once had to call the police to break up the crowds that would gather to hear Reverend Franklin preach.

There were many very talented people who made up the backbone of the community who were there because of segregation. It was a very prosperous community, because you had a number of black business people that had serviced that community for many years and were becoming affluent. This is one reason people talk about how Hastings was destroyed purposefully. That has always been the scuttlebutt within the community. The white man decided to get rid of Hastings because that community was becoming too strong.

People began to say, "They're going to get rid of us here," and others would laugh at it. When they look back, they feel it is true that this area was demolished for the freeway. It was very purposeful and destroyed the infrastructure of the people in that area. The disbursement to 12th street was like a migration of a people from one section of a country to another. They still had the same business people.

The record shop moved to 12th Street. I was about ten years old. I used to work there every weekend. My memories are of Saturday night on 12th Street, because the record shop would stay open very late. It was intense nightlife. This was from a child's eyes—seeing big cars and convertibles and sharp men. It was very exciting. My father never feared me standing right outside the record shop and watching. He never feared that something bad would happen to me.

My father's record shop had a regular pop and rhythm and blues section, and then it had a gospel section. My father developed this hatred against Sears and Roebuck. White society was beginning to get a piece of this black music for the first time. They were beginning to understand the marketability of black music. It drove him crazy that a person could now go to Sears and pay seventy-five cents and buy a record. He had the resentment of a person who thought, "What are you all interested in our stuff now for?" He didn't like that. He was right.

I can remember that one day in July 1967. My family lived in Highland Park, which is a few miles from 12th Street. We could look over the trees and see these clouds of black smoke coming from 12th Street. We also had begun to hear these news reports that something was happening over there. Daddy knew that there was something really brimming.

In the early parts of the riot, the first day, it seemed like kind of a fight that might somehow be contained. It was like some bad stuff happening, but it would blow over. I remember the tension during that time and my father conjuring up this bravado that he would be okay, that they weren't going to bother his record shop.

Everybody was watching television. Everybody was really intense about what was going on over on 12th Street. Older people remembered the race riots on Belle Isle in the 1940s. All of them knew that this was not a race riot. The news kept saying this was a race riot developing. That was one of my first experiences with how the media projects what they want. I was about twelve. It was so clear to my own eyes that white people were out there looting, too. Not to say that racial tensions didn't exist, but it wasn't black against white. It was the propertied against the non-propertied.

My daddy, after this first day, closed down the record shop, thinking that the police would contain this thing and it would all blow over. Then he said that he was going to get one of those signs that said "Soul Brother" and put it in his shop so that they wouldn't bother him. I remember teasing him about that, because he was like an old school black that didn't believe in this soul brother stuff, and here he was going to put up a "Soul Brother" sign to save his record shop. After the second day my father decided that he better take a pistol over there. He sat in the doorway and dared anybody to come in there. In the meantime we were watching it on TV, but we were involved in it because this is our father's livelihood. This is how we eat. As the days went on, it became obvious that his record shop was going to be caught up in this, too. The tension in the house built. He knew he could not save it.

One day we looked up and here was this army. They were stationed at this motel. I remember when the National Guard was out there and walking down the street. It was just like a movie. The army goes into an area, and you're the natives. It was a bizarre feeling that they're supposedly here to protect you, but you know that they might kill you too.

I walked down the street one morning, and here were soldiers. They were off-duty at the time, milling around, waiting for orders, drinking pop. I walked down the street to wave at them just like in the movies. I will never forget my mother snatching me back and saying, "Get over here." I've never been so scared in my life, because my mother understood. Here were the people that were here to save her husband's livelihood, but she feels compelled to keep me protected from them because she also understands that they might bring me harm.

At the tail end of the riot Daddy took my brother and me to look at the record shop. He just said, "Oh, Lord." It was like being in a war zone. Glass was all over the street. The record shop was just torn apart. Stuff was everywhere. It wasn't burnt down as he had feared, but had been totally looted. Tapes that he had for a generation were destroyed. It was like his whole life's work had been destroyed. I remember that feeling of witnessing my father witness that, of seeing him powerless over the situation, of the chaos because firemen and guardsmen were still running around. After that my mother says that he reopened the shop for a time. He was able to somehow pull it together, but it never did flourish. He ended up losing it shortly after that.

BIOGRAPHY

Marsha L. Mickens was born in 1954. Her father was Joe Von Battle, who owned a record shop at 3530 Hastings. He was one of the first black record producers/distributors in the United States, and for many years was the sole producer of the music and sermons of the late Reverend C. L. Franklin. Ms. Mickens was raised in Highland Park, Michigan. She is currently employed by the Wayne County Juvenile Court.

Numbers, dope, prostitution . . . everything! You could get anything. You could go to any barbershop on 12th Street and get anything you wanted. You just come in and make your order and come back in twenty minutes and pick it up . . . whatever it was.

I had a brother that had two books. He had a book of people that wanted stuff. You want a mink coat; write that over here. Now, he knowed dudes that stealed mink coats. That's how he made a living, just booking it up. He was a hustler. We call him a hustler; you'd call him a coordinator. He'd put the two people together, and he'd make ten percent for selling your stuff and a ten percent finder's fee from over here. He didn't do nothing, just sit up there . . . make two phone calls . . . boom, boom . . . get the money.

We had a dude what you'd call a "dog man." Used to walk the alleys . . . find out what kind of dog you've got. And I don't care how bad your dog was . . . he could steal your dog. Now, that's a fact. I don't know how he'd do that. People come in there and order . . . they want a female doberman. . . call "dog man," he'd know to go down on Edison between 12th and 14th . . . had a female doberman in the yard. He'd go down there and steal that man's damn dog. And he'd never get bit. I don't understand how he could do that.

We had two guys steal pianos. You want a piano, they get you a piano. I'm serious . . . anything . . . we'd get you anything. And you know, a car went like nothing. We'll get you a car in twenty minutes.

You had some guys come and meet you at the barbershop in the morning. They'd do that when I'd get there, "We're ready to play checkers." Had to put 'em out at night. Old man would just set right there and play checkers all day and all night. We had to make room for 'em. You had to have "X" number of square feet for the customers and" X" number of square feet for the checker players.

We could have stayed on 12th Street. The business people didn't want to go; that was in the plan. We didn't want to go. We wanted to stay there. They wouldn't allow us to stay there. They just told us we had to go. I asked Nicholas Hood in a meeting, "Where would you have me go?"

"They don't give a damn where you go, just got to go." So, we just had to go. And they didn't give us time, you know what I'm saying? They said, "You've gotta be out of here by Monday."

Cavanaugh was mayor during the riot. If we had had a different mayor. . . . Cavanaugh tried to be a nice guy. A different mayor might have. . . . I don't think the riot that day would have happened. It might have happened later in the year but not that day, because the police were aware that it was happening but they didn't come onto 12th Street. They didn't arrest nobody for a couple of days.

At that time I was open on Sunday and closed on Saturday. We moved out on Friday night and opened up Sunday morning up on the Boulevard.

The barber's the expert. The barber's a low-paid shrink. You tell me your problem and I'll solve it. It's easy, same as a shrink.

People have always had problems with their kids. And I don't know. . . . We never paid any attention to our parents. . . . I don't understand why we think our kids should pay attention to us. Everybody's always had problems with their kids. Nobody's ever had enough money . . . never. You look at the economic situation and nobody ever has enough money.

If you were a customer of mine and you didn't have the money, I'd give you a haircut rather than let you run a tab because, invariably, you'll lose your tab, and you'll lose your customer. It's easier for you to find another barbershop than it is to come and pay me.

Rather than do that, if you're a good customer, been coming around for years, what the hell, it's cut in a few minutes. I'd give you a haircut, no big deal. Then you'll have no reason not to come back when you get some money next time.

I've seen that happen just between friends. They borrow a guy's money. He don't have the money to pay 'em, so you avoid the guy. Ask for the money, and you gotta tell another lie why you can't pay him. So there's a friendship broken up for a couple of bucks.

So rather than have you lose your friendship, lose you as a customer, I cut your hair. What's it take but ten minutes. I'm not doing anything anyway. I cut your hair, you're cool with me; next time you need a haircut you'll come back.

BIOGRAPHY

Leon M. Bradley was born on November 16, 1923, and was raised in Flint, Michigan. He was best known as an ardent, twenty-two-year fan of the Detroit Pistons. Bradley was active in the Virginia Park community and was a member of the Citizens District Council. After retiring as a barber, Leon Bradley worked as a volunteer with youth at the Hutchins Middle School in the Virginia Park community. Mr. Bradley died on January 19, 1992. His widow is Jeanette Bradley.

William Lowell Hurt III was a teenager living on Glynn near 12th Street at the time of the 1967 civil disturbance.

WILLIAM LOWELL HURT III

We first came here when I was four or five. We lived here for a couple of years, and then we moved to D.C. for a year.

Coming back from D.C. was my first experience, let's see when was that . . . about 1959 or 1960. There were just three of us, my mom and two of my sisters. We took the Greyhound back, and we had to ride in the back of the bus. All the seats were taken, and I had to stand up. There were seats in the front of the bus, but I stood up from D.C. to Toledo. I couldn't sit up front, and the bus driver wouldn't let me sit on the floor in the back. I thought it kind of strange, because there were seats vacant in the front of the bus. I asked my mom, and she said we couldn't go up there. So I didn't make an issue of it.

They were real good, or real sly, in how they kept racism from us growing up in Detroit, whenever we went South. They would just tell us that the way things were done down there were different from the way they're done up here. But they never said it was because we were black and they were white and there was the racism. But we never stopped at restrooms. My mother would always carry all the toiletries we needed, and we'd have to stop on the side of the road and go to the bathroom. We never thought anything of it. We just called it country.

368

When we traveled to the South we'd always leave at two o'clock in the morning. It was a common practice, if blacks were traveling from the North to the South, they would always leave in the early morning, predawn, so that all of their nighttime driving would be done in the North, and all of the daytime driving would be done in the South.

I later found out that there were green books that literally had road maps for blacks traveling from the North to the South at that time. This was late 1950s or early 1960s, before they had the major interstates. There were two-lane highways that you did a lot of your traveling on. We'd just stop for gas, and that was it. We would carry all the food we'd need. That's probably why I like chicken, because chicken was a staple.

I never realized how anxious my parents always were. I always knew that their tempers were short, and they were always very nervous whenever they got to the South. But I always chalked that up to anticipation. You know, they'd been on the road so long and wanted to hurry up and get there because I'm in the back seat battling with my sisters, and I hated it. I never knew the fear that they experienced, of how dangerous it was traveling, whether it was daytime or nighttime.

And then, you know, being raised in Detroit, we were never subjected to individual racism. We could walk into the front door of any store, whether it was a white-run store or a black-owned store or a Jewish-owned store. We could walk in the front door and purchase anything we wanted.

I remember our cousins didn't like us to go anywhere with them because we didn't, as they said, know how to act. If we went to a store, they would always walk around to the back. The storekeepers would come out to the back and ask them what they wanted, and then bring it out to the back. Well, my sisters and I would just open the front door and walk into the store. Our cousins would always be crying, and we never knew why. The storekeepers would say, "Those are Burt's kids from Detroit . . . they don't know better." They wouldn't hold that against us. They'd just say we weren't trained properly.

In Detroit, the neighborhood I grew up in, the Boston-Edison area in the early '60s, was a very integrated area. My dad built a house on the corner of 12th and Glynn, and we moved into that in 1961. The first kid on the block I made friends with was a white guy. And he saw me coming, because he sold me this old bike that all of the other kids on the block had kept teasing him about. But I loved it. It was an old, big, balloon-tired, gray, dingy bike with a basket on the front handlebars. I bought it the first day I was there; and he was happy, and I was happy . . . and so we quickly became friends.

We lived in an area where on one side of 12th street, you had middle-class, black professionals. There were lawyers, doctors, judges, morticians, schoolteachers, professors, and insurance salesmen, and people who you would think are skilled trades. On the other side of 12th, beginning at Glynn between 12th and Woodrow Wilson, and heading north on 12th street, you had a lot of two-family flats and double-family-occupancy homes. You had a lot more of working class living in that area. You had a tremendous blend of educational, ethnic, income, of blacks, whites, Jews.

From Clairmount and 12th street almost down to the Boulevard, you had a complete shopping area. You had all kinds of men's clothing stores, women's clothing stores, supermarkets, millinery shops, and other small businesses. It was basically a community that was self-contained. You had pharmacies and drugstores and five- and-tens. Right on the corner of 12th and Glynn, on the northeast side, there was a little soda fountain; and it was called Cozy Corners.

Ernie Durham, who used to be the top deejay of WJLB, lived directly behind our house, on the corner of Boston and 12th. He used to give all kind of parties, and we'd drill these little holes in the back of his wooden fence and peer through them. He would have bands, and everybody would be in tuxedos or dinner jackets. We could see some of the Motown entertainers—Smokey Robinson, the Miracles, the Temptations. He was such a personality at that time and was really responsible for getting Motown and putting it on the map. Just sit in the alley and peer through the holes and watch him party. We had to have some kind of enjoyment as kids. So we did that.

12th street was fascinating because, like I said, you had doctors, lawyers, professional people. You had blue collar, you had pimps, prostitutes. It was nothing to see two prostitutes get into a fight over whatever, and we used to love it, because the women would tear each other's clothes off and be bare-breasted, naked, and screaming and shouting at each other, running up and down 12th. 12th street was really live. You'd see guys walking up 12th street with yellow suits and sharkskins and thick-and-thins. They're socks that were made out of silk. They had thick lines running through them and thin, silk lines—almost like stockings. You could buy all of this stuff at Louis the Hatter and some of the other men's clothing stores. So 12th street was not only a melting pot of lower- to upper- middle-income blacks . . . it was also a fashion center. It had to be one of the richest areas in the city, as far as culture at that time.

As a kid, we used to have bottle-top guns, where we would take flat pieces of board and take bicycle inner tubes and nail it down on one end of the board, a board maybe three to four feet long. On one end of the board was the inner tube. We'd cut the inner tube and nail it down, and then take one of those spring-action type of wooden clothespins that had the metal coil in the middle and tack it down on the opposite end.

We would stretch the rubber inner tube all the way down and catch it. We would walk around with sacks of bottle tops that we got out of the machines and set the bottle tops inside the rubber bands. You pulled the rubber band from the front of the board to the clothespin at the back, and set the bottle top inside of the end of the rubber band and hold it down with the clothes clip. When you'd press down on it and it would open, the rubber band would, being tight, spring forth and propel the bottle top out.

It's amazing no one got seriously injured the way those things would take off. But we'd have wars with kids on other streets, and instead of knives and guns we had bottle-top guns. They would cause a nice welt, if they hit you, and sometimes it would even cut the skin. For some reason, no one ever got injured seriously with them. I mean, it would sting like hell.

In the early '60s we were bused out to totally white areas in the city of Detroit, beyond Seven Mile and Livernois or Seven Mile and Southfield. They were taking a lot of the students who excelled, who had good grades. They bused kids to predominately white schools on the outskirts of the city of Detroit, integrated those schools. They didn't do it with Board of Education buses. We were assigned to those schools, and would take the city buses.

There were some negative responses, because all the black students that went to the school got off of city buses, and at that point in time, the city buses would pull up right alongside the school. They had city bus stops right in front of the school. Every morning these busloads of black students would get off the bus, and there would be all these white and Jewish students standing in line and milling around the outside. Bus after bus would pull up and there would be nothing but black students getting off of these buses.

We grew up in an area at a period in time where it was racially mixed. I mean, we didn't look at the white kids as being any different than the white kids that we played with in the neighborhood. We got in trouble, got chased by the police, hid on top of garages, hid inside of people's garages and basements, and there were white kids with us. So a lot of us didn't really think anything was strange about going to a school that was mostly white.

The negativity really didn't present itself until the riots in '67. That changed the whole complexion of that area. The riots were something that forced a lot of blacks out of that area, professional blacks. Some stayed, but a lot moved out. It definitely forced the whites out of that area to a greater degree. You saw a huge exodus of whites after the riots, or as a result of the riots.

I was about fourteen at the time of the riots. I remember the Sunday morning that the riots started. My uncle called over to our house about six o'clock that morning and told my dad and mom that they should get up and look at what's happening on 12th street. He said people have started rioting down around Clairmount, or just below Clairmount. He really didn't know what had caused that riot. We sat on our front porch that whole day and that following Monday and literally witnessed the riot move north up 12th street from Clairmount.

They were in the process of putting a Clark gas station on the corner. They had dug the foundation and had actually put the gas drums in and had filled the drums. The Clark station was getting ready to open that following week, the week of the riots. But it hadn't officially opened. These gas tanks were filled, and this was kitty-corner to our house. My mom, being the nervous sort of person that she was, once the riot started to get into full gear, the only thing that she could think of when the people started burning the buildings was that this gas station was going to explode and take our house with it.

But we sat there and watched people in the middle of July, walking up 12th street with fur coats on. Obviously they had stolen these things. We watched them pull, drag, the old guy who ran that shoe repair shop out in the middle of 12th Street and literally beat him mercilessly, simply because he was white.

We saw people looting, just breaking windows at the supermarket up the street on the corner above Calvert and 12th. A crowd gathered outside, and this one guy who was obviously leading them broke the window and was the first person in the supermarket. I recall how my friends and I always laughed about this because he was the first person into the supermarket and all he came out with was about two oranges. We saw people walking up and down the street with arms full of clothes, or jewelry or walking with television sets and radios they had looted.

Our parents, the kids' parents who lived on our side of 12th street, none of them took part in the rioting, none of them took part in the looting. Our parents were very, very strict. I'd have friends come down to my porch and watch what's happening because we were right on the corner of 12th. But even that got dangerous, because police would drive by and see five, six, or seven black male youths sitting on the porch, and they'd tell us to break it up.

They had something in that point of time called the "Big Four," and they drove around in these black Chryslers or Fords and were usually three white police officers with one black officer that was driving. Nobody messed with the "Big Four." They would whip your head on the spot. There was a certain amount of fear and through that fear a certain amount of respect for the "Big Four." No one liked them, but no one messed with them either.

We had outside of our home, on the corner, three National Guards. On the side of the house we had two. And between our house and the house that was next to us, we had another National Guard stationed. National Guards were stationed up and down the block and along 12th and Boston to protect our neighborhood from brick-throwing, rioting, and destruction. All of the moms in our block club would get together and make these guys huge dinners and would feed the soldiers every day. They would give them breakfast, lunch and dinner. That stopped abruptly.

Our living room was in the back of the house; and we had this big, huge, glass window that was a sliding glass door. You could come from the backyard into the living room of our house. A number of homes received threats, via bricks thrown through their windows with messages attached to them, saying that if you continue to feed the National Guard troops, your house will burn. So food stopped. Soldiers stopped getting fed.

We started writing a phrase on the side of the house, on the windows; and all store owners who wised up to what was happening would put the signs in their windows that said, "Soul Brother," or "I'm a Soul Brother," or something like that. That was almost like painting the blood over the top of the house to let death pass over, because they didn't mess with the houses that had those signs or the stores that had the signs.

There was a little party store right across the street on the other side of 12th, and my mom sent me out to the store to get some milk or something, and I came running out the side of our house. I ran out of the house and got into the middle of the street when the National Guard hollered, "Stop!" I literally froze in the middle of the street. They called me over and asked me where was I going, what was I doing; and I told them that, hey, I live right here and my mom was just sending me to the store. They made me go back in the house, made my mom or my dad come out and explain to them where I was going, what I was going for, and then stood there and watched as I went across the street to the store and came back.

Then one night, my younger sister was just an infant at that time, and they had pinned a sniper down on the roof of the building across the street on 12th. My mom got up about eleven-thirty or twelve o'clock. The police had turned off all of the street lights up and down 12th Street, so it was pitch black. My mom got up to go downstairs to get my sister a bottle. When she turned on the light in the living room, which was in the back with that big glass door, the light hit like a floodlight; and she got about two steps when the National Guard and the police said over a megaphone she had about five seconds to turn that light out or it would be blown out because it was giving their position away and illuminating them to the sniper. She turned the light out, and I remember how she crawled back up the steps. She was so scared. She made us sleep under our beds that night because of the gunfire. The next morning I got up, went out in the backyard, and saw spent shells. And our garage on the alley side was just riddled with bullets.

At first the riots were a matter of just looting stores and people roaming. Then it got real ugly. I mean, it turned more violent, where there were snipers and gunfire, and we were literally under martial law. If there was a group of four or five blacks walking down the street together, they were broken up. The police would stop them, break them up, and make some of them go a different way. It was really scary. I remember how firemen stopped coming into the neighborhood because they were being shot at. That is why you had so many buildings that were just gutted.

During the riots, I would sit on my porch and watch the people come up the street with all of the stolen goods they had looted from the stores down 12th Street.

There was this one time that this guy came up the east side of 12th, and I'm sitting on my porch on 12th and Glynn. We had this big front yard, and I was sitting out there with my mom, and the guy was walking on the east side of the street, and a lady walking on the west side of the street. This guy had watches all up his arm, in his pockets and his coat. He was shouting to this lady across the street. He got mad at her, and he reached up his arm and pulled a watch off and threw it at her. It landed right in the middle of our grass. He missed her and kept going.

All day long I just sat there and looked at that watch. I turned to my mom when he first did it, and before I could ask her, she said: "No, you can't have it. Just leave it there." I was like a cat watching a ball or piece of string. I was just fixed on that watch. I sat on my porch all day long to make sure no one else would see it and pick it up. Anytime anyone walked up the street that day, I'd run out and stand by that watch and just stand there until they walked away, and then go back and sit on the porch. Yes, I just stood over it and blocked it so no one would look down and see it. I sat on the porch all day long. 'cause when I went out and looked at the watch it was a Longines. It was a real, real nice watch. Here I am a young teenage kid, and I'm lusting after this watch.

So I sat there all day long until that evening and my mom had gone in the house. I went out and got the watch and put it in my book bag. I hid it and never wore the watch at home. Whenever I left home, I always had to carry it with me so that my mom would never find it in the house. But whenever I was out, I'd put the watch on. It was a great watch. I enjoyed it. It was amazing how that watch just had me fixed. I could not move. I did not want to leave the porch. I did not want to do anything else because I wanted that watch and I got it.

She never found out about it until I told her when I was grown, because I had lied to her. She asked me that evening what happened to the watch, and I said somebody had come and taken it. What I said was the guy came back and picked it up. It was believable and so she bought it. I not only had to hide it from her and my dad, but I had to hide it from my sisters, too, because they would have told. I couldn't have kept them happy long enough for me to keep the watch without them telling on me. I made sure that I wore it only when I wasn't around any members of my family.

I'll bump my head and I'll bump my head, but it's like this is going to be mine. And that's the way I am now in my business. I've had every reason in the world to do something else, but it is just like me sitting on the porch looking at that watch. It was something that I wanted. Not even my mom sitting there, and knowing what I had to do to keep it, didn't stop me from wanting and getting it.

BIOGRAPHY

William Lowell Hurt III was born on June 29, 1953, in Phenix City, Alabama. He moved to Detroit with his parents and four sisters in 1957. He is senior vice president of PR Networks, a public relations, marketing, and advertising firm in Detroit. The family-owned business includes his sister, Acquanetta Pierce, and cousin, John A. Graves. He and his wife, Jill, are parents of a daughter, Mercede.

DAVE BING

My first experience with Detroit actually occurred before I had ever visited Detroit and was a senior in college. In 1966 I was drafted by the Detroit Pistons as their number one player. However, I had mixed emotions at that point in time, because I didn't know anything about Detroit. I had the impression that I would be going to New York with the Knicks and didn't know anything about the Pistons' organization or the city.

On my first visit to Detroit I didn't really want to be there. Having been born and raised on the East Coast, and with New York City being the mecca, if you will, for both basketball and for media coverage, that's where I thought I should be. But getting drafted by the Pistons really turned out to be a blessing in disguise.

A very unique experience occurred when I first came to Detroit: none of the folks wanted me here. The player they wanted, and rightly so, was Cazzie Russell, who was a great player at the University of Michigan and was the number one overall draft choice into the NBA. Most folks here had seen Cazzie play from a collegiate standpoint and felt that he was what the Pistons needed to bring the organization back. It didn't happen that way. Therefore, I had something to prove immediately; and that was that I had talent, I could play. And I had to win folks over by performance. Through the years it's been a love relationship between myself and the people of the city since.

A real rude awakening in my first year here was the civil disturbance of 1967, and I saw this city come apart at the seams. In 1966 I lived out in the Eight Mile and Greenfield area, and that was considered a nice area of Detroit, where there were no real problems to speak of; and it was a good mixed neighborhood, with well-kept homes. The values of the homes were still pretty high at that time. I didn't realize until the third or fourth day the magnitude of the disturbance because the Light Guard Armory, where a lot of troops were gathering, was very close to my home. I could hear the heavy traffic and the tanks going up Greenfield as well as on Eight Mile. For the first time I realized just how serious the problem was. Based on what I saw on TV, and when I had a chance to go out afterwards to see the devastation, it really put me in a different kind of mind-set. That mind-set was there was going to be a hell of a lot of work to rebuild the city because it was torn apart.

The following year, I remember vividly that one of the healing processes was Detroit's amazing sports franchises. The Tigers won the World Series in 1968, and all of a sudden all of the negatives that occurred because of the disturbance seemed to start healing themselves. Black, white, suburb, and city started to come together for a common cause; and that was to root the Tigers on to a championship. We have been rebuilding ever since 1967, and we are still going through that process.

My family came from the South and had absolutely nothing. My father went to the seventh grade; my mother went to the ninth grade. But they were resourceful people, because in the times that they grew up, they didn't know where their next meal was coming from. They didn't know how they were going to make a car payment or house payment, and educating their kids above the high school level was something that was unheard of.

Out of my sibling group I was the first one to go to college, and that was a big thing. I went to college on an athletic scholarship. And even though my parents had always pushed academics when I was growing up, one of the things that was real rewarding to me was that my father came from a family of thirteen, and I used to sit and listen to a lot of the stories they would tell about how tough times were and how difficult it was to get out of the South and then try and make a new living in the North. About five of them came to Washington, five went to New York, and two went to Philadelphia, so most people came east. A lot of the second generation remained in the South.

During family reunions or family visits, I remember them sitting late at night. You would play like you were asleep and listen to the adults' conversation, and you would learn a lot. I found out that the very best education you could get was from older people, people with experience.

There was a lot of gamesmanship that folks had to go through: things that you did and said and acted in a certain way so that you could get by, so that you wouldn't be looked upon as a threat. You learn early on how to respect your elders, because those folks were pretty smart to have no formal education and to be in the South and to survive it and get out and start life all over again. You just pull your roots up and go somewhere where you don't know a damn thing about the area. You don't know anybody, and you start and you make it. A lot of the things that they talked about, the sub-par wages, the way folks were treated, the way you were looked upon, and all of it was negative. In spite of that, those folks made it and they always kept their dignity. I think that's extremely important. Regardless of how educated you are and how much money you've got, that doesn't give you dignity. You can be poor and uneducated, but you can be dignified.

You go back to the old folks; and they had a work ethic, I think, and a respect for themselves, for family, for human life that is damn near nonexistent today. Obviously that's why we are having a lot of the problems we are having. The extended family was norm. It's forced upon some folks, but that was a normal thing. You looked forward to having aunts and uncles, cousins, grandfather, grandmother; whether you were in the same house or a stone's throw from each other, you always had the support group. Now we've become bourgeois or middle class or whatever, and you want to disassociate yourself away from that where, in my opinion, that was the real strength.

Today it is common practice that if you're middle class, both parents are working in order to maintain that. Back then mothers weren't working; families were together. The breakdown of the family has been our quest to get these material goods. You've broken the family down completely. My mother never worked. We weren't rich. We were poor and didn't know it. We never had to worry about food on the table, a roof over my head, clean clothes to wear. That was never a concern of ours because my father, coming from the South, learned how to work with his hands early on. Getting a good job was never a problem for him. There was a work ethic there. We get to the next generation and I see it constantly, the same mistakes are being made over and over. It happened to black families, but now I see it happened to middle-class white families, also.

BIOGRAPHY

Dave Bing was born on November 29, 1943, in Washington, D.C. He is chairman and CEO of the Bing Group which includes Bing

Steel, a steel service center; Superb Manufacturing, Inc., a metal stamping plant; and Heritage 21, a construction management company.

Mr. Bing played professional basketball for twelve years and continues to serve the community as advisor to many youth groups. He received a B.A. degree from Syracuse University. He has three daughters and one grandson.

*After serving in World War II,
Ollie Foster moved to Detroit,
where he became an actively
contributing member of the
Virginia Park community.*

DISCUSSION ON VIRGINIA PARK COMMUNITY

OLLIE FOSTER, HERSCHEL L. RICHEY,
AND WALTER ROSSER

OLLIE FOSTER: The city had plans for the [Virginia Park, 12th Street] area, and they revealed them along about that time, 1960. Nobody trusted the city. They used to have the city come out and tell them all the plans. They were going to build some football fields in there, and they were going to have some baseball diamonds. The people said, "Where are all the people going to be when you do all of this?" There were a lot of apartment buildings at that time, and it was overcrowded.

I think the controversy in the area probably came from what you would call a melting pot. There were a number of union people. There was a lot of schoolteachers and things in that area. Even at that time there were some poor people who were on Aid to Dependent Children. Some block clubs didn't want renters to belong to the block club. Then you had some very militant people in there. I remember some of them, after the civil disturbance and New Detroit came into being. New Detroit gave them some jobs, and you wouldn't know they were the same people. They'd come out there reading things that New Detroit had told them to say. It was said in the community that if you raise enough hell, the city will pick you up and give you a job.

They had a master plan for the entire city, and this was the one that they were going to work on first. We were supposed to get forty-three million dollars. This was prior to the civil disturbance. The planning committee had not agreed on what they were going to do. Along about the same time, it was overcrowded because of all the apartment buildings in there. Whatever area you picked for development, that was one of the really controversial things. If you were on the committee, and it was a friend's area about to be taken, they'd come to you and say, "I didn't think you'd do this to me." It was some trying times. I remember Fred Thomas, they wanted to take his house. He thought I had voted to take his house.

They knew that civil disturbance was going to happen. I understand there were some people that were part of a watch committee that was supposed to alert the police if something jumped off. Blacks were feeling more and more that they were being disenfranchised, that they weren't getting their fair share.

HERSCHEL L. RICHEY: One month before the 1940s riot I had written an article that said that Detroit was a boiling pot ready to erupt at any time. The same condition prevailed in the 1960s.

WALTER ROSSER: Gentlemen, I think we've overlooked one critical element. The Virginia Park area, as I remember it in 1948, when I moved there, was one of the most attractive neighborhoods in the city of Detroit, structure-wise. The type of black families who were moving in were those who could accumulate a down payment on a house and buy it. The majority of the first black residents in the Virginia Park area were home buyers. Then suddenly the criminal vice element was relocated because of the highway construction in the Hastings area. This element relocated one hundred percent up to 12th Street. Southfield was opening, and the Jewish merchants had an opportunity to go out there and establish businesses. So here you've got a neighborhood of working, struggling black people trying to make it, and suddenly the entire vice community is dumped right in their midst.

HERSCHEL L. RICHEY: You had a much more crowded situation then, because you had numerous apartments there, dozens and dozens of apartments.

WALTER ROSSER: That's usually the case in any large city in America where a black community settles—that there's a housing shortage. They jam the people up by subdividing.

HERSCHEL L. RICHEY: They had one apartment there, remember the one on Seward and Woodrow Wilson? It was a nice apartment to begin with, but they began to cut it up, and it was rehabilitated.

They had planned to build a high-rise. The peculiar thing about it was that they got the government's permission, state's permission, city, but they didn't get the Virginia Park District Council permission.

When it came to us, we turned it down, so it never did happen. They were going to put a high-rise up. The concept at that time was, let's try to get rid of some of the apartments and maybe have only two-story buildings.

A funny thing happened during that time. They wanted to put in a shopping center. I was in favor of them putting a shopping center on the east side of 12th. They put it on the west side of 12th, which was a very good thing, I think, because we got rid of all those apartments over there. It was nothing but apartments over there.

OLLIE FOSTER: They were mostly owned by outside people or what we call absentee landlords, and they began at that time to drain them off, just get money and make no repairs or nothing like that. There was very little rehabilitation work done. In fact, I think a lot of them stopped paying city tax and all of that after blacks started coming in.

At that time it wasn't as much holdups and things. There was prostitution and gambling and numbers, but some people didn't mind numbers as bad. The only thing was when they had these runners picking up the numbers in what they call single action. Some of the block clubs didn't like that, because of the image for the youngsters that this was a way to make it, and we know well that it's not a good way make it. No illegal activity is the way to make it.

Along about that era was the time that the police became kind of corrupt. If you complained to them about something like that, them people knew it two hours after that. They'd come back some time and ask you, "Are you against this, are you against that?" The police told them, and I'll say that anywhere.

The police and community is what brought it about. I don't think they expected it to come off when it did. I think they was expecting something much larger than that to happen. You read how it happened: it was a blind pig place and they raided it. I guess they may have shoved somebody around, and that's when it started. But the police brutalized quite a bit at that point, and they were expecting something else to happen.

There was a lot of them blind pigs and what we called house-rent parties. A lot of times people didn't want it happening in their neighborhood, because what happens is that sometimes a guy goes there and loses all his money, and he's scared to go home. If he should happen to come out and see somebody walking alone, he's liable to take him some money.

HERSCHEL L. RICHEY: In the other riot, if you did some looting, you were shot. In 1943 I was standing on the porch of Great Lakes Insurance Company, and they broke into a store on the corner of Brush and Warren. I saw one fellow come out with a bottle of wine or liquor. The police came up at that time, and they just shot him and killed him.

That's what they were doing with looters back in that first riot, but they must have had orders not to shoot the people in this riot because they just carried out all kinds of material. A few of the kids in my neighborhood hid some of the stuff in my basement, and I didn't even know it. I found it, and I took it out, and I put it in the alley.

WALTER ROSSER: I believe you can't call them all criminals, but I refer to them as the night people, the people who more or less did what they called hustle. The pickpockets and the gambling hustlers and a group of youngsters who more or less looked to them as role models, as well as the youngsters who, like all youth in America at that time, were becoming anti-establishment, anti-authority. That mood got in them that the "pigs," as they called the police, apparently have orders not to crack down on us; so let's just go ahead and make a killing.

HERSCHEL L. RICHEY: I'm standing in Grace Church yard; and there were several people standing there watching the buildings across the street burn down, and they would fall in the street. I would say, "Why are they burning those houses down?"

One of the fellows said to me, and I think he probably was involved in this burning, he says, "Well, the house may belong to one of the brothers, one of the brothers might live in the house; but whitey owns it, and we're burning it down because he will be responsible for rebuilding it."

WALTER ROSSER: There was a nihilistic attitude amongst these street people and young people. They didn't particularly adhere to or follow any given ideology. Some called themselves militant, but the majority of them were nihilistic, just "anti" everything. When an occasion came for them to loot and steal and parade and claim themselves militants, they did so.

OLLIE FOSTER: I guess the word got out that they weren't going to burn any black guy's establishment because they said you were supposed to write on there "soul brother." I remember a Chinese had on his window, "Me soul brother too."

WALTER ROSSER: What really hurt me about this business is that it triggered off on a Sunday. The following day it was extremely hot. What few small neighborhood groceries that were spared were black owned. These guys raised their prices two to three hundred percent. I had to get in my car and drive way to Inkster. There's this black fellow that had this supermarket over there. I went out and loaded up my trunk with bread and milk and came back so my neighbor's kids could have milk and bread. Otherwise, if they bought in the neighborhood, where it normally sold for thirty-five cents a quart, these fellows were asking a dollar and ten cents or a dollar and a quarter for a quart. These were black merchants.

Another thing I suppose people don't realize: in the black community throughout America, ten years earlier you had *Brown* vs. *Board of Education*. There were great promises, and a lot of people just didn't see fulfillment of these promises and expectations. There was a mood of anger. Statistics will prove that at that time a great majority of the rioters were working here and held steady jobs. These were the people who they arrested. A good sixty-five percent had good paying jobs in the auto industry. Jerry Cavanaugh said it could never happen here, but he was thinking through the liberal perspective.

The National Guard in the 1967 riot was mostly composed of young men who did not want to get drafted into Vietnam. The majority of them were in the Guard because they didn't want to perform military service. I believe they pulled some units that were camped at Grayling. These guys are all from small rural communities out in Michigan where they don't communicate with or they don't know anything about black people. God knows what they had heard. They weren't in the very best of moods, and they weren't too well disciplined. There was as much difference as night and day in the areas where the troopers from the 101st were.

HERSCHEL L. RICHEY: They had a curfew at that time. My son and a kid next door, I guess they were young teenagers. The curfew didn't mean anything to them, but the National Guard stopped them and knocked them down. The kid next door was crying like a baby. They made them lie on the ground. It took me a week before I found out where my son was. They locked him in a pen over some place. I got in touch with some City Council people, and we finally found out where he was.

WALTER ROSSER: When President Johnson got tired of playing politics with Romney, they dispatched the 101st Airborne Division, and that ended it. Their presence alone seemed to give the people the impression that these guys are professional and they mean business, and they had better stop.

OLLIE FOSTER: You've got to remember that during that time there was efforts for civil rights all across the country. Martin Luther King and other people were beginning to say that we've had enough. We're not going to take it anymore. If you had anything in you at all, you had to be of that same philosophy that, I'm paying my taxes, I'm doing everything that every other citizen is doing, and I ought to be getting some of the spoils. People here were saying that, I won't take that. That was a part of that march here in 1963 that Franklin led along with other ministers. That we're not going to take this anymore. We want something different.

Until they started doing that in the South, many people in the North didn't realize just how segregated or how they were being discriminated against here. There were housing patterns, and you could only live here or live there, irrespective of how much money you had. Banks wouldn't loan you any money. I remember that I was selling real estate; and if no black lived in an area and you were trying to buy a house in there, this bank said we will not be the first one to break the neighborhood. It just went on that way. Of course, some of them bought on land contract.

These are the things that were happening. Ministers began to talk about it. Reverend Hill and Franklin and there were a couple of other ministers that began to talk about these things, that we ought to have what we are really entitled to. Ministers were coming from the South, and they were trying to get some help with the things that were happening to them. That made you realize more and more that the same thing almost was happening to you.

BIOGRAPHIES

Ollie Foster was born on February 20, 1919, in Burdette, Arkansas. He came to Detroit in 1937. He served in the U.S. Army during World War II, where he attained the rank of staff sergeant. He married Eleanor Franklin on March 10, 1946. Their two children are Cynthia Harris and Michael O. Foster. Mr. Foster has been active in the Virginia Park community and is past president of the Virginia Park Nonprofit Housing Corporation. He is on the board of the Virginia Park Community Investment Associates and the Citizens District Council. Ollie Foster is a real estate salesman. He is a member of Hartford Baptist Church.

Herschel L. Richey: See p. 236.

Walter Rosser: See p. 140.

George Romney was governor of Michigan from 1963–69. He was placed in a difficult position by the Johnson administration when he sought federal assistance in quelling the 1967 civil disturbance.

GEORGE ROMNEY

My legal advisor, Robert Danoff, called me because the mayor's office had called him. They had assured him that they thought they could handle the disturbance. They had handled one earlier in the year, so they thought could handle this one. It wasn't until the afternoon of July 23rd that he called and indicated that things were much more serious than they realized, and therefore they'd like our help, the state's help. Mayor Cavanaugh had requested the assistance of the state and National Guard. At 3:05 P.M., word was received that 360 troopers were at the Eight Mile Road Armory awaiting transportation. At 4:20 P.M., Mayor Cavanaugh requested the aid of the National Guard troops.

Well, if they requested two hundred ahead of time, they didn't request them with me. My recollection is that I was asked to make the National Guard available. It's true that there were some troopers at the armory, but the bulk of the troops were up at Grayling on summer training. And that was one reason it took time to get the troops down here, because they had to be transported from Grayling down. There were only these few that were in the armory at the time.

At 7:45 P.M., Mayor Cavanaugh issued a proclamation placing the city under curfew between 9:00 P.M. and 5:00 A.M. I don't know whether

386

he issued that or I did. I think I did. It's my recollection that I issued the proclamation on the curfew.

Cavanaugh and I had concluded there was no assurance that we could control it with just the police and the National Guard. The National Guardsman were not trained for a riot. I walked into his office and talked to Vice President Humphrey up in Minneapolis/St. Paul. Humphrey told him that we should call Clark. So I called Attorney General Ramsey Clark and requested national troops, and Clark said we'd get them. He didn't raise any questions at that point. You have to keep in mind that, at that point, I was ahead of Lyndon Baines Johnson in the presidential polls, so I was a possible political opponent for the presidency. At any rate, Clark started out by saying, "Yes, you can have them." Then he called back a few hours later—I'm sure this is after he had conferred with the president—and said they had to have a written request indicating that the riot was completely beyond our control.

I consulted with my legal advisor, Danoff, and he said, "If you submit a written request of that character, all of the insurance policies in this area will be voided." Then we began a series of discussions to try and convince them that I could not give them that sort of a thing. We finally worked out a compromise written request that didn't negate all of the insurance policies in the area. They eventually agreed on that basis to send the federal troops.

It took hours. It was quite a bit of delay. The Newark riot occurred before our riot, and President Johnson called the governor of New Jersey and offered to send the federal troops in. In my case they were insisting that I provide them this statement. There was a great contrast between how they handled Newark and us. As a matter of fact, subsequently, they studied the question of on what basis the federal troops should be made available if a governor requested them; and they concluded that all that was needed was an oral request from the governor, just what I had given them initially. So subsequently, they confirmed the fact that this holdup was completely unnecessary and unwarranted.

They didn't mention any federal statutes or anything at that point. They just indicated they wanted a written request indicating that the thing was completely out of control. Not only insurance policies would be nullified, but also we didn't know with certainty whether we could or couldn't have made it without federal troops. We concluded that we shouldn't take the risk of not being able to control it, because if we would have done that, things would have been worse.

In any event, eventually they agreed, and the president sent Cyrus Vance out here in advance with General Throckmorton. They arrived in the early afternoon, in advance of the troops. They were sent to take control of the situation, because the way things operate, if the mayor asks for the governor and the governor comes in, then the governor is in command. If the governor asked for national assistance and the president sends somebody in to take over on a national basis, then they are in command. So the minute Vance and Throckmorton arrived, they were in command, and Cavanaugh and I were subject to their decisions.

Well, the troops got in here, as I recall, during the afternoon. They got in shortly after Vance and Throckmorton got here. What Vance said was, he wanted to go out and assess the situation personally before deciding whether to commit the federal troops, so he and Throckmorton went out in a five-car convoy. It was dinnertime; and the rioters were getting hungry, I guess, so the magnitude of the disorder declined during the period they were out. So when they came back, Vance refused to send the troops out, the federal troops. We had them at Selfridge Field, but he refused to send them out.

After the dinner hour, Throckmorton and I were conferring, keeping in touch with Police Commissioner Nichols, and the rioting began to pick up again after the dinner hour. At about 9:00 P.M., I was convinced that the situation was still out of control and that we needed the federal troops on the streets. Throckmorton was with me when we were talking with Nichols and looking at the figures. I went in to see Vance at about 9:00 P.M.

We were all at police headquarters. At least Throckmorton, Vance, Cavanaugh, and I were. I went in to see him at about 9:00 P.M., as nearly as I can recall the time, and said: "Look, on the basis of these figures that we have, the situation is still out of control. Get those federal troops out in the area as rapidly as possible." He again confronted me with the same request that Ramsey Clark had requested of me in the morning—a written request indicating the situation was completely out of control. So we were right back to where we had the delay in the morning.

I finally said to him, "Look, if you want to blame this whole thing on me, blame it on me; but get those troops out in the riot area." Throckmorton backed up the fact that the situation had deteriorated. He had the assistant attorney general with him when I met with Vance. After I met with him and indicated that they could blame it on me if they wanted, he didn't say what he was going to do, but I'm sure he conferred with the White House. I'm sure he conferred with President Johnson, and the president made a broadcast about 10:30 P.M. In his broadcast he didn't blame me for it. He indicated he was ordering the troops out to deal with the riot. They didn't get out in the field until about midnight. In my opinion, we lost about a day that way as a result of this inability to satisfy first Clark and then Vance.

These troops that came in were good troops that were trained to deal with situations like this. They had riot training. They had dealt with such activities. It was very helpful to get them on the field. Once they got out there, the situation was brought under control.

Subsequently, the next day, in talking about what caused this and what might be done to prevent a reoccurrence and to compose relationships in the city, Vance and Cavanaugh and I discussed the creation of an interracial organization that might bring the representative leadership of the community together and establish communication and relationships that would avoid a subsequent occurrence of the same type. That led to the convening of the broad leadership group from the city to discuss the creation of such an organization. The leadership of the city thought it was a good idea. As a result of that, New Detroit was created. I was asked to call Joe Hudson and ask him to be the chairman of the first New Detroit organization. He agreed to serve as the first chairman. People viewed him as an objective man of integrity. I felt he was highly regarded by all the elements involved, and he did a good job.

What triggered the riot in my opinion, to a considerable extent, was that between urban renewal and expressways, poor black people were bulldozed out of their homes. They had no place to go in the suburbs because of suburban restrictions. They settled along 12th Street. The concentration of people on 12th Street was too great. So when that incident occurred, it was a spark that ignited the whole area. On the other hand, the problems in Detroit now are pretty much through the whole city, not just concentrated in one place. The population is not as concentrated, but the drug pushers and the prostitutes and the pimps and those people are the people in control, and those are the people the young blacks see all the time who've got money and so on. We've got serious problems down there, and I'm hopeful we'll get at them before it's too late.

BIOGRAPHY

George Romney was born on July 8, 1907, in Chihuahua, Mexico. Before his career in government he was managing director of the Automobile Manufacturers Assocation and Chief Executive Officer of American Motors. Mr. Romney served as governor of Michigan from 1963–69. He was the Secretary of the U.S. Department of Housing and Urban Development from 1969–72. Mr. Romney currently serves on the board of Points of Light Foundation and the Commission on National and Community Service. Throughout his life he has been active in the Church of Jesus Christ of Latter-Day Saints.

ROY WILDS

I found myself in the summer of 1967 looking at things that were happening across the country, things that were going on in Watts and Newark. I remember talking to a friend of my mother, and she said, "Do you notice there are people that are angry or whatever?"

I said, "I would be hard pressed to see why they should riot or anything like that, because everybody seems to be okay." Well, that very weekend, just a matter of days, I remember the National Guard and the state troopers coming in, and I remember watching folks loot and burn.

I stood back, and guys would say, "Come on, you might as well get some of this." I will not forget this guy on the corner of Linwood and Hazelwood. Between Hazelwood and Gladstone there was a drugstore. A guy broke into this drugstore and was bringing out this liquor, and he ran between myself and my best friend, Eugene Rogers, who I grew up with. We were standing there with our mouths open just looking, and I will not forget this National Guardsman pulling this rifle. He leveled it at this guy. He just pointed it at this guy, and the guy ran between us. The guardsman did not fire. He just looked. It was at that point in time that I told Gene: "Hey man, we'd better go home, because you know what? We could have been killed just that easily." We did leave the streets.

I remember that the A & P that I was working in was looted. It was on Linwood and West Grand Boulevard. It was closed. That Sunday I was supposed to work. I remember taking a bus there and going up and just looking at the store. The front window was all broken out. The barbecue sauce display that we had worked on very diligently was knocked over, and there was barbecue sauce everywhere. Of course, all the shelves were ripped off. The cans and canned goods and meat was all gone. So I went there around the time I was supposed to go to work, and I remember going into the store. Our boss was there. He said, "There's not a whole lot we can do, so let's just get a push broom and push this debris up to the front of the store."

So there were about three or four of us that were in the store the guys that worked stock and me. We were pushing this stuff down the aisle, and I happened to look up. And in the window, where a plate glass window used to be. There were four National Guards, and they had their weapons trained on us. At this point one of the guys in the next aisle said, "Hey man, I'm through with this," or something to that effect, and I just kept on sweeping or pushing all this sauce up the aisle, because there was sauce everywhere—floors, shelves, everywhere.

So, this guy says, "Halt, nigger!" I guess I stopped at that point, as did everyone else.

And I remember the assistant manager, I told you he was black, he came out, and he said: "That's okay. These are my boys."

And the guardsman said, "You too, nigger, you put your hands up!"

At that point in time, the manager came out and said, "What's going on?" He was in the little office. They didn't say anything to him. They just accepted the fact that he could have been the manager. Now, nobody was dressed except us. We were dressed like we were coming to work. I had a white shirt, tie, and my jeans on, and so did these other guys. We put on our aprons to keep our clothes clean.

I guess, at that point in time, it pretty much crystallized where I was in America and what I was about. You might not be in Selma, but people still harbor a lot of hatred and prejudice towards you simply because you're black. You're different than they are. Well, that kind of made me angry.

After I thought about it and the fact that I could have been killed, I discussed this with my mother, and she said, "Yeah, well, you don't even understand." She told me stories about what had happened to her in the South, how people tried to molest her, for example, because she was a very good-looking woman for any culture. "If your father was here, he would tell you worse stories because he left the South knowing that he was up against the odds. Why did you think he had to have the two degrees, one from college and then go to another college to get another degree, and never wind up doing what you are trained to do?"

I guess that I started to become bitter and angry about the conditions in my life. At the same time, on the political horizon, two people had emerged as being central to the African experience in America. Malcolm X was one and Martin Luther King. But, of course, by this time Malcolm had been assassinated as had been JFK. My mother did not clearly understand that the same kind of energy that took Malcolm's life also took Martin's life.

The first thing I had to learn to control, at that point, was my anger, because I was extremely angry. The next year, in 1968, when Martin was killed, I like lost it. I knew people who were, in fact, part of an armed struggle to eradicate police because there had been a lot of brutality, specifically to Afro-American males in the community. These people were just about saying, "Well, if I see a pig, I will off him." I wasn't part of that, but I was part of the faction of education, meaning not so much formalized, higher learning. . . . But let me share with you my experiences. Let me show you that we, in fact, all do have a commonality and a common destiny. That folks look at us for whatever reason in this life, but we have to be concerned about being the best people we can be. Somehow or other that wound up being economically sufficient. Some people might say that that was a doctrine of separatism, but to me it wasn't separatism. It was do for yourself and ourselves, and let's not become dependent upon the same person who is, in fact, shooting these bullets at us. I was already upset about the fact that I'm a taxpayer and those bullets were probably bought with taxpayers' money. So I'm not a suicidal idiot. I would not pay for folks to shoot at me. That kind of clarity started to come to me in terms of . . . we should be very, very concerned about how we operate in an economic sense as well. The arms struggle was not for me, because I'm not a killer, but I'm a person who believes in life and a person who believes in family and a person who believes in love. I'm more into . . . you have to love self first and understand who I am first before I can love anyone else, be they my brother, or be it the collective family of mankind.

I think that I got to the point where I felt very confident in knowing my history and knowing politically where I am. Once I was able to do that, then I was able to look at people straight and say: "Well, I'm not looking at a person who happens to be European or American. I'm looking at a person first, who may be female, who may be male, who may like me or who may dislike me." I was able to make those kinds of distinctions and feel good about making those kinds of distinctions. If a person was a bigot, they were a bigot. If a person liked me for me and was still a bigot, he was a bigot. Now, that's not to say that I was just turning a friendship totally down; but I would try to take them along, 'cause I would say, "If you really like me, let me enlighten you as I've had to enlighten others." At the same time, those kinds of abilities to make those assessments became keen for my survival.

So here I am today after a myriad of other things that have gone on in my life, like marriage, divorce, childbirth. I lost my mother, extended family growing, more formalized education. I still probably was more molded by those years that you mentioned from my birth to 1967 than I was by anything else. It set me on a path that I couldn't turn back if I wanted to.

BIOGRAPHY

Roy Wilds was born on October 24, 1947, a day when it snowed in Detroit. He graduated from Central High School. He received his degree in business and psychology from Mercy College. He worked at the University City "A" Citizens District Council. He was on the staff of the Detroit Urban League Male Responsibility Program, and is now working with young men at Don Bosco Hall. Roy Wilds is the father of a son—Amon-Ra Wilds.

As a conscientious objector during the Vietnam War, Gerald Wayne Smith was the target of harassment and accusations.

GERALD WAYNE SMITH

I had taken my physical on July 25th of 1968. That was a day before my eighteenth birthday. In my neighborhood, which was on the near west side of Detroit around the 29th Street-Buchanan area, so many young men were taken off to Vietnam it just obliterated our neighborhood. I could count maybe five or six or seven of these young men that I personally knew that were killed in Vietnam. As a result of my increasing political awareness during that time, I became a conscientious objector. I refused to go to war.

It was through the conscious building efforts of reading and studying and being around people with a political consciousness that I couldn't morally, with any conscience, go to a war that didn't represent my interest as an American citizen without justification, moral justification. Why should I kill? Why should I be used as cannon fodder to kill for a cause unknown, because no one knew why we were over there in the first place?

First I had to apply at the Selective Service board, apply for something called "CO status." I had to say that I felt that I could not kill anyone for any reason based upon any judgment on the part of an organized entity. It could be the American government, it could be the police force, or whatever. I said I was against all war because of my religious faith.

At that time Father Norman Thomas wrote my conscientious objector statement for me. I signed it. I went to Sacred Heart. When Norman Thomas had taken over that parish in 1968 from St. Patrick where he was an associate pastor, he was the first Roman Catholic priest to actually house what they called draft resisters in the church. These people had been drafted and then refused to go, so the FBI, or whoever the federal agents were at that time, would have to come into the church and remove these people. There was a big stink about that. I didn't reach that point.

Well, it would have been bad publicity for the federal government to go into a church. It wouldn't have been politically expedient or advantageous for them to go in there to do that, recognizing the high profile of the war itself and the disproportionate numbers of blacks and minorities in that war, and the historic nature of the church. It's the oldest black Catholic church in the city. That had a lot to do with it, as well as the political consciousness of the priest himself, Father Thomas, his as well as Bishop Gumbleton.

I had been visited at my mother's home on 29th Street by the Federal Bureau of Investigation. The FBI made it very hard on me for three years. It was very difficult for me to get a job. This was between 1968 and 1971. I had to go back to school. They thought I constituted some kind of serious threat out here in the community. It was a harassment. It was one of these sophisticated harassment techniques where you couldn't see it visibly with the eye, but you knew you were being affected by this.

Shortly thereafter, when I pledged and stated this CO status, it wasn't too long after that that the lottery came and my number fell, like 303, which was semisafe at that time.

It was also a point in time in which I had recently gone back to school full-time. During that time, between 1967–1970, I had worked for New Detroit. I had worked at the Model Cities Program. After those two tenures of employment, I had gone back to school to the University of Detroit.

I was involved in the student movement and political activities which were also monitored by the FBI. They took pictures of me, saying it was me when it wasn't me. They had photographed me allegedly doing certain things that wasn't me. At that time we had a team of three attorneys which you've probably heard of—Alex Allen, who is now a judge; Elliot Hall, who is a vice president of Ford Motor Company; and Dr. Edward Littlejohn, who is a law professor at Wayne State and who defended us. After going through these legal processes at the university as well as circuit court, we were found innocent of all charges.

As for me, they had photographed me and said Gerald Smith was tearing up the library. Gerald Smith did this and Gerald Smith did that. It wasn't me. We had to laugh. Somebody was tearing up the library, and it could have been an agent.

I was born on July 26 of 1950. At that time I was living at 9511 Oakland. That building is still there. It was upstairs from a gas station. My father at that time owned a shoe repair business on Gratiot Avenue. Interesting enough, one of his employees was Richard Austin. That was one of Richard Austin's first jobs, as a shoe shine boy for my father in 1939, I think. I lived there with my three other brothers, my mother, and father. We moved from Oakland to 29th Street, on the near west side. At that time he had opened up another shoe shop in southwest Detroit. It was called Tri-City Shoe Repair. It was right there between Ecorse, River Rouge, and Detroit. Very hard-working man. I think I was a semi-mistake, because I was born when he was fifty years of age. I have two half-brothers. My mother was much younger. He had four kids after he was forty, so his life was just beginning. I had two older brothers who were born in Bessemer, Alabama. One is still living in Birmingham; he's retired.

He was a very hard working man who left the South because of racial injustice, left the South because he was mulatto. He was caught betwixt and between. He had several problems with that. He was too light to be black and too dark to be white. The South was really still going through its antebellum period. He moved here to Detroit in 1933 or 1934. Then he met my mother, and they were married in 1940. From that union sprung four boys, all of whom are from Detroit. Their names are Ronald, Joseph, Maurice, and Gerald. My older brothers were Jacob, Jr., and Jose, who was my oldest brother. Both were from Alabama. Jacob came up for two weeks, and my father and he were riding the bus; this was in 1945. He was saying, "Yowsa," and my father told him, "You don't say that up here anymore." He just could not get ready for the North, so he moved back down South and has been there ever since.

My family started a baseball team, and we won several championships in the city of Detroit. My mother, as a matter of fact, managed five championship baseball teams. The men hated her. She never hit a baseball, never caught a ball, but she knew the game. She would have some of the players hit the balls at batting practice or field practice; and she would take these kids who were considered bad boys in the neighborhood and turn them around and organize them into a baseball team. She was also a den mother.

A few of her players went on to the major leagues. Ron Johnson, who used to play for the University of Michigan, he was our catcher. He played for the New York Giants. He owns a franchise of McDonald's in

New Jersey. Willie Horton was on the fringe at that time. Alex Johnson, Ron's brother, who won the American League batting title back in 1970, California Angels. We had a lot of guys. Julius Bender, who played the farm system for the New York Yankees. We had a lot of aspiring ball players on our team that went on, and we played against several major league baseball stars that came right out of Detroit, at Northwestern Field, as well as at Kronk. In the early 1960s we dominated this city regarding baseball. She was at the helm. I'll never forget: the newspaper headline said, "Vikings Win West Side Crown—Managed By A Woman." Men would just get so upset.

She knew the game; she knew the psychology of the game. She knew the mechanics. She coached and managed. She was the manager of the team. She came from a family of nine. She was very much involved with taking an interest in the neighborhood boys. They all called her Mrs. Smith: "Yes, Ma'am; no, Ma'am." None of this cussing or nothing like they're doing today. She was a little bitty woman.

We were in several leagues. One, we were in Parks and Rec class B and C. We were also in the West Side Optimists Club League that sponsored the teams at that time. All these leagues were integrated. We didn't have all-black leagues. At Kronk, they were by and large white leagues, because we're looking at the late '50s and early '60s. There was a discipline about the community with the Polish community that we got along fairly well. There were still the questions of fights, but there wasn't the kinds of wanton killings. Maybe a few gang fights, knife fights. If you go across the tracks, you don't enter certain territories.

In 1966 there was a Kercheval Street incident which was a mini-insurrection. There were some police and community relations problems. Ken Cockrel was involved in that. That's where Ken met Justin Ravitz, in 1966. Justin was a law student. Essentially what caused the insurrection here was bad housing, terrible police and community relations, crime problems, employment problems. Basically all the social ills that we're still talking about today were faced in that area over there. That area burned long before 1967. There was nothing to burn over there when 1967 rolled around. Cavanaugh was the mayor. It was also at that time that Detroit was named one of the model cities in the United States, one of the best cities to live in in the United States, and a year later the insurrections broke out.

The only major narcotic that I knew of that was out was marijuana, weed. It wasn't until after 1967 and 1968 that you had a high influx of "skag" or what they call heroin now or "mixed jive" as they used to call it back in those days. It's quinine and heroin mixed. It's called "penny caps" in red capsules; break them open and sniff them. It wasn't until after 1967 that you had a high influx of that. Used to call it "tooter for the snooter."

It doesn't take a genius to figure out the fact that people are still poor, people are still hungry. There's still a certain level of injustice and evil out here. Certainly racism plays a big part of it. There's still a real cleavage between the "haves" and the "have nots."

[The increase in crime is related to] shrinking economic opportunities, the war, the prevailing violence that was seen on TV every night. That it was okay to kill. Although the Congress didn't sanction it, they supported it. It was undeclared, but it was okay to kill. If violence is legitimate abroad, then violence should be legitimate at home. Just like today, you kill over a thirty-three-dollar barrel of oil, and you turn around and ask a kid why is he killing for a one- hundred-and thirty-three dollar jacket. What's the difference? Killing is killing. If two intelligent, reasonable persons can't sit down and negotiate and resolve these conflicts and mediate these conflicts, then the end result is war and death and destruction.

People were really starting to get disgusted about war at that time because it was really hitting home. It was coming to the neighbors. We had a draft. People knew that disproportionate numbers of the community were being taken and returning without the jobs that they left; those opportunities were gone. So what do you do if you have a family? Then there's another thing, why the teenage pregnancy rate had gone up, because it was said that if you were a father, if you impregnated a girl, chances are you wouldn't be drafted. So if you have children, you wouldn't be drafted. You go to school, you wouldn't be drafted. There was a variety of means and ways in which the black community was looking at how to avoid war. Some of those various ideas took root, getting a girl pregnant, going to jail for a little misdemeanor or felony, and they didn't take felons. They didn't draft felons. Didn't care what the record would say. Going back to school for those who were fortunate to do that. Getting married or having another relative over there that was in the immediate family.

Violence was sanctioned back in those days, and that's when the dramatic change that I saw happened in our neighborhoods, was that war. It was a war there but also the assault here, because of the resources being expended over there and not being channeled into the cities where it would have done the most good.

I see the same thing happening, this wanton assault against the black male. I really see that. It's just not exclusive to the black community. Now all poor people are suffering.

BIOGRAPHY

Gerald Wayne Smith is director of community development for WTVS/Channel 56 in Detroit. Mr. Smith serves on the faculty of Wayne State University in the Department of African Studies and was named U.S. Peace Corps "Black Educator of the Year" in 1990. A native of this city and graduate of the University of Detroit, he is pursuing graduate studies at Wayne State University. He served as a guest lecturer at the Nairobi International School of Nairobi, Kenya, and is included in the seventh edition of *Who's Who Among Black Americans*. He is host/producer of a radio talk show on WDTR. Mr. Smith is past chairman of the Friends of American Art and serves on many civic and human service committees.

When Walter L. A. Edwards was sent to Vietnam, he learned that the enemy could be behind you or next to you as well as in front of you.

WALTER L. A. EDWARDS

I joined the army in 1968, thinking that making that kind of a move first I would be able to pretty much choose my own direction there. That didn't work out. I should have just gotten drafted, but it was okay. I had good times and difficult times. I went to Vietnam right away, straight there.

[Going over there] was like being excited, nervous, scared, a whole bunch of emotions all at once. I didn't know what to expect really. When I got there, it wasn't quite what I expected. It was hotter. The water was brown. The sky seemed closer to the earth. It was kind of a pretty place. It was kind of an exotic place. Sometimes I wish I could go back there again, but only as Superman. It was kinda nice.

The first time you are in combat the two things that go through your mind are, "When have I ever been so scared before in my whole life?" and the other is, "When have I ever heard so much noise?" because it's really loud. It's not like going to the show. The war is over in ninety minutes there. This was a war that was a war within a lot of other wars. It's loud. It's for real. It's a war of nature, too. You've got to deal with the elements—snakes and bees and spiders and ants and all kinds of stuff. The water, the heat, the rain, the mud, the booby-traps, the freaks of nature, all kinds of stuff.

400

Sometimes fighting the enemy is not as bad as like fighting scorpions and centipedes that might be a foot long or rats that run over you in the middle of the night, so big that you don't know how big they were, maybe like small dogs or something. It gets kind of scary. Here at nighttime you've got streetlights or something, but out there it gets really, really black, pitch black. Sometimes you can't even get light in from the stars or the moon because of the foliage.

Sometimes you smell so many different kinds of beautiful flowers, and it's pretty, so pretty it's ugly; or it smells so sweet it stinks. Like you've got too many different flowers. It's like everybody taking all their perfume and opening them all at the same time and pouring it into a bowl and putting that on. It's just too sweet. It gets sickening after awhile.

Then all of a sudden you've got the war to deal with. Then you've got politics to deal with. You got racial tensions there to deal with. That's another thing I never noticed, that wasn't really mentioned too much in any of the movies that you see. There was a lot of that. A lot of Americans killed Americans. Sometimes if you were fighting side by side with somebody, and if you don't like them, don't let them get in front of you. It wasn't uncommon for a guy to have an M-16 bullet hole in the back of his head when the enemy is in front of him.

A lot of guys hated walking up in front of the line in case there were any booby-traps there. They would be the first one to draw the fire to them, so a lot of guys would walk in back. Some guys would have to unfairly walk up front. It wasn't always a decision that was fairly given to spread out amongst people. I heard of a case where this one lieutenant wanted this black guy to walk the point. This black guy felt like he was breaking, and he couldn't handle the worry anymore. He was pleading and crying, begging not to go back out in front no more. Since he wouldn't go back out and fight no more, the lieutenant shot him in the head. He really needed psychiatric help, is what he needed. But you have situations like that. Sometimes you have a lot of racial tensions that didn't make sense to me either once you have a common denominator like that.

When I first got there, some of my friends were white, and we got along real well. Then I started talking to some of the black guys; and they were, what they call, "blackenizing" me, making me more aware. They said I had too much white in me, so they started "blackenizing me." They meant well. I guess a lot of black guys there were getting unfair shakes as far as duty situations, as far as walking point, or being out in the field, or doing most of the fighting. The majority of the guys doing most of the fighting out there would be black.

I didn't really experience any racial discrimination myself per se, because I got along with everybody. But I had seen it happening in terms

401

of other things, such as racial slurs being made, and I heard of what types of statements had been stated about black people to the natives of that particular country that were there. Those things weren't too cool. The statements weren't too nice of things to say. I personally never really had any problems, I don't think. If my problems were with anybody, it was on a man-to-man basis, not because I was black and he was white.

It wasn't because of that, well, maybe one time. When I came back, some racial slurs were made at me. Then I kind of said something back. They were coming at me to attack me and stuff, and I had just been in the jungles about twenty-three months. A long time. I might have cut him a little bit. When you're in the jungles you become adjusted or adapted to any form of weapon or survival that you can. I wore two bayonets strapped to my side like Billy the Kid or something. I got pretty good with them. I learned the art of self-defense with a knife from a guy that took fencing over in Europe and another old sergeant that I made friends with when I first got there. I was still in Vietnam, but I was at a fighter base, going to a PX to get some pop or something. They made some racial remarks, and when they came at me I just let them have it. I didn't know what else to do besides that.

Other than that, I can't think of any per se, because I had a lot of friends that were white or Mexican or Hawaiian or something like that. Stateside and overseas. I never personally had any problems. A lot of those black guys that had problems, had them for different reasons. Sometimes they might have had a bad life, maybe some rough breaks. A lot of guys had good breaks too. I had a first general who was a black guy. A lot of black guys didn't get it really bad. Some did.

Some of the white guys got it bad. Like this guy that I sent to the hospital, he was a white guy from Alabama. The only reason I let him have it was because he kept on reading comic books, and I was trying to stop him from that habit. In the jungles, he's supposed to be watching my back and I'm watching his. He's constantly reading comic books. So I just stopped him with a "wait a minute vine." It's a long vine that if you aren't watching and it snags you as you're driving through the jungle, the first thing that comes out of your mouth is, "Hey, wait a minute." He's watching my front and I'm watching his back. So anyway, I saw this "wait a minute vine," and I pulled it as we were riding on the vehicle. He was through reading his book, so I let him have it. He went to the hospital in Japan. I think I did him a favor anyway, because he didn't have to fight anymore. He went to Japan to the hospital. It didn't kill him, though. If he had kept reading that comic book, he would have been dead probably.

Sometimes guys got shot up by their own men by accident, too. They called them artillery strikes. Either those people couldn't read maps well or didn't care and brought artillery down on their own men.

Or when you would call in the Air Force to give us some air strikes, they shot their own men. You couldn't tell nothing. Like I said, it's really noisy there. Sometimes you had a B-52 bomber dropping bombs in your area, but they're so high up you can't even see them. They could be hitting anywhere, and if you're in the wrong place at the wrong time. . . . You can't document any information like that. We definitely lost that war.

I wasn't like trying to be brave. I couldn't think of a time when I had been more afraid in my whole life. The only reason that I was shooting so many rounds off so fast and working so fast to try and survive was because I didn't want to get caught either. You're either in a hole or on an armored personnel carrier. You can be in a lot of places. You can be in a hole, behind a tree, or inside of a vehicle, or behind a vehicle. In my case I was behind a vehicle hiding behind a lot of explosives, so that didn't make much sense either. I didn't have anyplace else to hide.

When we came home, they treated us like dogs. They called us "baby killers" and things like that. It was mostly college students, friends you went to high school with. It happens. We handled it. They're trying to pay us back now, trying to be nice to us now. But it's too late really.

BIOGRAPHY

Walter L. A. Edwards, a.k.a. "SHKYPP," was born on September 25, 1947, in Detroit. He served in the U.S. Army from 1968–70. He has worked as a graphic artist for WTVS as well as advertising agencies. He is now an independent construction contractor, doing work primarily for the Detroit Board of Education. He is also a musician and plays several instruments.

INDEX

405

BOOKS IN THE AFRICAN AMERICAN LIFE SERIES